***Titles published***

*Fleeting Agencies: A Social History of Indian Coolie Women in British Malaya*, Arunima Datta

*The Indentured Archipelago: Experiences of Indian Labour in Mauritius and Fiji, 1871–1916*, Reshaad Durgahee

# Uncivil Liberalism

## Labour, Capital and Commercial Society in Dadabhai Naoroji's Political Thought

Vikram Visana

CAMBRIDGE
UNIVERSITY PRESS

**CAMBRIDGE**
**UNIVERSITY PRESS**

University Printing House, Cambridge CB2 8BS, United Kingdom

One Liberty Plaza, 20th Floor, New York, NY 10006, USA

477 Williamstown Road, Port Melbourne, vic 3207, Australia

314 to 321, 3rd Floor, Plot No.3, Splendor Forum, Jasola District Centre, New Delhi 110025, India

103 Penang Road, #05–06/07, Visioncrest Commercial, Singapore 238467

Cambridge University Press is part of the University of Cambridge.

It furthers the University's mission by disseminating knowledge in the pursuit of education, learning and research at the highest international levels of excellence.

www.cambridge.org
Information on this title: www.cambridge.org/9781009215541



First published 2022

Printed in India by Thomson Press India Ltd.

*A catalogue record for this publication is available from the British Library*

ISBN 978-1-009-21554-1 Hardback

*To my parents*

# Contents

*List of Abbreviations* xi

*Acknowledgements* xiii

Introduction 1

1 Sociality in an Imperial and Industrial Age 27

2 Sociality and the Parsis of Western India 51

3 Civil Society and Social Reform 72

4 Conceptualizing the Drain Theory 97

5 Making Commercial Society in India 123

6 Making Commercial Society in Britain 150

7 The Afterlives of Naoroji's Political Thought 184

Conclusion 202

*References* 208

*Index* 234

# Abbreviations

| | |
|---|---|
| BLAPAC | British Library Asia Pacific and Africa Collections |
| BLPES | British Library of Political and Economic Science |
| BUL | Bombay University Library |
| CUL | Cambridge University Library |
| *CW* | *The Collected Works of John Stuart Mill* |
| *CWMG* | *The Collected Works of Mahatma Gandhi* |
| ILHC | Islington Local History Centre |
| *JEIA* | *Journal of the East India Association* |
| *JNIA* | *Journal of the National Indian Association* |
| MSA | Maharashtra State Archives |
| NAI | National Archives of India |
| NMML | Nehru Memorial Museum and Library |
| RNP | Report on Native Papers, Bombay |
| UBL | University of Bristol Library |

# Acknowledgements

At the time of writing, this book has been almost a decade in the making and I have incurred many personal and professional debts over those years. Chief among these is to my Ph.D. supervisor, the late Chris Bayly. Chris and I met on a grey afternoon in October 2011 at St. Catherine's College for our first supervision. Scrutinising my statement of research, Chris remarked that he was keen to supervise the topic since he too had – in his characteristically understated language – 'an interest' in Indian liberalism. His seminal book on the topic, *Recovering Liberties*, was due for publication the next month. It was only at the conclusion of our meeting that he suggested I read it, having first rattled off a number of other scholars that I should consult. Afraid of being grilled on his book, I avoided telling Chris that I had already read the proofs in Cambridge's Centre for South Asian Studies. I need not have worried, as I quickly discovered, as Chris had a tremendous capacity for combining intellectual generosity with a self-effacing approach to teaching. He allowed his students' ideas to mature on their own terms with an occasional approving nudge in the direction of a resource or scholar to signal that you were headed in an interesting direction. Chris's example as a teacher has been as enlightening for me as his inestimable scholarship and I am immensely grateful for both.

For the final five months of my PhD, Shruti Kapila graciously took up the responsibility of supervision. Her conscientiousness in reading and understanding the whole work and its subsequent drafts in such a short window of time will forever be appreciated. Moreover, her intellectual dynamism and incisive comments undoubtedly improved the final product. Both Shruti and my external examiner, Faisal Devji, have produced agenda-setting work in South Asian political thought which, unflinchingly novel as it always is, continues to intellectually provoke. After my PhD, navigating the academy as an early career researcher was made much smoother by Edinburgh's Emma Hunter, whose generous mentorship and scholarly feedback was indispensable. Emma's own work on global histories of political thought in Tanzania and her ongoing research on East Africa's global connections continue to inspire.

I first began to think about political thought, liberalism and Naoroji during the last two years of my undergraduate degree at Cambridge when I had the great fortune of taking Richard Sarjeantson's specialist topic on 'utopian writing'. I am ashamed to admit that I ranked this choice last as part of my 'themes and sources' module options but, largely due to Richard's unfalteringly engaging seminars, the experience irreversibly shifted my historical interests in the direction of political thought. From there, I had the pleasure to be supervised by Joya Chatterji for the 'history of the Indian Subcontinent' paper during my final year, delving into Naoroji's *Poverty and Un-British Rule* for the first time as I tried to add some empirical ballast to an essay on Indian famines. My undergraduate dissertation on New Liberalism and British Idealism in India received great encouragement and support from my advisor, Eugenio Biagini, whose brilliant scholarship on liberalism I have engaged closely with ever since. I am thankful to all of these fine scholars for opening my eyes to new ways of looking at the past, all of which continue to shape my research.

The book has benefitted from generous external funding which made extended periods of overseas research possible. Many thanks to the Arts and Humanities Research Council, Economic History Society, and British Academy for facilitating numerous trips to Indian archives as well as enabling essential conversations with my peers at conferences and workshops. The work was also supported by timely and much appreciated internal grants from the George Macaulay Trevelyan, Holland Rose, and Members Funds at Cambridge's History Faculty as well as an International Networking Grant from the University of Huddersfield.

The lion's share of the archival work was conducted over the course of twenty months at the National Archives of India between 2012 and 2014. There, in the private papers section, Rajbala Jain was a consistent source of support in allowing me access to uncatalogued items and streamlining the occasionally cumbersome process of ordering individual documents. Shorter spells were spent at the Nehru Memorial Museum and Library, the Maharashtra State Archives, Mumbai University Library, and Sabarmati Ashram in Ahmedabad where staff were equally indispensable in locating documents. In particular, Tridip Suhrud was especially welcoming, helping me to navigate the Gandhi library and archives at Sabarmati. In the UK, staff at the British Library and Islington Local History Centre took a keen interest in the work, helping to excavate the British side of Naoroji's story. Likewise, colleagues at the universities of Birmingham, Bristol and Cambridge offered bespoke advice on where to locate sources on Naoroji's various political interlocutors. Without the conscientious support of librarians and archivists, histories such as this would be more challenging, more incomplete and far less enjoyable.

A small contingent of scholars have provided ballast to keep the project buoyant over the years. Feedback on chapters, papers, conferences, postdoctoral applications, book proposals and tips on new resources have been gratefully received. Thanks to Andrew Sartori, Jennifer Pitts, Gareth Steadman-Jones, David Washbrook, Georgios Varouxakis, Sebastian Conrad, John Hinnells, Teresa Segura-Garcia and Malcolm Deboo. Colleagues from the University of Edinburgh's Centre for Global History also provided a nurturing environment for an early career researcher looking to establish himself. Alongside Emma Hunter, Crispin Bates, Stephen McDowall, Felix Boecking, Talat Ahmed and Christopher Harding were important sources of advice and encouragement. The encouragement and collegiality of history colleagues at the University of Huddersfield has meant that the final stages of augmenting, completing and editing this manuscript have been far less frenzied than I would have anticipated from modern academic life.

Friends and fellow early career researchers across several institutions made my peripatetic years more enjoyable. In no particular order, thanks to James Roslington, Tom Simpson, Kate Boehme, Devyani Gupta, Jagjeet Lally, Sophie-Jung Kim, Patrick Clibbens, Maria Guagnin, Francesco Mari, Jean-Baptiste Pettier, Gesa Froemming, Marius Buning, Chelsea Sambells and Robert Piggott. Many important friends from beyond academia were there for me from start to finish and, more than once, tolerated my absences, flakiness and general inconsistency with good humour. A special thanks, then, to Oleg Loginov, Rahul Mansigani, Anthony Hollands, Joan Groizard, Nico Rosetti, Nadia and Rob Marshall-Keeys, Eleanor and Nick Boddy, Emily and Joe Price, Shamindrie Silva, Emma Dabbs, Ravin Thambapillai and Dan Underwood.

My family – Mum, Dad and Sachin – have made the ever-simmering background angst of the PhD and postdoctoral career much more manageable both emotionally and practically. It is the sort of support that many young South Asians committed to the humanities do not readily receive. For that and much besides I am truly thankful. In 2017, I met the man who is now my fiancé. Ryan has devoured primers on Indian history, graduating to weightier tomes and continues to take a passionate interest in all things South Asian. His own renaissance interests are communicated with such infectiousness that they have also given more than a little inspiration for future research. More than this, Ryan was a welcome distraction from research and writing. It helps that he is a whizz in the kitchen and that I think with my stomach. While finishing this manuscript, Ryan has been a partner in the truest sense of the word, so much so that I cannot imagine my next project without him.

# Introduction

In the summer of 1893, a communal riot erupted between Bombay's Hindu and Muslim communities over the issue of cow protection. In the aftermath, the *Pall Mall Gazette* interviewed the member of parliament (MP) for Central Finsbury for his views. The representative of this London borough was the 'Grand Old Man' of India, Dadabhai Naoroji, who had been elected on the Liberal ticket the previous year and was immediately catapulted to global fame as the first Indian MP in British history. Already several decades into his peripatetic political career between India and Britain, Naoroji's insight into these riots was no doubt influenced by similar incidents that took place between his own Indian Zoroastrian community – the Parsis – and some of Bombay's Muslims in 1851 and 1874. He answered the reporter by claiming that fanatics of every religious creed caused civil strife in many societies. However, to his mind, the real question was why these riots were usually confined to what he dubbed 'the lower orders' and under what circumstances could diverse populations live together peacefully?[1]

By this stage of his career, Naoroji had already formulated his iconic 'drain theory' of Indian poverty. Commonly understood as a critique of colonial economic extraction, the theory is widely regarded as an indigenous broadside against the political economy of empire and a formative step in theorizing Indian economic nationalism. This book contends that the retrospective reading of Naoroji's drain through the lens of anti-colonial nationalism has obscured the relevance of the theory's wider normative repertoire. By conducting a genealogy of Naoroji's thought, this book dramatically expands the political horizons of his drain theory from a local nationalist polemic to a global theory of sociality that took Britain's liberalism to task wherever it was applied. Put another way, Naoroji devised a materialist understanding of how individuals and communities from different cultural backgrounds could form bonds of social interdependence in a colonial age defined by doctrines of racial and cultural asymmetry. In using his

1 *Pall Mall Gazette*, 14 August 1893.

drain theory to draw attention to British liberalism's inability to socialize all of its subjects into an imperial civil society, Naoroji offered his drain theory as a new paradigm to replace the empire's uncivil liberalism.

As the book shows, Naoroji was an academic, economic and political migrant, and it was this mobile career that allowed him to inhabit an intellectual space that did not give the state or capitalist production primacy in the generation of ideas. By his reckoning, property and freedom were mutually constituted and required political vigilance and agency in order to guarantee their proper relationship. As such, he calibrated the politics of labour, capital and the state depending on the particularities of the locale he was addressing. However, the striking conceptual constant in Naoroji's drain was commercial sociality, which is to say, his understanding of society as a product of materialist interdependence resulting from the fair contractual exchange between free labour. Conversely, Naoroji regarded capitalist monopoly in all its forms as fatal to sociality. The formative local experiences in India and Britain that prompted Naoroji to make these novel connections, his reinterpretation of globally circulating ideas, and the insertion of these new concepts into the established canon of liberalism are the subjects explored in this book. In our own globalized world, characterized by connection but also by industrial exploitation, financialization and social fragmentation, it is hoped that the recovery of Naoroji's vision of a culturally plural society anchored in labour rights stimulates thinking on new alternatives to the uncivil liberalism of our own age.

## Indian Politics between the State and Capital

Decades of scholarship from the middle of the twentieth century on the struggle between imperialism and anti-colonial movements have tended to lump any critique of empire and the transition to freedom under the rubric of 'nationalism'. Between the 1950s and 1980s, scholarship on Indian politics in the age of empire made two major assumptions. The first presumed that, as in Europe, politics was primarily oriented towards the state; the second took a prosopographical approach which insisted that Indian actors derived their political interests from collective caste, class or ethnic identifications. For instance, Bipan Chandra's *Rise and Growth of Economic Nationalism* traces the collective politics of middle-class Indian professionals and their principled critique of colonial political economy. Chandra regarded indigenous interventions on colonial capitalism as a contiguous local theory in which Indians instinctively challenged borderless exchange and imperial heteronomy. The solution was to socially embed the market by the promotion of customs barriers and indigenous industry, thereby inscribing a national political-economic space.[2] A more recent riff on this argument is found in Manu Goswami's insistence that economic nationalism is a collective project made possible by 'the modalities of spatialization' and capitalist infrastructure that designate regions as units of state governance. Goswami concludes that the idea of the Indian 'nation' prefigured the emergence of nationalist politics around the 1870s. The 'superimposition and interpenetration' of socio-economic structures, state practices and cultural forms along with 'webs of irrigation and transportation networks' were among the 'modalities of spatialization' that came to constitute India as a unit of state governance and a distinctive political economy.[3] Goswami's account relies on a Polanyi-like reasoning in which the territorial nation was inscribed politically and made meaningful to the community through the physical boundedness of a national space which provided a counter-geography to the de-territorialized imperial economy.[4] Indian nationalism was thus a structural response to a penetrating colonial capitalism.

The account of a national bourgeoisie acting collectively against the pressures of colonialism in order to regenerate India was opposed starkly by the work of the so-called Cambridge School. Here the structural focus remained unswervingly on the political possibilities generated by the state. The instrumentalist account of the 'elite' stressed competition between regional Indian magnates and 'collaboration' with British officials in the pursuit of political and economic power.[5] In this perspective, the material incentives of the colonial state, deployed at an increasingly all-India level, produced a Namierite politics in which the normative and moral problems posed by capitalism and colonialism are written out of Indian concerns altogether.[6]

Ultimately, both of these approaches relied on the analytical trope of a 'Westernized middle class' educated in European ideas and driven by them to use nationalism as a vehicle to press their material or professional claims against the colonial state.[7] This heuristic left little room for intellectual agency and

---

[2] Bipan Chandra, *The Rise and Growth of Economic Nationalism in India: Economic Policies of Indian National Leadership* (New Delhi: People's Publishing House, 1966).

[3] Manu Goswami, *Producing India: From Colonial Economy to National Space* (Chicago, IL: University of Chicago Press, 2004), pp. 5–8.

[4] Ibid., pp. 18–19.

[5] Anil Seal, *The Emergence of Indian Nationalism: Competition and Collaboration in the Later Nineteenth Century* (Cambridge: Cambridge University Press, 1966); John Gallagher, Gordon Johnson and Anil Seal, eds., *Locality, Province and Nation: Essays on Indian Politics 1870–1940* (Cambridge: Cambridge University Press, 1973).

[6] Seal, *The Emergence of Indian Nationalism*, p. 22.

[7] For use of the trope of a 'Westernized elite' to explain nationalist politics, see Bruce Tiebout McCully, *English Education and the Origins of Indian Nationalism* (New York, NY: Columbia

unknowingly replicated the official view of British imperialists that in 'mimicking' European thinking Indians had fundamentally separated themselves from 'real' Indian traditions, customs and conservatism.[8] From the 1980s, the subaltern studies collective turned their attention to the ideas of Indian politics and nationalism in particular. They sought to balance historical accounts that they understood as 'colonialist and neo-colonialist' or 'nationalist and neo-nationalist'. By the collective's reckoning, elite bias had compromised the integrity of historical accounts of both empire and nationalism. The former had given undue emphasis to the influence of British colonial administrators, institutions and culture, while the latter had similarly overplayed the contribution of Indian elite figures, organizations and ideas.[9] Though the works of the collective were varied in their approach and conclusions, they did bifurcate the life-worlds of the urban elite and the rural peasant, representing the latter as an autonomous cultural and political realm defined by the semiotics of 'peasant consciousness'.[10]

In this rigidly demarcated model of 'authentic' and 'inauthentic' Indian politics, elite Indian thinkers were accused of carrying out the historicist programme laid before them by the 'West' and its version of modernity. Founded on an a priori rationalistic model of economy and society, Europe offered India an image of its own future. Thus, any political theory that Indian intellectuals envisaged was derived from the very structures of power-knowledge that culturally dominated and marginalized colonial peoples. In sum, the Indian bourgeois agenda could never represent the interests or values of the autonomous peasant consciousness of rural India.[11] However, by reaffirming the 'oriental peasant mentality' promoted by nineteenth-century ethnographers, Guha and his colleagues' analysis could not account for historical or intellectual change and insisted on the validity of the essentialist category of both the 'peasant' and the

University Press, 1940); Seal, *The Emergence of Indian Nationalism*; J. H. Broomfield, *Elite Conflict in a Plural Society: Twentieth-century Bengal* (Cambridge: Cambridge University Press, 1968); Eugene Irshick, *Politics and Social Conflict in South Asia: The Non-Brahman Movement and Tamil Separatism, 1916–1929* (Berkley, CA: University of California Press, 1969); Judith Brown, *Gandhi's Rise to Power, Indian Politics 1915–1922* (Cambridge: Cambridge University Press, 1972).

[8] For instance, see Valentine Chirol, *Indian Unrest* (London: Macmillan, 1910).

[9] Ranajit Guha, 'On Some Aspects of the Historiography of Colonial India', in Vinayak Chaturvedi, ed., *Mapping Subaltern Studies and the Postcolonial* (London: Verso, 2000), p. 1.

[10] The seminal account of 'peasant consciousness' is Ranajit Guha, *Elementary Aspects of Peasant Insurgency in Colonial India* (Durham, NC: Duke University Press, 1999).

[11] Partha Chatterjee, 'Whose Imagined Community?' in Gopal Balakrishnan, ed., *Mapping the Nation* (London: Verso, 1996), pp. 214–25.

urban intellectual in hock to European categories of knowledge.[12] As such, despite the theoretically sophisticated interventions of subaltern studies, Indian politics was still incapable of being conceptualized as anything other than a simulacrum of colonial power-knowledge through which no rupture with established modes of thinking was possible.

All of the aforementioned approaches to Indian history have been preoccupied with politics as a primarily structural phenomenon defined by national, statist or capitalist rubrics at the expense of understanding individual intellectual agency. More recent literature has rightly stressed the Indian capacity for creative and open-ended political thought within a capitalist economy and under a capitalogenic state as thinkers deployed vernacular ideas of dynasty, natural rights or sovereign labour in order to transform their societies.[13] Moreover, as Sudipta Kaviraj has observed, it is misleading to group colonial critics before the twentieth century under the collective 'nationalist' umbrella because they had not 'yet named a community which would take the responsibility of opposition to colonialism'.[14] As such, Naoroji's thinking developed a critical, radical and generalizable model to reform imperial liberalism by re-sequencing the relationship between labour and capital but it did not claim national sovereignty.

## Indian Political Thought between the Local and the Global

In the mid-nineteenth century, Indians were motivated by established local political interests and communitarian prestige to pursue opportunities generated by the Government of India's programme of political decentralization and bureaucratic expansion. But political and commercial interest did not preclude the use of the public arena as a space for dynamic and inventive debate. Jim Masselos showed that Bombay's municipal politics drew heavily on the social concerns of the urban

[12] C. A. Bayly, 'Rallying Around the Subaltern', in Chaturvedi, ed., *Mapping Subaltern Studies*, p. 121.

[13] Milinda Banerjee, '"All This Is Indeed Brahman" Rammohun Roy and a "Global" History of the Rights-Bearing Self', *Asian Review of World Histories* 3, no. 1 (2015), pp. 81–112; Milinda Banerjee, 'How "Dynasty" Became a Modern Global Concept: Intellectual Histories of Sovereignty and Property', *Global Intellectual History* (Advanced online publication [2020]), pp. 1–32; Michael O'Sullivan, 'Vernacular Capitalism and Intellectual History in a Gujarati Account of China, 1860–68', *Journal of Asian Studies* 80, no. 2 (2021), pp. 267–92; Layli Uddin, '"Enemy Agents at Work": A Microhistory of the 1954 Adamjee and Karnaphuli Riots in East Pakistan', *Modern Asian Studies* 55, no. 2 (2021), pp. 629–64.

[14] Sudipta Kaviraj, 'The Imaginary Institution of India', in Partha Chatterjee and Gyanendra Pandey, eds., *Subaltern Studies 7*, new edn (New Delhi: Oxford University Press, 1994), pp. 1–39.

and rural ratepayers and their professional representatives. Masselos identified the city's council debates and associational culture as a space for creative argument that incubated a diverse generation of nineteenth-century political and social thinkers.[15] Similarly C. A. Bayly's early work on Allahabad's merchant and service classes also stressed the contingency of these intermediate groups' fortunes on the social history of the towns in which new intellectual developments dovetailed with urbanization, marketization and the search for social capital.[16] Echoed in his later work on regional Indian patriotisms and liberalism, Bayly convincingly suggests that the political consciousness of Indian elites was contingent upon discernibly regional debates which mixed global and local political languages.[17] What this provided the colonized with was a diverse conceptual repertoire that might be deconstructed and reassembled in myriad new ways in order to make sense of their varied lives.[18]

The mixing of local and global political languages did not imply a flattening hybridity, however. Debate and argument thrived, and the 'cosmopolitan thought zones', which some scholars claim represented the shared social experience of a global public, did not preclude fierce conceptual contestation driven by cultural difference.[19] Indian intellectuals could have pronounced disagreements between themselves and the British over the same issue even when they claimed a common political lineage. As the final chapter of this book discusses, the same ideas were often appropriated by several different but linked parties in order to pursue radically divergent cultural and political agendas. Indeed, the over-reliance on networked conceptions of global intellectual exchange has occluded political thought that embraces what Nile Green terms 'heterotopia' – arrangements in which radical cultural difference is taken as accepted and intractable.[20] As we shall see, Naoroji was one such theorist whose drain theory attempted to resolve social tensions not

[15] J. Masselos, *Towards Nationalism: Group Affiliations and the Politics of Public Associations in Nineteenth Century Western India* (Bombay: Popular Prakashan, 1974).
[16] C. A. Bayly, *Rulers, Townsmen and Bazaars: North Indian Society in the Age of British Expansion, 1770–1870* (Cambridge: Cambridge University Press, 1983).
[17] C. A. Bayly, *Origins of Nationality in South Asia: Patriotism and Ethical Government in the Making of Modern India* (Oxford: Oxford University Press, 1998); C. A. Bayly, *Recovering Liberties: Indian Thought in the Age of Liberalism and Empire* (Cambridge: Cambridge University Press, 2012), p. 8.
[18] Bayly, *Recovering Liberties*, p. 33.
[19] Sugata Bose and Kris Manjapra, eds., *Cosmopolitan Thought Zones: South Asia and the Global Circulation of Ideas* (Basingstoke: Palgrave Macmillan, 2010).
[20] Nile Green, 'Waves of Heterotopia: Toward a Vernacular Intellectual History of the Indian Ocean', *American Historical Review* 123, no. 3 (2018), pp. 846–74.

through cultural cosmopolitanism but through the commercial interdependence of free labour.

Given the epistemic violence inherent in universalizing European ideologies like liberalism, the Indian process of reinterpretation could not be a straightforward process of hybridization or of reaching a common understanding. Especially pertinent to this study is Uday Singh Mehta's deconstruction of liberal theory. Mehta accuses the liberal canon of neglecting the colonial context alongside which liberalism was spawned. Thus, seemingly emancipatory liberal ideas must have a complex and fraught relationship with the exploitative practices of empire.[21] Mehta's thesis is that the 'exclusionary thrust' of British liberalism in the nineteenth century did not stem from political misapplication and manipulation but from the 'theoretical core' of the ideology itself.[22] Behind liberalism's putatively inclusive universal criteria was, according to Mehta, another 'thicker set of social credentials that constitute the real bases of political exclusion'.[23] An abstract a priori rationalistic model of society, devised in a European cultural milieu, was used as a schema against which to judge foreign peoples. In other words, when British liberals encountered the cultural and social difference of indigenous peoples, they were in the habit of seeing 'those experiences, those life forms, as provisional'.[24] Biologically, the colonized were regarded as rational human beings but the qualities necessary for political inclusion, citizenship and its corollary rights were to be deferred until they exhibited these attributes explicitly in their social organization and individual behaviour.

Similarly, Talal Asad's deconstruction of secularism critiqued the 'Western' liberal privatization of the sacred in an effort to purge potentially contentious claims of moral absolutism from the public sphere.[25] Not having taken a European historical trajectory, the Indian context was one in which religion would not easily be exorcised from civil society. These realities did not lead to an outright Indian rejection of liberalism but to an attempt to strip it of unsuitable attributes or, in Naoroji's case, reorient it to new political priorities. With this in mind, historians must remain attentive to Jennifer Pitts' and Duncan Bell's injunction that the political practice of liberalism resulted in the polyvalent deploying of

[21] Uday S. Mehta, *Liberalism and Empire* (Chicago, IL: University of Chicago Press, 1999), p. 5.

[22] Uday S. Mehta, 'Liberal Strategies of Exclusion', in Ann Laura Stoler and Frederick Cooper, eds., *Tensions of Empire: Colonial Cultures in a Bourgeois World* (Berkley, CA: University of California Press), pp. 60–1.

[23] Mehta, *Liberalism and Empire*, p. 61.

[24] Ibid., p. 191.

[25] Talal Asad, *Formations of the Secular: Christianity, Islam, Modernity* (Stanford, CA: Stanford University Press, 2003).

liberal theory in discrete contexts that could both justify and critique imperial rule.[26] Moreover, while liberalism's 'historical consciousness' could fire British imperialism's pro-consular imagination, it could likewise facilitate multiple and contested interpretations of history that colonial subjects used to sequence their own accounts of freedom and progress.[27] Similarly, Andrew Sartori has considered the appropriation and interpretation of globally circulating liberalism through what it seeks to describe and explain in a given place and time. Though Sartori develops a sophisticated Marxian sociology that links the material relations of production to the thinkability of certain liberal concepts, for the purposes of this book, it is his open-ended idea of the 'object orientation' of a concept and its 'denotative capacity' that is particularly useful when considering how globally circulating ideas were refashioned by Indian thinkers.[28]

Ideas are not only produced and received in particular contexts, but they live on in strikingly unpredictable ways in order to shape new futures.[29] As Dipesh Chakrabarty has astutely signalled, European ideas have a contradictory relationship to Indian modernity in that they are indispensable when trying to understand modernity in the subcontinent but also insufficient for understanding the societies of the Global South in their totality. These societies have been represented in European terms even though they represent a non-European historical trajectory. Indian thinkers were forced to struggle with this dichotomy, observing through the imperfect operation of liberalism in the subcontinent that the 'global currency' of Western ideas could 'no longer be taken for granted'.[30] As such, this study of Naoroji's thought deals with the 'afterlife' of European liberalism, to use Shruti Kapila's term, examining where it was enmeshed in unique Indian political realities and was transformed through 'ideological experiments' by Naoroji and those reinterpreting his ideas after his death.[31] Naoroji conducted his experiments first in India before exporting his remade liberalism to Britain and,

[26] Jennifer Pitts, *A Turn to Empire: The Rise of Imperial Liberalism in Britain and France* (Princeton, NJ: Princeton University Press, 2005); Duncan Bell, *Reordering the World: Essays on Liberalism and Empire* (Princeton, NJ: Princeton University Press, 2016), p. 21.
[27] Bell, *Reordering the World*, p. 123.
[28] Andrew Sartori, *Bengal in Global Concept History: Culturalism in the Age of Capital* (Chicago, IL: University of Chicago Press, 2008), p. 47.
[29] Faisal Devji, *Muslim Zion: Pakistan as a Political Idea* (London: Hurst, 2013), p. 8.
[30] Dipesh Chakrabarty, *Provincializing Europe: Postcolonial Thought and Historical Difference* (Princeton, NJ: Princeton University Press, 2000), pp. 22, 45.
[31] Shruti Kapila, 'Global Intellectual History and the Indian Political', in Darrin M. McMahon and Samuel Moyn, eds., *Rethinking Modern European Intellectual History* (Oxford: Oxford University Press, 2014), p. 270.

in so doing, subjected the imperial metropole to the critique of a distinctly Indian political thought.

## Agency, Structure and Anti-foundationalism in Global Political Thought

The approaches to global political thought sketched here do, in one way or another, show how the agency of political thinkers is facilitated or constrained by social, economic and political processes in an age of globalization. Similarly, this book conducts detailed evaluations of 'the social transformations that make specific intellectual practices and concepts plausible and meaningful across large spatial extensions', as Moyn and Sartori insist.[32] However, this work also relies on a new approach to intellectual agency that offers ample space for conceptual innovation without taking a rigidly anti-foundationalist attitude towards the process by which globally circulating ideas are appropriated and remade – which is to say that even after having reinterpreted the European canon in India in ways that may have rendered it unrecognizable to British counterparts, Naoroji's self-definition as a 'liberal' still made sense. His interpretation of liberalism recovered conceptual attributes that were immanent within the original liberal canon but which could only become discernible in India and in Indian hands. In order to better understand this seemingly paradoxical claim, a phenomenological approach to political thought is outlined here alongside more traditional approaches like contextualism.

Of particular relevance in Skinner's linguistic contextualism is his criticism that the history of ideas had focused too much on which thinkers had 'influenced' others. Skinner questioned whether authors who invoked other theorists were merely invoking a 'fashionable authority' in order to 'disguise ... some dangerous ideological commitment'.[33] This is pertinent for Indian thinkers operating under the cultural and psychological asymmetries of colonialism. To this extent I do not search for the 'invocation' of canonical thinkers in any of the sources analysed but focus on the 'illocutionary force' of the political languages which combine the meaning of the utterance with what the author is doing in making it vis-á-vis other thinkers. Here, the linguistic context reveals the ideological attitudes of the day

[32] Samuel Moyn and Andrew Sartori, 'Approaches to Global Intellectual History', in Samuel Moyn and Andrew Sartori, eds., *Global Intellectual History* (New York, NY: Columbia University Press, 2013), p. 24.

[33] Quentin Skinner, 'The Limits of Historical Explanations', *Philosophy* 41, no. 157 (1966), pp. 204–6.

and whether the author is endorsing or challenging them.[34] However, recognizing that there is no established canon of Indian social theorizing as in the 'West', Indian thought must be reconstructed from the various mediums in which it was debated and disseminated, such as newspapers, journals, speeches and letters.[35] Not unlike early modern Europe, which Skinner's research predominantly addresses, modern Indian ideas were deployed in abstract argumentation and theorizing; this similarity notwithstanding, Indian thought was also conceived and deployed in political practice and social experiments designed to realize imagined collective futures. When considering political thinker-actors like Naoroji who addressed a range of audiences across the empire in writing, speech and action, we need to supplement linguistic contextualism with analytical equipment that can take account of this diversity of political intervention in order to ascertain why some ideas became more tractable than others.[36]

In order to achieve this, the book borrows from realist and phenomenological approaches to political philosophy. First, in Raymond Geuss's political realism, action is defined by the imagination and to 'act' is a fundamentally revisionist move intended to create a new reality.[37] An imaginative act can capitalize on a political opportunity to do something completely revisionist without a speech-act having been uttered. Encouraging others to react to your actions, in line with your ideological designs, can encourage a favourable shift in the political status quo.[38] More than just 'opinion formation and discussion', the reality of politics is such that the contexts in which discussion and opinion formation take place are usually 'action-orientating'.[39]

Second, I adopt Martin Heidegger's concept of the life-world and his phenomenological tool analysis. His student Hans Georg Gadamer developed Heidegger's idea of life-world to produce a sophisticated understanding of how ideas interact with custom, experience as well as local institutional norms and

[34] Quentin Skinner, 'Meaning and Understanding in the History of Ideas', *History and Theory* 8, no. 1 (1969), pp. 42–6.
[35] Sudipta Kaviraj, 'Ideas of Freedom in Modern India', in Robert Taylor, ed., *The Idea of Freedom in Asia and Africa* (Stanford, CA: Stanford University Press, 2002), pp. 98–9; Bayly, *Recovering Liberties.*
[36] C. A. Bayly, 'Liberalism at Large: Mazzini and Nineteenth Century Indian Thought', in C. A. Bayly and Eugenio F. Biagini, eds., *Giusepp. Mazzini and the Globalisation of Democratic Nationalism 1830–1920* (Oxford: Oxford University Press, 2008), p. 355.
[37] Raymond Geuss, *Politics and the Imagination* (Princeton, NJ: Princeton University Press, 2010), ix.
[38] Ibid., pp. 15–16.
[39] Ibid., p. 3.

dynamics.[40] For Gadamer, it is the preliminary 'prejudices' derived from our life-world that inform the reader's approach to a given text. By the term 'prejudice' he means any type of fore-judgement necessary to make a claim of knowledge. This could be inherited tradition, institutional situatedness or superstition but it could just as easily be an awareness of the historical context in which a text was produced or training in a specialist subject. This results in a process in which the act of interpretation can draw upon custom and reason in equal measure. After all, traditions can only be reproduced through acts of preservation or modification for modern circumstances, and this required the reflective application of a calculating reason.[41] The act of interpretation is, therefore, dependent on ascertaining the fore-meanings and prejudices of the reader from their life-world.[42]

The problem of incongruity when elaborating a coherent system of political thought across multiple political and social contexts is partly remedied by such an approach. The force of pre-existing 'prejudices' means that the reader tends to oscillate between 'part' of the text and its 'whole'. The key concepts of a text are rendered meaningful to a reader insofar as they can address the predetermined expectations derived from her context. These expectations are not the same as ideology because they are informed as much by sentiment and prejudice as by conscious analysis. Thus, one's ethical values, beliefs and politics are almost always 'half-baked' in Geuss's words. Insofar as they show determinacy, they only do so in formalized, local contexts and are constantly in a state of flux.[43] In this understanding, politics is first and foremost a mediated but meaningful act in a particular historical, sociological, psychological and economic context. Our ideals or applied ethics, insofar as they are coherent, only enter into politics at a secondary level.[44] What is more, it is only through political acts that ideas are *made* convincing to larger constituencies that are not engaged in active social theorizing but have a set of pre-existing prejudices.[45] As such, concepts emerge while reading parts of the text in line with prevailing prejudices, and the meaning of the whole is retrospectively revised in terms of what emerges. This lends the

---

[40] Bayly, *Recovering Liberties*, p. 23; Hans-Georg Gadamer, *Truth and Method*, trans. Joel Weinsheimer (London: Bloomsbury, 2013).

[41] Gadamer, *Truth and Method*, pp. 292–4.

[42] Ibid., pp. 280–3.

[43] Raymond Geuss, *Philosophy and Real Politics* (Princeton, NJ: Princeton University Press, 2008), pp. 3–4.

[44] Ibid., pp. 2, 6–10.

[45] Emma Hunter, *Political Thought and the Public Sphere in Tanzania: Freedom, Democracy and Citizenship in the Era of Decolonization* (Cambridge: Cambridge University Press, 2015), pp. 10–11.

text a sense of coherence in the eyes of the reader and makes it suitable for making sense of, and providing solutions to, her 'prejudices'.[46] When tackling the issue of intellectual derivation, entering the hermeneutic circle through Gadamreian and Geussian perspectives implies that through their 'prejudice' the reader may become conscious of aspects of the text that the original author, through her own 'prejudice', unconsciously included.[47] Unconsciously included or not, these features are inherent to the text.

So far, we have considered the 'prejudices' of someone actively reading as the route by which conceptual characteristics hidden from the original author and buried in the text might be rendered legible. Naoroji, as an Indian political thinker-actor, turned to conscious theorizing of the drain in moments of epistemic crisis like famine or financial meltdown, as is discussed in Chapter 3, even as he was in the middle of a liberal project of social reform. Historians of political thought need to better understand how the life-world of lived liberalism could come under scrutiny in such moments of crisis but still retain its conceptual coherence *as* liberalism. I propose using Heidegger's tool analysis as a way of thinking about how extant ideologies occasionally fail to explain new historical events and in doing so open themselves to acts of radical conceptual recovery by the gimlet-eyed theorist.[48] Heidegger used the example of a workman hammering to illustrate how we interact with and cognize tools. This thought experiment can also be extended to ideologies as discrete political traditions that are tools for understanding our social environment and also provide the intellectual resources for changing it. Heidegger showed that an individual hammering a nail treats the hammer unthinkingly as equipment or, in other words, an object with a clearly established use connected to the workman's goal of joining two pieces of wood. So long as the hammer is connected to this goal – and can readily insert nails into wood – rarely would a person need to consciously theorize what a hammer is. As such, in day-to-day life the hammer's innate qualities other than its touch and colour are withdrawn from both thought and praxis. Heidegger posits that it is only when the hammer stops functioning (perhaps the handle falls off) that the act of hammering ceases to be a seamless process of untheorized equipment. Instead, we are faced with the

[46] Gadamer, *Truth and Method*, p. 197.

[47] Ibid., p. 198.

[48] To see how the tool analysis can be expanded in this way, see G. Harman, 'Technology, Objects and Things in Heidegger', *Cambridge Journal of Economics* 34, no. 1 (2010), pp. 17–25; G. Harman, 'The Well-Wrought Broken Hammer: Object-Orientated Literary Criticism', *New Literary History* 43, no. 2 (2012), pp. 183–202.

conscious shock of failure which reveals to us a new set of qualities that we did not previously realize the hammer had.

If applied to discrete ideologies, as bundles of subcomponents, we can use the tool analysis to mitigate some of the compartmentalization that linguistic contextualism promotes. As ideas circulate and settle in certain local contexts, it may well be that their inability to completely explain the strange social and political life of a particular place demands the reconstitution of these concepts. It is this failure in a moment of crisis that transforms liberalism from the intellectual equipment of empire into a conscious subject of indigenous theory. What cannot be lost sight of is the fact that the context does not define the entirety of liberalism or its meaning; neither can it be reduced purely to a set of relationships between their surroundings and the reader. The context merely allows a particular range of interactions and effects to occur which facilitate a reinterpretation of some components of the conceptual bundle, through the reader's 'prejudices', but not of others.[49] In this way, we can speak of Indian liberals' reinterpretation, ideological change and intellectual commitment across cultures and contexts without reducing Indian liberalism to an arbitrary grab bag of concepts used rhetorically by disgruntled colonial subjects to discredit imperial rule. By the same token, we cannot reduce Indian liberalism to a passive project of colonized minds seeking to fulfil the promises of a truncated European ideology in completely originalist terms.[50] Indians were legitimate liberals and conceptual innovators in equal measure.

## Liberalism

As the British Empire's 'official' liberalism revealed itself as increasingly sclerotic in the face of rapid social and economic change, Indian thinkers like Naoroji moved from being practitioners of an inherited political tradition to conscious theorists of their own liberalism. This book traces this process through Naoroji's social reformism of the 1840s and 1850s to his pivot to economic reform and labour republicanism from the 1860s until his death. Liberalism is of course a perennially difficult ideology to define, and its various mutations over the centuries, particularly over the course of the twentieth century, have led some, like Duncan Bell, to suggest that the term has become a catch-all for every progressive Western movement. According to Bell, the relevance and internal coherence of liberalism

[49] Harman, 'The Well-Wrought Broken Hammer', p. 191.
[50] Samuel Moyn, 'On the Nonglobalization of Ideas', in Moyn and Sartori, eds., *Global Intellectual History*, pp. 187–204.

were preserved by ideological sleights of hand like the incorporation of Locke into the canon in later years in order to shore up the contractarian basis of the ideology.[51] Yet there are discernible liberal commitments that we might identify and, in this sense, liberalism is no less dogmatic than its more recent ideological cousins.

Liberalism favours a loose institutional alliance encompassing free association, free press, formal equality, free labour and free trade in order to undergird its fundamental commitment to the principles of human liberty, individualism and progress.[52] In addition to intellectual and institutional commitments, we might also speak of a liberal sensibility that granted access and status to individuals and groups who demonstrated the characteristics listed earlier. Advocating a particular type of bourgeois sociability suited to the industrialized and commercialized world that emphasized generosity, compassion and tolerance also constituted liberalism's social firmament.[53] It was this constructive dimension of liberalism that Indians found particularly appealing in a country riven by social cleavages. In this way, Bayly offers a wide-ranging definition of Indian liberalism that encompasses 'arguments, projects and sensibilities which the English-speaking intelligentsia believed would give Indians freedom from despotic government, superstitious religiosity, social tyranny and economic backwardness'. He adds that 'Indian liberalism also comprised a sustained series of attempts to build up a civil society (then called a "public") by promoting civic responsibility, morality, Indian political representation, progressive religion and a free press'.[54]

In addition to this representational order, in which the characteristics of individuals are weighed against a bundle of attributes that allow liberal norms and institutions to operate successfully in a given culture, the materialist register of liberalism is especially significant for this book. Onur Ulas Ince's powerful study of the early modern social conditions of capitalism under which liberal theorizing emerged alerts us to liberalism's attempt to normatively legitimate the concrete relations of private property, market and exchange while eliding the coercive origins of capitalist expropriation. The present work recognizes liberalism's provenance in European capitalism but also that ideas break free of their intellectual nurseries in

---

[51] Duncan Bell, 'What Is Liberalism?', *Political Theory* 42, no. 6 (2014), pp. 682–715.

[52] Theodore Koditschek, *Liberalism, Imperialism and the Historical Imagination: Nineteenth-century Visions of Greater Britain* (Cambridge: Cambridge University Press, 2011), p. 1; Michael Freeden, *Liberal Languages: Ideological Imaginations and Twentieth Century Progressive Thought* (Princeton, NJ: Princeton University Press, 2005), pp. 1–5.

[53] Freeden, *Liberal Languages*, p. 1.

[54] C. A. Bayly, 'Empires and Indian Liberals', in Catherine Hall and Keith McClelland, eds., *Race, Nation and Empire: Making Histories, 1750 to the Present* (Manchester: Manchester University Press, 2011), p. 74.

acts of reinterpretation. This qualification notwithstanding, we must recognize the reciprocal but contradictory relationship between a liberal value system and capitalism as a specific institutional form.[55] Naoroji's early liberalism, addressed in Chapter 3, had regarded the maintenance of a dynamic and autonomous civil society in Bombay as the key to his Parsi minority's social and cultural progress. The philanthropy of Parsi business elites had created a middle-class public that was institutionally plural, freely associating and tolerant.[56] Later, however, in the midst of social and economic crises, this ideal would come under Naoroji's theoretical scrutiny and give way to a materialist model of commercial society predicated on a critique of colonial capitalism. The reciprocal relationship between market exchange and liberal values persisted in his thought but only after he came to appreciate British liberalism's misrecognition of actually existing capitalism.[57]

Naoroji's liberalism sought to remove the normative inconsistencies of colonial liberalism and also to reconcile the ideology with India's staggering cultural diversity. The colonial state had made communities or 'populations', rather than autonomous individuals, the passive objects of policy.[58] The initial task of liberal theory was not to find a way of representing Indian citizens or safeguarding their liberty but to abstract liberal subjects from extended kinship groups and maximize their capacity to enter into sociable relations so that something resembling an Indian people could be called into existence.[59] This raised the issue of balancing an as yet unrealized individualism with cultural diversity and uneven liberal capacities (understood as 'progress') between each community. For this reason, Jeremy Waldron's view that liberalism's vague and abstract notions of freedom need to be coupled with a 'requirement that all aspects of the social should either be made acceptable or be capable of being made acceptable to every last individual' also characterized the realism of Naoroji's theorizing.[60]

---

[55] Onur Ulas Ince, *Colonial Capitalism and the Dilemmas of Liberalism* (Oxford: Oxford University Press, 2018), ch. 1.

[56] Partha Chatterjee, 'On Civil and Political Society in Postcolonial Democracies', in Sudipta Kaviraj and Sunil Khilnani, eds., *Civil Societies: History and Possibilities* (Cambridge: Cambridge University Press, 2001), pp. 172–3.

[57] James Tully, *Public Philosophy in a New Key, Vol. II: Imperialism and Civic Freedom* (2 vols., Cambridge: Cambridge University Press, 2008), pp. 250–6.

[58] Chatterjee, 'On Civil and Political Society', p. 173.

[59] Bhiku Parekh, 'The Cultural Particularity of Liberal Democracy', *Political Studies* 40 (August 1992), p. 171; Nazmul Sultan, 'Self-Rule and the Problem of Peoplehood in Colonial India', *American Political Science Review* 114, no. 1 (2020), pp. 81–94.

[60] Jeremy Waldron, 'Theoretical Foundations of Liberalism', *Philosophical Quarterly* 37, no. 147 (1987), p. 128.

Naoroji's close engagement with the culturally neutral language of political economy was partly a result of his preoccupation with the underdetermined nature of the Indian social and the need to articulate a constructive programme of social interdependence which, at the same time, did not transgress the cultural boundaries of each Indian community. Capitalism did not, of course, arrive in India with the British. David Washbrook outlined the beginnings of an indigenous pre-colonial capitalism but emphasized that by the early nineteenth century it was ultimately reconfigured into a marketized mechanism of extraction by colonialism.[61] From its earliest days, this was a process in which indigenous merchants and power-brokers played a leading role.[62] Dipesh Chakrabarty's in-depth study of jute workers in Calcutta demonstrated that the new colonial capitalism had a metropolitan bias that proved itself unable and unwilling to transform multiple traditional Indian communities into a single modern society of individuals. The Indian labourer was not reified into his public and private self, nor was he decoupled from his religious, familial and rural moorings. Consequently, the political and social languages of the Indian working classes were decidedly customary, forcing capital to rely on modes of institutional coercion and disciplining instead of the self-regulation of modern market citizens.[63]

From the mid-nineteenth century this half-baked capitalist transformation relied upon an ethnographic state to manage Indian populations, which were still defined by 'custom'. This legal regime colluded in the rustication of Indians by passing commercial legislation that bifurcated Indian business into a world of 'modern' urban market agents and a 'traditional' world of Indian mercantile firms based on custom and kinship rather than contract.[64] In response, Naoroji's insurgent critique of British political economy was itself a constructive liberal programme to remedy these ills. In this way, his political thought would also contribute to twentieth-century debates on Indian development. As Benjamin Zachariah notes, by the twentieth century 'backwardness' was associated with colonial rule itself, and economic backsliding was seen as the source of India's social ills.[65]

[61] David Washbrook, 'Progress and Problems: South Asian Economic and Social History, c. 1720–1860', *Modern Asian Studies* 22, no. 1 (1988), 57–96.

[62] David Veevers, *The Origins of the British Empire in Asia, 1600–1750* (Cambridge: Cambridge University Press, 2020).

[63] Dipesh Chakrabarty, *Re-thinking Working Class History: Bengal 1890–1940* (Princeton, NJ: Princeton University Press, 1989).

[64] Ritu Birla, *Stages of Capital: Law, Culture, and Market Governance in Late Colonial India* (Durham, NC: Duke University Press, 2009), pp. 2–8, 28.

[65] Benjamin Zachariah, *Developing India: An Intellectual and Social History* (New Delhi: Oxford University Press, 2005), p. 5.

By the end of the Grand Old Man's career, he had popularized a materialist theory of constructive liberalism. In doing so, Naoroji contended that only free labour and the property it generated for itself could sustain an interdependent but culturally plural society based on freely established individual contracts.

## Republicanism

Naoroji's conviction that only free labour could achieve the promise of a liberal society points to what I have called his 'labour republicanism', in which workers had an absolute right to the wealth they had created by mixing their labour with nature. With this in mind, a point of conceptual clarification is necessary since it is conventionally assumed that liberalism and republicanism promote distinct principles of liberty. Philip Pettit and Quentin Skinner clearly distinguish between a negative concept of liberty predicated on non-interference, a positive concept of liberty that prizes self-realization and a republican iteration of liberty that values non-domination. Pettit is unambiguous in showing that republican liberty 'requires that no one is able to interfere on an arbitrary basis – at their pleasure – in the choices of a free person'.[66] While non-interference depends upon the absence of physical or political impediments, non-domination relies upon status. As such, what Skinner calls 'neo-Roman liberty' may avail itself of legal intervention in order to protect an individual from domination and dependence.[67] To be dependent was a status the Romans associated with slavery and was a term that, as we shall see, Naoroji repeatedly used to describe the condition of labour in the British world. While Skinner mostly explores neo-Roman liberty through its focus on political participation and civic virtue in a free state, he does acknowledge the economically normative thrust of some republican writers. For example, he observes that in the eighteenth century, Trenchard and Gordon state in *Cato's Letters* that 'where there is liberty, there are encouragements to labour, because people labour for themselves: and no one can take from them the acquisitions that they make', whereas if they live under an arbitrary will their trade is always at risk.[68] In this regard, though republicanism does not prioritize issues of economic justice,

---

[66] P. Pettit, *Republicanism: A Theory of Freedom and Government* (Oxford: Oxford University Press, 1997), p. 271.

[67] Quentin Skinner, *Liberty before Liberalism* (Cambridge: Cambridge University Press, 1997).

[68] Quentin Skinner, 'Freedom as the Absence of Arbitrary Power' in Cecile Laborde and John Maynor, eds., *Republicanism and Political Theory* (Oxford: Oxford University Press, 2008), p. 91; Eugenio Biagini has also noted the continued uptake of neo-Roman concepts by nineteenth-century British liberals in E. F. Biagini, 'Neo-Roman Liberalism: "Republican Values and British Liberalism, ca. 1860–1875', *History of European Ideas* 29, no. 1 (2003), pp. 55–72.

it does regard the possession of property – protected from arbitrary expropriation – as a guarantor of autonomy.

Such an understanding of free economy was critical to Naoroji's thinking because of the labour theory of value inherent in his drain theory. This posited that the generation of new wealth occurred only through the action of labour on the fruits of nature. Any attempt to exert arbitrary power over this process contravened natural law and, as such, labour republicanism was an expression of natural justice. In this case, we can think of justice as negatively conceived as an absence of mediation in the process of accumulation. For Naoroji, the mediation was almost always in the form of commercial or financial domination. Sometimes this was in the form of *imperium* and on other occasions in the form of *dominium*, to use Pettit's terminology.[69] Meaning public and private power respectively, both of these terms denoted forms of arbitrary will that could equate to types of economic domination. This phenomenon is commonly understood through the concept of monopoly. As with politics, the republican approach to economics is hostile to systems that promote bargains among a small number of self-interested groups.[70] This type of corruption could only be overcome by holding such forces acting against natural justice in check by a system of law and institutional balances that might transform the market into a realm of genuinely equal bargaining free from dependent exchange.[71] As we shall see, Naoroji's career between Bombay and London meant that what these checks and balances ought to be depended on the context he was addressing.

## Dadabhai Naoroji's Transnational Life

This book is not a comprehensive life history or biography but is the first to treat Naoroji as a conscious theorist of liberalism. This being the case, a chronological sketch of Naoroji's life between Bombay and London will help us situate the recovery of his ideas which follows. There are only a handful of book-length studies of Naoroji's life, all of which adopt the biographical approach. R. P. Masani's biography of Naoroji was published just over twenty years after the latter's death in 1917 and is more narrative than analytical in its approach.[72] Comparatively, Munni Rawal's study is effective in tracing the change in Naoroji's politics over

[69] Pettit, *Republicanism*, p. 140.
[70] Cass Sunstein, 'Beyond the Republican Revival', *Yale Law Journal* 97, no. 8 (1988), p. 1549.
[71] Stuart White, *The Civic Minimum: On the Rights and Obligations of Economic Citizenship* (Oxford: Oxford University Press, 2003), pp. 44–7.
[72] R. P. Masani, *Dadabhai Naoroji: The Grand Old Man of India* (London: George Allen & Unwin, 1939).

the years but is unable to integrate it into a single theoretical framework or isolate Naoroji's motivations. Rawal can only conclude that Naoroji was the 'intellectual child of European liberalism'.[73] More recently, Dinyar Patel's fluent and erudite account of Naoroji's life explores the Grand Old Man's drain theory but adds the qualification that Naoroji 'did not develop philosophically nuanced strains of political thought'.[74] Patel's biography suggests that Naoroji and his drain theory are both pioneers of 'Indian nationalism' but not contributors to a more generalizable theory of liberalism. Indeed, Patel's lengthy horizontal descriptions of Naoroji's international networks – without the vertical mining of particular nodes – have the effect of dispersing his intellectual agency, with Naoroji emerging as a political eclectic and opportunistic strategist.

Focusing exclusively on the conceptual genealogy and legacy of Naoroji's liberalism, this study draws upon initial forays into his political thought by C. A. Bayly and Theodore Koditschek. Both of these scholars have analysed discrete aspects of Naoroji's liberalism, with Bayly observing how Naoroji's 'statistical liberalism' used official figures to critique the ethnographic state and the epistemic violence of the colonizer.[75] Naoroji's statistical liberalism is explained in greater detail in Chapter 3 of this book and is reinterpreted as a way of quantifying deviations from natural justice and legitimate labour republicanism.[76] Koditschek has rightly identified Naoroji's 'radicalized Macaulayism' and its attendant liberal progress narrative as central to Naoroji's political programme in an age of 'philosophical history'.[77] Considerably expanding Bayly and Koditschek's initial insights, this book recovers Naoroji as a systematic theorist who, through his writings and his meaningful political action, left a legacy of nuanced political thought.

Born in Khadak, Bombay, into a poor family of Parsi *dusturs* (Zoroastrian priests) in 1825, Dadabhai underwent the initial stages of consecration into the priesthood in 1839. His priest father, Naoroji Palanji Dordi, could trace his family's ancestry to Zarthost Mobed, the first Zoroastrian priest to land in Navsari, Gujarat

[73] Munni Rawal, *Dadabhai Naoroji: A Prophet of Indian Nationalism, 1855–1900* (New Delhi: Anmol Publications, 1989), p. iii.

[74] Dinyar Patel, *Dadabhai Naoroji: Pioneer of Indian Nationalism* (Cambridge, MA: Harvard University Press, 2020), p. 8.

[75] C. A. Bayly, 'Liberalism at Large: Mazzini and Nineteenth Century Indian Thought', in C. A. Bayly and Eugenio F. Biagini, eds., *Giussepe Mazzini and the Globalisation of Democratic Nationalism, 1830–1920* (Oxford: Oxford University Press, 2008), p. 373; Bayly, *Recovering Liberties*, p. 105.

[76] Bayly, *Recovering Liberties*, p. 105.

[77] Koditschek, *Liberalism, Imperialism, and the Historical Imagination*, p. 294.

(the religious centre of the Parsis in western India). The family also continued to own ancestral agricultural lands in the nearby princely state of Dharampur.[78] While it was customary for the sons of *dusturs* to follow their father's vocation, Naoroji Palanji died only four years after Dadabhai's birth, leaving him in the care of his mother and uncle.[79] At age eleven, Dadabhai was married to Gulbai, the seven-year-old daughter of Sorabji Shroff.[80] Dadabhai's mother, Manekbai, insisted that the young boy go to the local vernacular school and, upon the recommendation of his schoolmaster, enrolled him in a free school operated by the Bombay Education Society. Ultimately, Naoroji would forego the priesthood and enrol in the Elphinstone College. Graduating in 1845, he would remain at the institution – first as an assistant master and then becoming an assistant professor of mathematics in 1848 (holding a professorship in mathematics and natural philosophy by 1855, the first Indian to hold such a senior post). By the 1850s, Naoroji was deeply involved in the philanthropy and social reform efforts of his Anglophile Parsi community; his direct influence over this programme was interrupted by an opportunity to travel to the United Kingdom in 1855 as a partner in Cama & Co – the first Asian firm established in Britain – during which time Naoroji was based in Liverpool as a commercial agent. Within three years, he had resigned his partnership and had returned to Bombay, only to go back to the British Isles a year later after having founded his own cotton trading outfit: Dadabhai Naoroji & Co. From this period, Naoroji's portfolio career gradually shifted from a businessman and academic to a professional critic of British rule in India. From a flurry of academic papers on Parsi and Indian culture in the early 1860s, Naoroji would pivot to issues of political economy after Bombay's financial crisis in 1864–5. It was during this seminal period that Naoroji's liberalism would engage with issues beyond India. From September 1863 to April 1865, he had a short sojourn in Bombay, returning to London with his family in tow in order to liquidate the struggling Dadabhai Naoroji & Co, fulfil his financial obligations to lenders and found the East India Association in 1866.

Indian political economy drew Naoroji back to Gujarat in 1871, where he embarked on a tour of the region with his colleague Naoroji Furdoonji to evaluate agricultural poverty. This Indian episode of Dadabhai Naoroji's life would also see him become *diwan* (prime minister) of the Indian princely state of Baroda in 1873, only to resign after the ruling monarch became embroiled in

---

[78] Masani, *Dadabhai Naoroji*, p. 20.

[79] 'The Hon. Dadabhai Naoroji,' in George Potter, ed., *The Monthly Record of Eminent Men*, vol. III, January to June 1891 (London: George Potter, 1891), p. 229.

[80] Masani, *Dadabhai Naoroji*, p. 30.

an assassination attempt on the British resident. Naoroji subsequently took up a position on the Bombay Municipal Corporation and Council from 1875 to 1876. This was a post he would occupy again from 1883 to 1886, during which time he was also appointed to the Bombay Legislative Council in 1885, the same year he co-founded the Indian National Congress. In March 1886, Naoroji sailed to Europe once again, this time with the intention of standing for election to the House of Commons. The Liberal Party's MP for Central Finsbury from 1892 to 1895, Naoroji was never able to replicate his success and after party infighting, he ran as an independent candidate for North Lambeth in 1906, garnering only 733 votes. In an impromptu trip to India, he presided over the Calcutta meeting of the Indian National Congress in December 1906 and demanded *swaraj*, or 'self-rule', but 'under British paramountcy'. Ambitiously, Naoroji hoped to continue his activism in Britain when he arrived again in London by January 1907, only to retire permanently to India in October of the same year after several months of deteriorating health. At the age of 91, Dadabhai Naoroji passed away on 30 June 1917 in Cumballa Hill, Bombay.[81]

## Sources

For the most part, commentary on Naoroji's drain theory has been based on a small body of published sources. Naoroji's *Poverty and Un-British Rule* (1901) is a compendium of his writings, speeches and letters and is the most widely consulted of his works.[82] In addition, there are two volumes of collected works of Naoroji's public pronouncements: Parekh's *Essays, Speeches, Addresses and Writings of the Hon'ble Dadabhai Naoroji* and Zaidi's curiously titled *The Grand Little Man of India: Dadabhai Naoroji, Speeches and Writings*.[83] Patel's recent biography of Naoroji is the only one to make extensive use of the Naoroji Papers at the Indian National Archive. However, even this substantial piece of scholarship omits the use of crucial evidence from the Naoroji collection, such as the substantial 'Notes and Jottings' files that add significant nuance to Naoroji's thinking on political and economic issues. The full collection numbers approximately 25,000 discrete items, including personal correspondence, newspaper cuttings, extracts, receipts, diaries, and notes and jottings by Naoroji. The majority of the collection comprises

---

[81] For a strictly chronological approach to Dadabhai's life, see Masani, *Dadabhai Naoroji*.

[82] Dadabhai Naoroji, *Poverty and Un-British Rule* (London: Swan Sonnenschein & Co, 1901).

[83] Dadabhai Naoroji, *Essays, Speeches, Addresses and Writings of the Hon'ble Dadabhai Naoroji*, ed. C. L. Parekh (Bombay: Caxton Printing Works, 1887); Dadabhai Naoroji, *The Grand Little Man of India*: *Dadabhai Naoroji, Speeches and Writings*, vol. I, ed. Moin Zaidi (New Delhi: Institute of Applied Political Research, 1985).

letters to Naoroji from a plethora of individuals and organizations touching on every aspect of politics, social reform, economics and religion. Approximately 3,200 items are copies of letters Naoroji sent to others.

While Naoroji's publications and his papers provide the core source material for this book, they are supplemented with material from the private papers of Naoroji's key interlocutors in Britain and India, such as the private papers of William Digby, George Birdwood and Gopal Krishna Gokhale.[84] The more limited collection of Naoroji correspondence at the Nehru Memorial Museum and Library was also consulted.[85] While this book does not rely upon the heuristic of the 'network' to interpret global political thought, the exchanges between Naoroji and other thinkers do provide one way of examining how Dadabhai's thought was interpreted by others. The penultimate chapter of this book shows how constituent parts of Naoroji's liberal theory were reinterpreted by his interlocutors but often for a range of divergent political projects.

The intellectual context of the period is also sketched through the British and Indian scholarly journals in which Naoroji's ideas were disseminated and debated. Among those consulted are *India: The Journal of the British Committee of the Indian National Congress*; the *Indian Spectator*; the *Journal of the East India Association* in London; the *Journal of the National Indian Association*; and the *Journal of the Poona Sarvajanik Sabha*.[86] Naoroji was also involved in a number of political and social associations in which he both co-operated and conflicted with fellow members. For instance, the minutes of the British Committee of the Indian National Congress (National Archives of India, New Delhi) and the British Committee of the Continental and General Federation for the Abolition for the State Regulation of Vice (The Women's Library, London School of Economics) have been consulted to evaluate the institutional context of Naoroji's ideas and politics over a range of issues.[87] The personal papers of key British officials have also been employed in order to ascertain institutional and bureaucratic opposition

---

[84] London, British Library Asia Pacific and African Collections (BLAPAC), William Digby Papers, MSS Eur D767; BLAPAC, George Birdwood Papers, MSS Eur F216; BLAPAC, Gopal Krishna Gokhale Papers, IOR Neg 11697–11710.

[85] New Delhi, Nehru Memorial Museum and Library (NMML), Dadabhai Naoroji Collection, vols. I–II.

[86] *India: A Journal for the Discussion of Indian Affairs* (London, 1890–1921); *Indian Spectator* (Bombay: 1880–1913); *Journal of the East India Association* (London: 1867–1941); *Journal of the National Indian Association* [*Indian Magazine* from 1886] (London, 1871–1933); *Quarterly Journal of the Poona Sarvajanik Sabha* (Pune, 1866–1920).

[87] NAI, Minutes of Meetings of the British Committee of the Indian National Congress, reels 1 to 3, accession number 1940-1943; London, British Library of Political and Economic Science, London School of Economics (BLPES), The Women's Library, British Committee of the

to parts of Naoroji's programme. For example, the official papers of Sir Lewis Pelly shed significant light on Naoroji's career as prime minister of the Baroda state and how his thought developed through an often fraught relationship with colonial administrators.[88]

In wanting to better understand how Naoroji's political thought was inextricably intertwined with his political action and oriented towards both the Indian and British publics, the newspapers of both countries were examined in detail. Over thirty national and local newspapers in the United Kingdom reported on different aspects of Naoroji's politics, and much of this reportage was transmitted back to India, where the indigenous press reflected on its implications. For instance, W. T. Stead's *Pall Mall Gazette* and the *Freeman's Journal* are two prominent examples that routinely documented how Naoroji's thought informed radical politics in both London and Ireland. Together, this wide array of source material has been used to reconstruct Naoroji's intellectual milieu and life-world between India and Britain. His individual agency within this ecology was defined by the co-constitution of 'prejudice', conscious theorizing and meaningful action.

## Structure of the Book

Chapter 1 summarizes the exclusionary logic of 'official' colonial liberalism towards Indians as well as British debates around the civil and commercial registers of modern society. It also discusses Victorian romanticism's critique of liberalism and utilitarianism. The object of the chapter is to show that liberalism and liberal political economy were not inherently closed to more generous interpretations about the ideology's efficacy in non-European contexts. The ideas of British thinkers on commercial and civil society like Adam Smith, David Hume, John Stuart Mill and Henry Sumner Maine are parsed and put into dialogue with romantic critics like Thomas Carlyle and John Ruskin. The chapter concludes with an exploration of how some Indian thinkers were able to produce a creative tension between these antagonistic British traditions by using romantic conceptions of individual will and heroism to bring about a historical acceleration and counter the gradualism of colonial liberals.

Chapter 2 outlines the nineteenth-century Parsi life-world out of which Dadabhai Naoroji emerged and the attendant 'prejudices' which informed his reinterpretation of liberalism. Through a detailed examination of Parsi faith,

---

Continental & General Federation for Abolition of Government Regulation of Prostitution, 3BGF.

[88] BLAPAC, Lewis Pelly Collection, MSS Eur F126.

commerce, social affairs and communal tensions with fellow Indians, this part of the book explains how Bombay's Parsi community was intensely concerned with how to ensure civil peace through sociality in ways that also maintained cultural distinctiveness. In addition, the chapter reveals how Anglophile economic and professional elites in the community were drawn into imperial forms of civil association that lubricated the wheels of trade and imperial preferment. This spawned a middle-class Victorian attentiveness to civic munificence and philanthropy in an effort to sustain a plural public sphere in which civil and commercial association, both within India and across the British Empire, might freely be pursued through social organizations like the Freemasons or political and intellectual outfits like the India Reform Society.

Chapter 3 turns to the fragility of the Parsi world during the middle of the nineteenth century as a series of scandals among the community's traditional elite on the Parsi *panchayat* and a chain of communal riots destabilized the community. The social reform agendas of Dadabhai Naoroji, Naoroji Furdoonji, Kharshedji Cama and others are examined in order to show how they critiqued the practices of some of their co-religionists and community elders. This involved replacing the fiat of the Parsi *panchayat* with a civil society based on autonomous liberal self-fashioning and individual property ownership. The chapter therefore details Naoroji's leadership in matters of cultural education, reform of illiberal religious practices as well as female education and female inheritance as a form of liberal intervention to encourage the community's social improvement through individual self-reliance. The chapter also draws attention to Naoroji's particular attitude to these questions by comparing his liberal arguments with those of competing liberals like Behramji Malabari.

Chapter 4 plays a pivotal role in the book's argument by explaining the turning point in Naoroji's liberalism from social reform to economic reform. As financial catastrophe struck Bombay and Naoroji's own business fortunes, the fragile commercial taproot of Parsi philanthropy and Bombay's social peace was called into question by Naoroji, colleagues like Dinshaw Wacha and the wider Parsi public sphere. The chapter recounts how Naoroji's transnational business experiences, lawsuits in London and observation of recurrent regional famines prompted him to focus more closely on political economy as the source of India's social problems. He embarked on a period of sustained statistical inquiry in the Gujarati countryside with his collaborator Naoroji Furdoonji and also to study the conditions of Indian prisoners with European colleagues. The goal here was to calculate the basic level of individual subsistence of an Indian worker and what he might be able to produce under conditions of free labour. This process allowed

Naoroji to abstract the individual Indian labour from a medley of ethnographic colonial classifications. Dadabhai Naoroji concluded that sociality arose overwhelmingly from reciprocal commercial relationships between individual producers and consumers but that such a commercial society was undermined by the colonial state's monopolistic expropriation of labour's rightful property. Naoroji identified exorbitant civil service salaries as well as the land revenue and council bill systems as the cause of the drain from India and also the reason the individual Indian labourer was consigned to semi-feudal bondage rather than economic autonomy.

Chapter 5 commences with Naoroji's application of his newly conceived drain theory to Indian politics. It elaborates how he attempted to reform the bureaucratic colonial state and its monopolistic fiscal and financial practices by proposing a new system of simultaneous examinations for Indian and British candidates for the civil service. In addition, this section also examines Naoroji's career as prime minister of the princely state of Baroda and how he tried to reform corruption within a royal court that exerted an arbitrary power over the peasantry and the land revenue of the state. Contrary to the accounts of other scholars, the chapter uses these two interventions in Indian politics to show how Naoroji was not concerned with democratic representation and self-government. Indianization of the bureaucracy, by a class of dutiful bourgeois technocrats such as himself, on the other hand, would put an end to labour's domination by corrupt vested interests and engender Indian sociality.

Chapter 6 considers Naoroji's application of the drain theory's conceptual repertoire and his politics of labour republicanism to the social and economic debates taking place in Great Britain, Ireland and Africa between 1860 and 1910. Departing from accounts that show Naoroji navigating the representational order to win the Central Finsbury constituency in 1892, this chapter, instead, shows how he used his ideas to win over the radical wing of the Liberal Party and his overwhelmingly working-class constituents. In this respect, the chapter develops the account of Naoroji's transnational experience from previous sections in order to take a closer look at how he used his ideas at a global, national, constituency and municipal level. Using the drain theory in order to speak to issues of Irish Home Rule, municipal reform, livery and guild reform, co-operative politics and the taxation of ground rents and more, the chapter explains how Naoroji achieved prominence in Britain through political debate as a global thinker. The chapter also sketches the engagement of Irish Land Leaguers, social democrats, American populists, campaigners for African self-government and others with Naoroji's ideas. Finally, a close examination of his writings and political action shows that he regarded the labouring masses of Great Britain, Ireland and British Africa as living in a state of economic domination akin to Indians. Naoroji's solutions aligned with those that he proposed for the Raj, that of enacting a programme of anti-trust reform buttressed by industrial courts that empowered workers to arbitrate the relationship between financial capital and labour. Unifying the principles of his drain theory across transnational contexts, he regarded these anti-monopoly reforms as analogous to his proposed Indianization of the colonial state, suggesting a functional equivalence in his thinking for the Indian labour and the British proletarian.

The final chapter reveals the ideological twists and turns the drain theory made as it was appropriated by a new generation of Indian thinkers. From Gandhian village economics to left-wing industrial developmentalism, this chapter shows how Naoroji's liberalism was cannibalized and deployed in a panoply of divergent political projects. Even so, it was the normative language of Naoroji's labour republicanism that united these disparate re-inscriptions of the drain theory. The chapter traces the residual influence of the drain theory in the political thought of Mahatma Gandhi, Jawaharlal Nehru, Chakravarty Rajagopalchari and other prominent Indian thinkers. Among the biggest takeaways of this Indian reception history of Naoroji-ism after 1920 is the paradox that his programme of constructive sociality was linked to an Indianization of the state's technocracy that undermined the idea that state sovereignty was distinct from society. The long-term legacy of this relationship was to throw Indian politics on to a sociocentric vision that made aspects of the drain theory simultaneously amenable to secular developmentalists like Nehru and – more curiously – radical religious conservatives like Gandhi.

# 1 Sociality in an Imperial and Industrial Age

In February 1866 the retired Scottish physician and colonial administrator Sir John Crawfurd launched an epistemic assault on the alleged racial and cultural incapacity of Asians for 'progress'. Delivered at the London Ethnological Society, Crawfurd's paper 'On the Physical and Mental Characteristics of the European and Asiatic Races of Man' enumerated the racial and sociological deficiencies of Asians, from their physical weakness to the inferiority of their literary output, invoking prominent utilitarian and liberal intellectuals like James Mill to bolster his argument. Dadabhai Naoroji had arrived in the United Kingdom eleven years earlier as a cotton trader based in Liverpool and by 1859 had relocated to London, where he was firmly enmeshed in the city's intellectual associations and political life. Taking exception to what he regarded as Crawfurd's libellous attacks on Asian culture, Naoroji launched a scholarly counter-attack a month later in his own paper entitled 'The European and Asiatic Races'. The indignant Parsi offered copious examples of Asian literary and political genius. However, in instances in which India did display 'illiberal' tendencies, Naoroji interpreted and deployed his own selection of liberal concepts in order to historicize Indian development through a comparative stadial theory of 'progress' and so counter Crawfurd's orientalism and racism.[1]

The subsequent chapters of this book explore Naoroji's engagement with liberalism and how ideological experimentation with this ideology allowed him to innovate a universal theory of plural sociality. Even though European liberals did not fully integrate cultural or class difference in practice, in Naoroji's estimation liberalism was open to conceptual experimentation and held out the potential for a more solidaristic politics. This chapter examines the writings of British liberals, political economists and their critics across the long nineteenth century in an effort to conceptually disaggregate forms of liberal sociality under the two

[1] Dadabhai Naoroji, 'The European and Asiatic Races: Observations on the Paper Read by John Crawford, Esq., F. R. S.', read before the Ethnological Society, 27 March 1866, in Dadabhai Naoroji, *Essays, Speeches, Addresses and Writings of the Hon'ble Dadabhai Naoroji* ed. C. L. Parekh (Bombay: Caxton Printing Works, 1887), pp. 11–13.

broad headings of civil and commercial society. The rationale here is to evaluate liberalism's capacity to promote sociality across different cultural and class groups using the variety of thinkers we know Naoroji to have read. In so doing, the immanent potential Naoroji recognized in these traditions is outlined before we turn to how he renovated them in India. The account begins with the attempts of colonial officialdom to contain Indian political and economic aspirations through strategies of cultural quarantine via the 'official' liberalism of the Raj. The chapter moves on to discuss how ideas of civil society, based on individual character, and commercial society, based on economic interdependence, each promoted its own version of sociality. This part of the book also notes how some Indians dipped into British romanticism's critique of utilitarianism's pleasure and profit motives in order to seed liberal and commercial doctrines with civic virtue predicated on the nobility of free labour. What is more, in leading by example, romanticism's admiration of 'great men' convinced some Indians that individual self-overcoming through sheer willpower could rupture the liberal continuum of gradualist historical development in which indigenous peoples and the European working classes had been politically relegated to the 'imaginary waiting room of history'.[2]

## The 'Official' Liberalism of Colonial Rule

By the second half of the nineteenth century, the 'official' liberalism of the colonial state established an ethnographic legal regime that reified Indian castes into incommensurable ethnic groups ruled by their respective customary laws.[3] Indians had to be governed according to their various customs, so the argument went, because the birth of modern reason was uniquely European and owed its success to the non-reproducible sequence of social and legal 'progress' from Roman antiquity to the Industrial Revolution. This departed from the Enlightenment's focus on natural law and its commitment to the universal rationality of mankind. If this development did not stall the global liberal telos, it did at least apply the brakes to the pace of 'progress' and on the continued legitimacy of a 'civilizing mission' based upon the tutelage of 'Western' institutions like Christianity, education and commerce. The comparative jurist Henry Sumner Maine was the main theorist of this new circumscribed liberal dispensation. Maine attacked natural rights theorists, utilitarians and those who claimed to have developed a universal 'science of man'. In Maine's view, these misguided individuals postulated a non-historic,

[2] Dipesh Chakrabarty, *Provincializing Europe: Postcoloniality and the Critique of History* (Princeton, NJ: Princeton University Press, 2000), p. 8.

[3] Nicholas Dirks, *Castes of Mind: Colonialism and the Making of Modern India* (Princeton, NJ: Princeton University Press, 2001).

'unverifiable condition of the race'. Though state of nature theories varied with regard to the 'prae-social state, and as to the nature of the abnormal action by which men lifted themselves out of it', Maine insisted that there was still a 'great chasm' which he believed 'separated man in his primitive condition from man in society'.[4] Likewise, Maine may have admired utilitarianism's legal rationalism but questioned the universal applicability of the pleasure–pain–happiness principle and whether distant cultures would comprehend a clarified system of jurisprudence derived from it.[5]

Returning to the primordial origins of political obligation, Maine identified the power of the *pater familias* as the origin of state and society. As states grew larger and more complicated, they expanded personal rights to create a social order based on free association rather than compulsion, or, in Maine's terms, there had been a movement from 'Status to Contract'.[6] India would become an important comparative case study for Maine's continued analysis. He had served on the Indian law commission in the mid-1860s, studying the development of Indian society, and in 1871 published his *Village-Communities in the East and West*, which postulated that English institutions and laws had disrupted traditional Indian culture. While in Western aristocracies the Roman influence had transformed early law codes into secular civil and political institutions, in India Brahmins remained resolutely religious and displaced military and political authority.[7] Maine believed that utilitarian attempts to rationalize Indian law codes according to European precedents disfigured a religiously bound Indian culture. Modern liberalism was inapplicable to the Indian context because modern reason was predicated on individual contracts liberated from religious obscurantism and injunction.[8] Rather, traditional societies were characterized by corporatist structures where religion and law intermingled to form the basis of individual agency, whereby the social became the privileged domain of understanding India to the exclusion of the political or economic.[9] India, Maine postulated, 'knows nothing of individuals'.[10]

---

[4] Henry Maine, *Ancient Law: Its Connections with the Early History of Society and Its Relation to Modern Ideas* (London: John Murray, 1861), p. 111.

[5] R. C. J. Cocks, *Sir Henry Maine: A Study in Victorian Jurisprudence*, new edn (Cambridge: Cambridge University Press, 2004), p. 136.

[6] Maine, *Ancient Law*, pp. 163–5.

[7] Ibid., pp. 9–18.

[8] Karuna Mantena, *Alibis of Empire: Henry Maine and the Ends of Liberal Imperialism* (Princeton, NJ: Princeton University Press, 2010).

[9] Henry Maine, *Village Communities in the East and East, with Other Lectures, Addresses and Essays*, 3rd edn (London: John Murray, 1890 [1871]), p. 9

[10] Maine, *Ancient Law*, p. 258.

Maine's India was paradigmatic of the claims made by more biological conceptions of racial difference. Nevertheless, in its sociological focus it was also much more theoretically flexible with regard to isolating institutional or cultural flaws that could be existentially remedied. Moreover, Maine never offered a detailed theory of how the shift from status to contract occurred in Europe, thereby leaving the door open for reinterpretations of this thought. Consequently, as I show in the next two chapters, both colonial officials and Indians fell back upon liberal institutions as a means to intervene in Maine's closed cultural system. Specifically, political economy became a route into the social, allowing for its internal transformation and bypassing the need to directly challenge religion or custom. The examination of Parsi inheritance in Chapter 3 shows how this intellectual space was seized upon by a community with strong commercial traditions, which simultaneously used the language of social reform and political economy in order to promote the continued cohesion and prosperity of their minority.

In political economy a similar shift took place from commercial tenets based on natural law to those adapted to the historical sociology of a society. On the one hand, a Mainite orthodoxy textured colonial officials' views of legitimate and illegitimate commerce. By the late nineteenth and early twentieth centuries, business legislation such as the Negotiable Instruments Act (1881) and Indian Companies Act (1882) sought to demarcate a modern marketized economy of largely European capital from that of vernacular traders. Defined by the Hindu undivided family, colonial lawmakers understood traditional commercial enterprises to be characterized by extended kinship networks. These were defined and regulated according to 'traditional' personal laws quarantining them from the public sphere of contractual agents by placing them in the private realm of customary culture.[11] On the other hand, political economy metamorphosized from a science predicated on the rubric of natural law and the primacy of the physical world into a system of investigation that increasingly foregrounded human agency, institutions and historical context.[12] According to Margaret Schabas, the watershed moment in this 'denaturalisation' was the publication of J. S. Mill's *Principles of Political Economy*.[13] Physiocracy and Malthusianism continued to channel the overwhelming influence of nature,

[11] Ritu Birla, *Stages of Capital: Law, Culture, and Market Governance in Late Colonial India* (Durham, NC: Duke University Press, 2009).

[12] Margaret Schabas, *The Natural Origins of Economics* (Chicago, IL: Chicago University Press, 2005).

[13] John Stuart Mill, 'The Principles of Political Economy with Some of Their Applications to Social Philosophy, Books I–IV' [1848], in John Stuart Mill, *The Collected Works of John Stuart Mill* [hereafter *CW*], vols. II–III, ed. John M. Robson, intro. V. W. Bladen, online edn (33 vols., Toronto: Toronto University Press, 1965).

and even David Ricardo emphasized commerce's reliance on natural endowments and local climate when determining what each region of the world would produce most economically.[14] Though both Maine and Mill moved from natural law to sociological analyses, the latter's account of the historical evolution of societies and their attendant political economies was more dynamic than Maine's rigid legal institutionalism.

Mill accounted for the need to tailor any given science of political economy to specific 'states of society' rather than the dictates of natural law and owed his historical methodology, which rejected biological determinism, to Auguste Comte's positivism.[15] Mill acknowledged a qualified human nature but totally denied a pre-social natural right deriving from it, insisting that man's nature was not constituted as 'if he were to live as an individual and no other humans existed'. There were a different set of attributes that might be called human nature that arise exclusively from 'living in a state of *society*, that is, forming part of a body or aggregation of human beings, systematically co-operating for common purposes'.[16] Mill identified the affective deficiencies of both the 'civilized' poor and the 'uncivilized' indigenous peoples in tandem. These groups were seen as having not yet developed the habits and ethos of sustaining sociality. However, for each group the correct combination of social, political and educational institutions would cultivate the appropriate bonds and desires for a socially oriented character to develop.[17] Thus, Mill used the terms 'state of society' and 'state of civilization' interchangeably. Both were defined in his *System of Logic* as 'the simultaneous state of all the greater social facts or phenomena' of a people and in which 'there exist Uniformities of Coexistence between the states of the various social phenomena'.[18] The impression given is one in which correct intervention with the appropriate pedagogic mechanisms could improve the socialization of the British working classes and colonized subjects. In the meantime, Mill admitted that in India 'custom' served a purpose in protecting the weak from the strong and

---

[14] Schabas, *The Natural Origins*, p. 116.

[15] Cheryl B. Welch, 'Social Science from the French Revolution to Positivism', in Gareth Steadman Jones and Gregory Claeys, eds., *The Cambridge History of Nineteenth Century Political Thought* (Cambridge: Cambridge University Press, 2011), p. 191.

[16] John Stuart Mill, 'On the Definition of Political Economy; and on the Method of Investigation Proper of It', in *Essays on some Unsettled Questions of Political Economy* [1844], in Mill, *CW*, vol. IV, p. 283 (emphasis in original).

[17] Inder Singh Marwah, 'A Matter of Character: Moral Psychology and Political Exclusion in Kant and Mill', (unpublished Ph.D. thesis, University of Toronto, 2002), pp. 147–8, 153; Georgios Varouxakis, *Mill on Nationality* (London: Routledge, 2002), p. 55.

[18] Varouxakis, *Mill on Nationality*, pp. 55, 62.

that full competition was a phenomenon of more fully developed societies. In such circumstances, the laws of political economy remained operative so long as they took account of 'the actual affairs of life' and considered what would happen in a society where 'competition falls short of the maximum'.[19]

Naoroji seized upon Mill's concept of the 'state of society' to counter Crawfurd's condemnation of Indians as backward, mendacious and despotic. Insisting that contemporary Indian laws differed from Europe because they were fitted to an alternative stage in social development, Naoroji showed that this sociology was not indicative of innate failings, nor did it indicate the inapplicability of European norms of governance. Naoroji also alerted Crawfurd to the fact that some Indian 'falsehoods' were not evidence of the incapacity of Indians to form a cohesive society based on mutual trust and contractual obligation. Drawing on Jeremy Bentham, Naoroji attested that falsehoods may be allowed to misdirect a murderer, to save a life in the case of a lying physician or to foster cohesion through exaggerated compliments or urbanity. Indeed, in most states of cohesive society removed from the communitarian bonds of custom, certain types of falsehood were a social duty.[20] Naoroji buttressed this argument by showing that the ancient Indian law codes, the *Institutes of Manu*, had mandated truthfulness where it related to issues of social cohesion, that is to say, where individuals were to take pleasure in 'truth' when it pertained to 'justice'. If chastisement of mendacity was the order of the day, it should not be in a moralizing but 'in a legal mode'.[21] Where Crawfurd saw immemorial stasis, Naoroji recognized that there was an opportunity to intervene in the dynamic state of society in order to re-sequence social phenomena in such a way that might facilitate progress to the next stage. Both Naoroji's early commitment to social reform and his later focus on political economy would depend upon the favourite tool of liberal intervention: education.[22]

Other British and Indian critics of 'official' liberalism drew on J. S. Mill but they also re-worked Maine in a way that stripped him of his legal determinism. Some historians have pointed to the German historical school, most closely associated with Friedrich List, as providing the tools with which Indians challenged the heteronomy of colonial liberalism by prioritizing the state-enforced political boundaries of a national Indian economy over that of borderless trade.[23]

[19] Mill, 'Principles of Political Economy, Books I–II', in Mill, *CW*, vol. II, pp. 233–6.
[20] Naoroji, 'European and Asiatic Races', p. 11.
[21] Ibid, pp. 11–12.
[22] Ibid, p. 19.
[23] Manu Goswami, *Producing India: From Colonial Economy to National Space* (Chicago, IL: Chicago University Press, 2004), p. 215.

This was certainly true by the late nineteenth century, particularly among Bengali nationalists like Benoy Kumar Sarkar, who were less enamoured of liberalism.[24] However, List's German *National System of Political Economy*, published in 1846, was not available in Britain until 1885, with the only English-language version available in the United States in 1856.[25] By contrast, British economists like T. E. Cliffe Leslie were embarking on historicist analyses of the Irish economy and the challenges it faced using methods derived from Mill and Maine.[26] Leslie admitted that 'my line was taken ten years before I ever saw a German book on economics. So far as my method is taken from anyone, it is taken from Sir Henry Maine'.[27] Leslie's *Land Systems and Industrial Economy of Ireland, England the Continental Countries* became a major work of comparative historical economics for western India's political economists like Naoroji's interlocutor and fellow Elphinstone College graduate, Kashinath Trimbak Telang.[28] Leslie's appeal in having inductively studied the historical origins of Irish poverty was his cultural sensitivity. He adhered to the Ricardian laws of production but complicated economic orthodoxies around material self-interest, insisting that people were also governed by their cultural inheritance:

> [T]he germ from which the existing economy of every nation has been evolved is not the individual, still less the personification of an abstraction, but the primitive community – a community one in blood, property, thought, moral responsibility, and manner of life; and that individual interests itself, and the desires, aims, and pursuits of every man and woman in the nation have been moulded by, and received their direction from, the history of that community.[29]

Since the political and social interests of many Hindu thinkers like Telang were to preserve the cultural integrity of their community while reforming it along liberal lines, Leslie's English historical economics was instructive in overcoming

[24] C. A. Bayly, *Recovering Liberties: Indian Thought in the Age of Liberalism and Empire* (Cambridge: Cambridge University Press, 2011), p. 131

[25] Gerard M. Koot, *English Historical Economics, 1870–1926: The Rise of Economic History and Neomercantilism* (Cambridge: Cambridge University Press, 1987), pp. 32–3.

[26] Ibid., p. 39.

[27] Ibid., pp. 46–7; Anon, 'Political and Economical Heterodoxy: Cliffe Leslie', *Westminster Review* 64 (October 1883), p. 492.

[28] K. T. Telang, 'Free Trade and Protection from an Indian Point of View', in K. T. Telang, *Selected Writings and Speeches of K. T. Telang* (Bombay: Manoranjan Press, 1916), p. 116.

[29] T. E. Cliffe Leslie, 'On the Philosophical Methods of Political Economy' (1876), in T. E. Cliffe Leslie, *Essays in Political Economy*, 2nd edn (London: Longman, Green & Co, 1888), pp. 171–80.

the Mainite stasis of 'official liberalism' without sacrificing its historicist and contextualist method. It tailored political economy, as an instrument of social change, to an Indian context in which 'everything was so liable to become stereotyped by custom'.[30] Other important historical economists like James Edwin Thorold Rogers were also well known to Naoroji and refrained from culturally relativizing economic theory but suggested, like Mill, that a more subtle appreciation of local context was needed.[31] Rogers's *History of Agriculture and Prices in England* was a compendium of wages between 1259 and 1793 and became hugely popular with labour unions and socialists in Britain on account of its ability to trace the historical evolution of wages and inequality rather than viewing poverty as an intractable contemporary problem associated with an un-reformable deficit in individual or class character.[32]

## Character and Civil Society

If the inability to establish individual contracts was regarded as hobbling indigenous societies, then the Victorian concept of 'character' also encapsulated the sociological credentials that defined model liberal subjects. Character enjoyed wide purchase across the British political spectrum during the nineteenth century and emphasized the traits of material and mental independence, self-restraint, thrift, perseverance and philanthropy. The Victorians put a premium on the cultural character traits of the well-socialized liberal subject for the same reason that Adam Smith and his intellectual fellow travellers in the Scottish Enlightenment examined the social bonds generated by mutual sympathy and commercial contract. Both were driven by the bourgeois anxiety that the atomistic individualism that resulted from urban and industrial progress would fragment society.[33] In contrast to the Scottish Enlightenment's belief that self-interest and utility produced an automatic socialization, the bourgeois moralism of character demanded an interiorization and cultivation of the self so that individuals avoided mean self-interest and actively promoted sociability.[34]

---

[30] Telang, 'Free Trade and Protection', pp. 116–17.

[31] Koot, *Historical Economics*, p. 65; Dinshaw Wacha to Naoroji, 30 September 1887, in R. P. Patwardan, ed., *Dadabhai Naoroji Correspondence*, Vol. II, Part I: *Correspondence with Dinshaw Wacha* (2 vols., Bombay: Allied Publishers Private Limited, 1977), pp. 35–6.

[32] Koot, *Historical Economics*, pp. 67–8; J. E. Thorold Rogers, *A History of Agriculture and Prices in England from 1259 to 1793* (7 vols., Oxford: Clarendon Press, 1866–1902).

[33] James Vernon, *Distant Strangers: How Britain became Modern* (Berkley, CA: University of California Press, 2014), p. 101.

[34] Dror Wahrman, *The Making of the Modern Self: Identity and Culture in Eighteenth-century England* (New Haven, CT: Yale University Press, 2004), pp. 265–311.

Intellectual and political weight was added to popular discourses of good character by writers like Alexis de Tocqueville. His sociology of American democracy and its reliance on 'middling' social attributes was a major influence on Mill and prefigured his commentary on comparative states of society. Tocqueville's anxieties about the need to counteract the majoritarian and intellectually stultifying potential of mass democracy and mass society were also reflected in Mill's work. Tocqueville's treatises were read closely by the pioneers of India's new municipal politics during the second half of the nineteenth century, like Naoroji's Parsi colleague and Municipal Commissioner of Bombay, Pherozeshah Mehta.[35] Tocqueville's key contribution to this field was to link the cultural traits of Americans, or their capacity for retaining 'civic virtue' in the midst of the Jacksonian second-party system, with the civic tutelage that emanated from the 'art and science of association'.[36] The 'middling' character of the average American – their desire to amass wealth through hard work, independence and self-restraint – was at the core of their willingness for individual combination instead of collectivism.[37] This spontaneous drive to voluntary association between individuals free from state or community sanction is what we would term 'civil society'. This link was also a moderating influence. It was necessary because of individualism's flattening by mass society but also because, at the other extreme, individualism encouraged a retreat into a life of private egoism at the expense of public spiritedness. Tocqueville was keen to demonstrate the dual advantages of civil society. First, voluntary association, as a force of political and social activism, was able to solve local problems while preserving liberty by inviting citizens into forms of political participation that instilled civic virtue and freedom of thought. Second, in order to prevent state interference in the regulation of social relations, an indirect system of socialization was necessary. America's cultural predisposition to voluntary association facilitated just such a process in which '[f]eelings and ideas are renewed, the heart enlarged, and the understanding developed only by the reciprocal action of men one upon the other'.[38] The axiomatic antithesis of this process of socialization between different social and commercial interests was Tocqueville's account of the French old regime. Here, the community of interest

---

[35] P. M. Mehta, 'The Bombay Municipal Reform Question of 1871', a speech read at the Bombay branch of the East India Association, in P. M. Mehta, *Speeches and Writings of the Honourable Sir Pherozeshah M. Mehta*, ed. C. Y. Chintamani (Allahabad: The Indian Press, 1905), p. 105.

[36] J. G. A. Pocock, *The Machiavellian Moment: Florentine Thought and the Republican Tradition* (Princeton, NJ: Princeton University Press, 2016), pp. 537–8.

[37] A. de Tocqueville, *Democracy in America*, trans. G. Lawrence (New York, NY: Harper & Row, 1966), pp. 539–41.

[38] Ibid., p. 515.

between the regional governance of the nobility and the people was severed when the monarchy granted special fiscal and legal privileges to the aristocracy, realigning them away from the civil realm and closer to that of the dynastic state.[39] As Chapter 3 clarifies, when it came to the subject of social reform among the Parsis of India, the dichotomy set up was between horizontal socialization, despite cultural differences, against corrupt vertical hierarchies that prevented a genuine sociality from emerging.

The character analogy could also express desirable bourgeois attributes in an economic register. Between the Enlightenment to the Industrial Revolution, the world of work came to substitute that of leisure as the ethical sphere in which one demonstrated moral probity. The character discourse was also suspicious of the sustainability and long-term utility of commercial self-interest unalloyed by ethical guidance. The fear was that, eventually, the enterprising spirit of some humans might stagnate or give way to private greed.[40] The promoters of good character intended to remedy this by imbuing individual enterprise with a consciously ethical vector. In this vein, opposed to the virtues of character stood the 'residuum', the bottom 10 per cent of the working classes. In the franchise debates of the 1860s, John Bright insisted that the residuum could not be enfranchised because of its 'hopeless poverty and dependence ... such as to give no reasonable expectation that they would be able to resist the many temptations ... [that] men would offer them at periods of election'.[41] In Britain, the popular perception was that the residuum's poverty was a sign of its low character, which in turn, so the circular argument went, marked their inability to engage in industrial activity. While ethnic and religious identities may have been replaced, the class-based register of character is inescapable; indeed, it was expressed and thought of explicitly as the contractualism of 'official' liberalism. James Thompson's study of nineteenth-century British civil society reveals that legitimate 'public opinion' was regarded as coterminous with the views of the salaried, professional and propertied middle classes as those who epitomized good character. This bourgeois public expressed its opinion as a national cohort of consumers who expected open and honest contractual dealings with the nation's producers in the labouring classes.[42] This went hand in hand

---

[39] A. de Tocqueville, *The Old Regime and the French Revolution* trans. S. Gilbert (New York, NY: Doubleday 1955), p. 136.

[40] Stefan Collini, 'The Idea of "Character" in Victorian Political Thought', *Transactions of the Royal Historical Society* 35, no. 1 (1985), pp. 41–4.

[41] *The Times*, 27 March 1867.

[42] James Thompson, *British Political Culture and the Idea of 'Public Opinion', 1867–1914* (Cambridge: Cambridge University Press, 2013), pp. 42–4, 56–7.

with middle-class Britons imagining themselves as a nation of unencumbered free traders.

The producers of the nation, however, could fulfil the conditions of good character and liberal subjectivity based on the quality of their labour and the ownership of property which guaranteed their autonomy. The language of republicanism and natural law suffused the way in which producers like yeoman small-holders, artisans and tradesmen were lauded by liberal thinkers like Mill as representing 'sturdy independence' in contrast to the dependent and mindless wage-slavery of the factory system and tenant farming.[43] Indeed in the public moralizing of the day, the economic independence of the property-owning producer was viewed by radical liberals and Gladstonians as a sign of self-sufficiency and mental independence which equalled that of the bourgeois consumer.[44] Mill's moral economy also subordinated profit seeking to the task of 'training intelligence' in a tone that substituted independent commercial participation for the political participation of the republican tradition. The cares of the peasant proprietor, Mill writes, 'are that he takes his fair share of the business of life; that he is a free human being, and not perpetually a child, which seems to be the approved condition of the labouring classes according to the prevailing philanthropy'.[45] Similarly, in the context of the debate on Ireland, John Bright believed that it was a 'great mistake' to suppose that 'land is really only intended to be in the hands of the rich'. Directly invoking John Locke, he concurred that a proprietary yeomanry should form the liberal backbone of any country. 'There is no country in the world', Bright insisted, 'in which there are only great landowners and tenants, with no large manufacturing interest to absorb the population, in which the degradation of the cultivating tenant is not completely assured.'[46] Chapters 3 to 5 turn to the relationship between character, sociality and civil peace and to Naoroji's eventual preference for the exclusively economic nexus of consumers, producers and civil association

[43] J. S. Mill, *Chapters and Speeches on the Irish Land Question* (London: Longmans, Green, Reader, and Dyer, 1870), p. 2.

[44] Eugenio F. Biagini, *Liberty, Retrenchment and Reform: Popular Liberalism in the Age of Gladstone, 1860–1880* (Cambridge: Cambridge University Press, 1992), pp. 87–8; Chris Clarkson, *Domestic Reforms: Political Visions and Family Regulation in British Columbia, 1862–1940* (Vancouver: University of British Columbia Press, 2007), p. 24; Robert Lloyd Kelly, *The Transatlantic Persuasion: The Liberal-democratic Mind in the Age of Gladstone*, new edn (London: Routledge, 1990), pp. 46–7.

[45] Biagini, *Liberty, Retrenchment and Reform,* p. 86; Mill, 'Principles of Political Economy, Books I–II', in Mill, *CW*, vol. II, p. 260.

[46] John Bright, 'House of Commons, Mar. 14, 1868', in John Bright, *Speeches on Questions of Public Policy by the Right Honourable John Bright MP*, ed. James E. Thorold Rogers (London: T. Fisher Unwin, 1898), pp. 202–3.

shorn of cultural criticism. Naoriji's early career in social reform was preoccupied with the indispensability of good character and its attendant economic skills for creating an Indian civil society. However, as communal rioting and economic crisis undermined this project, Naoroji would re-work his idea of a civil society into a new vision of commercial society based more rigidly on the reciprocal contracts generated by production, consumption and trade under conditions of non-domination. In shifting the focus from the cultural deficits of character to the institutional deficits that allowed economic monopoly to thrive, Naoroji hoped to move his civil activism away from the potentially incendiary cultural critiques of other Indian communities.

## Natural Law and Commercial Society

Using political economy to intervene in liberal theory offered those living under uncivil liberalism an opportunity to accelerate the development of sociality without engaging in excessive cultural introspection. Chapter 4 shows how Naoroji understood this process after 1865 as resulting from the fair formation, holding and exchange of property through contract. In nineteenth-century Bengal, Naoroji's contemporaries had critiqued the sovereign violence of the colonial state by combining concepts from natural law and theology; in Bombay, however, Naoroji arrived at an Indian index of progress by intermingling natural law with a materialist historicism.[47] Accepting the historical and cultural differences between India and Britain, the ability to claim a natural law basis for reform was essential to Naoroji's allegation that poverty in both countries was a direct consequence of subversion of natural justice. Nevertheless, tensions remained between the doctrine of natural law, as an abstract pre-legal entitlement, and the historical contextualism touted by Cliffe Leslie, to say nothing of Mill's qualified utilitarianism that 'rejected the idea of abstract right as a thing independent from utility' and prefiguring any historical 'state of society'.[48] Naoroji's ability to invoke natural law and positive law together, alongside tenets of nineteenth-century liberalism, requires some conceptual explanation before we can detail his thought.

Naoroji had explained India's poverty as the result of the 'unnatural treatment' of British rule.[49] What he called for, as we shall see, is the restitution of 'natural law'

[47] Milinda Banerjee, 'Sovereignty as a Motor of Global Conceptual Travel: Sanskritic Equivalents of "Law" in Bengali Discursive Production', *Modern Intellectual History* 17, no. 2 (2020), pp. 487–506.

[48] Mill, 'On Liberty', in Mill, *CW*, vol. XVII, ch. I, para. 11.

[49] Dadabhai Naoroji, *Poverty and Un-British rule in India* (London: Swan Sonnenschein & Co, 1901), p. 203.

and 'justice' to the British world with special regard to the operation of commerce.[50] He claimed restoration to this natural economic liberty as the 'natural right' of British-born Indians.[51] Moreover, as later chapters make clear, Naoroji understood individuals operating within the natural law of the market as the means by which value and property were fairly created, secured and exchanged. Adam Smith's doctrine of natural law and commercial sociability was a conceptual repertoire available to Naoroji that could be disembedded from its European provenance in order to reconfigure nineteenth-century liberalism in its Indian context. The following discussion also indicates how Naoroji reconciled Smith's notions of commercial society with Maine and Mill's historicism.

The thinkers of the Scottish Enlightenment like Hume and Smith were more concerned with the conditions of possibility for liberty and sociability under an already-existing civil government. Like Naoroji, who accepted imperial sovereignty, these thinkers did not prioritize or explain the origin of authority and political order in their writings.[52] From Adam Smith came the most rigorous and well-known account of the role of commercial utility in fostering human sociality, a state of affairs that was sustained by the innate human tendency to justice. 'All members of human society', Smith insisted, 'stand in need of each other's assistance, and are likewise exposed to mutual injuries.' It was generally beneficial, therefore, if reciprocity arose 'from love, from gratitude, from friendship, [and] from esteem'.[53] In the absence of these inconsistent sentiments, the more reliable alternative was that society could 'subsist among different men, as among different merchants, from a sense of its utility, without any mutual love or affection'.[54] This state of affairs was upheld by justice predicated on an individual's 'natural resentment' and universalized to the whole community through Smith's doctrine of human 'sympathy'.[55] Unlike Hume, who regarded justice as driven exclusively by utility maximization, and emerging from the conventions of civil authority, Smith recognized that some form of prior consensus had to have emerged in

[50] Dadabhai Naoroji, 'On the Commerce of India', read before a meeting at the society of arts, London, 15 February 1871, in Naoroji, *Essays, Speeches, Addresses and Writings*, p. 126; Naoroji to W. Martin Wood, 28 November, n.d., National Archives of India, New Delhi [hereafter NAI], Dadabhai Naoroji Papers [hereafter DNP], N-1 (3140).

[51] Naoroji, *Poverty and Un-British Rule*, p. 203.

[52] Paul Sagar, *The Opinion of Mankind: Sociability and the Theory of the State from Hobbes to Smith* (Princeton, NJ: Princeton University Press, 2018), p. 101.

[53] Adam Smith, *The Glasgow Edition of the Works and Correspondence of Adam Smith: The Theory of Moral Sentiments*, ed. D. D. Raphael and A. L. Macfie (Oxford: Oxford University Press, 1976), II.ii.3.1.

[54] Smith, *Theory of Moral Sentiments*, II.ii.3.2.

[55] Ibid., II.ii.2.1–4.

order for those conventions to have been formalized. Thus, Smith regarded the resentment that one feels when seeing a party impose themselves upon another or their possessions, and the resulting desire for punishment, as the natural motive behind the justice that buttressed commercial society.[56] In Britain, such a theory of natural law operated within the bounds of established civil authority but was essential for socializing a population of 'strangers' born of rapid urbanization and rural dislocation. In India, it was all the more important to indigenous thinkers living under the authority of an established ethnographic state whose legal regime replicated social dislocation by legislating only on behalf of endogamous caste and kinship groups. It was assumed by the late nineteenth century, especially after the 1857 rebellion, that interfering in India's many customary traditions risked civil strife. This book makes clear that the attraction of commercial society to Naoroji was that it charted a middle path between the society of pure friendship and that of pure violence. More than this, it facilitated the growth of an effectively contractual society through a tacit concord. That is to say, contract was the outcome of social and economic processes operating according to natural law rather than a conscious commitment to civil peace.

Alongside Smith's model of commercial society sat his well-known stadial theory of historical development, which might appear to loosely prefigure Maine's anthropological historicism. Superficial similarities notwithstanding, Smith's moral theory was characterized by intentionalism and was focused on the self-interested and utility-driven interactions between the human mind and the nexus of economic needs. This was the original basis of civil authority in the earliest pastoral stage of economic development. Smith would have regarded Maine's idea that authority was inherited from the archaic family and then projected historically through Roman law – as contract – into ever more rational stages of European society as over-determined and not borne out by historical observation.[57] In his four-stage theory, Smith emphasized that it was commerce and trade that birthed modern liberty in the final stage. However, it was the specific quality of shifting political authority that, through happenstance, maximized individual commercial utility. From the perspective of society as a whole, the consequences were often unintended. For instance, Smith postulated that immediately after the fall of the Western Roman Empire it was Europe's semi-free cities, particularly in Germany and Italy, and their independent artisanal, trading and merchant classes that

---

[56] Sagar, *Opinion of Mankind*, pp. 171–3.

[57] Istvan Hont, *Politics in Commercial Society: Jean-Jacques Rousseau and Adam Smith*, ed. Béla Kapossy and Michael Sonnenscher (Cambridge, MA: Harvard University Press, 2015), pp. 47–55.

pioneered foreign trade. Here, a vestigial neo-Roman republicanism survived and facilitated the rule of free town dwellers and free markets from which the benefits of security and civility flowed.[58] The active and participatory civic virtue of the classical republican account was replaced by one that resulted from a much larger nexus of utility processes that did not depend upon cultural cultivation or social rank.[59] This stood in stark contrast to Montesquieu and some of his late-nineteenth-century British adherents who insisted that the liberties of the German *Volk* had been crystallized in a feudal system that was later exported to the British Isles by the Anglo-Saxons.[60] Montesquieu's biological and racial qualities did not require political or commercial participation to uphold.

In Smith's account, neo-Roman liberties did give way to rustication through the rise of feudalism in the Middle Ages, which resulted in agricultural accumulation and baronial infighting as aristocrats acquired significant judicial and military power. Feudal hierarchies were only dissolved by chance when the extent of baronial wealth forced its productive expenditure on luxury, resulting in effective rural to urban investment. The baronial patronage of retinues of dependent villeins gave way to the indirect encouraging of independent economic activity and the restoration of some semblance of economic non-domination promoted through the influence of the towns.[61] Serfs were thus freed and a rural division of labour instituted whereby peasants became wage labourers or, crucially, independent small proprietors.[62] Given this knowledge of the past, upholding the natural human proclivity to act upon one's material needs through economic activity was what produced the commercial interdependence of sociality. Though he is not regarded as a providential natural law theorist in the same way as John Locke, Smith did still insist upon the maintenance of law and justice in such a way as to maximize the human capacity to fulfil natural wants through the protection of property and the deterring of predation. In this way, Smith's account of the sociable individual depended upon a liberal account of economic activity that was free from external interference; however, it equally relied upon a vestigial republicanism which insisted that modern economic relations had to move beyond the monopolistic character of feudal dependency.

---

[58] Istvan Hont, *The Jealousy of Trade: International Competition and the Nation-State in Historical Perspective* (Cambridge, MA: Cambridge University Press, 2005), pp. 107–8.

[59] Hont, *Politics in Commercial Society*, p. 20.

[60] Hont, *The Jealousy of Trade*, pp. 105–6.

[61] Ibid., p. 108.

[62] Smith, *The Wealth of Nations*, books I–III (London: Penguin, 1982), pp. 496–514.

## Natural Born Englishmen and Commercial Society

If the Scottish Enlightenment proffered a natural basis for sociality incubated by a rational civil administration inclined towards justice, then English Whiggism accounted for this process through the unique qualities of English historical development. Such was Thomas Babbington Macaulay's account of the rise of commercial society which featured repeatedly in Naoroji's speeches and writings – so much so that Theodore Koditschek has labelled Naoroji's entire intellectual programme 'radicalized Macaulayism'.[63] For Macaulay as for Smith, British civility was founded upon a commercial society characterized by a division of labour, freely contracting producers and consumers, as well as foreign trade. However, Macaulay was not committed to a science of development or a natural law account of the origin of property.[64] He was a pragmatic reformer committed to preserving the felicitous English institutions that had arisen from a mixture of historical contingency and timely legislation. This account achieved global significance with Macaulay's interpretation of the Magna Carta as a political model of sociability that was transposable to British subjects around the world. In his epic *History of England*, Macaulay suggests that with the signing of the Great Charter in 1215 the historical trajectory of the disparate tribes of Britain was transformed by the 'first pledge of their reconciliation ... won by their united exertions, and framed for their common benefit'. This compact sowed the seed of England's future liberty and commercial prosperity that all native-born Englishmen might claim as their natural right.[65] For Macaulay the result was emphatic: 'In no country has the enmity of race been carried further than in England. In no country has that enmity been more completely effaced.'[66]

Naoroji accepted that the advent of British rule in the subcontinent represented the bequeathing of this Whig romance to India. Macaulay's English liberty was for Naoroji also the birthright of all Indians. Just as Macaulay had traced the beginnings of English progress to the Magna Carta, so too did Naoroji trace India's liberty to the moment Indians became British subjects in 1669 with

[63] Theodore Koditschek, *Liberalism, Imperialism and the Historical Imagination: Nineteenth-century Visions of Greater Britain* (Cambridge: Cambridge University Press, 2011), p. 294.
[64] Thomas Babbington Macaulay, 'Copyright' [a speech delivered to the House of Commons on 5 February 1841], in Macaulay, *The Miscellaneous Writings and Speeches of Lord Macaulay*, vol. 4 (London: Longmans, Green & Co, 1880).
[65] Israel Finestein, 'A Modern Examination of Macaulay's Case for the Civil Emancipation of the Jews', *Transactions and Miscellanies (Jewish Historical Society of England)*, vol. 28 (1981–1982), p. 43.
[66] Thomas Babington Macaulay, *The History of England from the Accession of James the Second*, vol. I (5 vols., London: Longmans, Green, Reader & Dyer, 1877 [1848–59]), p. 8.

the Company's acquisition of Bombay. Naoroji noted that 'the moment a people come under the British Flag they are free "British fellow citizens"'.[67] Likewise, Naoroji's colleague in India, the Parsi social reformer Behramji Malabari, suggested that because the 1669 Charter identified the island of Bombay as an extension of the Royal Manor of East Greenwich, British-Indian subjects were even entitled to representation in parliament.[68] Naoroji accepted the pluralism of English liberty as coterminous with the sovereignty of the English crown even though the United Kingdom was a composite nation. The 'word England, or Britain', Naoroji wrote to Lord Welby to clarify his views, 'is always used by me as embracing the United Kingdom.'[69] As far as Naoroji was concerned, the Scots, the Irish and the Indians were all inextricably a part of the historical unfolding of English liberties. Thus, Naoroji never consented to the view that the Queen's proclamation of 1858, which guaranteed every Indian's religious and cultural liberty, was a British ploy to keep India quiescent.[70] On the contrary, he viewed it as a formal and explicit statement of the rights of Indians as British subjects or, as many Indian liberals dubbed it, a 'Great Charter' for India.[71] Indeed, for Naoroji the principles of 1858 were laid down even earlier by Macaulay himself in the 1833 Charter Act, wherein 'no native of the said territories [India], nor any natural born subject of His Majesty resident therein, shall, by reason of his religion, place of birth, descent, colour or any of them, be disabled from holding any place, office or employment under the said [East India] Company'.[72]

For Naoroji, the 1858 proclamation was the 'grand and glorious charter of our liberties' since it encapsulated 'the germs of all that we aim at now, of all that we can desire hereafter'. He was so convinced of the transcendence of this moment as a blueprint for English liberty that he suggested that every Indian child commit the

---

[67] 'Grant of the first East India Company of the Island of Bombay', from 27 March 1669, NAI, DNP, notes and jottings, group 7: political, serial number 16.

[68] 'Mr Dadabhai Naoroji', *Indian Spectator*, 17 March 1889.

[69] Naoroji to Lord Welby, 15 February 1896, in Naoroji, *Poverty and Un-British Rule*, p. 343.

[70] On how Indians used the 1858 proclamation to advocate for equal rights, see also Sukanya Banerjee, *Becoming Imperial Citizens: Indians in the Late Victorian Empire* (Durham, NC: Duke University Press, 2010), pp. 42–50; Milinda Banerjee, *The Mortal God: Imagining the Sovereign in Colonial India* (Cambridge: Cambridge University Press, 2018), pp. 77–9.

[71] Naoroji to Lord Welby, 3rd November 1897, in Naoroji, *Poverty and Un-British Rule*, p. 434; 'India's Interest in the General Election', read before a meeting of the Bombay Presidency Association, 29 September 1885, in Naoroji, *Essays, Speeches, Addresses and Writings*, p. 293.

[72] Naoroji's 'Presidential address', second Indian National Congress, Calcutta, 1886 in Dadabhai Naoroji, *The Grand Little Man of India: Dadabhai Naoroji, Speeches and Writings*, vol. I, ed. Moin Zaidi (2 vols., New Delhi: Indian Institute of Applied Political Research, 1985), pp. 13–14.

proclamation to memory.[73] The Bengali critic of empire Surendranath Banerjea also recognized that it was only after 1858 that calls for Indian representation at the national level became conceivable. As in Macaulay's description of the Magna Carta, Banerjee believed that nationalist politics 'were the natural and legitimate product of the public activities that had preceded [the 1858 Proclamation]'.[74] The equivalence between the 1858 proclamation and the Magna Carta operated on two levels. First, it was a compact delineating duties and rights between the sovereign and her Indian subjects. Among these duties was the guarantee of an Indian's natural right to fair commerce and trade. Second, in Naoroji's interpretation, like the Magna Carta the proclamation conceptualized the disparate castes and creeds of India into a single cohort of potential subjects to whom 'English liberties' were promised – thus amalgamating Hindus, Muslims and Parsis under a common legal status on equal terms.[75]

This 'transcendent episode' of Britain's national story offered Indian reformers a model for liberty and sociality under the auspices of a global English story defined by the moderate statesmanship of masculine figures, like William of Orange, who maintained the delicate compact and eschewed the extremes of ostensibly effeminate religious fanaticism or hyper-masculine radicalism.[76] Juxtaposed with William's wisdom was James II's blindness to the fundamental laws that bound good governance, prosperity and liberty together. James recognized that Irish and English animosity was based on differences of character but he did not realize that these differences could be allayed if the issues of ignorance and wealth inequality were solved. Ireland lacked a judicious reformer who might allow the innate capacities of the Irish as human beings to flourish.[77] If such organization was undertaken, Macaulay believed, a natural transition would occur in which 'religious animosity ... would itself fade away'.[78] Attuned to the needs of his west Indian context, Naoroji would appropriate Macaulay's English political romance and hybridize it with Mill and Maine's contextualism and Smith's doctrines on the natural human drive for material betterment accompanied by its unintentional consequences of civil peace through commercial society. This would allow Naoroji

---

[73] Ibid., p. 14.

[74] Surendranath Banerjea, *A Nation in the Making: Being Reminiscences of Fifty Years of Public Life* (Bombay: Oxford University Press, 1963 [1925]), pp. 61–2.

[75] R. P. Masani, *Dadabhai Naoroji: The Grand Old Man of India* (London: George, Allen & Unwin Ltd, 1939), p. 56; Naoroji's speech at the annual dinner of the London Indian Society, *Sheffield and Rotherham Independent*, 7 September 1896.

[76] Koditschek, *Liberalism, Imperialism, and the Historical Imagination*, pp. 12, 131.

[77] Macaulay, *The History of England*, vol. I, pp. 393, 537–8.

[78] Ibid., p. 393.

to conscript law and political economy as pedagogic institutions intended to accelerate India's historical evolution while simultaneously demanding immediate redress in the commercial sphere through a language of natural law and justice. It was fitting then that alongside his Macaulyite contextualization of 1858 as a moment in English world history, Naoroji repeatedly quoted Macaulay's 1833 'the Government of India' speech in which a 'well-governed' India 'wearing our broadcloth, and working with our cutlery' was regarded as an infinite improvement over dependent feudal peasants 'performing salaams to English collectors and magistrates'. Britain had allegedly bestowed its traditions of political liberty to India but had forgotten that 'to trade' freely with 'civilized men' was a seamless form of socialization and reciprocity that avoided the need 'to govern' a fragmented population of 'savages'.[79]

In more recent times, the various bourgeois ideals of civil peace through commercial society discussed earlier were summarized by Jurgen Habermas, who spoke of the long-distance 'continuity of contract' generated by global trade. In order to maintain the reciprocal flow of international trade, bourgeois public opinion became the arbiter of a regulatory framework that best facilitated production and consumption. This led to a 'depersonalized state authority' eschewing direct social regulation by coercion and embracing a bureaucratic management of the capitalogenic processes underlying society after which 'public authority' was compelled to 'legitimate itself before public opinion'.[80] This process was expressed in terms of the natural economic laws of the 'free market' as a realm independent of direct interference or domination.[81] While searching for a durable basis for civil peace, a similar pivot in Naoroji's thinking from direct social and cultural reform to the indirect management of market relations through economic reform is the theme at the heart of this book. But in the age of colonial monopoly capitalism, and in comparison to Habermas's anodyne account, Naoroji's story is one of a political radicalism that sought to restore to labour its status as the natural producer of property, capital and contract – and so – the originator of modern market citizenship.

---

[79] Thomas Babbington Macaulay, 'Government of India', 10 July 1833, in Thomas Babbington Macaulay, *The Works of Lord Macaulay: Speeches, Poems and Miscellaneous Writings* (12 vols., London: Longmans & Co, 1898), p. 584; Macaulay quoted in Dadabhai Naoroji, *Poverty and Un-British Rule*, p. 277; Hansard, HC Deb, 14 August 1894, vol. 28, c. 1055; Naoroji's annotated copy of Macaulay's 1833 speech in 'Macaulay extracts', NAI, DNP, E-72 (90).

[80] *Jürgen Habermas, The Structural Transformation of the Public Sphere: An Inquiry into a Category of Bourgeois Society, trans. Thomas Burger (Cambridge: Cambridge University Press, 1992)*, pp. 15–25.

[81] Ibid., p. 25.

## Romanticism's Critique of Commercial Society

The fear that commercial society was a soulless mechanism that substituted individual virtue for utility was best articulated by English romantics like Thomas Carlyle and John Ruskin. As Naoroji engaged with political economy and liberal historicism, his biographer Rustom Masani tells us that he was also exposed to Carlyle's criticism, going on to compare Naoroji's establishment of reform-minded newspapers in Bombay to the preaching friar in Carlyle's *Sartor Resartus*.[82] Some Indian thinkers appropriated key tropes of the romanticists' lexicon in such a way as to reimagine and salvage aspects of liberalism. Both Carlyle and Ruskin idealized the 'hero', or public man, as a force for social transformation, and this trope appealed to India's small, educated and reform-minded intelligentsia who sought to catalyse the historicist timetable through exemplary intervention in the social order.[83]

Commercial society's fixation with pleasure and profit, at the expense of virtue and real utility, irked both Carlyle and Ruskin. To many, this echoed civic-humanist and republican critiques of the servility of the industrial world and the narrowing of human faculties on the factory floor. All this stood in stark contrast with the active self-cultivation of the classical Greek *polis* or Roman *civitas*.[84] Yet Alexander Jordan's detailed study of Carlyle's thought has recently re-positioned the romantic as a defender of 'useful labour' that sought to rediscover republican virtues in a reconstituted world of 'just industrialism'.[85] Carlyle laid out this political philosophy unambiguously in the serialized story of *Sartor Resartus* from 1833.[86] Invoking Aristotle, Carlyle recasts man from a political animal into a 'Tool-using Animal' who created the world by his 'Productive Industry'.[87] This type of autonomous creative labour stood in contrast to the monopolistic 'Feudalism and Preservation of the Game' that characterized the combine of the 'Overgrown Monsters of Wealth' whose membership included 'big Capitalists, Railways Directors, gigantic hucksters, kings of scrip, *without* lordly quality, or other virtue

[82] Masani, *Dadabhai Naoroji*, pp. 62, 75.

[83] Bayly, *Recovering Liberties*, pp. 160, 168; for the archetypal account, see Thomas Carlyle, *On Heroes, Hero-Worship, and the Heroic in History* (London: James Frasier, 1841).

[84] John Burrow, *A Liberal Descent: Victorian Historians and the English Past* (Cambridge: Cambridge University Press, 1985), pp. 65–7.

[85] Alexander Jordan, '"Noble Just Industrialism": Saint Simonism in the Political Thought of Thomas Carlyle' (unpublished Ph.D. thesis, European University Institute, Florence, 2015).

[86] W. J. Mander, *British Idealism: A History* (Oxford: Oxford University Press, 2011), pp. 25–6.

[87] Thomas Carlyle, *Sartor Resartus* (Oxford: Oxford University Press, 1987), pp. 32–5.

except cash'.[88] Carlyle condemned mechanistic analyses of human nature, state and society that focused on the 'physical, practical, [and] economical condition' of individuals 'as regulated by public laws'.[89] Political-economic laws were but 'outer semblances' of what were really the inner dictums of the human soul, and the former could never be a practical 'Law of Union for a Society of Men'.[90] Real freedom allowed individuals to cultivate their character and spirit through an exercise of their individual will, as well as allowing social sanctions to correct them when they strayed from a morally righteous path.[91] The fact that human existence was 'compassed round with Necessity' meant that industry was indispensable but it could only have real meaning as a liberated 'Voluntary Force' of virtuous world-building labour.[92] To this extent the labourer was a heroic figure, 'the real backbone of society', as Carlyle put it, and through his 'brotherhood' with the rest of the industrial classes could claim to be – both materially and morally – the foundation of the modern community.[93]

Ruskin expanded on Carlyle's critique, attacking the instrumentality of economic relations in numerous works.[94] *Unto This Last*, published in the 1860s, influenced the incipient labour and co-operative movements of the period, selling 200 copies per annum by the late nineteenth century.[95] Ruskin could not accept that capitalism promoted the social welfare of all. True wealth had to be collective, but in reality, individual profit was 'equally and necessarily the art of keeping your neighbour poor'. Consequently, accumulation 'does not therefore necessarily involve an addition to the actual property, or well-being of the state in which it

---

[88] Ibid., p. 92 (emphasis in original); Thomas Carlyle, 'Latter Day Pamphlet No. I: The Present Time' [February 1850], in *Latter Day Pamphlets* (London: Chapman & Hall, 1897), pp. 49–52, 230–1.
[89] Thomas Carlyle, 'Signs of the Times' [1829], in Thomas Carlyle, *Critical and Miscellaneous Essays*, vol. I (4 vols., London: Chapman & Hall, 1887 [1838–57]), p. 480.
[90] Thomas Carlyle, *Past and Present* (Boston, MA: Charles C. Little & James Brown, 1843), p. 32.
[91] Ibid., p. 212.
[92] Carlyle, *Sartor Resartus*, p. 140.
[93] Thomas Carlyle, 'Excursion (Futile Enough) to Paris', in *The Last Words of Thomas Carlyle: On Trade-Unions, Promoterism and the Signs of the Times* (Boston, MA: Dana Estates & Company, 1892), p. 182; Thomas Carlyle to Robert Peel, 19 June 1846, in *The Collected Letters of Thomas and Jane Welsh Carlyle*, vol. 20 (Durham, NC: Duke University Press, 1970–), pp. 211–12.
[94] Gill Cockram, *Ruskin and Social Reform: Ethics and Economics in the Victorian Age* (London: Bloomsbury, 2007), p. 7.
[95] Ibid., p. 11.

exists' but established 'the maximum inequality in our own favour'.[96] Ruskin promoted a deeper consideration of the process of accumulation and the nature of its subsequent expenditure. The 'real value [of wealth] depends on the moral sign attached to it', Ruskin claimed as he hitched materialism and spirituality together.[97]

Ruskin also believed that the industrial economy of his day was inherently mercantilist. Political economy proper was that which cultivated the freedom of state and its citizen, whereas the existing fetishization of individual accumulation culminated in a monopolistic index of private wealth's command of labour.[98] To compensate, Ruskin proposed that wage labour could not be left to the dictates of the market but should be founded on a pre-determined fair price for work.[99] Markets ought to be socially subservient; the fact that they were not was why men of business were seen as lacking virtue, whereas doctors or soldiers could claim some honour. The capitalist had a 'duty, not only to be always considering how to produce what he sells, in the poorest and cheapest forms, but how to make the various employments involved in production, or transference of it, most beneficial to the men employed'. The capitalist could indeed be a hero, or public man, if his motives ceased to be 'wholly personal'.[100] Detailed in Chapter 3, Naoroji's business career epitomized Ruskin's ideal and set an example for commercial practices that were apt to promote sociality through fair dealing and contract. Naoroji would also echo Ruskin's love of artisanal labour, which utilized and cultivated the natural talents of the worker, in contrast to the mindless division of factory labour. The Parsi entrepreneur promoted co-operative production as an interdependent relationship between producer and consumer in a way that favoured socially beneficial uses for commodities.[101]

## Conclusion

By exploring British debates on civil and commercial ideas of sociality, we have uncovered a range of positions on civility for an industrialized world. Although these British interlocutors may have engaged in mutual critique and regarded their respective ideas as incommensurable, this chapter has endeavoured to show

[96] J. Ruskin, 'Unto This Last', in J. Ruskin, *Unto This Last and Other Writings*, ed. Clive Wilmer (London: Penguin, 1997 [1862]), pp. 181–2.
[97] Ibid, p. 187.
[98] Cockram, *Ruskin and Social Reform*, pp. 48–9.
[99] Ruskin, 'Unto This Last', p. 169.
[100] Ibid., p. 178.
[101] Cockram, *Ruskin and Social Reform*, p. 56.

how there were significant thematic and conceptual overlaps around issues of monopoly, autonomy, as well as the ideal of a reciprocal and fair contract. Outside of the colonial context, British reflections on the modern public seemed to be defined more by class considerations than those of race or culture. It is easy to see why many Indian observers of these debates may have accepted that there was no a priori exclusion of non-Europeans from the social ideals promoted by political economists, liberals and romantics. Indian liberals engaged with these traditions expressly because they rendered themselves useful to a dynamic process of ideological experimentation, allowing them to bypass the language of race, culture and caste – instead, substituting it with that of class and non-domination.

The rest of this book explores how the alterity of the Indian context enabled these British traditions to be interspliced with each other as well as seeded with Indian insights. The result was to reinvigorate liberal political economy in such a way that made new collective futures of sociality thinkable across the empire. Unsurprisingly, the open-ended nature of this experimentation meant that Indian thinkers often had radically different takes on an intellectual tradition. Naoroji's western Indian colleague Mahadev Govind Ranade narrated the career of a fellow social reformer and predecessor, Rammohan Roy, through the trope of Carlyle's 'hero' but did not evaluate the latter's economic critique despite the fact that both Ranade and Roy had much to say about colonial economics.[102] Moreover, Ranade found Adam Smith to be little more than a purveyor of abstract dogma, whose descriptions of natural economic laws were 'literally true of no existing Community'.[103] In stark distinction to Naoroji's ideal of commercial society that innovated ideas of free labour akin to Carlyle's 'just industrialism', Indian religious reformers like Keshub Chandra Sen read Carlyle and his writings ascetically as a call to positive renunciation and introspective spiritualism.[104] More than anything else, these examples demonstrate the extent to which European traditions were reinvented in accordance with the array of 'prejudices' that constituted the diverse life-worlds of the subcontinent.

Naoroji's Parsi community in western India was one such life-world. The minority had demonstrated a pronounced cultural Anglophilia throughout

---

[102] M. G. Ranade, 'Raja Rama Mohana Roy', in Mahedeva Govind Ranade, *Religious and Social Reform: A Collection of Essays and Speeches*, ed. M. B. Kolasker (Bombay: Gopal Narayan & Co, 1902), pp. 118, 122–3, 128.

[103] M. G. Ranade, 'Indian Political Economy', in M. G. Ranade, *Essays on Indian Economics: A Collection of Essays and Speeches* (Madras: G. A. Natesan & Co, 1906), p. 10.

[104] Keshub Chandra Sen, 'The Love of God', read at the Unity Church, Islington, 1 May 1870, in Sophia Dobson Collet, ed. *Keshub Chunder Sen's English Visit* (London: Strahan, 1871), p. 368.

the first half of the nineteenth century, indicative of their fruitful commercial relationship with the British. With rich Parsi benefactors forming a vanguard class of philanthropists and investing in the creation of a plural public in Bombay, appeals to Victorian doctrines of bourgeois character and commerce became inseparable from Parsi ideals of civil society. It was this world that Naoroji was born into and for which he became a prominent social reformer and philanthropist. The next chapter turns to this early Parsi preoccupation with public munificence and civil society.

# 2 Sociality and the Parsis of Western India

Regarded as exemplary entrepreneurs, professionals and philanthropists by the early decades of the nineteenth century, the Parsis of western India were the toast of the town. The very model of Victorian good character, they were known for their Anglophilia in matters of domesticity, dress and leisure which had developed through a sustained process of negotiating British cultural norms in an effort at community self-fashioning.[1] Similarly, British officials cooed about the Parsis as models of colonial loyalty. This mutual admiration was born in part due to the community's historical role as a comprador class facilitating the penetration of European capital into the west Indian hinterland. Common self-interest notwithstanding, there was a genuinely held belief that the Parsis were agents of liberal reform and 'civilization' in India and abroad. Henry Bartle Frere, as the Governor of Bombay from 1862 to 1867, even mooted the idea of encouraging Parsi emigration to East Africa as agents of progress. An ardent admirer of Henry Maine's historical sociology, Frere imagined the Parsis as a vanguard community that might develop more 'backward' indigenous cultures.[2]

This chapter explores the nineteenth-century Parsi reformist debates which informed Dadabhai Naoroji's early liberal politics. While Frere and his British colleagues' admiration for the Parsis was motivated by a long-standing relationship with the community as a comprador class, the following argument reveals a Parsi life-world in flux which would give new Parsi debates a critical edge.[3] As such, this chapter traces the contours of the Parsi life-world in religion, commerce and institutional politics from the mid-eighteenth century to the mid-nineteenth century. While historians have outlined the social and political context of Parsi life

[1] Simin Patel, 'Cultural Intermediaries in a Colonial City: The Parsis of Bombay c. 1860–1921' (unpublished Ph.D. thesis, University of Oxford, 2015).

[2] *Native Opinion*, 4 May 1873; C. A. Bayly, *Recovering Liberties: Indian Thought in the Age of Liberalism and Empire* (Cambridge: Cambridge University Press, 2011), pp. 174–5; for Bartle Frere as a student of Maine, see James Jaffe, *Ironies of Colonial Governance: Law, Custom and Justice in Colonial India* (Cambridge: Cambridge University Press, 2015), p. 261.

[3] Bayly, *Recovering Liberties*, pp. 118–23.

in western India, this chapter does not aspire to a comprehensive social history of this minority.[4] Instead, it focuses specifically on motivations and methods of civil association in order to identify the inherited political and social 'prejudices' which informed Naoroji's future thinking on sociality.

The years of Bombay's 'modernization' were formative for Naoroji. Traditionally, the so-called Cambridge school of Indian history regarded the existence of urban politics as evidence of a creeping European modernity that incentivized Indian elites to take up new positions in the expanded educational and political establishments of the presidency towns.[5] A handful of early studies attempted to investigate the modern Indian city as a more negotiated space within an overarching 'Western' modernity; conversely, some of the post-independence historiography fixated on the cultural authenticity of the peasant and the village over the colonial city.[6] More recent accounts have factored in 'imperial globalization' in order to explain the spread of European governance, technology, political economy and divisions of labour, and how they were actively negotiated and appropriated by Indians.[7] The emphasis on the class-based exercise of power in Bombay has offered an explicitly materialist reading of the city's social history linking the uneven development of city planning and economic interests.[8]

The importance of 'modernity' in pioneering Bombay's civic munificence and public culture is well taken; nevertheless, this chapter also draws attention to Parsi proclivities in this direction that preceded Bombay's modernization. The origins

---

[4] Eckehard Kulke, *The Parsees in India: A Minority as Agent of Social Change* (Munich: Weltforum Verlag, 1974), pp. 93–4; John R. Hinnells, *Zoroastrianism and the Parsis* (London: Wardlock Educational Co, 1981); Jesse S. Palsetia, *The Parsis of India: Preservation of Identity in Bombay City* (Leiden: Brill, 2001); see collected essays in John R. Hinnells and Alan Williams, eds., *Parsis in India and the Diaspora* (London: Routledge, 2008); Patel, 'Cultural Intermediaries in a Colonial City'.

[5] Anil Seal, *The Emergence of Indian Nationalism: Competition and Collaboration in the Later Nineteenth Century* (Cambridge: Cambridge University Press, 1966), pp. 11, 14–15, 18, 80–2.

[6] Narayani Gupta, *Delhi Between Two Empires, 1803–1901* (New Delhi: Oxford University Press, 1981); C. A. Bayly, *Rulers, Townsmen and Bazaars: North Indian Society in the Age of British Expansion, 1770–1870* (Cambridge: Cambridge University Press, 1983); Mariam Dossal, *Imperial Designs and Imperial Realities: The Planning of Bombay City, 1845–1875* (New Delhi: Oxford University Press, 1991); Veena Talwa Oldenberg, *The Making of Colonial Lucknow, 1856–77* (Princeton, NJ: Princeton University Press, 1984); for a historiographical overview, see Janaki Nair, 'Beyond Nationalism: Modernity, Governance and a New Urban History for India', *Urban History* 36, no. 2 (2009), pp. 327–8.

[7] Prashant Kidambi, *The Making of an Indian Metropolis: Colonial Governance and Public Culture in Bombay, 1890–1920* (Aldershot: Ashgate, 2007), pp. 1–9.

[8] Sandip Hazareesingh, *The Colonial City and the Challenge of Modernity: Urban Hegemonies and Civic Contestations in Bombay, 1900–1925* (Himayatnagar: Orient Black Swan, 2007), p. 8.

of Parsi social reform in Bombay stretch into the eighteenth century, and the roots of public philanthropy can be witnessed in other centres of Parsi settlement like the Gujarati town of Surat. The social controversies surrounding community identity and leadership were between Parsi traditionalists and Western-educated liberals. If 'Western' concepts were appropriated in this debate, they were interpreted through local politics and hashed out during genuine differences of opinion about the efficacy of community governance and sociality. While these debates overlapped significantly with concerns about profit, prestige and power, they cannot be reduced to them. In the same vein, European pedagogy alone cannot account for Naoroji and his coevals' liberalism; rather, local politics provided the environment in which the explanatory power of particular liberal concepts failed while others emerged as more useful.

## Dadabhai Naoroji and Zoroastrianism

A principal feature of the Parsis and their community politics was the self-conscious retention of their Zoroastrian faith in a country where other much larger religious groups predominated. This was a social theme with which Naoroji was intimately acquainted through his priestly ancestry. Fleeing Islamic persecution in Iran, the Parsis arrived in Gujarat around the eighth century CE. They remained small-scale artisans, merchants and farmers until the arrival of the European trading companies in the seventeenth century.[9] Zoroastrians believe that the priest Zarathustra was the first great prophet of the major world religions. Ahura Mazda, the supreme deity, is the creator but is not recognized by Zoroastrians as all-powerful and all-good because of the continuing presence of Angra Mainyu (evil) over which Ahura Mazda lacks control. However, the world was created such that evil could eventually be vanquished. History is thus an ongoing temporal battle between good and evil, and Zoroastrians are bound both ethically and devotionally to pursue honest transformation of the world in favour of the good. This was epitomized by the mantra of 'Good Thoughts, Good Words, Good Deeds' contained within the concept of *asha* which signified a temporal order of righteousness, veracity and justice that stood in stark opposition to *druj*, or falsehood.[10]

[9] Hinnells and Williams, 'Introduction', in *Parsis in India and the Diaspora*, p. 1.

[10] Ibid., pp. 12–13; Dosabhai Framji Karaka, *History of the Parsis*, vol. II (2 vols., London: Macmillan & Co, 1884), p. 194; Mitra Sharafi, *Law and Identity in Colonial South Asia* (Cambridge: Cambridge University Press, 2014), p. 71; T. M. Luhrmann, 'Truth and Tolerance', *Parsiana*, 7 October 2012.

Ethically, Zoroastrians were enjoined to actively preserve order and moderation as the motive principle of all human endeavour.[11]

Parsi virtues of individual self-fashioning and good character synergized with the bourgeois individualism of Victorian Britain. Masani, Naoroji's biographer, would pen a survey of Zoroastrianism dubbed *The Religion of the Good Life* that drew direct parallels between the Zoroastrian 'code of ethics' and the good habits of liberal individualism. Masani exclaimed that the Parsi endeavour to vanquish evil 'builds character' and was a process of 'self-improvement' and 'self-sacrifice'. In this reading, Parsis were, more than any other Indian community, animated by 'industry and the spirit of citizenship', both of which manifested themselves most clearly in the community's extensive philanthropy.[12] Reflecting an unabashed Anglophilia, these sentiments also demonstrated the minority's anxieties around maintaining the plural and tolerant social order that had originally granted them 'asylum'.[13] Like the Jews, Naoroji believed that the Parsis ought to be lauded for maintaining their cultural specificity in a foreign land where, owing to external circumstances, they were compelled to promote forms of multicultural sociability.[14] This abiding concern would animate Naoroji's political thought until his death.

Little is known about Naoroji's life as a student at Elphinstone College.[15] Nevertheless, he had so distinguished himself there that the President of the Board of Education, Erskine Perry, proposed to send Naoroji to Britain in 1845 to study for the bar. However, the paranoia around young Parsis converting to Christianity prevented Naoroji from going to England and he took up an academic role at the Elphinstone College instead.[16] What Naoroji's academic career reveals is his preference for teaching subjects by placing a particular interpretative paradigm on the social state of India. He highlighted the class summaries for history and geography from the 1853–4 Report of the Board of Education. Together, these subjects explained both the physical and sociological reasons for the state of

---

[11] John R. Hinnells, *Zoroastrians in Britain: The Ratanbai Katrak Lectures, University of Oxford 1985* (Oxford: Oxford University Press, 1996), p. 13.

[12] Rustom Masani, *The Religion of the Good Life: Zoroastrianism* (London: George Allen, 1954 [1938]), pp. 13–14.

[13] Dadabhai Naoroji to Dinshaw Wacha, 28 January 1889, in R. P. Masani, *Dadabhai Naoroji: The Grand Old Man of India* (London: George, Allen & Unwin Ltd, 1939), p. 301.

[14] Dadabhai Naoroji, 'The European and Asiatic Races: Observations on the Paper Read by John Crawford, Esq., F. R. . S.', read before the Ethnological Society, 27 March 1866, in Dadabhai Naoroji, *Essays, Speeches, Addresses and Writings of the Hon'ble Dadabhai Naoroji*, ed. C. L. Parekh (Bombay: Caxton Printing Works, 1887), p. 24.

[15] Masani, *Dadabhai Naoroji*, pp. 33–4.

[16] Ibid., p. 39.

commerce in different parts of the world. Naoroji particularly approved of the following passage:

> [T]he characters of the various inhabitants of the earth; of their productive industry, -whether pastoral, agricultural, manufacturing, or commercial, - as depending on physical and political conditions. In fact Geography, History and Political Economy, by their reciprocal interdependence, naturally form, as it were, a '*tria juncta in uno*'. (Emphasis in original)

Equally, in the examiners' reports of 216 student essays, Naoroji was pleased to see that there was a good mix of historical and economical scripts. Essays were then read before the class, as a lesson in both history and political economy, in order to elicit discussion and critique.[17]

What we do know is that during his time at Elphinstone College, Naoroji continued to explore his Zoroastrian heritage in the context of the Parsi experience of Indian multiculturalism. One of the most influential works was the Gujarati treatise *The Duties of Zoroastrians* which Naoroji claims reinforced in him the Zoroastrian virtues of 'pure thought, pure speech, pure deeds'.[18] Naoroji searched for these ideals in European texts as well. Watts's *The Improvement of the Mind* was cited as forever settling Naoroji's mode of thought and expression on account of its simplicity and forthrightness, and so Naoroji 'bade farewell to the fine and flowery'. Watts was a clergyman and had elaborated a set of instructions that promoted the use of logic and simple conscientious activities to improve one's knowledge. He preached against dogmatism, in favour of recognizing the frailties and imperfectability of human nature, and learning through interaction and conversation with others as a means of testing private opinions. In short, the book advocated self-education and self-cultivation.[19] Naoroji also studied Ferdowsi's *Shahnameh* (the *Book of Kings*) repeatedly throughout his childhood, recalling that he read the Persian epic in its Gujarati translation to Parsi audiences as a boy and he 'need hardly say that these readings had much to do with the formation of [his] character'.[20] The *Shahnameh* recounts the history of Greater Iran from the

---

[17] 'Review [Report] of the Board of Education. Bombay 1853–4. With Special Reference to the Elphinstone College', National Archives of India, New Delhi [NAI], Dadabhai Naoroji Papers [DNP], notes and jottings, group 3: Education, serial no. 11.

[18] Masani, *Dadabhai Naoroji*, p. 34.

[19] Ibid., pp. 34–5; Isaac Watts, *The Improvement of the Mind: Or a Supplement to the Art of Logick* (Edinburgh: D Shaw, 1801 [1727]).

[20] Naoroji, 'A Chapter of Biography', in Dadabhai Naoroji, *The Grand Little Man of India: Dadabhai Naoroji, Speeches and Writings*, vol. II, ed. Moin Zaidi (2 vols., New Delhi: Indian Institute of Applied Political Research, 1985), p. 213.

creation of the world to the Islamic conquest. Ferdowsi insisted that the history ought to be seen as a contingent whole from which people could abstract lessons for good conduct in life.[21] Justice, honour, truth and order are valorized in the epic alongside piety, patriotism, charity and family life. The important fact to remember is that as a history of Persian politics and life in the Zoroastrian religious tradition, it was intended as a manual for daily life. In Naoroji's time the *Shahnameh* was held up as just such a guide to instruct Parsis from within their own literary traditions. One commentator noted that Ferdowsi, in the true Zoroastrian spirit, 'combines vigour, simplicity and purity of expression' and that the text's ideals were not mere myth, panegyric or 'vague abstractions' but 'embodied in flesh and blood'.[22] Naoroji would continue to be fascinated by various interpretations and translations of the epic throughout his life, even asking colleagues to translate and verify themes from the original Persian.[23]

Naoroji also sent books and pamphlets emphasizing the nobility, rationality and liberality of Zoroastrian traditions to European interlocutors.[24] He encouraged the Professor of Persian Language at Oxford University, Lawrence Heyworth Mills, to disseminate knowledge on Zoroastrianism more widely in the United Kingdom. Mills translated the *Zend Avesta* (Zoroastrian scripture) into English and secured donations via Naoroji for more research from wealthy Parsis in Bombay, encouraging him to start a class in Zoroastrianism in London for both Parsis and non-Parsis.[25] This was an extension of the early nineteenth-century programme of rediscovering and 'rationalizing' the tenets of Zoroastrianism in the face of Christian missionary activity, which had attempted to portray non-Protestant faiths as idolatrous and irrational. The Bengal Renaissance from the late eighteenth century witnessed a rationalist Hindu response to these critiques as a way of defending indigenous religion. Given the diasporic dimension of the Zoroastrian community, the Parsi engagement with religious reform was transnational in scope.[26] Pioneering individuals like Kharshedji Nasarwanji Cama

---

21 Quoted in Mahmoud Omidsalar, *Poetics and Politics of Iran's National Epic, the Shahnameh* (New York, NY: Palgrave 2011), pp. 112–13.

22 P. B. Watcha, *Firdousi and the Parsis. What We Owe to Him* (Bombay: n.p., 1911), pp. 52, 59.

23 S. Z. A. Balkhi to Naoroji, 31 August 1900, New Delhi, NAI, DNP, B-18 (31); Balkji to Naoroji, 9 September 1900, NAI, DNP, B-18 (32).

24 Edwin Greaves to Naoroji, 5 January 1893, NAI, DNP, G-103.

25 Lawrence H. Mills to Naoroji, 15 September 1888, NAI, DNP, M-127; Mills to Naoroji, 28 September 1888, NAI, DNP, M-127 (2).

26 For Bengal's Hindu reformism, see David Kopf, *The Brahmo Samaj and the Shaping of the Modern Indian Mind* (Princeton, NJ: Princeton University Press, 1979); Brian Hatcher, 'Remembering Rammohan: An Essay on the (Re-)emergence of Modern Hinduism', *History of Religions* 46, no. 1 (2006), pp. 50–80.

and Meherwanji Framji Panday created the Society for the Amelioration of the Conditions of the Zoroastrians in Persia, after new Iranian Zoroastrian refugees arrived in India from the 1830s. Charitable works were undertaken on behalf of Iranian Zoroastrians, such as the building of dispensaries and poorhouses.[27] Simultaneously, in India, Cama established the Mulla Firoz Madressa for the teaching of *Zend*, Pahlavi and Persian to young Parsis.[28]

The social and demographic decline of their co-religionists in Iran was a constant reminder of the potential fate that could befall the Parsi minority. Zoroastrian reflection on the converging political challenges around their minority status in both regions contributed to what Afshin Marashi has dubbed the 'Persian cosmopolis', with Parsi merchants taking a leading role in forging South–South intellectual connections.[29] The new Zoroastrian refugees who continued to trickle into India from the 1830s were fleeing the Shah of Iran's illiberal policies, with the levying of the *jizyah* (the tax on non-Muslims) seen as an especially oppressive imposition. By 1854, Bombay's Parsis had established the Association of Zoroastrians in Persia to investigate and ameliorate the condition of their Iranian counterparts.[30] The association's leading voice, Manekji Limji Hataria, travelled to Qajar Iran on a fact-finding mission in March–April of the same year. His report entitled *A Parsi Mission to Iran* detailed the social conditions of the 7,200 Zoroastrians remaining in the kingdom. Laws prejudicial to Zoroastrians encouraged conversion to Islam through financial incentives (such as differential inheritance rights), prohibited trade and access to bazaars and imposed humiliating civic penalties (such as limiting the height of Zoroastrian homes relative to Muslim homes).[31] However, by 1882 a successful Parsi campaign and delegation to the Shah had succeeded in convincing him to exempt Iranian Zoroastrians from the tax. The activism against Iran's coercion of religious and social status through the *jizyah*'s assault on Zoroastrian property was among the major public debates that informed Naoroji's developing thoughts on commerce, poverty and sociality.[32]

---

[27] Dosabhai Framji Karaka, *History of the Parsis*, vol. I, p. 55.

[28] *Parsee Voice* 1, no. 19 (2004), p. 1.

[29] Afshin Marashi, *Exile and the Nation: The Parsi Community of India and the Making of Modern Iran* (Austin, TX: University of Texas Press, 2020).

[30] Mary Boyce, 'Manekji Limji Hataria in Iran', in N. D. Manochehr-Homji and M. F. Kanga, eds., *K. R. Cama Oriental Institute Golden Jubilee Volume* (Bombay: K. R. Cama Oriental Institute, 1969), pp. 19–31.

[31] M. L. Hataria, *Rishale Ej Har Shiyaate Iran*, published in 1865 and serialized and translated in *Parsiana*, August 1990 to January 1991.

[32] Karaka, *History of the Parsis*, vol. I, pp. 82–5.

## Parsi Sociality and Commerce

As a coastal entrepôt and multicultural centre of commerce, the life-world of Bombay's public men was markedly different from the presidency's hinterland, which incubated more conservatively minded thinkers in cities like Pune (though certain figures like Gopal Krishna Gokhale and Mahadev Govind Ranade managed to bridge both).[33] From the sixteenth and seventeenth centuries, first under Portuguese and then British rule, Bombay developed its diverse and commercial character largely due to Indian Ocean trade and opium exports to China.[34] The inheritance of Portuguese and British corporate institutions and early law courts meant that a system of civil law and commercial law co-exited alongside community courts like the Parsi *panchayat*. This created a distinct legal ecology in which debates about the limits of political, social and economic jurisdiction and authority developed a secular and pragmatic tone.[35] The political and legal plurality of Bombay was especially useful to the Parsis since their Zoroastrian faith did not possess a corpus of theological law or centralized religious institutions for resolving local disputes.[36] Furthermore, unlike many Hindu and Islamic traditions, there was no Zoroastrian religious sanction on taking disputes to outside authorities.[37] It was in such an environment that the Parsi *panchayat*, set up under British patronage, received semi-official recognition from the local government in 1778.[38] The following two paragraphs clarify the interlocking registers of commercial contractualism and associational culture that defined the Parsi life-world in Naoroji's time.

The Parsis had established themselves as a force in western Indian commerce from an early stage owing to the initial weakness of colonial political power and the dearth of liquidity of European merchants.[39] Even before the arrival of the British, the Parsis fulfilled a comprador role for Portuguese and Dutch trade in and around Surat in Gujarat. However, the fragmentation of Mughal authority in and around Surat, piracy and increasing English trade in the Red Sea and Persian

33 Bayly, *Recovering Liberties*, pp. 116–17.
34 Ibid., p. 43.
35 Ibid., p 117.
36 Sharafi, *Law and Identity*, p. 75.
37 Ibid., p. 76; S. T. Lokhandwalla, 'Islamic Law and Ismaili Communities', *Indian Economic and Social History Review* 4, no. 2 (1967), p. 172; Lauren Benton, *Law and Colonial Cultures: Legal Regimes in World History* (Cambridge: Cambridge University Press, 2002), pp. 113–14.
38 Bayly, *Recovering Liberties*, p. 119.
39 Rajnarayan Chandavarkar, 'Bombay's Perennial Modernities', in Jennifer Davis, Gordon Johnson and David Washbrook, eds., *History, Culture and the Indian City: Essays by Rajnarayan Chandavarkar* (Cambridge: Cambridge University Press, 2009), p. 16.

Gulf slowly choked Parsi traders off from both internal and external markets.[40] As Parsis relocated to the relative stability of Bombay under the East India Company, their commercial activities became increasingly determined by the political and economic privileges they enjoyed from their British governors. In Bombay, international commerce continued to be the source of Parsi prosperity, although now it was closely allied to British commercial and political interests. Parsi shipbuilding flourished from 1736 when the East India Company encouraged Lowjee Nusserwanjee Wadia to establish himself in Bombay as a timber trader and carpenter.[41] The expansion of Company trade into Asia opened up new opportunities for Parsi brokerages both into the Indian hinterland and to China. By 1756, the first Parsi firm was established in Canton – the only port in China open to foreigners at the time – and focused mainly on importing Indian cotton in exchange for tea, silk and porcelain.[42] Bombay became a global trade hub, receiving ships laden with coffee, gold and honey from Arabia as well as salves and ivory from the African littoral.[43]

Commerce and politics went hand in hand for the Parsis, who were now trying to establish themselves as an independent community in Bombay. Services to the Royal Navy by Wadia's descendants earned them grants of *inam* lands in Bombay from the Company.[44] Many of the most prominent merchants were not involved in trade in their own right, however, but were guarantors or brokers to British trade or involved in shipping.[45] While many mercantile families became exorbitantly wealthy by brokering for European firms, a position of dependence on trade carried out by external parties also exposed some merchants to extensive liabilities. Those who continued to prosper like Hormusji Bomanji Wadia were forced to pay the debts of Parsis involved in more fragile enterprises like those engaged with Forbes, Forbes & Co.[46] Yet in the early nineteenth century, the Company continued to rely on native brokers to facilitate trade and thus a contractual reciprocity persisted. Some Parsi

[40] David L. White, 'From Crisis to Community Definition: The Dynamics of Eighteenth-century Parsi Philanthropy', *Modern South Asia* 25, no. 2 (1991), p. 307.
[41] Rusheed R. Wadia, 'Bombay Parsi Merchants in the Eighteenth and Nineteenth Century', in Hinnells and Williams, eds., *Parsis in India and the Diaspora*, p. 122.
[42] Ibid., p. 123.
[43] S. M. Edwardes, *The Gazetteer of Bombay City and Island*, vol. I (3 vols., Bombay: The Times Press, 1909), pp. 412–5.
[44] *Public Department Diary of the Bombay Government*, 1792, vol. 100, Mumbai, Maharashtra State Archives (MSA), p. 21.
[45] *Gazetteer of the Bombay Presidency, Ahmedabad*, vol. 4 (Bombay: The Times Press, 1879), pp. 64–70.
[46] Jamsetjee Jeejeebhoy to David Jardine, 18 March 1851, Bombay, Bombay University Library (BUL), Jamsetjee Jeejeebhoy Letterbooks, vol. 384, p. 37.

financiers also dabbled in trade themselves. For instance, in 1829 the government accepted the demand of native merchants, led by the Parsi Framji Cowasji to keep its own cotton presses closed for five months a year in order to prevent the Chinese market being flooded with English goods and harming those Indian merchants who were themselves exporters.[47] Aided by their European connections, the Parsis also handsomely met mutual obligations within the Parsi community, in the interests of social solidarity and prosperity. For example, in 1833 the first Parsi baronet, the merchant-prince Jamsetji Jeejeebhoy, and his European colleagues advanced 100,000 rupees at a negligible rate of interest to Hormusji Dorabji so as to help him pay his Hindu moneylenders.[48]

By the beginning of the nineteenth century, opium was by far the most lucrative Parsi export and allowed merchants to amass vaster fortunes than previously imagined.[49] The first half of the century also witnessed the extensive migration of young Parsis from Gujarat to pursue a career in trade and finance in Bombay.[50] The opium and cotton trades, more than any other, enabled Bombay's Parsi merchants to trade on their own account. Jeejeebhoy had himself diversified into exporting opium to China in partnership with Jardine Matheson & Co and also independently.[51] By the 1840s, however, the alliance between European and Asian capital, based on mutual needs and obligations, began to break down, scuppering the short boom enjoyed by Parsi traders. The penetration of European capital, agency houses and, most destructively, steamers undermined Parsi brokers and shipping. Increased duties on ships between India and China made native shipping immensely costly, slowly prejudicing insurers and surveyors against Indian shipping.[52] To accentuate Parsi economic woes, the supply of cotton and that of other cash crops dwindled during the price depression of the late 1830s and 1840s.[53] As commercial ties and obligations between the British and the Parsis weakened, other enterprising communities including Khoja Muslims, Jains, Jews

[47] Commercial Department: 1830/11, MSA, pp. 139–49.

[48] Jeejeebhoy to James Matheson, (undated) August 1833, MSA, Jamsetjee Jeejeebhoy Letterbooks, vol. 351, p. 5.

[49] Jesse S. Palsetia, 'The Parsis of India and the Opium Trade in China', *Contemporary Drug Problems* 35, no. 4 (Winter, 2008), p. 654.

[50] Kulke, *The Parsees in India*, p. 56.

[51] JeeJeebhoy to William Jardine, 12 April 1838, BUL, Jamsetjee Jeejeebhoy Letterbooks, vol. 358, p. 66.

[52] JeeJeebhoy to Alexander Colvin, 30 December 1840, BUL, Jamsetjee Jeejeebhoy Letterbooks, vol. 385, p. 359; JeeJeebhoy to Captain Colgan, 19 July 1841, BUL, Jamsetjee Jeejeebhoy Letterbooks, vol. 370, p. 180.

[53] B. R. Tomlinson, *The Economy of Modern India: From 1860 to the Twenty-first Century* (Cambridge: Cambridge University Press, 2013), p. 34.

and Hindu Banias began to corner traditional sectors of the Parsi export trade.[54] Increasingly, Parsis diversified into speculative investments or manufacturing, leading to the growth of the first indigenously run cotton mills in Bombay by the early 1850s. Parsi entrepreneurs were attempting to hedge against the volatility associated with the export of primary commodities and, simultaneously, establish businesses independent of European capital and oversight.[55]

Although the mutual benefit and reciprocity Parsis enjoyed with the government and European traders were declining, existing Parsi riches and new mill wealth allowed prominent merchants to secure political stability for their community through philanthropy. In 1827, Indian notables, including Jeejeebhoy, had joined with the British government to set up the Bombay Native Education Society and the Elphinstone Institution scholarships, with the baronet contributing 18,000 rupees.[56] Similarly, the construction of the Jamsetji Jeejeebhoy Hospital between 1840 and 1852 was evidence of the immense utility of Parsi philanthropy in providing the basic infrastructure of civic governance in Bombay. By the time of his death, it was estimated that Jeejeebhoy spent 2,459,736 rupees on philanthropic projects.[57] Framji Cowasji had also attempted to secure a clean water supply for parts of Bombay, funded from the revenues of his estate, and committed his children in his will to continuing the project.[58]

Parsi investment in the fabrication and maintenance of an Indian public was intended to institutionally buttress a nascent multicultural civil society. However, this zeal was not confined to the major presidency capital of Bombay. In the Gujarati city of Surat, the local Parsis also mirrored the international philanthropy of the Association of Zoroastrians in Persia. In October 1862, the Surat Lancashire Relief Fund was established to aid cotton millworkers in Britain laid off on account of the American Civil War and disrupted cotton imports from the south.[59] Both regions were heavily dependent on the textile industry. The international and inter-community quality of this new philanthropy marked a qualitative departure from

[54] Edwardes, *Bombay City*, p. 435; Jamsetjee Jeejeebhoy Sons & Co to Jardine Matheson & Co, 19 July 1854, BUL, Jamsetjee Jeejeebhoy Letterbooks, vol. 361, p. 224.

[55] Rajnarayan Chandavarkar, *The Origins of Industrial Capitalism in India: Business Strategies and the Working Classes in Bombay*, new edn (Cambridge: Cambridge University Press, 2002), p. 241.

[56] J. R. P. Mody, *Jamsetjee Jejeebhoy: The First Indian Knight and Baronet, 1783–1859* (Bombay: n.p., 1959), p. 172.

[57] *Bombay Times*, 16 April 1859.

[58] Koshru Navrosji Banaji, *Memoirs of the Late Framji Cowasji Banaji* (Bombay: Bombay Gazette Steam Printing Works, 1892), pp. 29–31.

[59] *Bombay Gazette*, 17 October 1862.

the eighteenth-century Surati practice of local 'gifting' as a means of knee-jerk crisis management for destitute Parsis.[60] Routine philanthropy secured religious prestige and favour with the British, but it also created a cosmopolitan social environment that promoted mutual recognition and reciprocity.[61] The power of commercial success was that it could still be used to mediate social relations in the absence of direct links with British capital. The Parsis recognized the usefulness of the mid-Victorian ideal of a public-minded masculinity, grounded in the intertwined Christian notions of social duty and charitable giving, while emphasizing the Zoroastrian tenets that demanded the same.[62]

## Social and Political Associations between India and Britain

Parsi personal law – those that dictated the community's norms of marriage, divorce and inheritance – was subject to the civil jurisdiction of the community's *panchayat*. In the absence of Zoroastrian religious courts, and owing to the community's strong commercial links with Europeans, the government had supported the institution's mediation of social and religious disputes as well as its provision of social welfare. By 1818, elected lay members were added to the membership as debates about religious rites arose.[63] In these early years, the essentially liberal and consultative nature of the *panchayat*, when all male members of the community met to discuss issues in the *anjuman* (assembly or association), was reported as follows:

> [T]his little council decides all questions of property, subject, however, to the Recorder's Court; but an appeal seldom happens, as the panchaït is jealous of its authority, and is consequently cautious in its decisions. It superintends all marriages and adoptions, and inquires into the state of every individual of the community.[64]

---

[60] White, 'From Crisis to Community Definition', p. 313.

[61] J. R. Hinnells, 'The Flowering of Zoroastrian Benevolence', in H. Bailey, A. D. H. Bivar, J. Duchesne-Guillemin and J. Hinnells, eds., *Papers in Honour of Professor Mary Boyce, Homages et Opera Minora,* vol. 10 (11 vols., Leiden: Brill, 1985), pp. 261–326.

[62] Boyd Hilton, *The Age of Atonement: The Influence of Evangelicalism on Social and Economic Thought, 1785–1865*, new edn (Oxford: Oxford University Press, 2001), p. 104; Jesse S. Palsetia, 'Partner in Empire: Jamsetjee Jeejeebhoy and the Public Culture of Nineteenth-century Bombay', in *Parsis in India and the Diaspora*, pp. 81–2; Palsetia, 'Parsis of India and the Opium Trade', 665; Govind Narayan, *Mumbai: An Urban Biography from 1863*, trans. Murali Ranganathan (London: Anthem Press, 2008 [1863]), p. 203.

[63] Bayly, *Recovering Liberties*, p. 119; Sharafi, *Law and Identity*, p. 78.

[64] Maria Dundas Graham Callcott, *Journal of a Residence in India* (Cambridge: Cambridge University Press, 2012 [1813]), p. 41.

In 1791, the *anjuman* passed a resolution granting itself, a secular and civil body, the power to administer certain Zoroastrian rites, including marriage and divorce. This led to a series of liberal reforms regarding the rights of Parsi women, including sanctions against bigamy and the ability to remarry if her husband was absent for a period of ten years without her consent or in the case of sterility and impotence.[65] In essence, Parsi associational and legal traditions came to subordinate religious authority to civil jurisdiction.

Parsi secularism in matters of personal law came about as a result of Parsi associational culture. By the 1830s and 1840s conservative tendencies in the *panchayat* and its transformation into a nepotistic, hereditary and arbitrary authority delegitimized it in the eyes of an increasingly vocal group of young Parsi professionals.[66] This educated group sought to create alternative loci of associational culture within their community, like the Parsi Law Association from 1855, which could preserve and restore the consensual civil jurisdiction enjoyed by the community by petitioning the colonial government to establish new civil and matrimonial courts to challenge the arbitrary authority wielded by the *panchayat*. Associational culture extended beyond the confines of the community as well, in order to create a consensual educated public opinion that opposed the orthodox elements that had captured the *panchayat*. But as sporadic communal rioting and religious intolerance in Bombay would reveal, concerns about social consensus and civility would apply to inter-communal relations as well.[67] For instance, Naoroji and his colleague Naoroji Furdoonji were the leading lights of the Bombay Association, founded in 1852 to petition the Government of India on behalf of local stakeholders, consisting mostly of large landowners, industrialists, merchants and professionals.[68] These organizations would provide a fertile environment for Naoroji and other Indians to disseminate their views, honing their liberal sensibilities and making connections with analogous British associations.

Bombay's wider associational culture also allowed Parsis to promote solidarity with the metropolis's other religious communities. Most notable among these was Freemasonry, which scholars have already linked with the attempted nurture of

---

[65] B. B. Patell, *Parsee Prakash: Being a Record of Important Events in the Growth of the Parsee Community in Western India, Chronologically Arranged*, vol. I [Gujarati] (3 vols., Bombay: Duftur Ashkara Press, 1888), pp. 870–5.

[66] Bayly, *Recovering Liberties*, p. 119.

[67] J. Masselos, *Towards Nationalism: Group Affiliations and the Politics of Public Associations in Nineteenth Century Western India* (Bombay: Popular Prakashan, 1974).

[68] *Minute of Proceedings of the Bombay Association* (Bombay: Bombay Association, 1852), pp. 18–19.

'supra-national communities' across the British Empire.[69] Naoroji was affiliated with such lodges in Bombay and London and received his first taste of cosmopolitan association during his earliest days in Liverpool, befriending temperance reformers and fellow cotton traders like Samuel Smith, with whom he attended local literary associations.[70] Naoroji's partner in business and social reform, K. R. Cama, extolled the fraternal pluralism of masonic associationalism, noting that one could become a Freemason regardless of creed so long as one was a monotheist. A Freemason was 'a brother to that extent for all the purposes of Freemasonry, although he may not be a brother by consanguinity, nationality, or religious profession'.[71] The absence of a prophet or scriptural doctrine meant that Freemasonry was a 'cosmopolitan religion', and the holidays of each individual religion, like Parsi New Year, were all celebrated. To Cama's mind, this made the masonic lodge conducive to the creation of a 'kind and sympathetic and forbearing spirit' which was 'the genuine secret and beauty of our institution'.[72] Acceptance into this rarefied associational world was, however, predicated on a display of good character. Despite the middle-class underpinnings of its membership, Cama promoted Parsi associationalism as an inclusive, pluralist and ascriptive vision of sociability:

> Freemasonry is described to be a moral institution veiled in allegory and illustrated by symbols. The institution differs from other religious systems in this respect, that, unlike the latter, it has no born members. A Christian or a Zoroastrian, or a Mahomedan or a Hindoo's children take their father's religion by right of birth; not so the children of a Freemason in Masonry. The members in a Masonic body are elected after strict enquiry and a rigid voting ballot when they are of mature age, and have proved themselves morally worthy.[73]

Trans-imperial political associations between India and Britain emerged as early as the 1830s, becoming valuable interstitial spaces for intellectual exchange.

---

[69] J. Harland Jacobs, *Builders of Empire: Freemasons and British Imperialism, 1717–1927* (Chapel Hill, NC: University of North Carolina Press, 2007), p. 11.

[70] F. R. W. Hedges, Secretary to the Royal Masonic Institution to Naoroji, (undated) April 1890, NAI, DNP, H-80; The Crusaders' Lodge to Naoroji, 18 January 1893, NAI, DNP, C-293; North London Masonic Benevolent Ball to Naoroji, 14 November 1894, NAI, DNP, N-136; Margot D. Morrow, *The Origins and Early Years of the British Committee of the Indian National Congress, 1887–1907* (unpublished Ph.D. thesis, University of London, 1977), p. 80.

[71] K. R. Cama, 'Zoroastrians and Freemasonry', in K. R. Cama, *The Collected Works of K. R. Cama*, vol. I (2 vols., Bombay: K. R. Cama Oriental Institute, 1968), p. 360; Karaka, *History of the Parsis*, vol. I, p. 149.

[72] K. R. Cama, 'Freemasonry among the Natives of Bombay', *The Collected Works of K. R. Cama*, vol. I, pp. 387–8; Cama, 'Zoroastrians and Freemasonry', p. 362.

[73] Cama, 'Zoroastrians and Freemasonry', p. 372.

The earlier incarnations of British–Indian political cooperation, however, had very asymmetrical origins. Quakers founded the British Indian Society in 1839 with the patronage of the Lancashire cotton interests and aimed to abolish slavery in the United States by destroying American cotton cultivation via competition. As such, they encouraged the production of cheap Indian cotton for British manufactures and demanded the extirpation of the East India Company for carrying out costly military expansion and being contrary to sound free trade principles. Indian co-operation was based on the society's support for the permanent settlement of taxes on rural landlords which large landowners approved of on account of the progressively decreasing rental burden.[74] The fact that the society died out by 1846, when Chartism and Anti-Corn Law agitation dominated political debate in Britain, shows the extent to which it owed its intellectual dynamism and political momentum to an Indian interest but one which did not seek to socially transform the Raj or seriously consider Indian agency.

Newer associations linking Britain and the empire did promote a co-operative, collaborative and interdependent exchange of ideas around mutually acknowledged imperial issues.[75] British politicians and imperial activists like John Bright and John Dickinson used the renewal of the Company's charter in 1853 to raise important issues about its principles of governance. Dickinson was mostly concerned with the British dealing with Indian princely states in good faith by upholding mutual agreements and granting Indian sovereigns maximum autonomy. He set his sights on bringing 'the real nature of our Indian Administration' and what he regarded as the mismanagement of middle men to the attention of parliament and the British public.[76] Similarly, Bright wanted to bring an end to the un-scrutinized rule of the Company by creating an Indian secretary of state and a council of five answerable to parliament and public opinion.[77] Dickinson formed the India Reform Society in 1853 in order to lobby the legislature, and Bright's association with the society gave the organization access to a network of MPs. Meanwhile, Dickinson's Indian contacts gave him access to local reports, and statistics from that Bright diligently

[74] S. R. Mehrota, 'The British India Society and Its Bengal Branch, 1839–46', *Indian Economic and Social History Review*, 4 (June 1967), pp. 131–54; Rosina Visram, *Asians in Britain: 400 Years of History* (London: Pluto Press, 2002), p. 123.

[75] Andrew Thompson, 'The Power and Privilege of Association: Co-ethnic Networks and the Economic Life of the British Economic World', *South African Historical Journal* 56, no. 1 (2006), p. 46.

[76] John Dickinson, *India: Its Government under a Bureaucracy* (London: Saunders and Stanford, 1853), p. 1.

[77] John Bright, *Speeches on Questions of Public Policy*, vol. I, ed. James E. Thorold Rogers (2 vols., London: MacMillan & Co, 1868), p. 50.

deployed in parliamentary debate.[78] By 1865, however, the society was defunct thanks to Dickinson's writing on princely states rousing negative feelings towards him among imperial mandarins in Calcutta and retired Anglo-Indians at home.[79]

It was in this spirit of cooperation, through already-established bourgeois-imperial networks, that Indians established their own political associations in late-nineteenth-century Britain. These institutions were not simply debate halls where civility was discussed (there were talks on social duty, imperial citizenship and public service) but were also sites of lived experience in which cultural pluralism was practised and expanded to outlying – though still overwhelmingly middle-class – groups.[80] The first wholly indigenous and multicultural initiative was Naoroji, Womesh Chunder Bonnerjee and Badruddin Tyabji's London Indian Society of 1865. The society's objective was to debate 'political, social, and literary subjects relating to India with a view to promote the interests of the people of that country'.[81] Its longevity into the twentieth century was ensured by the flow of new Indian students into London and because the society was independent of both colonial and Indian National Congress agendas.[82] In December 1866, Naoroji also set up the East India Association, with its head branch in London and connected branches in the presidency towns of India, in conjunction with retired Anglo-Indian officials. The task of this organization was to pick up where the India Reform Society had left off, to supply parliament and the British public with facts about the true condition of India.[83] Associational links traversing the empire allowed the transfer of 'people, funds, and information' between branches and a pooling of local knowledge and ideas.[84] Several friends of India in parliament, including John Bright, joined and cooperated with Naoroji's association, raising the issue of the decentralization of administration

[78] Bayly, *Recovering Liberties*, p. 127.

[79] Robert Harrison, 'Dickinson, John (1815–1876)', rev. Peter Harnetty, *Oxford Dictionary of National Biography*, Oxford University Press, 2004; online edn, October 2007 (http://www.oxforddnb.com/view/article/7606, accessed 7 May 2015).

[80] Carey Anthony Watt, *Serving the Nation: Cultures of Service, Association, and Citizenship in Colonial India* (Oxford: Oxford University Press, 2005), pp. 1–2, 7.

[81] Jonathan Schneer, *London: The Imperial Metropolis* (New Haven, CT: Yale University Press, 1999), p. 186.

[82] Naoroji amendments to the 1898 London Indian Society prospectus, 1903, NAI, DNP, L-100 (23).

[83] 'Introduction', *Journal of the East India Association* [hereafter *JEIA*] 1 (1867), p. 2; 'Rules', *JEIA* 1 (1867), p. 8; Dadabhai Naoroji, *On the Duties of Local Indian Associations in Connection with the London Association*, (London: W. Clowes & Sons, 1868).

[84] Arthur Downing, 'The Friendly Planet: "Oddfellows", Networks, and the "British World" c. 1840–1940', *Journal of Global History* 7, no. 3 (2012), p. 414.

in India in 1868 and again in 1877.[85] Indian liberals like Bonnerjee offered talks on 'Representative and Responsible Government for India', while some former British officials offered more prosaic presentations on topics like 'Transport in India'.[86] While the association's membership grew to over 1,000 by 1871, by the 1880s it was overwhelmed by the Anglo-Indian civil service and military element that drove the organization into more conservative and Anglo-centric perspectives.[87] Nevertheless, while it lasted, the association facilitated a bourgeois sociability between Indians and sympathetic Britons from all castes and creeds.

As Indian critics of empire flourished in Britain and in the subcontinent, so-called British improvers of India became ever more reliant on their expertise in the last quarter of the century. Though cultural asymmetries were not levelled by this reliance of European expertise on Indian knowledge, it did allow Indians to leverage themselves into positions of greater epistemic agency. It also allowed for greater cooperation on two major fronts of Indian social 'improvement' – female education and health – both of which were promoted through the language of political economy. For instance, the social reformer Mary Carpenter founded the National Indian Association in 1870 with the Bengali social and religious reformer Keshub Chandra Sen.[88] Carpenter made four trips to India between 1866 and 1876, visiting female schools and inspecting prisons as a means of fulfilling the 'white woman's burden' by elevating 'helpless Indian womanhood' to a better condition.[89] Female education in India was a means of emancipating Indian women from Asian patriarchy and retraining them to fulfil their duties as mistresses of Victorian domesticity and motherhood without sacrificing their culture.[90] Domestic rationality and companionate family life was a type of liberal

---

[85] Mary Cumpston, 'Some Early Indian Nationalists and Their Allies in the British Parliament, 1851–1906', *English Historical Review*, 76 (April 1961), p. 281.
[86] W. C. Bonnerjee, 'Representative and Responsible Government for India', *JEIA* 1 (1867), pp. 157–99; Hyde Clarke, 'Transport in India', *JEIA* 3 (1869), pp. 157–70.
[87] Visram, *Asians in Britain*, p. 124.
[88] Committee book of the Indian Association of Bristol, National Indian Association minute books, council and committee meetings, (undated) October 1870, London, British Library Asia Pacific and Africa Collections (BLAPAC), MSS Eur F147/1, f. 1.
[89] Antoinette Burton, 'The White Woman's Burden: British Feminists and the Indian Woman, 1865–1915', *Women's Studies International Forum* 13, no. 4 (1990), pp. 295–308; Ann Schwan, '"Dreadful Beyond Description": Mary Carpenter's Prison Reform Writings and Female Convicts in Britain and India', *European Journal of English Studies* 14, no. 2 (2010), pp. 107–20.
[90] Antoinette Burton, 'Fearful Bodies into Disciplined Subjects: Pleasure, Romance and the Family Drama of Colonial Reform in Mary Carpenter's "Six Months in India"', *Signs* 20, no. 3 (1995), pp. 545–74.

schooling every bit as important as that of the classroom. The result of this liberal pedagogy, as British reformers saw it, would be to elevate the social stability and prosperity of the future Indian race.

Carpenter's National Indian Association also ran a scheme to house Indian students with British families. This was partly a means of subordinating impressionable Indians under the paternalism/maternalism of English hospitality and manners.[91] Consequently, Keshub Chandra Sen complained of Carpenter's 'incessant directions about the usages and etiquette of English society'.[92] Naoroji was already acquainted with Mary Carpenter in the 1860s, eventually leading to his introduction to Florence Nightingale.[93] His Parsi colleague Behramji Malabari also maintained a long partnership with Carpenter on issues of female education in India and relayed information to her about the condition of women in Hindu society. From 1871, Naoroji was fully involved in the organization of Carpenter's Indian National Association and by the 1880s decided to drop references to the uniquely 'female' character of its work and to set up a superintendence committee which could provide guardians for Indian students in Britain subordinated to the committee's control.[94] The guardians also relayed written reports back to Indian parents on their children's comings and goings and the association largely institutionalized Carpenter's hectoring disposition.[95] Later this control was extended to living allowances, whereby an indebted student was permitted to draw on his deposit with his guardian but would immediately forfeit the value of the deposit until the deficit was repaid.[96] Elizabeth Manning, who ran the scheme, was fully aware that some Indians 'do not like to be under the committee' but still insisted that 'we are convinced that some aid is important in this connection'.[97]

---

[91] Julie F. Codell, 'Reversing the Grand Tour: Guest Discourse in Indian Travel Narratives', *Huntingdon Library Quarterly* 70, no. 1 (2007), pp. 173–89.

[92] Quoted in John A. Stevens, 'Colonial Subjectivity: Keshub Chandra Sen in London and Calcutta, 1870–1884' (unpublished Ph.D. thesis, University College London, 2011), pp. 133–4.

[93] Naoroji to Florence Nightingale, 29 July 1867, London, British Library, Nightingale Papers, Add. MSS 45800, ff. 129–32.

[94] Committee meetings on 25 February 1885 and 13 May 1885, National Indian Association minute books, London, British Library Asia Pacific and African Collections (BLAPAC), MSS Eur F147/4.

[95] Committee meeting on 25 May 1887, National Indian Association minute books, BLAPAC, MSS Eur F147/5; 'Superintendence of Indian Students in England', *Journal of the National Indian Association* (September 1885), p. 407.

[96] Committee meetings on 5 December 1888, National Indian Association minute books, BLAPAC, MSS Eur F147/5.

[97] Elizabeth Manning to Naoroji, 5 July 1890, NAI, DNP, M-54 (7).

Indians endorsed these paternalistic schemes explicitly because they fostered sociability while maintaining cultural distinctions. Indian parents were concerned about their children's financial security, the temptations of the metropolis, and of religious and cultural miscegenation. C. P. Lalkaka asked Naoroji to act as guardian while his son studied for the Bar in London, bemoaning the young man's 'tender heart' and propensity to become a 'dupe to self desiring persons'.[98] Superintendence committees also provided a financial safety net which allowed Indians successful access to legal, bureaucratic and medical instruction.[99] Elizabeth Manning was also aware of the liberal desire among reformist Parsi families to use the Victorian household as a model of the companionate nuclear family. Her papers contain a copy of Veerbaiji F. Vicaji's essay on the ideal home, which outlined not only the modern woman's duties but also the man's mutual obligations to his wife.[100] Simply put, this was an attempt to inculcate the traits of British good character while maintaining cultural difference. Naoroji told fellow Parsis coming to Britain, however, that they would 'feel at home' at Manning's because of her hospitality but also thanks to the fact that Indian guests were encouraged to maintain their customary dress and observe their respective cultural practices.[101]

Manning and Naoroji's cosmopolitan intentions are best exemplified by the Northbrook Indian Club, which was originally set up as a sub-committee of the National Indian Association with the intention of providing the sort of cordial social and scholarly environment that the National Liberal Club ended up providing by default. Mooted in 1879, the club operated independently from the Indian Association by 1881, though managerially there was an overlap of personnel between the two organizations.[102] Europeans viewed such organizations from an associational perspective as well, in the hope of promoting the exchange of radical ideas and the crystallization of a radical politics in London. The temperance activist Rev. W. B. Banyard sought to promote the 'means of the people' of Britain and India and thought that the Northbrook Club, situated in South Kensington,

---

[98] C. P. Lalkaka to Naoroji, 10 June 1889, NAI, DNP, L-12a.

[99] Committee meeting on 2 November 1900, minutes of meetings of the British Committee of the Indian National Congress, vol. v, microfilm reel 3, accession number 1943, NAI, Private Archives Section, p. 30.

[100] Veerbaiji F. Vicaji, translated from Gujarati, *Home: Its Duties and Comforts* (Bombay: Parsee Girls' School Association, 1888), Cambridge, Cambridge University Library (CUL), Elizabeth Adelaide Manning Correspondence and Papers, MS Add. 6379/30.

[101] Naoroji to Pestonji Dadabhoy, 13 April 1883, NAI, DNP, N-1 (118); Muncherji K. Lalkaka to Naoroji, 4 November (undated), NAI, DNP, L-13 (13).

[102] *The Times*, 6 August 1881; Committee meeting on 24 February 1886, National Indian Association minute books, BLAPAC, MSS Eur F147/4.

was poorly located. He pressed Naoroji to promote a new club which met 'City requirements' and which would 'infuse a new element and an almost new tone into City life'.[103] A serialized travelogue written by an 'educated Hindu' made it abundantly clear how empowering the British club was. During his short stay he met Professor William Hunter at the National Liberal Club, the anti-opium campaigner Dr Farquharson, and many Indians at the Northbrook Club.[104] More significantly, however, he compared the 'Club in the civilized West' to the 'chowpal' in India where the village community would vigorously discuss their collective affairs. In this way, many middle-class Indians did not see themselves as outsiders in the world of British clubs and associations but as updating some of their traditions for the civil sphere. Indian professionals had merely substituted debates on Irish Home Rule for those on the 'exactions of the moneylender' and 'champagne' for the 'simple *huka*'.[105]

## Conclusion

The Parsi life-world out of which Naoroji emerged was already engaging in forms of social experimentation that sought to maximize civil association in culturally diverse contexts where Parsi minority status put the community at a numerical disadvantage. The claims of Christian missionaries prompted a reformist zeal among a new generation of Parsis who were keen to point out Zoroastrianism's seamless integration into the Victorian ideal of social modernity. However, the quest for a plural civil society in which Parsis could retain their identity and social status without being subject to the arbitrary whims of fellow Indians or their own *panchayat* was also driven by the minority's anxiety around the plight of Iranian Zoroastrians. It was no coincidence that Parsi philanthropy was indebted to the dual registers of social and commercial association which combined charity with commercial virtue, character and public-mindedness.

In the midst of these developments Indian professionals were also building institutions of trans-imperial association in which young Parsi professionals played a pioneering role. Freemasonry, scholarly associations and Anglo-Indian foster homes for Indian students were places where a liberal sensibility was incubated

---

[103] Minutes of the society, 17 May 1869, London, Royal Society of Arts Library and Archive (RSA), Royal Society of Arts, minute books, November 1869–June 1870, RSA/AD/MA/100/12/01/116; W. B. Banyard to Naoroji, 12 September 1888, NAI, DNP, B-40; Banyard to Naoroji, 10 May 1890, NAI, DNP, B-40 (28).

[104] 'First Impressions of an Educated Hindu of England and Parts of Europe', *Indian Spectator*, 1 April 1888, p. 274.

[105] Ibid., p. 273.

and practised through meaningful acts. Indian agency in these colonial realms was also defined by a conscious attempt to make European counterparts dependent on Indian input while also protecting cultural difference. The consequence was the authoring of a particular type of private autonomy that was upheld not by law but by interdependence. Moreover, the sorts of virtuous character attributes that one had to demonstrate in this associational culture were also those that allowed Parsis to become successful entrepreneurs in spaces where they enjoyed relative security and freedom. These spaces were in turn sustained by the public philanthropy that commercial prosperity made possible. The Iranian episode demonstrated the extent to which the stifling of public autonomy also undermined the material conditions under which Parsi beneficence flourished and through which private autonomy and character might continue to thrive. The fragile epiphenomenal relationship between private and public virtue – between the social and commercial domains of Parsi society – would be debated among Bombay's Parsi community during the middle of the nineteenth century.

Naoroji emerged from this Parsi life-world in the vanguard of social and commercial reform during a period in which Parsi and wider Indian customary practices were coming to be regarded as detrimental to the private and public autonomy under which civil society was maintained. The arbitrary authority of the *panchayat* would once again be at the heart of this debate but so too would the role of women in social improvement in all Indian communities. Naoroji's influential interventions in these debates are the subject of the next chapter.

# 3 Civil Society and Social Reform

In February 1885, Naoroji commemorated the life and legacy of the recently deceased Parsi philanthropist Kharshedji Nasarvanji Cama, who had bankrolled a number of Naoroji's reform and educational organizations in Bombay during the 1840s and 1850s. Reminiscing about what prosperous Parsi reformers achieved in these times and the type of civil society they had promoted, Naoroji remarked that 'the state of society' before these philanthropic efforts had appeared decidedly 'peculiar'. Liberal education subsequently opened the minds of young men to 'new ideas and thoughts' about their 'social and ... other duties and relations'. These pioneering professionals backed with money from wealthy Parsi businesses had challenged the traditional hierarchies of priestly, patriarchal and *panchayati* obligation. By the 1860s the *panchayat* seemed to epitomize all the community's illiberal traits, monopolized as it was by conservative orthodox families that sought to use their influence to arbitrarily arrest the pace of change. As far as Naoroji was concerned, it was the 'moral' and 'self-bondage' of his co-religionists that enabled these forms of domination.[1]

Anxieties around cultural and moral bondage animated the social reform agenda of Naoroji and his colleagues from the 1840s to the 1860s. First, the *panchayat*'s status-based monopoly of what constituted the legitimate parameters of Parsi social conduct came under increased scrutiny as community notables discredited themselves through scandal and corruption. Second, communal rioting in Bombay revealed the fragility of the city's social concord, prompting a search for ways to maintain inter-communal harmony. The Victorian character discourse was reconfigured in this context to promote individual self-regulation and self-restraint through a programme of liberal tutelage. However, given the desire of Indian communities to preserve their cultural distinctiveness, this was to be executed in accordance with the life-worlds of respective religious groups. Because cultural backsliding was associated with the exercise of arbitrary power by

[1] 'The Late Mr. C. N. Cama', *Times of India*, 9 February 1885.

orthodox elites, Naoroji and his allies' account of liberty and society developed a republican inflection.

As guardians of the domestic sphere, Indian women emerged as the lynchpin of the new social order with female uplift seen as a way of inculcating rational self-fashioning and self-reliance among future generations. This chapter also explains how female education was aligned with projects of cultural uplift that sought to inculcate self-mastery using the didactic pedagogy of Parsi, Hindu and Muslim cultures. The result would be the sequencing of each community in accordance with a model of non-coercive self-regulation and sociability from which pacified inter-communal relations would automatically emerge.[2] The chapter concludes by exploring Naoroji's insistence on fairer inheritance laws for women and how he recognized that commerce and property also played a constitutive role in his model of multicultural civility.

## The Demise of the Parsi *Panchayat* and Communal Tensions

Bombay's Parsi community was in a state of existential crisis by the mid-nineteenth century as priests, community elders and young professionals wrangled over the cultural and religious boundaries of the minority. Initially catalysed by the proselytizing efforts of Christian missionaries in the 1820s, the situation came to a head in 1839 when two Parsi boys attending Rev. Dr John Wilson's school were converted to Christianity, sparking condemnation and outrage from the Parsi *panchayat*. Though the *panchayat* appealed to the high court and petitioned the government for redress, they were rebuffed, and the conversion episode dealt a heavy blow to the legitimacy of the institution and its ability to define and defend the boundaries of the group's common religious identity. The attempt to modernize on their own terms in the face of aggressive Christianization has been singled out as the prime reason Parsis turned to social reform.[3] More than this, social reform through elite philanthropy and pedagogy was intended to birth a new sociality in the void left by an ever more sclerotic *panchayat* and rapidly deteriorating inter-community relations in Bombay.

[2] Catherine Hall and L. Davidoff, *Family Fortunes: Men and Women of the English Middle Class, 1780–1850* (London: Routledge, 2002); Dror Wahrman, *The Making of the Modern Self: Identity and Culture in Eighteenth-century England* (New Haven, CT: Yale University Press, 2004); Michael Mason, *The Making of Victorian Sexuality* (Oxford: Oxford University Press, 1994); John Tosh, *A Man's Place: Masculinity and the Middle-class Home in Victorian England* (New Haven, CT: Yale University Press, 1999).

[3] Eckehard Kulke, *The Parsees in India: A Minority as Agent of Social Change* (Munich: Weltforum Verlag, 1974), pp. 93–4; Jesse S. Palsetia, *The Parsis of India: Preservation of Identity in Bombay City* (Leiden: Brill, 2008).

The *panchayat*'s authority continued to decline through the nineteenth century, culminating in the Parsee Marriage and Divorce Act and Parsee Succession Act of 1865.[4] Both acts borrowed from British legislation, infusing it with an admixture traditional Parsi customs and progressive measures. These new laws were the fruit of the Parsi Law Association (1855–64), a pressure group led by Naoroji's close collaborator on issues of religious reform and education, Naoroji Furdunji.[5] The movement developed from tensions dating to the late 1830s when the older generation of *panchayat* members had refused to regulate their own social usages by practising bigamy and nepotism and calling the liberal self-image of the community into question.[6] The tipping point came in 1836 when a senior member, Naoroji Jamsetji Wadia, resigned on the grounds that other members of the *panchayat* were arbitrarily dispensing selective justice and practising bigamy themselves whilst presuming to adjudicate on the social affairs of the lower orders or choosing to ignore community anxieties entirely. Another *panchayat* member, Framji Cowasji, complained of the institution's ambivalence, adding that 'under such circumstances' the Parsis 'are forced to act independently of the Punchyat [*sic*]' and if this continues 'it will be impossible for the Punchyat [*sic*] to punish them for defying its authority'.[7] While the marriage and inheritance laws succeeded in substituting matrimonial and civil courts for the *panchayat*, they had put the final nail in the institution's coffin and left a gulf in matters of day-to-day social arbitration.

Those young Parsis who, like Naoroji, had benefitted from English education in Bombay believed that the *panchayat*'s function and diktat could be fulfilled voluntarily in the civil sphere through education and the inculcation of good character. Thus, while European education furnished the abstract concepts of the ideal liberal subject, local politics provided the context in which it was appropriated and put to work for indigenous needs. During the first half of the century, reform efforts enjoyed catholic patronage thanks to the Parsi community's immense

[4] Sorabjee Shapoorjee Bengalee, ed., *The Parsee Marriage and Divorce Act 1865* (Act no. XV of 1865), *The Parsee Chattels Real Act* (Act no. IX of 1837), *The Parsee Succession Act* (Act no. XXI of 1865), *with an Appendix and Guzerattee Translation* (Bombay: Parsee Law Association, 1868).

[5] Kulke, *The Parsees in India*, pp. 67–8; Palsetia, *Parsis of India*, pp. 214–18.

[6] C. A. Bayly, *Recovering Liberties: Indian Thought in the Age of Liberalism and Empire* (Cambridge: Cambridge University Press, 2011), p. 119.

[7] Manockjee Cursetjee, *The Parsee Panchayet, Its Rise, Its Fall and the Causes That Led to the Same: Being a Series of Letters in the Bombay Times of 1844–5, Under the Signature of Q in the Corner, Published at the Request of Some Gentlemen of the Parsee Community and with the Permission of the Author* (Bombay: L. M. De Souza, 1860), p. 24.

success in commerce. The political question of the day was the social function of the community's wealth and the benefits of philanthropically established civic institutions in sustaining public space and lubricating sociability. These community concerns were played out across the prosperous Parsi communities of western India. In 1860s Surat, the local Parsis had invested their faith in the leadership of the *nagarsheth*, the head of the local Hindu and Jain banking castes, who had also demonstrated municipal munificence and public-spiritedness. This selection marginalized the orthodox *modi*, who was the traditional head of the local Parsi community.[8]

In Bombay, the effectiveness of charitable works in sustaining inter-communal harmony was seriously questioned after the Parsi–Muslim riots of 1851 and 1874. Depictions of the Prophet Mohammed in Gujarati-language Parsi publications, *The Illustrated Mirror of Knowledge* in 1851 and *The Renowned Prophets and Nations* in 1873, sparked violence before and during the Muharram festival and further intensified the existing commercial rivalry between the two communities over the opium trade. Ismaili Khoja Muslims had been particularly successful at edging out Parsi competitors in the China trade.[9] In 1851, the riot was sporadic, over the course of several weeks, claiming one life and injuring over twenty.[10] Across three days in February 1874, the civil violence was more concentrated and severe, leaving seven dead, fifty injured and causing more than 32,000 rupees in damages.[11] These events further undermined Parsi faith in their traditional leaders causing Western-educated Parsis to question the social development of other communities, particularly their 'lower orders' or 'the very dregs and scum of society', as the press dubbed them. Fears were stoked of a 'chronic' religious divide between the two communities, as the Muslims were seen as 'more and more in the wrong' with 'every day that passes'.[12] What was even more shocking to the Parsi intelligentsia was their *panchayat*'s demand following the 1851 riot that all Parsis refrain from participating in the Shia Muharram festival in the coming weeks.[13] This seemed to signal a distressing lack of commitment to Bombay's cultural

---

[8] *Bombay Gazette*, 17 October 1862.

[9] Rajnarayan Chandavarkar, *The Origins of Industrial Capitalism in India: Business Strategies and the Working Classes in Bombay*, new edn (Cambridge: Cambridge University Press, 2002) p. 62.

[10] A Parsee, *The Mahomedan Riots of Bombay in the Year 1851* (Bombay: Bombay Samachar Press, 1856), pp. 69–71.

[11] Dinshah Ardeshir Taleyarkhan, *The Riots of 1874: Their True History and Philosophy* (Bombay: Vining & Co, 1874), pp. 2–3.

[12] *Bombay Times and Journal of Commerce*, 29 November 1851.

[13] Ibid., 25 October 1851 and 26 November 1851.

pluralism. While anger was directed at the British authorities for failing to protect the Parsis, far more scathing opprobrium was reserved for the Parsi leaders who hid in their homes and did nothing to safeguard their community.[14] Alternatively, the average Parsi who defended his property against rioters was valorized as a paragon of honourable masculinity.[15]

When violence flared up between the two communities again in 1874, the communal tone of the reportage and loud disappointment in the government's response became more trenchant. The police admitted that they could not be expected to 'cope with all disturbances breaking out first in one quarter and then another' and a deputation to Governor Philip Wodehouse resulted in his refusal to garrison the city with soldiers unless the police totally failed.[16] This time violent reprisals from Parsis were more extensive than in 1851, and the community had to account for its behaviour. Dinshah Taleyarkhan's eyewitness account of the events insisted that 'Parsi cases were confined to a few of the uncultivated order, who would not feel quite gratified in letting the Mahomedan rioters escape unchallenged'.[17] The more outraged sections of the Parsi community now called for a total ban on the Muharram celebrations, arguing that it was not central to the faith of most Muslims. Educated Parsis argued against such a move, believing it to set a worrying precedence for religious freedom in the city.[18] Echoing the general trend of educated liberal opinion during the century, Taleyarkhan directed his displeasure at the colonial state for being run by a monolithic class of foreign bureaucrats who could not understand the 'heterogenous [*sic*] mass of the country'.[19]

What communal conflagration had invoked in many Parsis was a demand for the state to nurture a liberal society that was also sensitive to India's diversity. The various communities of the city had to be individually transformed into 'future civilized and independent bodies of people' and it was felt that until 'the different races in India are improved by a better cultivation of their moral and intellectual faculties, it is the imperative duty of the Government to duly protect the religious feelings of any section of the Indian community from being violated'. This was a duty Taleyarkhan believed the government of the Bombay Presidency had

[14] Masani, *Dadabhai Naoroji*, p. 64.
[15] Dosabhai Framji Karaka, *History of the Parsis*, vol. I (2 vols., London: Macmillan & Co, 1884), p. 105.
[16] Taleyarkhan, *The Riots of* 1874, pp. 2–9.
[17] Ibid., p. 16.
[18] Ibid., pp. 23–4.
[19] Ibid., p. 30.

singularly failed to honour.[20] If the state ought to midwife modern civil society into existence, then it was also to police transgressions of civil peace during the gestation. This was all the more pressing since civic philanthropy in Bombay was increasingly insular and directed towards conservative religious establishments or festivals. Liberals like Framji Cowasji demanded that the values of good character be universalized more forcefully even among Parsis. The class divide between the wealthy Parsi families who lived in the Fort area of Bombay and those who lived beyond it, and who had participated in the riots, meant that the latter class was still regarded as suffering from arrested social development.[21]

Naoroji maintained that the problem of communal violence was not due to living cheek by jowl with other faiths but the Hindu and Muslim lower classes' lack of character. When Hindu–Muslim riots erupted in Bombay in 1893 over the issue of cow protection, Naoroji reassured the British public that in 'every place in the world there is always one set of men who are fanatical ... in the lower classes principally, whether they are Parsees, Hindoos, Christians, or Mahomedans, it doesn't matter'. Naoroji's argument was that tensions were 'entirely confined to the lower classes' of each different community and hinted at there being a 'deeper cause' than immutable hatreds.[22] Echoing Naoroji, the Parsi press blamed poorly educated Muslims who were incapable of social uplift because of bondage to their conservative community leaders. They were condemned in language that resembled the liberal Parsi attack on their own *panchayat*.[23] Shortly following the riots, Naoroji's Parsi colleague and political correspondent for the *Indian Spectator*, Dinshaw Wacha, reiterated the case for character in liberal and neo-Republican terms. If liberal self-cultivation promoted duty, the function of this virtue was to empower free will under the shadow of elite and orthodox attempts at self-interestedly monopolizing the power of social regulation. He compared this to 'the tyranny of the French kings and nobles' whose absence of social duty not only promoted revolution but planted the seeds of the 'relentless vandalism' of Jacobin social anarchy as well.[24]

---

[20] Ibid., pp. 32, 34.

[21] Douglas Haynes, *Rhetoric and Ritual in Colonial India: The Shaping of a Public Culture in Surat City, 1852–1928* (Oakland, CA: University of California Press, 1992), p. 38; Koshru Navrosji Banaji, *Memoirs of the Late Framji Cowasji Banaji* (Bombay: Bombay Gazette Steam Printing Works, 1892), pp. 26, 96; *Rajdan Parast*, 15 February 1874, week ending 21 February 1874, Report on Native Papers, Bombay [RNP]; *Jam-e-Jamsed*, 12 March 1874, week ending 14 March 1874, RNP.

[22] *Pall Mall Gazette*, 14 August 1893.

[23] *Rastgoftar*, 22 February 1874, week ending 28 February 1874, RNP.

[24] *Indian Spectator*, 28 January 1894.

The language with which the *panchayat* was abandoned in favour of a constructive civil society became ever more scathing. A letter in the *Bombay Times* poured scorn on those who continued to believe in arbitrary social regulation and distinctions of status when it came to managing character. 'To what a pretty pass the world would come', it ruminated 'if a body of men were to constitute themselves the keepers and guardians of other people's consciences and reputations.'[25] Likewise, Sorabji Shapurji fulminated on the inability of Parsis to rise to the challenge of social duty through autonomy from any external or institutional will. He claimed that the 'truly useful element – restraint – which is the mainstay in the formation and conduct of society' was not 'owned by' the majority of Parsis.[26] What little character Parsi society demonstrated, Shapurji thought, came from mimicking the British in order to secure preferment – it was not the same as being one's own person. Parsis needed to recognize that 'society' could only arise from 'self-growth'.[27] Mass education for all communities thus became the watchword of liberal reformers, and the necessary virtues to be inculcated were explicitly linked to liberal self-mastery but also of republican self-ownership. Shapurji concluded that 'in making progress towards civilization, which brings about the institution of society, a man becomes a gentleman'. The gentleman was 'a man of truth, lord of his own action, and expressing that lordship in his own behaviour, not in any manner dependent or servile either on persons, or opinions, or possessions'.[28] While this process began within the Parsi community, by focusing on women as domestic instructors, the educated elite also looked beyond their own religion as communal violence recurred.

## Female Education

In the late 1840s, Bombay's philanthropists approached Naoroji to champion the work of education and social reform in the city. Naoroji's colleague at Elphinstone, Professor Joseph Patton, Erskine Perry, the Brahmin businessman and philanthropist Jagannath Sunkersett and Jamsetjee Jeejeebhoy all urged Naoroji's participation in the social and political issues of the day.[29] The conservative leaders of the Parsi community would still have to be won over, however. Jeejeebhoy

[25] *Bombay Times and Journal of Commerce*, 1 July 1848.

[26] Sorabji Shapurji, *The Evil Social Customs at Present Prevalent among the Parsees and the Best Means of Eradicating Them* (Bombay: Ripon Printing Press, n.d.), pp. 40–1.

[27] Ibid., p. 40.

[28] Ibid., pp. 41–2.

[29] Munni Rawal, *Dadabhai Naoroji: A Prophet of Indian Nationalism, 1855–1900* (New Delhi: Anmol Publications, 1989), p. 5.

organized an interview between Naoroji and Dosabhoy Munshi, recognized to be one of the most conservative magnates of the day. Munshi questioned Naoroji's reforming zeal, convinced that women needed a bare minimum of education to fulfil their duties as wives and mothers. 'What do females want education for?' he questioned Naoroji, since 'it will only spoil them. You see, you should not supply more oil to a lamp than it can bear'. It was left to Jeejeebhoy to reassure him that Naoroji only desired to give women 'a moderate education' so that women should receive no 'more knowledge than they want'.[30]

Partly in concession to conservative opinion, Jeejeebhoy's Parsi Benevolent Institution opened four vernacular schools for girls which precluded English as a medium of female instruction.[31] Yet the institution was among the first major educational organizations that usurped institutional and public functions from the *panchayat*'s traditional remit.[32] Concurrently, in 1848 with the aid of Parsi notables like Kharshedji Nasarwanji Cama, Naoroji founded the Students' Literary and Scientific Society (SLSS) in conjunction with Elphinstone College.[33] This was a revival, in a recalibrated form, of the moribund Native Literary Society founded in 1841 to promote European learning of which Naoroji was president.[34] In 1849, the SLSS opened six schools for girls of its own which educated twenty-four Hindus and sixty-six Parsis.[35] The SLSS was innovative in that it was the first association in which likeminded 'reformed' men could forge a collective identity and carve out an intellectual space that was denied them in the public sphere.[36] The society also facilitated dialogue between Indian vernacular and Western knowledge by actively promoting a comparative approach to literary studies.[37] As such, the central society's library possessed both English-language works and vernacular translations. A network of vernacular branch societies also contributed talks, accessed the library and made up the central association's audiences. Literature in

[30] Extract about the meeting from *Indu Prakash*, 23 March 1885, enclosed in Sorabji B. Munshi to Naoroji, 1 March 1902, National Archives of India, New Delhi, Dadabhai Naoroji Papers [DNP], M-210 (25).

[31] Karaka, *History of the Parsis*, vol. I, pp. 288–9.

[32] Jesse S. Palsetia, 'Partner in Empire: Jamsetjee Jeejeebhoy and the Public Culture of Nineteenth-century Bombay', in John R. Hinnells and Alan Williams, eds., *Parsis in India and the Diaspora* (London: Routledge, 2008), p. 91.

[33] Palsetia, *Parsis of India*, p. 142.

[34] Bayly, *Recovering Liberties*, p. 121; Masani, *Dadabhai Naoroji*, p. 43.

[35] Ibid., pp. 142–3.

[36] Veena Naregal, *Language Politics, Elites, and the Public Sphere: Western India under Colonialism* (London: Permanent Black, 2002), pp. 225, 233.

[37] C. A. Bayly, 'Indian Thought in the Shadow of Macaulay', Macaulay Lecture, Loughborough, 24 October 2013.

the library included Guizot's *Histoire de la Civilisation en France*, Arnold's *Lectures on History* and S. S. Wagle's translation of Buckle's *History of Civilization*.[38] The society's talks demonstrate Naoroji and his colleagues' desire to engage with European knowledge and 'rationalize' Indian practices on non-sectarian lines as well as providing a forum to inculcate the educated elite with a sense of social duty. Among the first talks was Naoroji's 'duties of a teacher' in 1849.[39] The institution was dubbed a 'mutual improvement society' in which discrete religious groups could progress by the example of their neighbour and the methods of learning were adapted to the abilities of each community.[40]

Within these educational societies, reforming the condition of women was a key objective and one that far exceeded the conservative requirement for producing dutiful wives and homemakers. For instance, Naoroji's fellow Elphinstonian and business partner, Ardeshir Framji Moos, delivered a talk 'on morality' while a book of 'moral songs' was made available for the girls' schools and prizes distributed for academic achievement in liberal academic subjects on a par with men.[41] Female vernacular education, seeded with Western knowledge, was as much about the development of character and the fulfilment of public duties as it was about domestic obligations. As Bombay's educated male professionals searched for the 'virtuous member of society', it was decided that women had public as well as private duties to fulfil.[42] As Naoroji would later attest before the Indian Education Commission, the point of mass education was the 'cultivation and development' of the 'whole nature – material and moral – moral in its widest sense of all human conditions' of Indians. Parallel education in the 'political, social, and religious' spheres was necessary because 'these conditions, as they exist, act upon and influence, by all their forces, the education of every individual child ... and therefore the whole country'.[43]

[38] 'List of Books Presented to the Society from Various Englishmen and the Bombay Board of Education, in July 1850', in *Third Report of the Students' Literary and Scientific Society and Its Vernacular Branch Societies* (Bombay: Bombay Gazette Press, 1852), pp. 54–6

[39] *Proceedings of the Students' Literary and Scientific Society*, 1854–5 and 1855–6 (Bombay: Bombay Gazette Press, 1857), p. 4.

[40] Ibid., pp. 26–8.

[41] Ibid., p. 2; *Proceedings of the Students' Literary and Scientific Society*, 1856–7, 1857–8 and 1858–9 (Bombay: Bombay Gazette Press, 1860), pp. 23–4; *Bombay Times*, 2 April 1859, 30 June 1860, 11 April 1861.

[42] *Bombay Times*, 31 March 1858.

[43] 'A Note Submitted to the Indian Education Commission of 1882 by Dadabhai Naoroji. 16 Sept. 1882, Bombay', Evidence taken before the Bombay provincial committee and memorials addressed to the Indian education commission, 1884, Asia, Pacific, and Africa Collection, British Library, London [BLAPAC], IOR/V/26/860/6.

In contrast to Naoroji's hybridized methods, by the 1860s English education for girls was also promoted by reformers who drew more on the European missionary tradition, leading to the founding of the Alexandra Native Girls' Education Institution in 1863.[44] Naoroji's Parsi colleague and confidant Behramji Malabari was one of the most vocal activists for spreading English manners and customs among women, as well as invoking state intervention to ban child marriage and the Hindu custom of prohibiting widow remarriage.[45] Malabari had begun his childhood education at an Anglo-Vernacular school but following his mother's death opted to join the 'Irish Presbyterian missionary school' instead. Here Malabari threw himself into the study of all things English under the tutelage of Rev. Dixon and his wife.[46] He did not attend any of the government's higher education institutions, and his insights on 'Englishness' and reform were inflected through an overwhelmingly missionary perspective. This led him to conclude that all political and economic progress in India was dependent on every community aping the social usages of English culture first.[47] Malabari's semi-sardonic study of the condition of Gujarat insisted that 'the inner life' of a people and the 'moral and social forces that work among them' were exclusively due to their 'habits, customs, [and] manners'.[48] Compared to Naoroji, there was less here of the liberal sociological analysis of Mill, who placed considerable influence on the reformatory power of public institutions in a given state of society. In his missionary zeal for cultural reform, Malabari confined women to the home not unlike the Hindu cultural conservatives he deplored. He refuted Naoroji's logic for liberal female education, denying the public role of women:

> [T]he predominating tendency of public schools for girls is to turn out as first-class products of learning and general accomplishments, rather than to raise them to a standard of efficiency, which will fit them to cope with work peculiarly their own, in the government of a home, and in all that makes home sacred; because the centre-piece is a woman cultured in just that sort of education which helps her to fill the position assigned to her in the sphere of wifehood and motherhood.[49]

[44] Kulke, *Parsis in India*, pp. 84–5.
[45] Dayaram Gidumal ed., *The Life and Life-work of Behramji M. Malabari* (Bombay: Education Society Press, 1888), p. 26.
[46] Ibid., xxxiv–xxxvi.
[47] Ibid., pp. 143–4.
[48] Behramji M. Malabari, *Gujarat and the Gujaratis: Pictures of Asian Men and Manners Taken from Life,* 3rd edn (Bombay: W. H. Allen & Co, 1889 [1882]), pp. viii–ix.
[49] 'The Higher Education of Women', *Indian Spectator*, 15 January 1888.

Malabari's vision for female education regurgitated the separate spheres ideology of the Victorian middle classes.[50] For Malabari, the 'pomp and blazonry' of the female intellectual was to the 'detriment of more real and useful work' in the household. What was wanted was the 'professional woman' who was 'recognized as the mistress of her home'.[51] The 'professional woman' was one who was educated and trained in fields that mirrored the nurturing and motherly duties of the domestic sphere – of these nursing featured most prominently.[52]

In other Indian communities as well, the failure of the state to act neutrally on such questions meant the return to religious reform in which community could advance on its own lines. Mahadev Govind Ranade noted with dismay Malabari's failure to elicit massive legal intervention and urged 'the cleansing fire of a religious revival' instead. However, as we shall see, Naoroji's methods were not predicated on religion as the sole sociological criterion through which socialization might be achieved. Conversely, Ranade was insistent that any grassroots Indian reform should avoid the 'cold calculations of utility' and so had to be sequenced through individual faith.[53] This held out the prospect of unified action eventually because all Indian faiths and castes were 'alike defective' in their injustices.[54] Other Parsi reformers like Mancherjee Bhownaggree, Naoroji's political rival who became a Tory MP in 1895, corroborated the views of Malabari and his British associate Mary Carpenter. Bhownaggree paid lip service to Naoroji's success in founding vernacular schools but demanded that all future education must be solely in English.[55]

Bhownaggree and Malabari eagerly encouraged the education of Indian girls as nurses as well.[56] In honour of his late sister, Bhownaggree set up the Avabai

---

[50] Hall and Davidoff, *Family Fortunes*.

[51] 'The Higher Education of Women', *Indian Spectator*, 15 January 1888.

[52] Antoinette Burton, 'The White Woman's Burden: British Feminists and the Indian Woman, 1865–1915', *Women's Studies International Forum* 13, no. 4 (1990), p. 296; Ruth Watts, 'Mary Carpenter and India: Enlightened Liberalism or Condescending Imperialism?', *Paedagogica Historica: International Journal of History and Education* 37, no. 1 (2001), pp. 207–8.

[53] M. G. Ranade, 'Social Legislation in Social Matters', in M. B. Kolasker, ed., *Religious and Social Reform: A Collection of Essays and Speeches – Mahadeva Govind Ranade* (Bombay: Gopral Narayen & Co, 1902), p. 93.

[54] M. G. Ranade, 'The Bombay Social Conference, 1900', in M. G. Ranade, *The Miscellaneous Writings of the Late Hon'Ble Mr. Justice M. G. Ranade*, with an Introduction by Mr. D. E. Wacha (New Delhi: Sahitya Akademi, 1992 [1915]), pp. 236–7.

[55] M. M. Bhownaggree, 'The Present Condition and Future Prospects of Female Education in India', read at a meeting of the National Indian Association on 26 March 1885, *Journal of the National Indian Association* [hereafter *JNIA*] 172 (1885), pp. 229–30.

[56] B. M. Malabari to Naoroji, 19 June 1885, DNP, M-32 (78).

Bhownaggree Home for Nurses in Bombay in 1891. Bhownaggree had long campaigned for government support so that English nurses could train their Indian counterparts and for the latter to receive English-language instruction as well.[57] While straightforwardly Anglophile reformers like Bhownaggree and Malabari put themselves at the mercy of British missionaries and ceded public life to European men, Naoroji's attitude was subtly different. For instance, his daughter Maki was encouraged to go beyond nursing and studied medicine at Edinburgh and Dublin.[58] Naoroji used his colleagues in Scotland and Ireland, like Alfred Webb, to help secure every avenue of support for training both his daughter and son, Ardeshir, as doctors.[59] Naoroji even planned for her to have her own medical practice in London until her mother demanded her return to India.[60] Naoroji was well aware that he had exceeded both the orthodox Parsi and British missionary preferences for women's roles by allowing his daughter beyond the sphere of domestic duty.

Naoroji's championing of a rationalized vernacular, neither desiring wholesale Anglicization nor vernacular isolation, was indicative of the late-nineteenth-century liberal's belief that Indian knowledge required reinvigoration through dialogue with the scientific temper of European writing. Yet it was also a concession to India's pluralism, the value of Indian literature and the belief that reforming zeal could not trump cultural attachments but had to work through them. Naoroji was never in any doubt that this pragmatic method was still liberalizing, however. C. M. Kharshedji, the son of Manakji Kharshedji, who had founded the Alexandra Institution, wrote to Naoroji in 1912 claiming that it was his father's pioneering efforts in English education that marked the 'beginning of liberal female education' and that vernacular education merely taught writing and arithmetic and did not contain the 'mental and moral discipline' of real 'Western' education. Naoroji replied defending the ability of rationalized vernaculars imbued with Western themes and concepts to reform character.[61] At a meeting of the East India Association in London, he also castigated European interlocutors for advocating wholesale Anglicization. After all, India had 'its own ancient literature and own languages' which contained a wealth of instruction. English and the

[57] General Department 53/1890, comp. 287, part I; General Department 54/1890, comp. 287, part II, Maharashtra State Archives, Mumbai, India [MSA].
[58] Masani, *Dadabhai Naoroji*, p. 186.
[59] Alfred Webb to Naoroji, 20 October 1896, DNP, W-41 (2); Webb to Naoroji, 26 October 1896, DNP, W-41 (3).
[60] Masani, *Dadabhai Naoroji*, pp. 186–7.
[61] Kharshedji summaries the contents of previous exchanges between the two in this letter, C. M. Kharshedji to Naoroji, 2 October 1912, DNP, C-301 (7).

Indian vernaculars ought to inform each other and be taught side by side.[62] This pragmatic attitude was also expressed in Naoroji's desire to reform caste through education so that 'irrational' caste practices and their 'baneful' effects, like infant marriage, would diminish but maintained that reformers had to be cognizant of the common attachment to caste identity.[63]

## Religious Reform

The 1851 riots directly catalysed the Parsi intelligentsia's mission to gentrify and socialize the 'lower orders' of the community. Aided by K. N. Cama's patronage, Naoroji founded the fortnightly newspaper *Rast Goftar* (Herald of Truth) to discuss the ramifications of the civil strife. Future editions branched out into diverse discussions of social reform and development.[64] The same year also saw Naoroji's founding of the Rahnumae Mazdayasan Sabha (guides on the *mazdayasnan* path society) with Naoroji Furdoonji in an effort to 'purify' Zoroastrianism of its putatively 'foreign' and 'backward' rituals and customs.[65] Both institutions were a continuation of Naoroji's desire to create a vernacular public sphere in which free-flowing debate would rationalize Parsi culture. Indeed, Furdoonji hoped that the Mazdayasan Sabha could renovate tradition from within by seeding it with only the most relevant European concepts.[66] *Rast Goftar* was pitted against the community's conservative press in the shape of *Jam-e-Jamshed*, which was founded in 1832. Naoroji regarded his publication as a liberal journal rather than a 'newspaper' and pressed all the articles published therein to convincingly disseminate some 'social' or 'political ... principle'.[67] However, the *Rast*'s intellectual integrity as one pole of opinion within a contested yet autonomous public sphere could not be compromised. Thus, Naoroji refused to clandestinely interfere with the editorship of the paper even when it ran afoul of other liberal publications, only permitting himself to write an opinion piece as a reader.[68] Its public function was so important to Naoroji that he agreed to publish and circulate it at his own

[62] Naoroji's comments during the discussion following George Simmons, 'The Advantages of Encouraging the English Language to Become the Colloquial Tongue of India, with a Practical System for its Development', *Journal of the East India Association* [*JEIA*] 3 (1869), pp. 172–6.
[63] Discussion following R. H. Elliot, 'On the Beneficial Effects of Caste Institutions', *JEIA* 3 (1869): 177–88.
[64] Palsetia, *Parsis of India*, p. 280.
[65] *Rahnuma-e-Majdisna Sabha* [Gujarati] (Bombay, 1861).
[66] *Proceedings of the First, Second, and Third Meetings of the Rahnumae Mazdayasnan Sabha* (Bombay: Duftur Ashkara Press, 1851), p. 9.
[67] Naoroji to Kharshedji Cama, 3 July 1857, DNP, N-1 (9).
[68] Naoroji to Kharshedji Cama, 21 October 1856, DNP, N-1 (5).

private expense when the paper's accounts were in the red, with Naoroji and Cama losing ten thousand rupees publishing the initial issues.[69]

Naoroji understood the public sphere in essentially Habermasian terms. Rational arguments ultimately prevail, and consensus is arrived at through a mixture of sound reasoning and convincing argumentation.[70] The efficacy of the public sphere and of uninhibited political debate as a means of cultural equipoise – to bring about a change in attitudes without social unrest – was indispensable in the shadow of civil violence. Kashinath Trimbak Telang observed that 'in politics, argument goes a great way' whereas in matters of cultural reform the debate becomes bogged down in affective appeals to tradition and rationality is sacrificed.[71] A rational 'public' was 'necessarily unanimous' in politics.[72] In his private scribbles reflecting on postal strikes in the United Kingdom, Naoroji also concurred that 'free speech' was a form of socialization that led to inevitable 'combination' through rational habits. If everyone agreed on an issue, there was unified thought and action, and in conditions of disagreement, 'irrational' elements would 'soon recognize that and change their ideas'.[73] This meant, however, that while journals could pontificate on matters of supra-communal politics, such as lobbying the government for more educational funding or economics, they would have to confine religious and cultural controversies to their own respective communities in which the cultural terms of debate were uniform. Hence Naoroji only presumed to intervene in issues of Parsi religious custom but could only encourage Hindus and Muslims to follow suit.

Naoroji's 1861 paper on the 'Parsee religion' portrayed Zoroastrianism as inherently rational and attributed any 'backward' tendencies to foreign accretions.[74] In its attribution of religious corruption to the mixing of Hindu and Muslim customs with Parsi rituals, Naoroji's religious reform was firmly within the tradition begun by the Hindu revivalist Brahmo Samaj founded in 1828 and the Islamic reformist movements in the middle of the century. Each group identified

---

[69] Naoroji to Kharshedji Cama, 4 June 1856, DNP, N-1 (1); Uma Das Gupta, 'The Indian Press 1870–1880: A Small World of Journalism', *Modern Asian Studies* 11, no. 2 (1977), p. 219.
[70] Jürgen Habermas, *The Theory of Communicative Action,* vol. I (2 vols., Boston, MA: Beacon Press, 1984), p. 101; Jürgen Habermas, *The Structural Transformation of the Public Sphere: An Inquiry into the Category of Bourgeois Society* (London: Polity Press, 1989).
[71] K. T. Telang, 'Must Social Reform Precede Political Reform in India?', in K. T. Telang, *Selected Writings and Speeches of K. T. Telang* (Bombay: Manoranjan Press, 1916), p. 289.
[72] Ibid., p. 290.
[73] Notes on Free Speech and Other Topics, DNP, notes and jottings, group 9: social, serial number 5.
[74] Dadabhai Naoroji, 'The Parsee Religion', read before the Liverpool Literary and Philosophical Society, 18 March 1861 (London, 1862).

the other as the source of their cultural decay and reform could only emanate from within the community. Naoroji argued that Europeans were incorrect in assigning idolatrous practices to Zoroastrians and that the fire they appeared to worship was in fact a deist symbol for nature and its God. Having its own concepts of sin, heaven and hell, Zoroastrianism was a 'dialectical faith capable of social improvement' like Christianity.[75] Furdoonji also tried to historicize Zoroaster like the Christ.[76] Yet there are two aspects of Naoroji's paper that suggest his defence of Zoroastrianism had a broader purpose than the valorization of his own community. Naoroji singled out a 'separate caste' of uneducated priests who were 'ignorant of the duties and objects of their own profession' as the cause of social backwardness. This critique was certainly transposable to other major faiths of India. Priestly influence was particularly baneful because of its control over women's education.[77] Appealing to his British audience, these critiques echoed the Cobdenite polemics against corrupt aristocracies in Britain with Macaulay's account of British history attesting to the fact that priestly influence was banished by free speech or 'wise laws ... and enlightened public opinion'.[78] The reform agenda achieved wider purchase through liberal Parsi societies and publications. The *Times of India* contained numerous reports of conservative *dasturs* being heckled and labelled a 'disgrace' at the Mazdayasan Sabha, with some of its columnists demanding updated scripture to educate the public in their true spiritual and moral duties.[79]

Though Naoroji regarded borrowed Hindu practices as detrimental to Zoroastrianism, he did not believe Zoroastrianism was inherently superior to Hinduism. Read in conjunction with his paper on 'Parsee Religion', Naoroji's 'The European and Asiatic Races' elevates educated Parsis to a vanguard status in the quest for social development due to their willingness to borrow from European knowledge and insists that Hindus can replicate this programme.[80] Naoroji saw ancient Hindu literature as 'vast and varied ... in all departments of human knowledge' but admitted the 'fertile soil' had been 'neglected' in more

[75] Bayly, *Recovering Liberties*, p. 174; Naoroji, 'The Parsee Religion', pp. 20–2.
[76] Nowrozjee Furdoonjee, 'On the Existence and Era of Zoroaster', *Bombay Times and Journal of Commerce*, 26 April 1861.
[77] Naoroji, 'The Parsee Religion', pp. 1–2.
[78] Thomas Babington Macaulay, *The History of England from the Accession of James the Second*, vol. I (5 vols., London: Longmans, Green, Reader & Dyer, 1877 [1848–59]), pp. 3–4.
[79] 'The Parsee Religious Reform Movement', *Times of India*, 29 April 1881, 30 April 1881 and 2 May 1881.
[80] Dadabhai Naoroji, 'The European and Asiatic Races: Observations on the Paper Read by John Crawford, Esq., F. R. S.', read before the Ethnological Society, 27 March 1866, in Dadabhai Naoroji, *Essays, Speeches, Addresses and Writings of the Hon'ble Dadabhai Naoroji*, ed. C. L. Parekh (Bombay: Caxton Printing Works, 1887), pp. 1–25.

recent times.[81] Naoroji cited oriental scholars like Max Müller on the progress made by Hindu civilization in mathematics and the 'rational sciences' like medicine.[82] The Sanskritic scholar Theodor Goldstücker was invoked to show that the ancient Indian language was 'of wonderful structure, more perfect than Greek, more copious than the Latin, and more exquisitely refined than either'.[83] Most importantly, however, while Naoroji attributed the stalling in the further development of Sanskrit to foreign invasions, as with his own community he blamed the Muslim priesthood's will to power and ignorance rather than Islam itself, adding that this 'mischief' was true the world over.[84]

In Hindu history Naoroji also identified the promotion of characteristics of self-regulation and a rational legal regime. Reflecting Maine's link between the rise of individual contract and 'progress' through the historical agency of inherited legal norms, Naoroji suggested that Hindu law did indeed promote the individual honesty and reciprocity necessary for contractual relations. Quoting from the *Institutes of Manu*, he emphasized that India had always exalted truthfulness in the civil sphere by enjoining 'pleasure in truth' but also constraining honest public chastisement of an individual 'to a legal mode'. Naoroji directly compared this to Jeremy Bentham's description of truth in his 'theory of legislation', which states that persistent falsehoods lead to 'erroneous' judgements and 'misplaced expectations', the consequences of which were the breakdown of trust and the 'dissolution of human society'.[85]

## Cultural Education

Naoroji was also a keen promoter of a wider cultural pedagogy and actively promoted the translation of modern classics of European science into the Indian vernaculars. Pyare Lal of Buretha undertook this work, dedicating his book *Animal Kingdom* to Naoroji, while also writing his own vernacular histories of the *Agriculture of India* and the *Natural History of India* all priced at one rupee 'for the benefit of the country'.[86] However, Naoroji believed that Indian literary classics and modern Indian culture were an equally useful tool of social education, and he recognized an immanent rationality in their cultural and legal precedents.

[81] Ibid., pp. 1–2.
[82] Ibid., p. 5.
[83] Ibid., pp. 5–6.
[84] Ibid., p. 6.
[85] Ibid., p. 11; J. Bentham, *The Theory of Legislation*, ed. C. K. Ogden (London: Paul, Trench, Trübner & Co, 1931[1840]).
[86] Pyare Lal of Buretha to Naoroji, 11 January 1894, DNP, P-244.

For instance, he supported the literary work of A. K. Ghose, an Indian student in the United Kingdom during the 1890s, who informed Naoroji about his London-based Nava Bharat Sabha (New India Association) of Indian students at Oxbridge, describing them as 'staunch followers' of Naoroji's 'political teachings'.[87] It was in his capacity as a reformer that Naoroji reviewed and advised on the civic merit of Ghose's poetry, which he published under the pseudonym 'Judius'.[88] Ghose regarded poetry, in the right hands, as an expression of noblest spirits of the human soul, particularly with regard to the moral elevation of womanhood as the backbone of civilization. He noted that it was the Hindus who 'deified' woman in their literature first and that the more recent attempts of European positivists to elevate womanhood actually followed the Indian example. In an increasingly materialistic age, Ghose also suggested that poetry balanced the atomistic impulse of scientific secularism that risked denigrating 'the finer nature of man'.[89] The beauty of poetry, like Naoroji's attempts to suffuse Indian vernaculars with modern concepts, was that it relied on an admixture of reason and the reader's affective bonds with her own varied history, language and tradition more than Malabari's state intervention or Ranade's religious revivalism did. Concepts were subsumed and repackaged in ways that were meaningful to a plurality of Indians, and it was the coming together of 'inspiration, imagination, association of ideas, association between words and sentiments, faculty of harmony, and taste' that constituted real poetry. Unlike the orator who must consciously choose his words to appeal to a rationally engaged mind, the poet composed in whatever style reflects 'the truest picture of his own heart'.[90]

In addition to supporting Ghose, Naoroji's own endeavours relied on the didactic and non-coercive power of artistic expression like drama. In the wake of religious riots, western Indian intellectuals were worried about the moral monopoly of priestly instruction leading to zealotry rather than reason.[91] Pherozeshah Mehta admitted that the British were right in stating that intellectualism alone could not impart social and political morality to Indians. However, striking a very different tone to Hindu counterparts like Ranade or Telang, for Mehta this was only true when public morality was inextricably bound up with theology. Mehta assured his British critics that as education and commerce progressed, the 'moral realm' would

[87] A. K. Ghose to Naoroji, 24 March 1898, DNP, G-36 (1).
[88] A. K. Ghose to Naoroji, 11 May 1898, DNP, G-36 (3); Judius, 'Poetry, Poets, and Poetical Powers', *Westminster Review* 149, no. 6 (1898), pp. 667–79.
[89] Judius, 'Poetry, Poets, and Poetical Powers', pp. 677–9.
[90] Ibid., pp. 671–7.
[91] M. G. Ranade to G. K. Gokhale (undated), BLAPAC, Gokhale Papers, IOR Neg 11705.

become independent of religion and 'poetry, history and philosophy' would more effectively mould the Indian mind.[92] In the absence of a fully literate and educated population that could read and interpret great texts – religious or secular, English or vernacular – in a rational way, Naoroji believed drama to be a form of public education that, unlike religious orthodoxy, was amenable to mental cultivation without risking dogmatism. Since literature worked by directly 'conveying the thoughts of others by words', it required a fully developed mind to interpret and contextualize those words in a non-sectarian way. By contrast, 'drama' supplied 'the object lessons' of a dutiful life by emulation.[93]

The Parsis pioneered stylistically European but culturally and linguistically plural theatre in Bombay from the 1850s deploying literature and music in English, Gujarati, Urdu and Hindi.[94] Naoroji's fellow Elphinstonians started a dramatic club specializing in English-language plays alongside the vernacular contributions of the Parsi theatre company, which had begun by translating Shakespeare from 1853. The theatre company tailored performances for women in an attempt to foster independence of mind. A vernacularized version of *The Taming of the Shrew* revealed the intellectual coercion of Indian women through the monopoly of knowledge exercised by Brahmins and Hindu astrologers.[95] For Naoroji, drama's power lay in its 'imitation in the way of action' and the way it tapped into people's 'natural' impulses. The 'chief test of the dramatist's art', Naoroji opined, was that 'unity of action' persisted throughout the narrative and that every vignette 'should form a link in a simple chain of cause and effect'.[96]

Naoroji claimed to be drawing this lesson from ancient Indian dramatic criticism, a tradition dated to at least the third century BCE and which was 'purely native', according to Naoroji, with 'no evidence of Greek influence at any stage of its purposes'. Kalidas was for Naoroji the 'brightest of the gems of genius', while Bhavabhuti was likened to an Indian Shakespeare. Indian dramatists appealed to humour, pathos, 'the grander aspects of nature' and notions of self-sacrifice as the 'condition both of individual perfection and of the progress of the World'. Mutual affection and the loftiness of character that overcame the extreme

---

[92] P. M. Mehta, 'On the East India (laws and regulations) Bill, Clause 6', read at the Bombay branch of the East India Association, 27 April 1870, *JEIA* 5 (1871), pp. 64–5.

[93] Naoroji, 'Notes on Indian Drama and Plays', DNP, notes and jottings, group 2: art and culture, serial number 7.

[94] Palsetia, *Parsis of India*, pp. 184–5; Kathryn Hansen, 'Languages on Stage: Linguistic Pluralism and Community Formation in Nineteenth-century Parsi Theatre', *Modern Asian Studies* 37, no. 2 (2003), pp. 381–405.

[95] *Bombay Times*, 23 February 1857, 30 November 1858, 9 April 1859 and 28 April 1858.

[96] Naoroji, 'Notes on Drama', DNP, notes and jottings, group 2: art and culture, serial number 5.

selfishness of 'barbaric' peoples were particularly inculcated.[97] As such, ancient Indian drama had achieved a level of sophistication both in style and in its purpose of elevating the minds of Indians to a rational appreciation of their social obligations. Indeed, Naoroji considered plays suitable for educating the British public as well in order to awaken their duties to fellow subjects in India. In 1900, S. B. Wagle of the London Indian Society consulted Naoroji on a performance in which personifications of India and Britannia would enact the former's woe and the latter's dutiful response in a perfected empire.[98]

Naoroji's artistic pluralism contrasted sharply with the literary preoccupations of some of his contemporaries. For instance, Romesh Chunder Dutt, the Bengali Hindu and economic historian, valorized a pristine Hindu past in his own novels. Dutt's 1902 *The Lake of Palms* was intended as a book in the Anglophone tradition that idealized a Hindu past without confronting India's Islamic heritage.[99] Dutt emphasized that the spirit of progressive history was ever present in Indian civilization from its inception to the modern day and spun the indomitable living spirit of India as originating in a Hindu golden age that continued despite subsequent Muslim iconoclasm in the Middle Ages.[100] Muslims and Muslim history were at best marginalized or even held to be suspect in such a chronology.[101] Alternatively, Jotirao Govind Phule's movement for low-caste uplift critiqued the spiritual and temporal ascendency of Brahmins. In 1855, he penned a drama entitled *Tratiya Ratna* tracing the deception of the *ryot* by the wicked Brahmin to the moment of the Aryan invasion. In this narrative the religious elite was successfully opposed in recent history by the martial Maratha yeomanry, particularly during the reign of the seventeenth-century Hindu king Shivaji Bhosale.[102] This narrative was also exclusionary since its rural anti-Brahminism appealed to Hindu kingship and Vedic symbols that isolated the attributes of the Kshatria warrior caste as the highest aspiration for the low-caste majority.[103]

---

97 Ibid.; 'Indian Drama', DNP, notes and jottings, group 2: art and culture, serial number 6.

98 S. B. Wagle to Mr Mehta and Mr Mullick, copy to Naoroji, 6 May 1900, DNP, W-14 (9).

99 Sudhir Chandra, 'The Cultural Component of Economic Nationalism: R. C. Dutt's "The Lake of Palms"', *Indian Historical Review* 12, nos. 1–2 (1985–6), pp. 108–9.

100 Ibid., pp. 109–113.

101 Mushirul Hasan, 'The Myth of Unity: Colonial and National Narratives', in David Ludden, ed. *Contesting the Nation: Religion, Community and the Politics of Democracy in India* (Philadelphia, PA: University of Pennsylvania Press, 1996), p. 201.

102 Rosalind O'Hanlon, *Caste, Conflict and Ideology: Mahatma Jotirao Phule and Low-caste Protest in Nineteenth-century Western India* (Cambridge: Cambridge University Press, 1985).

103 Ibid., p. 277.

Naoroji's artistic preoccupations appeared anodyne but they were an important counter-influence to increasingly popular historical and literary forms emerging from the more conservative hinterland of the Bombay Presidency, especially from the towns of Pune and Nasik. The reign of Shivaji was a preoccupation of numerous western Indian and Hindu critics of empire from social reformers like Ranade to violent insurrectionists-cum-Hindu nationalists like Vinayak Damodar Savarkar.[104] Shivaji's example of model kingship could be used to marginalize Muslims in much the same way as Dutt's literature. Ranade promoted the renewal of Maratha histories known as the *bakhar*, claiming them as a form of linear and progressive political history akin to the Macaulayite tradition. In reality, the narrative was prone to hyperbole, extended scene-setting and partisan attachment. Nevertheless, this was not regarded as affectation but a commitment to detailing 'plausible situations', the 'mood of personalities' and 'credible and appropriate dialogue'.[105] Yet for both Ranade and Savarkar the *bakhar*s provided a suitable alternative to religious and puranic histories with their heroes, sages, gods and kings from Hindu cosmology, with the former retorting that these texts 'did not contain much matter for real history. Mythologies, scraps of ancient and modern history, local geography, and morals, are all jumbled together in these works in an extricable confusion ... the very rudiments of political history are missing'.[106] In documenting Shivaji's rule, the *bakhar*s are not overtly communal in tone.[107] However, the narrative is that of the carving out of a Hindu sovereignty in the face of Mughal 'tyranny', while Ranade regarded them unproblematically as 'the birth of Indian history and prose' and a 'secular history' that was 'stripped of religious garb'. These accounts were ambiguous, and descriptions of the epics as defined by the 'struggle for political and religious freedom' could and were interpreted as anti-Muslim polemics.[108]

Muslim modernizers like Sayyid Ahmed Khan also sought the renovation of their faith through introspective education as the solution to their political and cultural backsliding. Regarding Islam as inherently rational and scientific from its earliest inception in the age of the Prophet, Khan believed that these features were forgotten in more recent times. Islam did not need to discover modernity

---

[104] Vikram Visana, 'Savarkar before Hindutva: Sovereignty, Republicanism, and Populism in India c. 1900–1920', *Modern Intellectual History* (FirstView, 2020), pp. 1–24.

[105] Prachi Deshpande, *Creative Pasts: Historical Memory and Identity in Western India, 1700–1960* (New York, NY: Columbia University Press, 2007), p. 28.

[106] 'Maratha Bakhars or Chronicles and Grant Duff's History of the Marathas', *Quarterly Journal of the Poona Savarjanik Sabha* 1, no. 2 (October, 1878), p. 14.

[107] Deshpande, *Creative Pasts*, p. 48

[108] Ibid., p. 16.

in European thought but merely required the European example as a means of apologetic rediscovery of itself rather than a reconciliation of oriental tradition with occidental progress.[109] This intellectual autarky, however, rendered the associational culture pioneered in cities like Bombay and Surat as irrelevant to the Muslim community's needs. Indeed, Sayyid Ahmed's Muslim modernity was framed apolitically because Muslims had been gradually excluded from public power since the demise of the Mughals. Though friendly, Naoroji and Sayyid Ahmed differed on the latter's isolation from the liberal lobbying of diverse but largely Hindu organizations like the Indian National Congress, which Naoroji co-founded in 1885.[110] One cannot escape the conclusion that Naoroji's continued engagement with social reform into the late nineteenth century reveals his commitment to character cultivation as a route to sociality. Nevertheless, the middle of the century witnessed Naoroji's priorities pivot decisively to the economic sphere in which dominated labour was the primary obstacle to the emergence of a tacit social concord.

## Right to Property and Inheritance

Considerations of economics and property influenced Naoroji's early social reform even before his 1860s pivot to political economy. Since the 1830s, the Parsis had lobbied for and successfully secured exemptions from personal laws applying to marriage, succession, inheritance and charitable giving. For Hindus and Muslims, the rules pertaining to these issues were codified according to colonial interpretations of endogamous customary practices. Educated Parsis had lobbied for reform of their laws due to their perception of themselves as a more 'progressive' community not beholden to the bondage of custom and arbitrary adjudication by religious elites. These concessions were intended not to blindly ape British laws – indeed they lobbied for exemptions from certain British precedents – but to maintain the Parsi trajectory of social development.[111]

Framji Patel, a guiding light in the founding of the Elphinstone College and in female education, co-founded the first institution devoted to legal reform with Naoroji Furdoonji. The Parsee Law Association was established in 1855 at the behest of prominent members of the Parsi intelligentsia with Naoroji playing a key role lobbying the Law Commissioners and Secretary of State in the

[109] Faisal Devji, 'Apologetic Modernity', *Modern Intellectual History* 4, no. 1 (2007), pp. 61–76.
[110] Syed Ahmed Khan to Naoroji, 15 January 1894, DNP, S-301.
[111] Mitra Sharafi, *Law and Identity in Colonial South Asia: Parsi Legal Culture, 1772–1947* (Cambridge: Cambridge University Press, 2014). p. 128.

United Kingdom.[112] This was another organization that emerged in the vacuum created by the decline of the Parsi *panchayat*. The Parsis were governed by British common law, meaning that inheritance via primogeniture applied to the Parsis even though traditionally property was distributed between surviving relatives. By 1837, the community had secured the Immovable Property Act, replacing the English tradition of primogeniture, rendering intestate property as 'chattels real' governed by the English doctrine of leasehold interests. The deceased's widow would inherit one-third of the property, with the remainder split equally between the male and female children.[113] In the wake of this precedent, the Law Association had taken up the issue of married women's property rights. Parsi marriages were governed by the British norm of coverture, which meant that a woman's legal rights were subsumed into those of her husband. She relinquished her property and earnings into his control and, crucially, abrogated the right to enter into individual contracts.[114] Furdoonji emphasized the historically progressive treatment of Parsi women by pointing out that they were not subject to coverture before British rule. The ethnographic state and misapplied British precedents had robbed Parsi women of the autonomy they had previously enjoyed. Colonialism imposed a litany of abuses in which insolvent husbands had appropriated their wives' property only to see it taken as collateral by their non-Parsi creditors. In another instance, Furdoonji Sorabji Parekh had left his four granddaughters sufficient property to live autonomously of their husbands but under common law only two were allowed to receive their share. The social economy was also undermined when jilted men successfully sued their wives for control of her inheritance with the legal fees subtracted from the overall value of the property.[115] While the more conservative-minded Parsis from the rural hinterlands of the Bombay Presidency sought to dilute the Law Association's demands for equal inheritance for women, a compromise was reached which ultimately did improve the female right to inheritance.

---

112 Anon, *The First Indian Member of the Imperial Parliament, Being a Collection of the Main Incidents Relating to the Election of Mr. Dadabhai Naoroji to Parliament* (Madras: Addison & Co, 1892), p. 3.

113 'Act IX of 1837, Passed by the Right Honourable Governor General of India in Council, on 15 May 1837', India Acts 1834–40, BLAPAC, IOR/V/8/31; Karaka, *History of the Parsis*, vol. II, p. 297; Palsetia, *Parsis of India*, pp. 201–3.

114 Mary Lyndon Shanely, *Feminism, Marriage and the Law in Victorian England, 1850–1895* (Princeton, NJ: Princeton University Press, 1989), pp. 8–9.

115 'Mr. Nowrozjee Furdoonjee's Letter', 1862–3, government of India bill to amend law for Parsees, with supporting papers, copies for further supporting papers dating from 1798, BLAPAC, IOR/L/PJ/5/400.

The Parsee Law Association's suggestions resulted in the Parsee Marriage and Divorce, Parsee Chattels Real, and Parsee Inheritance Bills that were duly passed into law as the Parsee Intestate Succession Act in February 1865. The primary effect was that widows and daughters of Parsis dying intestate in the Bombay Presidency were now entitled to a share of property rather than a subsistence moiety, but this was still only a quarter that of male heirs.[116] The logic of distribution was also equalized by abolishing English common law distinctions between chattels real, leasehold, freehold, realty and personalty along with the doctrine of primogeniture.[117] The new law took significant aspects of social governance away from the *panchayat* in Bombay and the orthodox *modi* in Surat and institutionalized it in tribunals administered by a high court judge, accessible to all and open to appeal. The 1865 provisions explicitly framed the new rights in terms of the Parsi woman's renewed capacity to exercise her will free of domination or dependence on her husband. The act maintained that no 'person shall by marriage acquire any interest in the property of the person whom he or she marries, nor become incapable of doing any act in respect of his or her own property, which he or she could have done if unmarried'.[118]

Naoroji kept copies of all progressive Parsi legislation, approvingly noting down its emancipatory provisions.[119] His commitment to fostering wider Indian sociability encouraged him to consider the transposability of these reforms to other Indian communities. His copious extracts from a reprint of William Jones's translation of *The Mahommedan Law of Inheritance* seem to suggest that Naoroji was examining the Islamic tradition for evidence of progressive inheritance laws for women.[120] Professor Almeric Rumsey comments in the preface of this work that the Muslim law of inheritance 'comprises beyond question the most refined and elaborate system of rules for the devolution of property that is known to the civilised world'.[121] Naoroji concurred, noting down all the instances in which customary Islamic inheritance corresponded to the Parsi precedent set in India.

---

[116] *Bombay Times*, 13 May 1861; 'Letter of Nowrozjee Furdoonjee to the Parsee Law Commission', 28 April 1862, Judicial Department 1863: 20/143:314–31, MSA.
[117] Cited in Sharafi, *Law and Identity in Colonial South Asia*, p. 150
[118] Ibid., p. 158.
[119] The Parsee Chattels Real Act; the Parsee Succession Act; the Parsee Marriage and Divorce Act, DNP, notes and jottings, group 8: legislation/judiciary, serial number 3.
[120] Extracts from *Siraj-al-Dīn Muḥammad ibn Muḥammad al-Sajāwandī, Al Sirajiyyah; or, The Mahommedan Law of Inheritance*, trans. Sir William Jones with notes and appendix by Almaric Rumsey (London: Thacker, Spinck & Co, 1869 [1792]), found in 'Mahamadan Inheritance by Almeric Rumsey', DNP, extracts, E-72 (93).
[121] Al-Sajāwandī, *Mahommedan Law of Inheritance*, p. iii.

There was 'no right of primogeniture' and a daughter would receive a full half share of intestate property if she was an only child. If there were sons, daughters received half as much as their brothers, which was twice as generous to female siblings as the Parsi provision. Naoroji also observed that female autonomy was upheld since the 'woman's property does not become the property of the husband' as with coverture. He also thought it noteworthy that only one-third of an estate could be bequeathed outside of the community through a written will with two-thirds remaining intestate and distributed to widows, sons and daughters, thereby ensuring the independence of the community's social economy.[122]

## Conclusion

The primary categories of colonial governance – religion, caste and gender – were precisely those that Parsi social reform engaged with.[123] Though Parsi thinkers like Naoroji did not trace the colonial genealogies of these categories, much less try to provincialize Europe, they did scrutinize them as if such a world of cultural difference could not long cohere peacefully under customary forms of arbitrary regulation. Naoroji and his colleagues' attacks on the *panchayat*, personal law and priestcraft were accompanied by grassroots reform movements that pointed to colonial negligence for not actively promoting the sociable relations of a civil society. Taken in conjunction with Hindu and Muslim reform movements, this attitude marked a seminal moment in Indian political modernity that brought about a recognition of either the state's subordination or its complete irrelevance to social questions. Whether it was lobbied to legislate positively on social reform or whether Parsis took it upon themselves to invest in Bombay's civic institutions, political government – by its presence or its absence – was a bolt on to the primary question of social regulation. As Prathama Banerjee has noted, unlike Europe's conceptual distinction between state and society, in India the state becomes the subject of political action because it is fundamental in the conceptualizing of Indian society. This mutual constitution of state and society has rendered the social–political binary more fluid as both political and social categories are deployed to define Indian sociality.[124]

---

[122] 'Mahamadan Inheritance by Almeric Rumsey', DNP, extracts, E-72 (93).

[123] Nicholas Dirks, *Castes of Mind: Colonialism and the Making of Modern India* (Princeton, NJ: Princeton University Press, 2001).

[124] Prathama Banerjee, 'The Abiding Binary: The Social and the Political in India', in Stephen Legg and Deana Heath, eds., *South Asian Governmentalities: Michel Foucault and Question of Postcolonial Orderings* (Cambridge: Cambridge University Press, 2018), pp. 81–105.

During the period discussed in this chapter, Naoroji was in the vanguard of widely held and publicly discussed views about character development under conditions of individual autonomy and its salutary effect on socialization. This commitment relied overwhelmingly on the Parsi community's capacity to fund the political associations, newspapers and pedagogic institutions that were to incubate a modern Parsi society but also serve as an exemplar for other Indian communities. In these considerations, social economy – the ability for communities to retain property and distribute it somewhat equitably in order to maintain the autonomy of their members – was also the subject of lobbying. As the entrepreneurial taproots of Parsi philanthropy and social reform came under threat from the 1860s, the understanding of civil society as a form of proprietary autonomy would come increasingly to the fore. It is to this crisis of social reform during economic recession that we now turn.

# 4 Conceptualizing the Drain Theory

In the National Archives of India, sequestered within Naoroji's personal papers, is a scrap with the Grand Old Man's scribblings on social issues. On this page, Naoroji announces that 'every political question is a labour question'. This is followed by a hastily jotted rationale: 'Heritage of the Earth. Labour of Individual. Guidance of Nature. Our own Body'. Naoroji concluded this stream of consciousness with the ethical injunction that 'every human being must find nourishment. Present system unfair'.[1] Naoroji's ideas about these natural economic laws were developed in the years following the apotheosis of Parsi philanthropy and social reform in Bombay. This chapter is concerned with the events that caused Naoroji's politics of sociality to shift from social reform and cultural education to economic reform. Two decades of economic crisis and famine in western India during the 1860s and 1870s prompted this step change and culminated in Naoroji's interrogation of British political economy. This culminated in Naoroji's famous 'drain theory' of Indian poverty and its materialist account of poverty under capitalist monopoly as the antithesis of commercial society and, therefore, sociality.

Forerunners of the drain or 'tribute' paid by India to Britain can be traced back to the early-nineteenth-century religious and social reformer, Rammohun Roy. Dadabhai's senior classmates at Elphinstone, like Bhaskar Tarkhadkar who wrote under the pseudonym of 'A Hindoo' in the *Bombay Gazette* during the 1840s, also spoke of the plundering history of British rule which rendered Indians 'poorer and poorer'.[2] Most historians have defined Naoroji's variant of the drain theory as the system by which the national resources of India were appropriated via the council bill system, whereby Indian exports were paid for by council bills obtained in London, which were in turn exchanged for rupees at Indian exchange

[1] 'Labour Questions', New Delhi, National Archives of India, Dadabhai Naoroji Papers [DNP], notes and jottings, group 9: social, serial number 20.

[2] J. V. Naik, 'Forerunners of Dadabhai's Naoroji's Drain Theory', *Economic and Political Weekly* 36, nos. 46/47 (2001), pp. 4428–32; 'A Hindoo', *Bombay Gazette*, 10 August 1841, cited in C. A. Bayly, *Recovering Liberties: Indian Thought in the Age of Liberalism and Empire* (Cambridge: Cambridge University Press, 2012), p. 125.

banks to finance production and export. Since these rupees came partly from the Indian land revenue, the indigenous population was, through taxation, financing the extractive mechanism of British firms but receiving none of the profit. The essence of the argument was that the surplus drained away could have been invested in the economic development of India. This excess of outgoing wealth over domestic accumulation and investment was dubbed 'the Home Charges'.[3] This is a perfectly accurate description of Naoroji's understanding of the colonial mechanism, but neither it nor the earlier descriptions of British plunder goes any way to untangling the complex relationship between capital, labour and poverty in Naoroji's understanding of commercial society. This book contends that Naoroji's paradigm explains economic exploitation but more interestingly also foregrounds poverty, resulting from monopolistic market practices, as a rusticating process due to arbitrary interference with natural law. The removal of such monopoly constituted a restoration of natural justice.

In abrogating the promises of commercial society, British monopoly stifled the conditions under which labour productivism and international trade might produce social interdependence predicated on free economy and property ownership. It is in this sense that Naoroji regarded the economic system as 'un-British', since it reneged on the original promise of English liberty and instead practised the uncivil liberalism under which India laboured. This theory was predicated on a set of calculations about individual subsistence in a particular social and economic context. Only after this was understood could one ascertain the magnitude of economic production needed to allow the creation of surplus value which crystalized as the property or capital required to sustain commercial society. It is only from this statistical vantage point that Naoroji could appreciate how British monopoly impinged on what he regarded as the otherwise natural functioning of the Indian market. What follows in the next section is an account of how Naoroji arrived at this calculation of Indian poverty as an index of economic dependence and de-socialization.

## Economic Crisis and the Threat to Civil Society

From 1864 to 1865, Bombay was convulsed by a deep financial and liquidity crisis that left scarcely any mercantile family of the city untouched. The commercial

[3] Sugata Bose and Ayesha Jalal, *Modern South Asia: History, Culture and Political Economy* (London: Routledge, 1998), pp. 100–1; Bipan Chandra, *The Rise and Growth of Economic Nationalism in India: Economic Policies of Indian National Leadership* (New Delhi: People's Publishing House, 1966), pp. 101–2; S. Ambirajan, 'Economic Thinking of Dadabhai Naoroji', in P. D. Hajela, ed., *Economic Thoughts of Dadabhai Naoroji* (New Delhi: Deep and Deep Publications, 2001), pp. 20–1.

demise of wealthy Parsi households undermined the financial support of educational projections, civic improvement and even the newest apparatus of Parsi civil society – the vernacular journals and newspapers. This episode was not confined to the economic realm but had a lasting impact on the psychology and confidence of Bombay's mercantile communities. Writing in the *Bombay Gazette*, one concerned Parsi observed that the community was 'in a most unhealthy state, that the flush of fever is mistaken for a sign of health; and though disease may be arrested, it will too probably run its course, working its own cure at last only by some exhaustive process'.[4] The crisis promoted a keener public interest in commercial affairs and debates over moral economy.

After the comparative commercial stagnation of the 1840s and new investments in textile mills and manufacturing of the 1850s, Parsi capital was presented with an opportunity during the American Civil War to re-establish their former success in the export of raw cotton. Between 1860 and 1864 cotton trading in Bombay reached its apogee, buoyed by the British demand for Indian cotton in the wake of the American conflagration. The government encouraged the cultivation of Indian cotton, experiments to grow better-quality cotton and investment in commercial infrastructure. Within one year of the war's outbreak, India accounted for 75 per cent of cotton imported into Britain.[5] High cotton prices and the resulting influx of bullion into India meant that in the early 1860s the initial enthusiasm for Parsi cotton mill construction was drowned out by a wave of speculative investment.[6] By the end of 1864, there were 31 banks, 16 financial associations, 8 land reclamation companies, 10 shipping companies and 20 insurance companies in Bombay, while 62 joint-stock companies proliferated where there were none in 1855.[7] A precarious property bubble developed as native banks turned their attention to new sources of bumper profits.

Among the most ambitious outlets for speculative capital were the expensive projects for land reclamation in the city. The largest of these were the government-sponsored Back Bay scheme, and Wacha would later describe 'the fashion among the prominent financiers of the day that the most influential bank should have at

[4] W. F. M., 'A Few Elementary and Practical Considerations in Political Economy Chosen for Applications to the Present Commercial State of Bombay', *Bombay Gazette*, 7 January 1865.

[5] Dwijendra Tripathi, *The Oxford History of Indian Business* (Oxford: Oxford University Press, 2003), pp. 101–2.

[6] Rajnarayan Chandavarkar, *The Origins of Industrial Capitalism in India: Business Strategies and the Working Classes in Bombay*, new edn (Cambridge: Cambridge University Press, 2002), p. 245.

[7] Rekha Ranade, *Sir Bartle Frere and His Times: A Study of His Bombay Years, 1862–1867* (New Delhi: Mittal Publications, 1990), p. 80.

its elbow an equally influential financial and that as corollary or appendix to both, there should be a powerful reclamation company'.[8] Upon the war's conclusion, cotton prices plummeted and Bombay's financial institutions and enterprises unravelled, sending the city into an economic tailspin. Overleveraged enterprises collapsed taking their investors' wealth with them. Wacha observed that there

> was no such thing as banking in the real sense of the term. It was only a business of advancing loans to all and sundry on personal security and the security of worthless documents...the intrinsic worth of which was simply the value of the paper which certified what the paid-up capital was.[9]

Bombay would rebound as Parsis hedged against fluctuations in cotton prices by increasing investment in cotton mills on an even larger scale than the 1850s.[10] In addition to commercial pragmatism, this was also a part of a new moral economy of industrialism over speculation. The psychological impact of the crisis on Parsi commercial magnates should not be underestimated. The fortunes of many of the great mercantile families would never recover and this was a blow to the prestige of a community that was regarded as the toast of the town earlier in the century. Families that had long been associated with philanthropy in the city were no longer in a position to fund the infrastructure projects, educational and healthcare schemes that had brought them renown among the British and their own community alike.[11] Jeejeebhoy suffered heavy losses, while his brother went bankrupt. Naoroji's business partners and fellow social reformers, the Camas, suffered similar losses.[12] In the 1870s, conservative Parsis clung nostalgically to the memory of their community as a class of 'native brokers' not only facilitating European trade but in regular intercourse with European society.[13] Even in the early twentieth century Wacha reminisced about the great broker families of the 1850s, listing across two pages the ones who had met their demise by 1866. Wacha wistfully commented that 'alas, one can never forget those great merchants and public-spirited citizens of the epoch-making fifties'.[14] The social anxiety which

---

[8] Dinshaw Wacha, *A Financial Chapter in the History of Bombay City*, new edn (Bombay; A. J. Combridge & Co, 1910), p. 35.

[9] Ibid., p. 45.

[10] Chandarvarkar, *The Origins of Industrial Capitalism*, p. 65.

[11] Wacha, *A Financial Chapter*, p. 209; Govind Narayan, *Mumbai: An Urban Biography from 1863*, trans. Murali Ranganathan (London: Anthem Press, 2008), p. 135.

[12] J. Masselos, *Towards Nationalism: Group Affiliations and the Politics of Public Associations in Nineteenth Century Western India* (Bombay: Popular Prakashan, 1974), p. 54.

[13] *Bombay Gazette*, 5 May 1870.

[14] D. E. Wacha, *Shells from the Sands of Bombay: Being My Recollections and Reminiscences, 1860–1875* (Bombay: Bombay Chronicle Press, 1920), pp. 626–7.

plagued the Parsis was the abiding belief that the instability of financial capitalism had led to the transfer of wealth to less public-spirited groups:

> [T]he great name which Bombay bears for generosity and benevolence is owing chiefly to the Parsis. Then, again, the character of Parsi charity, not neglecting the special interests of its own community, has always been catholic, while, with the solitary exceptions of Mr. Premchand Raichand and the late Mr. Gokaldas Tejpal, benevolent Hindu and Mahomedan gentlemen have restricted their charities to objects specially benefitting their own respective races.[15]

Large Parsi landholders in Surat also suffered in the speculative frenzy and saw their property pass into the hands of rival Indian communities and Europeans.[16] Even the British press was critical of European investors having profited from the crisis at the expense of the Parsis, without reinvesting the profits in Bombay's economy.[17]

While these economic travails dealt a blow to Parsi prestige and ignited anxieties about the funding of the social reform, the community never lost sense of its role as warden of the 'public good'.[18] Yet the fear of the 'social wreckage and ruin' through economic imprudence haunted Parsi public opinion sufficiently to result in an explicit shift away from financial to industrial enterprises.[19] The necessity of accumulating capital that could not be siphoned off by less public-minded communities became a Parsi priority if social reform was to be effective. The Parsi press thought it necessary 'to administer some wholesome advice to the Native merchants to induce them to make a good use of the money in the interest of *bona fide* trade, and not to squander it in mere speculation, as they did about three years ago'.[20] As 'the edifice of industrialism' was substituted for the 'detritus' of finance, Wacha suggested that this development was the only 'solid foundation' upon which the prosperity of the community could rest.[21]

By the mid-1860s Parsi debate centred on the rise of a new industrial capitalism. Part of this interest came from its perceived ability to create abstract

---

[15] Dosabhai Framji Karaka, *History of the Parsis*, vol. II (2 vols., London: Macmillan & Co, 1884), p. 271.
[16] Ibid., p. 260.
[17] 'The Catastrophe in Bombay', *Pall Mall Gazette*, reprinted in *Times of India*, 25 July 1865.
[18] Karaka, *History of the Parsis*, vol. II, p. 263.
[19] Wacha, *A Financial Chapter*, p. 24.
[20] *Jam-e-Jamsed*, 11 May 1868, week ending 18 May 1868, Report on Native Papers, Bombay [hereafter RNP].
[21] Dinshaw Wacha, *The Life and Work of J. N. Tata*, new edn (Madras: Ganesh & Co, 1915 [1914]), pp. 3–5.

labour by transforming landless peasants into proletarian wage-earners. However, labour scarcity had always been a perennial conundrum for mill owners and a significant problem for industry since Indian capital was both scarce and often risk-averse, forcing managers to rely on labour-intensive production. Promoting labour flexibility at all costs had led to sectionalism among workers both at the factory and in their neighbourhoods, preventing the emergence of a cohesive and homogeneous working class.[22] The massive influx of capital during the cotton boom had momentarily demonstrated that a large demand for labour could be generated, holding out the possibility of disciplining the 'lower orders' of all communities through the management of abstract labour on the factory floor.

The labour demand quickly plateaued owing to the difficulty of reinvesting the vast quantities of surplus cash in productive enterprises.[23] Commentators observed that during the boom only some capital was used in the employment of labour, while the rest was taken out of the country, inappropriately invested in speculative schemes or hoarded by businessmen.[24] Similarly, in the wake of the crash a vast amount of labour was thrown out of employment, and it dawned on Indian industrialists and the government alike that accumulated capital ought to be used in more reproductive enterprises.[25] The upshot was that capitalism based on reproductive labour, manufacture and trade was increasingly emphasized as a more legitimate form of economic activity.[26] Indeed, the notion of social wealth as a tool for creating proletarians from peasants achieved the same rhetorical purchase as Parsi philanthropy had as a means of modernizing Bombay. Communities were not considered 'the richer for having more money' unless it was used to 'support labour'.[27]

The crisis generated new debates in the Parsi public sphere that pivoted from charity and pedagogy to industrialism and class when considering how to overcome the insularity of Indian custom. Although this did not exactly echo Naoroji's eventual critique, it was against the backdrop of this economic discussion about trade and industry as the 'source' of civilization that Naoroji would make his own

---

[22] Chandavarkar, *The Origins of Industrial Capitalism*, p. 332.
[23] 'The Catastrophe in Bombay'.
[24] *Jam-e-Jamsed*, 9 December 1868, week ending 12 December 1868, RNP.
[25] *Annual Report of the Bombay Presidency*, 1864–5, pp. 56–7.
[26] Wacha, *The Life and Work of J. N. Tata*, p. 93.
[27] W. F. M., 'A Few Elementary and Practical Considerations in Political Economy Chosen for Applications to the Present Commercial State of Bombay', *Bombay Gazette*, 7 January 1865; W. F. M., 'A Few Elementary and Practical Considerations in Political Economy Chosen for Applications to the Present Commercial State of Bombay II', *Bombay Gazette*, 9 January 1865.

theoretical intervention.[28] Indeed, it was from the 1860s that Naoroji began to quote Macaulay's dictum that it was far better 'to trade with civilized men' than rule dependent feudal peasants 'performing salaams to English collectors and magistrates'.[29]

## Indigenous Capital, *Homo Economicus* and Finance

As a businessman between 1855 and 1865, Naoroji learned about the workings of trade within the British Empire first-hand by developing his ideas on individual economic agency and the joint company. Before 1855 there were no Indian firms operating in Britain, prompting Muncherji Hormusji Cama, Kharshedji Rustamji Cama and Naoroji to pioneer Indian business in the metropole even though Naoroji had no previous commercial experience.[30] He initially settled in Liverpool where the auxiliary branch of the firm was established after the London branch and with the overall head office in Bombay. Naoroji's thinking on imperial trade was not reducible to personal profit maximization; indeed, the day-to-day business chatter in his correspondence is intermingled with more abstract discussions about economic theory. While his business endeavours were earning him a living, he also situated Indian entrepreneurship within larger social considerations. For instance, a business partner in Bombay, N. J. Moolla, offered mundane reports of Naoroji's investments in government treasuries. Alongside this, Moolla mentions a lecture on currency and bimetallism at the Bombay chamber of commerce that Naoroji will find interesting and promises to obtain a copy of the talk, before finishing the letter with a prosaic commentary on Naoroji's outstanding debts.[31] These idiosyncratic interests prompted Muncherji Cama to complain that Naoroji was a 'philosopher' rather than a straightforward business partner.[32]

Naoroji's concern for fair business practices led to one occasion in which he refused to forward a shipment of reel-threads acquired in England to another Bombay firm because it was of shorter length than specified. Head office showed

[28] 'Trade as a Source of Civilization', *Bombay Gazette,* 30 September 1853.

[29] Thomas Babbington Macaulay, 'Government of India', 10 July 1833, in Thomas Babbington Macaulay, *The Works of Lord Macaulay: Speeches, Poems and Miscellaneous Writings* (12 vols., London: Longmans, Green & Co, 1898), p. 584; Macaulay quoted in Dadabhai Naoroji, *Poverty and Un-British Rule in India* (London, 1901), p. 277; Hansard, HC Deb 14 August 1894 vol. 28, c. 1055; Naoroji's annotated copy of Macaulay's 1833 speech in 'Macaulay Extracts', DNP, E-72 (90).

[30] R. P. Masani, *Dadabhai Naoroji: The Grand Old Man of India* (London: George Allen & Unwin, 1939), pp. 71–2.

[31] N. J. Moolla, Cama, Moolla & Co to Naoroji, 31 January 1888, DNP, C-27 (66).

[32] Masani, *Dadabhai Naoroji*, p. 73.

consternation at Naoroji's refusal to tolerate such minor discrepancies when it came to the realities of the business world.[33] Masani attributes this to Naoroji's personal morality rather than an attention to the specific dynamics of Indian commerce. In this vein, Masani adds that the Camas and Naoroji parted ways in 1858 because Naoroji had been, from the first, opposed to the firm's alcohol and opium trade because of its deleterious impact on society.[34] However, Naoroji's earliest correspondence with K. N. Cama tells a different story. In 1856, Naoroji perused medical textbooks in an attempt to convince his colleague that 'moderate' consumption of opium had no negative health impact on the Chinese who bought it.[35] Naoroji subsequently asked whether the Chinese partaking of opium was really any different to the prodigious beer drinking in England, adding that these questions did not stem from his personal feelings on narcotics but that he felt 'it necessary in justice to [their business] partners to probe the questions thoroughly'.[36]

Naoroji would split from the Camas due to differences of opinion on business practices and establish his own firm under the name Dadabhai Naoroji & Co with Jamshedji Palanji Kapadia and Pestonji Rattanji Colah in 1860.[37] By 1862, there were at least four Indian firms operating in Britain, all of them Parsi.[38] Naoroji's new firm refused to engage in the common practice of accepting commissions from both the client firm (which made orders via Naoroji) and vendor firm (from whom Naoroji purchased the goods). He believed that with such economic practices his firm could not be seen as supervising the work in a disinterested and conscientious way, exclaiming that 'I am paid for the work by the buyer, I cannot be paid by the seller as well'.[39] Naoroji's probity as a model of fair business practices seems to have been effective. Upon his death in 1917 the commercial press pointed out that while the chief of the Bank of England's discount office sneered at Naoroji's politics, he did comment that Naoroji 'met all his engagements [following the economic crisis] in 1866, a thing comparatively few in the East were able to do' and this earned Naoroji a reputation as a man of 'strict integrity'.[40]

[33] Ibid, p. 74.
[34] Ibid.
[35] Naoroji to K. R. Cama, 4 June 1856, DNP, N-1 (1).
[36] Naoroji to K. R. Cama, 9 October 1856, DNP, N-1 (4).
[37] Masani, *Dadabhai Naoroji*, p. 77.
[38] *Lloyd's Register of British and Foreign Shipping, 1862/3* (London: Wyman & Sons, 1862), pp. xv–xix.
[39] Masani, *Dadabhai Naoroji*, pp. 78–9.
[40] *Investor's Review*, 17 July 1917, cited in Masani, *Dadabhai Naoroji*, p. 94; 'The Hon. Dadabhai Naoroji', *Biographical Magazine*, February (1887), pp. 6–7.

Naoroji's idiosyncratic business practices were intended as an example to counteract the pejorative representations of the 'dishonest' Indian bazaar while making the case that Indian businessmen were both rational and capitalist.[41] The debate ignited by the Bombay Cotton Act of 1869 provided an opportunity for Naoroji to argue in favour of the rationality of Indian economic agency and the falsehood of European representations of Indian commerce. The 1869 act left the 1863 Cotton Frauds Act in place despite Indian protests. The British millocracy had long complained of adulterated cotton from the United States and India, but existing enforcement practices in India tended to harass cotton exporters rather than the *ryot*s and rural moneylenders who were responsible for the adulteration.[42] The 1863 act criminalized the mixing of different types of cotton for one branch of commerce even though such behaviour was not a criminal act in its own right.[43] British supporters of the legislation claimed that this did not insult Indians since the level of adulteration in consignments of cotton from Bombay did not exceed those from the United States.

This prompted Naoroji to ask why, in that case, the Indian context demanded exceptional legislation. Compiling his own statistics from the Liverpool and Manchester chamber of commerce reports and the cotton supply association, Naoroji showed that there was neither any evidence nor clamour for penalizing Indian exporters.[44] He observed that the market imposed universal honesty and rationality because it accounted for adulteration via price. His experience in Liverpool showed that first 'samples are drawn, and the sale made according to those samples'. Naoroji explained that if 'the cotton is any mixture, or of inferior quality, the valuation is made accordingly, and the buyer pays his price not upon any mere marks or representations from the sellers, but upon his own judgement of the parcel'. Bombay merchants were thus more motivated than anyone else to

---

[41] Ritu Birla, *Stages of Capital: Law, Culture, and Market Governance in Late Colonial India* (Durham, NC: Duke University Press, 2009), p. 16; Chandra Mallampalli, *Race, Religion and Law in Colonial India: Trials of an Interracial Family* (Cambridge: Cambridge University Press, 2011), p. 73.

[42] *Report of the Commission Appointed to Enquire into the Working of the Cotton Frauds Act (1863); with Minutes of Evidence and Other Appendices* (Bombay: n.p., 1875), appendix A: minutes of evidence, Mumbai, Maharashtra State Archives (MSA), revenue department, 1875, vol. 27, number 501.

[43] Peter Harnetty, *Imperialism and Free Trade: Lancashire and India in the Mid-Nineteenth Century* (Vancouver: University of British Columbia Press, 1972), p. 111.

[44] Dadabhai Naoroji, 'The Bombay Cotton Act of 1869', paper read at a meeting of the East India Association on 21 December 1869, *Journal of the East India Association* [hereafter *JEIA*] 3 (1869), pp. 189–92.

export quality goods.[45] Since both parties were equally subject to the competition of the market, the Liverpool merchant never bothered to check if a consignment was marked 'Native Shipped' or not because he had already agreed to a price based on a sample. Naoroji noted that his own firm sold Indian cotton at the highest price yet achieved in the British marketplace.[46] In this way, Naoroji inverted the colonial discourse on irrationality, asking if the British capitalist was 'so green that he pays the price of fair for inferior cotton ... because the shipper chooses to call his cotton anything he likes?' If so, this was 'really giving very poor credit to the intelligence and business ways of the people of Liverpool and Manchester'.[47] Not only did the bill impugn Indian capital but it also harmed 'the most important trades', as far as Naoroji was concerned, which was those engaged in export.[48] Exports would constitute a major pillar of Naoroji's thought because they were seen as the only way of adding value to commodities after they had been fabricated by mixing labour with nature.

The importance of Naoroji's distinction between socially productive and less socially productive types of economic activity became more pronounced during and after Bombay's economic crisis. Naoroji realized that it was not merely unfair representations of, but also the inequity of certain types of economic practice, that undermined Indian trade and obstructed the formation of commercial society. Before the crisis, as a social reformer, Naoroji had continued the Parsi tradition of philanthropy by using the profits from his business to patronize a library of Sanskrit books for Elphinstone College. He also started a new fund for giving English education to Parsi girls and a Zoroastrian fund for Parsis in Europe in 1861.[49] However, the inability of Naoroji's Bombay clients to meet their payments after the financial collapse in Bombay and the bankruptcy of Kapadia resulted in the demise of Dadabhai Naoroji & Co.[50] Naoroji had put up his own capital as collateral for the debts of other Indian firms in Britain in order to enable Indian business to save face.[51] Surplus funds for patronizing social reform and civil society evaporated in the process. For instance, Naoroji established the Canning scholarships for Indian universities, which received 50,000 rupees from Naoroji

[45] Naoroji, 'The Bombay Cotton Act', p. 198.
[46] Ibid., p. 204.
[47] Ibid., pp. 203–4.
[48] Ibid., p. 197.
[49] Masani, *Dadabhai Naoroji*, p. 79.
[50] *The Times*, 22 October1867.
[51] Masani, *Dadabhai Naoroji*, p. 93.

and 25,000 rupees from K. N. Cama in 1864, but these were cancelled after Bombay's crisis.[52]

This crisis of capitalism fundamentally changed how Naoroji thought about social reform; he even wrote in 1868 to the Secretary of State for India imploring the government to fill the hole left by Parsi philanthropy. Naoroji admitted that Bombay's merchants had 'established and supported Schools for the last 17 years without aid from Government' on a scale unparalleled elsewhere in India. However, by 1868 Naoroji reported that 'many of the principal friends of education are suffering from the effects of four successive Commercial Crises, and are unable to do now what they have always readily and willingly done, and would have, but for their crippled means, as readily come forward to do on the present occasion'.[53] The private funding of education had decreased by 24,260 pounds in the Bombay Presidency between 1866 and 1867 when imperial funding was only 4,661 pounds.[54] Yet the government continued to throw the cost of primary education for girls onto local patrons, and Naoroji's appeals for the state substituting indigenous philanthropy were rebuffed. Doubling down on tried and tested methods in the presidency, British officials tried to coax more public expenditure from wealthy Indians, insisting that greater government funding for female normal schools would only be acceded to if the 'native community' could match the 15,520 rupees of monthly state expenditure.[55]

Naoroji's re-establishing of his firm after the crisis did not see him return to his former prosperity, leaving his more modest means incapable of bankrolling reform. The collapse of major Indian banking institutions like the Asiatic Banking Corporation and the Central Bank of Western India in 1866 resulted in a dearth of credit for many of his Parsi colleagues and Bombay businesses in general. Even by 1870 the only two remaining Indian joint-stock banks had a meagre capitalization of 500,000 rupees.[56] Indian merchants were forced to increasingly depend upon the European exchange banks and their access to London's capital markets.[57]

[52] *Manchester Times*, 5 March 1864; 'The Hon. Dadabhai Naoroji', in George Potter, ed., *The Monthly Record of Eminent Men*, vol. III, January to June 1891 (London: George Potter, 1891), p. 233; Anon, *The First Indian Member of the Imperial Parliament, Being a Collection of the Main Incidents Relating to the Election of Mr Dadabhai Naoroji to Parliament* (Madras: Addison & Co, 1892), p. 4.

[53] Naoroji to Sir Stafford Northcote, 5 February 1868, DNP, N-1 (17).

[54] *Statement of the Moral and Material Progress of India, 1866–7*, Asia, Pacific, and Africa Collection, British Library, London [BLAPAC], IOR/L/PARL/2/153, p. 57.

[55] Herman Merivale, India Office to Naoroji, 21 February 1868, DNP, M-107 (1).

[56] A. G. Chandavarkar, 'Money and Credit', in Dharma Kumar and Meghnad Desai, eds., *The Cambridge Economic History of India* (Cambridge: Cambridge University Press, 1983), p. 779.

[57] Ibid., pp. 782–3.

Naoroji wrote to his business partner H. R. Schroff lamenting the fact that the firm's current 'capital in hand' was the only investable capital they could lay their hands on and some of this they had to save 'to be prepared for any other contingency'. Naoroji believed that they had to secure as much capital as possible so that they might be 'more independent' of brokers, with the 2,500 pounds lent to them by Kapadia already locked up with a brokerage. He ordered Schroff to get the brokers to release the full advance to them as soon as possible since it could be put to use in undertaking business.[58]

Meditating on these liquidity issues and their long-term structural roots prompted Naoroji to identify interstitial financial institutions, like those that had proliferated during the share mania, as corroding the profitability of legitimate traders in the real economy and impeding the accumulation of Indian capital. Banking was regarded as particularly problematic. Prior to the crisis, Naoroji had engaged in a public spat with exchange banks that refused to accept shipping documents deposited by Cama & Co in India and insisted that Indian firms draw bills of exchange and have them accepted by the recognized broker.[59] On holding on to the documents, the Asiatic Bank arbitrarily insisted that it could claim 'the surplus of certain collateral securities against bills of exchange' even though the full amount for those bills had already been tendered. The surplus appropriated would be used to 'the liquidation of other liabilities which they hold against the drawer'.[60] Naoroji pointed out that Cama & Co incurred the liabilities in Bombay transactions in which Naoroji & Co had no part. Where was the justice in impeding the trade of a solvent firm and undermining mercantile credit generally?[61]

Editorials in the *Times of India* under the editorship of Robert Knight, a critic of British policy in India, supported Naoroji's position by showing that the banks and brokers were 'merely intermediate' in transactions and unless one party defaulted they had no business distorting trade because they had no way of knowing what 'was needful to square the acceptor's account with the drawer'.[62] Additionally, pursuant to Dadabhai Naoroji & Co's bankruptcy, Naoroji had tried to recover the profits of ongoing trades in order to meet his obligations, but banking institutions profited from the bills of exchange deposited with them by Naoroji in order to defray separate debts owed to them by his company. A similar case was bought against the Asiatic Banking Corporation and Central

[58] Naoroji to H. R. Schroff, 26 March 1869, DNP, N-1 (18).
[59] Masani, *Dadabhai Naoroji*, p. 94.
[60] *The Times*, 18 September 1865.
[61] *Times of India*, 25 September 1865.
[62] Ibid., 3 October 1865.

Bank of Western India, which demanded eleven bills of exchange that Naoroji had deposited with his recently deceased cotton supplier in Bombay, Pestonji Kharshedji Shroff. This was despite the fact that the 1,048 bales of cotton the bills were for had never been shipped to Naoroji.[63] In 1868, Naoroji sued the London-based 'Chartered Bank of India, Australia and China', a major financier of colonial trade, in order to recover these proceeds.[64] These were for the remittance of 3,248 pounds to Dadabhai Naoroji & Co; however, when the firm stopped payment in 1866 following bankruptcy, these funds were used to defray 8,335 pounds of debt from other bills of exchange of which the firm was an endorsee or holder.[65]

Naoroji's lawyers claimed that no contract of mutual credit had been entered into but the court concluded that such a contract existed implicitly when 'merchants mutually have dealings together, and each gives credit to the other' and when a bankruptcy takes places the calculations of those credits would inevitably end in a debt that should be repaid. What impacted on Naoroji's conception of the unfairness of a trade was the court's conclusion that it was 'clear that in order to constitute a mutual credit, it is not necessary that there should be credits connected with and dependent on one another'.[66] That is to say, profits from one equitably contracted transaction could be used to cover the debts of entirely separate transactions on the whim of the mediating European bank and in so doing they absconded with Indian capital they had no part in producing.

The difficulty Naoroji's friends experienced in financing their own enterprises persisted well into the 1870s and 1880s. Ardeshir Framji Moos complained that his plan for a sugar factory collapsed from lack of investment and that not a single Indian was able to buy shares in the enterprise.[67] In the 1870s, keen to set an example for indigenous entrepreneurship, Mehta and Telang established a soap factory in a risky act of 'self-sacrifice' only to lose 'every pie of money'.[68] In the late 1880s, Naoroji received a complaint from Moolla, who was so desperate for

[63] Dadabhai Naoroji vs. Asiatic Banking Corporation, 25 November 1865, C16/290/N48, *National Archives*, London.
[64] 'Dadabhai Naoroji and Another *v.* The Chartered Bank of India, Australia and China, 4 May 1868', in *The Law Journal Reports for the Year 1868*, vol. 37 (London: Edward Bret Ince, 1868), pp. 221–5.
[65] Ibid., p. 222.
[66] Ibid., p. 225.
[67] Ardaseer Framjee Moos during discussion following W. Martin Wood, 'The Conditions and Methods of Industrial Progress in India', read at the Framji Cowasji Institute, Bombay branch of the East India Association, in *JEIA* 9 (1877–8), p. 68.
[68] P. M. Mehta, speech at the 1902 'Ahmedabad Industrial Exhibition', in P. M. Mehta, *Speeches and Writings of the Honourable Sir Pherozeshah M. Mehta*, ed. C. Y. Chintamani (Allahabad: The Indian Press, 1905), p. 747.

funds to keep his business going that he offered to transfer the equity of his five-storey Bombay home to Naoroji in exchange for a cash loan.[69] Naoroji attempted to aid the legitimate trade of his colleagues after 1866 by helping Indian merchants circumvent brokerages and banks, thereby avoiding the expensive tying up of Indian capital in intermediary institutions.[70]

Naoroji's preference was for direct exchange between producers and consumers, avoiding unproductive middlemen. However, as a businessman and promoter of Indian trade in the context of the post-1866 dearth of capital, Naoroji felt that he had to speculate in the financial sector himself in order to generate the liquidity for international trade. He did this by buying and selling Indian government bonds, waiting for them to mature so as to reap a profitable lump sum.[71] On other occasions, Naoroji received the interest from the bonds or deposited an amount of 'rupee paper' with banks as collateral for a loan.[72] This 'native' credit was used to finance an eclectic array of trades between Britain and India, including that of printing and dyeing machinery, carpets and – curiously – *dhotis* (a loincloth worn by Indian men that resembles baggy trousers) for the India Office.[73] Naoroji also offered short-term loans with the promise of a profit share in the enterprises they were funding. One surreal example was a 1 per cent share of profit, in addition to interest, on a 3,000-rupee loan for Moolla's alpaca farm.[74] Carrying these formative commercial experiences forward, Naoroji turned his critical gaze towards the British Raj's wider political economy. Innovating new methods of quantifying wealth per capita in rural India, Naoroji would challenge the ethnographic assumptions of 'official liberalism' and the debilitating effects of financial monopoly.

## Statistical Liberalism and 'Improvement'

The empiricist tradition of critiquing Indian 'despotisms' re-emerged after 1815, originating among a small coterie of civil servants and army officers 'schooled in the Scottish Enlightenment', and was adapted by Indians into a 'statistical

---

69 N. J. Moolla, of Cama, Moolla & Co to Naoroji, 27 March 1888, DNP, C-27 (77).
70 A. F. Moos to Naoroji, 12 January 1885, DNP, M-171 (10).
71 Naoroji to A. F. Moos, 2 January 1885, DNP, N-1 (210).
72 Bank of England to Naoroji, 6 May 1891, 18 June 1891 and 13 August 1894, DNP, B-36; B-36 (1); B-36 (6).
73 A. F. Moos to Naoroji, 27 April 1885, 2 February 1885 and 27 January 1884, DNP, M-171 (48); M-171 (23); M-171 (19).
74 N. J. Moolla, Cama, Moolla & Co to Naoroji, 7 January 1889, DNP, C-27 (113).

liberalism'.[75] Enlightenment empiricism was also harnessed by Victorian liberals to renovate institutions that might 'improve' what they regarded as corrupted societies. Alongside healthcare, education and village sanitation, the condition of Indian jails attracted significant attention. It was within this particular debate that Naoroji developed his own 'statistical liberalism' that calculated Indian levels of subsistence and capacities for production.

John Lawrence, the new Indian Viceroy, appointed the Indian jail committee of 1864 whose report spawned the debate on the condition of prisoners and the prospects for rehabilitation.[76] Lawrence's 'improvement' agenda was backed by social reformers in Britain like Mary Carpenter and Florence Nightingale but had a wider appeal among Indian governors who saw the possibility of grafting European modernity onto Indian roots. Richard Temple of the so-called Punjab school of colonial governance during the 1840s and 1850s had established organizations like the Punjab Agri-horticultural Society in 1851 in order to promote capitalist, market-orientated farming on indigenous lines.[77] While scientific societies such as this promoted the acculturation of Indian economic knowledge, the codification of customs in the Punjab civil code intended to create a population of peasant proprietors, emancipated from the burdens of high taxation and indebtedness to moneylenders, free to cultivate and accumulate as an archetypal yeomanry.[78] According to Temple, this was the historical condition of many of the Indian cultivating classes but more recently prevailing customs had created a 'slavish obedience' and prevailing 'indolence'.[79] However, some cultivators had been institutionally disciplined by the British revenue system into showing renewed independence and industry by the adoption of transferable rights and by making material improvements in irrigation, roads and canals.[80] Temple noted that this newly reinvigorated neo-Roman yeomanry contracted freely by substituting custom with 'some sense of free citizenship'.[81]

---

[75] Bayly, *Recovering Liberties*, p. 105; N. Furdoonjee, 'The Trade of Cabul', *Asiatic Journal and Monthly Register* (September 1838), p. 73, cited in Bayly, *Recovering Liberties*, p. 120.

[76] 'Minute by the Governor General', in *Measures Taken to Give Effect to the Recommendations of a Committee Appointed to Report on the State of Jail Discipline and to Suggest Improvements* (Calcutta: Superintendent of Government Printing, 1867), BLAPAC, IOR/V/23/9, p. 1.

[77] Jagjeet Lally, 'Trial, Error and Economic Development in Colonial Punjab: The Agri-horticultural Society, the State and Sericulture Experiments, c. 1840–70', *Indian Economic and Social History Review* 52, no. 1 (2015), p. 3.

[78] Ibid., p. 4.

[79] Richard Temple, *India in 1880* (London: John Murray, 1880), pp. 107–8.

[80] Ibid., p. 109.

[81] Ibid., p. 108.

Lawrence and like-minded officials approached prison reform with the same institutional agenda. The education of women, reformatories for juvenile offenders and productive convict labour characterized the main topics of the 1864 report, with the prison becoming a site of 'improvement' for the creation of individual autonomy and civil relationships.[82] There was a unified logic of 'improvement' running from the Punjab school's considerations of political economy and the later debate on the role of prisons. For example, the most vocal agitator for reformatory prisons, Frederic J. Mouat, the inspector-general of gaols in lower Bengal, also praised the work of the Agri-horticultural Society.[83] These ideas were disseminated to other reformers of varied interests in plural scholarly organizations like the Society for the Encouragement of Arts, Manufactures and Commerce of which Naoroji was a member from 1868.[84]

Mouat had led the call for the 'conversion of jails into schools of industry' since the 1850s, claiming that there was no contradiction between 'maintenance of the strictest discipline' and the sort of work that would enable prisoners to 'earn an honest livelihood on release' and 'repay the whole cost of their maintenance'.[85] Critics of this system decried convict labour and Mouat's 'remunerative theory' that led to prison officials procuring goods at the cheapest price in order to sell at the highest.[86] The heavy strains placed on weak prisoners meant that labour was categorized into 'light', 'middle' and 'hard' with a monetary value attached to an hour's worth of each grade of work.[87] Unlike the outside world, in the

---

[82] 'Minute by the Governor General', pp. 1–2; David Arnold, 'The Colonial Prison: Power, Knowledge and Penology in Nineteenth Century India', in *Subaltern Studies 8: Essays in Honour of Ranajit Guha*, eds. David Arnold and David Hardiman (New Delhi: Oxford University Press, 1994), pp. 148–84.

[83] Quoted in David Arnold, 'Agriculture and "Improvement" in Early Colonial India: A Pre-history of Development', *Journal of Agrarian Change* 5, no. 4 (2005), p. 526.

[84] Naoroji listed as a member in *Journal of the Society for Arts* 16, no. 794 (1868), p. 232; Frederic J. Mouat, 'Our Prison Labour as an Instrument of Punishment, Profit, and Reformation: An Episode in the Prison History of Lower Bengal', read at a meeting of the society for the encouragement of arts, manufactures, and commerce on 21 February 1872, London, Royal Society of Arts Library, minutes of the society, November 1871 to June 1872, RSA/AD/MA/100/12/01/118.

[85] F. J. Mouat, *Report on the Statistics of the Prisons of the Lower Provinces of the Bengal Presidency for 1861, 1862, 1863, 1864 and 1865* (Calcutta: Superintendent of Government Printing, 1868), p. 17.

[86] A. P. Howell, *Notes on Jails and Jail Discipline in India, 1867–8* (Calcutta: Superintendent of Government Printing, 1869), pp. 46–7.

[87] David Arnold, 'Labouring for the Raj: Convict Work Regimes in Colonial India, 1836–1939', in Christian Giusepp. de Vito and Alex Lichtenstein, eds., *Global Convict Labour* (Leiden: Brill, 2015), pp. 211–12.

Indian jail various castes and communities were mixed together, and from this undifferentiated group jail statistics on labour were collated.[88] The 1864 report observed that it was impossible to compare the living conditions and productivity of the Indian prisoner to the general population because 'there exist no known data' that corresponded to 'the labouring classes in this country'.[89] On the other side of the prison walls, peasant and proletarian, individual and community were indistinguishable.[90]

Naoroji waded into the jail debate amidst broader questions about social reform. This was largely owing to Mary Carpenter's preoccupation with the social condition of Indian women and her Indian National Association's prioritizing of 'better prison discipline and juvenile reformatories' as the subjects around which Britons and Indians ought to 'co-operate'.[91] Mouat's ideas featured prominently in Carpenter's talks on prison reform at Naoroji's East India Association.[92] She recalled her visits to gaols in Ahmedabad, Surat, Pune and Calcutta where inmates involved in artisanal work 'looked as cheerfully engaged in their occupations as free labourers'.[93] Not only did British 'improvers' contribute to theorizing institutional interventions into the Indian social but Carpenter's fame also helped bring official statistics to public attention, giving Indian 'statistical liberalism' greater legitimacy. Surendranath Banerjea and the vernacular press praised Carpenter for having brought both the condition of Indian prisoners and also the official statistics in the jail reports to public attention.[94] Official statistics on jails were the only available form of data in which Indians were enumerated as individuals and whose labour was not tinctured by social considerations of caste and community. For Naoroji, as far as questions of individual economic agency were concerned, the irony was that the Indian jail represented something closer to natural economic laws and free economy than did the Indian economy under colonial liberalism.

---

[88] Ibid., pp. 210–1.
[89] *Committee ... on the State of Jail Discipline*, pp. 3–4.
[90] Dipesh Chakrabarty, *Re-thinking Working Class History: Bengal 1890–1940* (Princeton, NJ: Princeton University Press, 1989); Chandavarkar, *The Origins of Industrial Capitalism*, p. 398.
[91] Committee Book of the Indian Association of Bristol, October 1870, BLAPAC, MSS Eur F147/1.
[92] Mary Carpenter, 'Education and Reformatory Treatment', talk delivered on 9 June 1868, printed in *JEIA* 2 (1868), p. 301; 'On the Work Done by Her for Female Education in India', *JEIA* 4 (1870), pp. 175–82.
[93] Carpenter, 'Education and Reformatory Treatment', p. 302.
[94] Surendranath Banerjea in Howell, *Notes on Jails*, pp. 75–6; *Mitrodaya*, 14 March 1869, week ending 20 March 1869, RNP; *Chandrodaya*, 13 December 1869, week ending 25 December 1869, RNP.

Naoroji's earliest reference to the idea of a drain of capital from India was in his 1867 paper 'England's Duties to India'.[95] This concept was quantitatively fleshed out in a paper delivered in 1870 called 'The Wants and Means of India' and another in 1871 entitled 'On the Commerce of India'. The two papers calculated India's exports and imports per capita by simply dividing the total quantity of international trade by population and then comparing the figure to comparable statistics for the United Kingdom, Ireland and the United States.[96] Prisoners are not mentioned in these papers and it was not until Naoroji's 1871 testimony before the East India Finance Committee (1871–3) that he publicly detailed his use of prison statistics.[97] However, the process of collecting and analysing jail data occurred as early as 1868 on behalf of the East India Association's support of Henry Fawcett and his lobbying for a royal commission to investigate the condition of India.[98] In his testimony, Naoroji utilized the reports on jails from Bombay, the North-Western Provinces, the Central Provinces and Punjab to calculate 'the cost of living, for the bare necessaries of life'.[99] Naoroji gleaned information on individual standards of living from other sources as well, using the medical inspector's recommended basic diet for labourers emigrating from Calcutta.[100] From these figures Naoroji calculated the bare minimum of consumption per capita in terms of food, clothing and bedding for the average Indian. He also supplemented these calculations, using his colleague Kazi Shahabuddin's research on the individual cost of living for agricultural labour in Ahmedabad in 1868, concluding that the 'necessary consumption' of the free labourer would be about 45 rupees per annum, excluding provision for social needs.[101] Echoing the discourse on prison conditions and reform, Naoroji was calculating the minimum prerequisite consumption needed to reproduce labour. These calculations were combined with those in Naoroji's papers on India's international trade from 1870 to 1871 in his seminal 1876 paper titled the 'Poverty of India'.[102]

---

[95] Dadabhai Naoroji, 'England's Duties to India', in Dadabhai Naoroji, *Essays, Speeches, Addresses and Writings of the Hon'ble Dadabhai Naoroji*, ed. C. L. Parekh (Bombay: Caxton Printing Works, 1887), pp. 26–50.

[96] Dadabhai Naoroji, 'The Wants and Means of India', in ibid., pp. 97–111; 'On the Commerce of India', in ibid., pp. 112–36.

[97] Dadabhai Naoroji, 'Financial Administration of India', in ibid., pp. 137–59.

[98] Discussion following Robert Knight, 'India: A Review of England's Financial Relations Therewith', 3 March 1868, *JEIA* 2 (1868), p. 278; Masselos, *Towards Nationalism*, p. 108.

[99] Naoroji, 'Financial Administration of India', p. 158.

[100] Bayly, *Recovering Liberties*, p. 195; Naoroji, 'Financial Administration of India', pp. 158–9.

[101] Naoroji, 'Poverty of India, Part I', pp. 184–90.

[102] Dadabhai Naoroji, 'Poverty of India, Part I and II', read before the Bombay branch of the East India Association, 28 February 1876 and 27 April 1876, in Naoroji, *Essays, Speeches, Addresses, and Writings*, pp. 160–276.

Shahbuddin's rural research was used for agricultural statistics because, in contrast to jail figures, official rural data was more concerned with revenue extraction and systematizing a Malthusian attitude to the Indian countryside. Individual labour and productivity were obscured by the colonial state's simple interest in aggregate revenue from particular ethnic groups. Naoroji pointed out that no system of economic administration could possibly function in accordance with the laws of political economy without 'complete knowledge' of the subjects it purported to 'improve'. Indians were not incapable of commercial society; rather, it was the case that the British had not properly understood the context in which a non-Western capitalism might develop.[103] Ranade also observed this failure, noting that in Britain a 'vast mass of her population consists mostly of wage-earners', whereas Indian peasants 'are not wage-earners'.[104] The revenue settlement perpetuated a semi-feudal monopoly in which taxation was set arbitrarily because the state was also the national landlord.

Naoroji demanded that a second set of figures be given for the total quantity of unskilled labour and the relative size of the working and non-working populations divided by sex and age. Additionally, the earnings per capita should be given but subdivided according to classes of work as in the jail statistics. Finally, the government ought to calculate the number of labour hours expended in each class of work so as to understand how many days of the year each wage rate was earned.[105] This would reveal where the natural capacity of labour was being realized, where the cycle of production and consumption was reproductive and where it was hindered. For Naoroji, only when these recommendations for acquiring knowledge about the individual Indian labourer were accepted would one be able to 'ascertain the real average income of the unskilled labourer, who forms the majority of the population, and upon whose labour depends the subsistence of the nation'.[106]

The 'erroneous' assumptions of colonial statistics were designed to uphold a residualist model of economic management. Colonial officials assumed that the *ryots* were governed exclusively by custom, rather than the material rationalities of *homo economicus*, and as such they had minimal wants. In this view, a rent that resulted in the 'satisfaction' of basic subsistence was by definition a 'fair rent'.[107]

---

[103] Naoroji, 'Financial Administration of India', p. 145.

[104] M. G. Ranade, 'The Re-organization of Rural Credit in India', read at the first industrial conference in Pune, 1891, in Mahadev Govind Ranade, *Essays on Indian Economics: A Collection of Essays and Speeches* (Madras: G. A. Natesan & Co, 1906), pp. 64–5.

[105] Naoroji, 'Financial Administration of India', pp. 157–8.

[106] Ibid., p. 158.

[107] Ibid., p. 148.

Naoroji believed that this was the governing principle behind the application of Ricardo's differential rent axiom in India. In Ricardo's theory, the cost of production on the lowest quality of land determined the value of the commodity. Thus, if more fecund land yielded a larger harvest at the same cost of production, then the surplus was an unearned increment and the state could justly claim it as rent without harming the productivity of the farmer.[108] However, the primary principle to take into account when establishing a just rent was, for Naoroji, its capacity to increase 'production and prosperity' in relation to the relative investment and labour of the individual farmer.

Examining the Bombay revenue settlement, Naoroji found that the state effectively appropriated a fixed amount of the cultivator's net produce rather than a proportion. He gives an instance in which a farmer having invested 100 rupees in good-quality soil reaps 172 rupees 42 paise in produce of which 72 rupees 5 paise is the net produce. A cultivator who invests the same amount in a lower-quality soil reaps 127 rupees 6 paise of which 27 rupees 6 paise is the net produce. The state assesses the lowest-quality soil as the base rent and takes 5 rupees 13 paise from the second cultivator, leaving him 75 per cent of his net production, or 21 rupees 8 paise. In accordance with Ricardian theory, the state then leaves the cultivator of the top-quality soil with only 21 rupees 8 paise, while absconding with 66 per cent of his net produce.[109] Naoroji's discovery was that the colonial state's monopoly functioned like that of the banks that had appropriated Naoroji's property. They both distorted the natural accumulation of Indian capital through the exercise of 'mischievous' arbitrary economic influence over the market. If labour was not proportionately rewarded, it was not incentivized to expand the cycle of production and consumption, the substitution of contract for status and the creation of a commercial society.[110]

## The Land Question and the Labour Theory of Value

The famines that afflicted western India between 1868 and 1869 drew Naoroji's attention to agriculture and the land question as part of his enquiry into the condition of Indian labour. In Rajputana, the North-Western Provinces, the Punjab, the Central Provinces and Bombay, over 3,000,000 perished during this period.[111]

---

[108] David Ricardo, 'On Principles of Political Economy and Taxation' [1817], in David Ricardo, *The Works and Correspondence of David Ricardo,* vol. I, ed. Pierro Sraffa (11 vols., Cambridge: Cambridge University Press, 1951), ch. 2.

[109] Naoroji, 'Financial Administration of India', pp. 146–8.

[110] Naoroji, 'Poverty of India, Part I', p. 161.

[111] William Digby, *Prosperous British India* (London: Fisher Unwin, 1901), p. 127.

The exodus of workers from Bombay compounded the departure of thousands during the financial collapse.[112] The colonial state's dogmatic laissez-faire attitude also led to reductions in state expenditure on public works, even in the midst of the droughts of the late 1860s.[113] That the Government of Bombay's reassessment of the presidency's land values occurred in 1865, serendipitously with the city's boom and bust, only encouraged Naoroji to make the connection between rural travails and colonial mismanagement.[114] Moreover, the impact of British laissez-faire policies in the Rajputana states and neighbouring Gujarat particularly interested Naoroji given his ancestral farms in Dharampur, a princely state in the Surat Agency to the southwest of Navsari.

The British agents supervising the native administration of these regions blamed the loss of life on absolute scarcity, drought and the lethargy of Indian princes and their failure to build public works that gave peasants the opportunity of earning enough to buy food.[115] However, Naoroji teamed with Naoroji Furdoonji to refute these claims, showing that in times of famine collectors managed to increase the state's revenue on account of scarcity-induced price inflation.[116] A similar pattern was observed when drought struck Ahmedabad and Surat in 1864, with revenue increasing by 106,124 pounds over the previous year.[117] Official opinion resorted to its ethnographic rationale in explaining why relief works 40–50 miles away from affected villages were not used. It was claimed that this was because *ryot*s 'dreaded the inconvenience of labouring in an unaccustomed way more than hunger'.[118]

Naoroji and Furdoonji's rural fact-finding expedition to Gujarat and the Deccan used detailed questionnaires to ascertain from peasants themselves the relationship between famine and colonial policy.[119] They asked *ryot*s in Kaira, Broach, Surat and Bulsar about their views on the real causes of famine and

---

112 *Report of the Indian Famine Commission 1878, Part 3: Famine Histories* (Calcutta: Superintendent of Government Printing, 1880).

113 H. Fukazawa, 'Agrarian Relations: Western India', in *Cambridge Economic History*, p. 194; David Hall-Matthews, *Peasants, Famine and the State in Colonial Western India* (London: Palgrave Macmillan, 2005).

114 Peter Harnetty, 'Cotton Exports and Indian Agriculture, 1861–1870', *Economic History Review* 24, no. 3 (1971), p. 422.

115 'Report of the Political Administration of the Rajpootana States, 1868–9' (Calcutta: Superintendent of Government Printing, 1869), BLAPAC, *Selections from Records of Government, 70–74*, 1947 a. 2043, pp. 105, 109.

116 *Moral and Material Progress, 1868–9*, BLAPAC, IOR/L/PARL/2/153, pp. 40, 42.

117 *Moral and Material Progress, 1864–5*, ibid., p. 14.

118 *Moral and Material Progress, 1868–9*, ibid., p. 42.

119 Bayly, *Recovering Liberties*, p. 195; 'Furdoonjee and Naorojee in Gujarat', *Amrita Bazaar Patrika*, 16 February 1873.

deprivation and whether official accounts of failed rains, princely misgovernment and the economic irrationality of Indians were fair. The advantage of this method was that it enquired after the economic conditions of individuals rather than groups in order to paint an accurate picture of the Indian as an economic agent and his potential for greater production. One question entered into the costs of production and the size of the resultant surplus: 'Does the assessment generally leave a surplus to the cultivator or occupier, after satisfying the demands of the Government and paying the costs and charges of cultivation?' Others asked about instances of physical coercion by officials and the role of moneylenders.[120] In Nariad, they recorded complaints about the collectors assessing the revenue demand on the prevailing inflated price even during times of famine. In Kaira district the subjection of alienated land to a quit-rent under the Summary Settlement Act was found objectionable in principle.[121] Both instances represented an arbitrary land tax entirely detached from the consumptive needs of those being assessed and, as a corollary, the productive investment in capital and labour hours made by those working the land.

Naoroji's evidence before the Select Committee on East India finance in 1873 made full use of what he and Furdoonji had learned during their expedition. The testimony sketches an incipient labour theory of value at the heart of Naoroji's political economy and one that was foundational to his perceptions of natural law and justice. Naoroji was asked, in a Ricardian vein, whether the land revenue was actually a surplus rent from superior landowners to the state that did not affect the amount paid by cultivators to their landlords. Naoroji disagreed with the premise of the question, insisting that he 'consider[ed] the whole of the land revenue to be paid by the cultivator'.[122] Naoroji added that in native states like Travancore, where the British system of revenue farming was replaced by a direct system of collecting a fixed proportion of revenue from producer-proprietors, productivity and state revenue increased.[123] From 1835 a formal *ryotwari* system was introduced in the Bombay presidency where no fixed assessment existed at all, the only principle being that the assessment officer should not demand more than the cultivator's ability to pay.[124]

[120] 'Mr. Nowrozjee's Questions', *Native Opinion*, 16 February 1873.

[121] 'Travels in Guzerat', *Native Opinion*, 16 February 1873.

[122] 'Dadabhai Naoroji Examined, 11 July 1873', in *Third Report from the Select Committee on East India Finance; Together with the Proceedings of the Committee, Minutes of Evidence and Appendix* (Calcutta: Superintendent of Government Printing, 1873), BLAPAC, IOR/L/PARL/2/210, p. 505.

[123] Ibid., pp. 510–11.

[124] Fukazawa, 'Agrarian Relations: Western India', pp. 185–6.

The irrationality of the British revenue settlement in not taking the differentials of individual investment into account, in addition to the arbitrariness of taxes like quit-rent, had no relation to productive capacity at all. Thus, the producer-cultivator enjoyed 'no security of property at all'. In absconding with an unjustly large share of peasant production, the colonial state significantly diminished Indians' powers of consumption so that they enjoyed 'no security for life'. Indian property was annihilated by 'England's own grasp'.[125] Based on his own study, the average production per capita in India as a whole was merely 20 rupees compared to the 40 rupees Naoroji had calculated as the jail cost of living.[126] Thus, it was not drought that was the cause of starvation but the inability of Indian labour to reproduce itself and profit from its work. This led to an ever-increasing depression of the purchasing power of rusticated peasants, thereby preventing the consumption of grains from districts not affected by famine.[127]

In a final polemical broadside, Naoroji noted that famines were particularly devastating in India because the British were preventing their own merchants from enjoying the natural development of capitalist investment. Naoroji suggested that no incentives for capital investment in productive and distributive capacity would ever exist in a country where the state revenue system financed trade.[128] In a move aimed at delegitimizing the role of banking in international trade, Naoroji argued that Anglo-Indian trade was financed via the presidency banking system, whose capital stocks came in large part from Indian taxation. In this mechanism, the land revenue system was used to appropriate a disproportionate amount of Indian agricultural product through taxation or taxation in kind in order to finance the export of that same commodity to Europe. Cunningly, Naoroji made this point by reframing the comments made by James Westland, the viceroy's finance minister. Westland had admitted that the Indian money market was inextricably tied up with the Government of India's balances. Over 10,500,000 rupees of the presidency banks' capital was forwarded to British merchants and naturally, Naoroji observed, the profit from these trades would not return to the peasants.[129]

[125] Naoroji, 'Memorandum on a Few Statements in the Report of the Indian Famine Commission 1880' to Sir Louis Mallet, Undersecretary of State for India, in Naoroji, *Essays, Speeches, Addresses, and Writings*, p. 484.

[126] Naoroji, 'Poverty of India, Part I', p. 190.

[127] Naoroji, 'The Causes and Cure of Famine in India', speech at the Free Church in Croydon, 31 April 1901, in Dadabhai Naoroji, *The Grand Little Man of India: Dadabhai Naoroji, Speeches and Writings*, vol. I, ed. Moin Zaidi (2 vols., New Delhi: Indian Institute of Applied Political Research, 1985), p. 235.

[128] Naoroji, 'On the Commerce of India', p. 122.

[129] 'Evidence of Dadabhai Naoroji', in *First Report of the Royal Commission on the Administration of the Expenditure of India; With Minutes of Evidence* (London: Her Majesty's Stationary Office, 1896), BLAPAC, IOR L/AG/49/5 part II, pp. 162–3.

The *ryot* was never properly remunerated for his creation of value in the first place, and his own labour was used against him to finance the process of exploitation so that no capital investment was required in India. This distorted the cycle of production and consumption and obstructed any development of a natural and fair contract not only between British and Indian merchants but also among Indian producers. It was the colonial state that stripped Indian labour of its innate productive agency and relegated workers to exploited and asocial 'helots' extracting raw produce for British industry. As dependent 'hewers of wood and drawers of water', these people were regarded as artificially suspended in forms of the semi-feudal bondage that Parsi social reform had sought to escape.[130]

## Conclusion: Comparing Naoroji and Locke's Labour Theories of Value

In linking the origin of property to the primordial act of mixing labour with nature, Naoroji's political economy is distinctly Lockean. John Locke theorized that the origins of the rights-bearing individual and civil government lay squarely in the domain of property since the God-given labour power of every male denoted 'a property in his own person'. The inalienability of this natural property meant that every man had an inherent right to personal sovereignty. From this sprang the necessity for political combination as a conscious agreement to protect property, otherwise known as the social contract.[131] Locke added that 'it is labour indeed that puts the difference of value on every thing' in a society in which 'ninety nine hundredths' of the 'products of the earth useful to man' are 'the effects of labour'.[132] Clearly, there is no evidence of providentialism or a contractual basis of civil government in Naoroji's equivalent theory, and in this sense it is unlikely that he derived his insights from Locke but instead gleaned them from his examination of the economic condition of India. If Locke did directly influence

[130] Naoroji, 'England's Duties to India', p. 35; Naoroji, 'East India Revenue Account, Amendment for a Full and Independent Parliamentary Enquiry, 14 Aug. 1894', in Naoroji, *Poverty and Un-British Rule*, p. 282.

[131] John Locke, *An Essay Concerning the True Original and Extent of Civil Government* (Dublin: George Bonham, 1798), p. 34; John Locke, 'Second Treatise on Government', *Two Treatises of Government* [1689] in Peter Laslett, ed., *Cambridge Texts in the History of Political Thought* (Cambridge: Cambridge University Press, 1988), pp. 381–3.

[132] Locke, *Extent of Civil Government*, pp. 36–5, cited in Andrew Sartori, *Liberalism in Empire: An Alternative History* (Berkley, CA: University of California Press, 2014), p. 13; see also Neal Wood, *John Locke and Agrarian Capitalism* (Berkley, CA: University of California Press, 1984), pp. 38–9, 113; Karen I. Vaughn, 'John Locke and the Labor Theory of Value', *Journal of Libertarian Studies* 2, no. 4 (1978), pp. 311–26.

Indian thinkers, it seems to have been through his moral philosophy in *An Essay Concerning Human Understanding*, which was studied as part of the syllabus at the Elphinstone College.[133]

Andrew Sartori has also identified a Lockean register of political economy developing in Bengal during the Great Rent Case of 1865 in which the claims of Bengali peasants for fair rent and occupancy rights faced legal challenge. Ultimately, it was concluded that Bengali landlords could not claim the entirety of the differential rent as defined by Ricardo since agricultural workers had mixed their labour with the land. Basing their political-economic claims on customary right, Bengali peasants had sketched a vernacular liberal framework for economic justice.[134] Since what was traded was 'materialized labour', the agent could assert 'an absolute juridical right' over it.[135] However, Sartori also emphasizes that he is not using Locke in a 'provenantial sense' but is acknowledging that Locke's theory 'involved serious reflection on his contemporary social realities' during the exclusion crisis of late-seventeenth-century England. A similar attention to social interdependence in Bengal generated a Lockean theory of value. Sartori's sophisticated Marxian history prioritizes capitalist social relations as the condition of possibility for the uptake of liberal concepts, and it is the sphere of circulation alongside commodity exchange in Bengal's agricultural market that allows globally circulating concepts of political economy to be thinkable.[136]

In contrast to Bengal, Naoroji's turn to a labour theory of value was liberal in that it sought to manage the social world through political economy. His eventual arrival at this perspective was the product of a protracted series of social debates that were not reducible to viewing property and the relations of production as a Marxian base or substructure.[137] It is difficult to paint Naoroji as a Marxian socialist intellectually, however much a part of his network contained socialist allies. In Bengal, Sartori makes clear that beyond proprietary claims, the indigenous discourse 'was in no obvious sense liberal'.[138] Naoroji, in seeking to establish a society of freely associating individuals, was consciously committed to a wider liberal worldview that was campaigning for the restoration of natural justice as a prerequisite to sociality. It is also this determined focus on the origins of pluralist

---

133 'Review of the Board of Education, Bombay 1853–4: with Special Reference to the Elphinstone College', DNP, notes and jottings, group 3: education, serial number 11.

134 Andrew Sartori, *Liberalism in Empire*, chs. 2–4.

135 Ibid., p. 13.

136 Ibid., pp. 8–9.

137 Karl Marx, *A Contribution to the Critique of Political Economy* (Moscow: Progress Publishers, 1977 [1859]), ch. 2.

138 Sartori, *Liberalism in Empire*, p. 196.

interdependence, rather than the origins of civil government, that marks Naoroji out from Locke and reflects the nineteenth-century intellectual climate in which the primacy of the social was reflected in self-conscious theorizing of the social more than the political.[139]

For Locke, inconvenient mediation in natural law took another form. The need to arbitrate the natural process of mixing labour with nature only arose after the advent of money. In a pre-monetary society, there was little concern about the right to property or the apportionment of accumulated property since the basic ownership of livestock, foodstuffs or land was small scale and largely subsistence based. As Locke comments, the origin of ownership over commodities from the commons was easily conceivable from how 'the spending it upon our uses bounded it'. This 'easily seen' process of production and consumption 'left no room for controversy about the title, nor for the incroachment [*sic*] on the right of others'.[140] The growth of the monetized economy facilitated exchange but also accumulation via the mediation of price as an indirect and abstract system of value. As a result, the easily legible system of pre-monetary natural law blurred and required an institutionally administered and neutral system of justice, in the form of civil government, to arbitrate conflict and uphold the security of property.[141]

In Naoroji's world, the modern state and a highly financialized economy were established facts of life. In buying into the Whig interpretation of British 'progressive' global government, Naoroji was not working on a retrospective theory of political obligation or consent like Locke's. Given his commitment to Parsi, and, later, Indian business, Naoroji was not formulating a wholesale critique of capitalism either. What was at stake was the protection of the free exchange between producers and consumers from external economic dependence. Naoroji's intellectual innovation in this regard was to frame mediation in this relationship not as a negative externality of the abstract values and indirect relationships inherent in the use of money but as a product of institutional monopoly over labour. These insights were applied to both Indian and British workers in order to pioneer a radical liberal politics that united Indian and British labour in a common critique of capitalist monopoly for the first time. This new politics is the subject of the next two chapters.

---

[139] Karuna Mantena, 'Social Theory in the Age of Empire', in Sankar Muthu, ed., *Empire and Modern Political Thought* (Cambridge: Cambridge University Press, 2012), pp. 324–50.
[140] John Locke, 'Second Treatise on Government', *Two Treatises of Government* [1689], in Peter Laslett, ed. *Cambridge Texts in the History of Political Thought*, vol. II, p. 51.
[141] Ibid., p. 131.

# 5 Making Commercial Society in India

The Irish Home Rule question was catapulted to the top of the British political agenda in 1868 with William Ewart Gladstone making it a centrepiece of his election campaign. As a result, the Irish land question flourished in British public debate around the same time that Naoroji was conceptualizing his labour theory of value. It is hardly surprising that in Naoroji's comparative political economy, British commentary on the condition of Ireland was an ever-present foil to the situation in India. Moreover, the elite commentary on Irish agrarian distress, tenancy rights and British rule was an important historical antecedent to Naoroji's own concerns since questions of Irish proprietary right resembled those of the subcontinent.[1] Nevertheless, Naoroji parted ways with major policy interventions on the Irish question by influential pundits like J. S. Mill who initially advocated land nationalization, switching later to a doctrine of owner-occupation, or persisted with archaic economic doctrines like that of the wage fund. Sensitive to the Irish debate but not repeating it, Naoroji charted his own vision for commercial society that reinstated natural justice by minimizing the colonial state's financial monopoly.

By the late 1880s, Naoroji was in regular correspondence with Irish Land Leaguers like Michael Davitt, co-operating with him in movements for land reform in England.[2] However, it was the economic writings of individuals who linked land issues with pauperization in the United Kingdom that bear striking resemblance to Naoroji's own critique, and the most significant among these was Henry Fawcett,

---

[1] C. A. Bayly, 'Ireland, India and the Empire: 1780–1914', *Transactions of the Royal Historical Society* 6, no. 10 (2000), pp. 377–97.

[2] Dinshaw Wacha to Naoroji, 10 July 1888, R. P. Patwardan, ed., *Dadabhai Naoroji Correspondence*, Vol. II, Part I: *Correspondence with Dinshaw Wacha* (2 vols., Bombay: Allied Publishers, 1977), pp. 101–2; 'Extracts from Mr. Davitt's Speech at St. James' Hall', New Delhi, National Archives of India, Dadabhai Naoroji Papers [DNP], notes and jottings, group 1: accounts/economic/trade, number 23; English land restoration league to Naoroji, 14 January 1890, DNP, E-54 (4); Land law reform association to Naoroji, (undated) January 1895, DNP, L-20 (2).

with whom Naoroji was well acquainted since the 1860s.[3] In many ways, Fawcett's views about Irish tenant farmers echoed those of his intellectual mentor, J. S. Mill, and the student of his political economy, J. E. Cairnes. Fixity of tenure and the right of the labourer to a fair share of the value he had produced featured prominently in these discussions.[4] Mill also castigated absentee landlords for facilitating a system of unilateral transfers from Ireland to Britain that resulted in deteriorating terms of trade and an increase in the cost of Irish imports – a paradigm Naoroji cited in his own drain theory.[5] Consequently, in 1868 Mill advocated land nationalization in Ireland, but by 1870 this was replaced by a gradual transfer of land to a productive yeomanry of co-operative farmers who could reap rewards proportional to their investment and labour.[6]

Fawcett's publications on land addressed the question of labour and poverty in general and linked them to liberal subjectivity. For Fawcett, pauperism in Britain was a grim reality of the Malthusian trap but it also resulted from deleterious economic arrangements and government mismanagement.[7] Although he did not advocate the sort of labour radicalism that Naoroji's British politics would adopt, he did link the growth of human character and the 'development of man as a moral and responsible being' with the generative properties of a well-functioning

[3] R. P. Masani, *Dadabhai Naoroji: The Grand Old Man of India* (London: George Allen & Unwin, 1939), p. 104; Fawcett present at Robert Knight's reading of 'India: A Review of England's Financial Relations Therewith', 3 March 1868, *Journal of the East India Association* [*JEIA*] 2 (1868), p. 278; Naoroji shared a platform with Fawcett and Jacob Bright with J. S. Mill in the audience at a suffrage meeting at St James' Hall reported in the *Englishwoman's Review*, 1 April 1871; Fawcett also sat on the East India finance committee in 1871; see *Report from the Select Committee on East India Finance; together with the Proceedings of the Committee, Minutes of Evidence and Appendix, 18 July 1871*, London, British Library, Asia, Africa, and Pacific Collection [BLAPAC], L/PARL/2/208.

[4] J. E. Cairnes, 'Ireland in Transition', *The Economist*, 21 October 1865; H. Fawcett, 'The Land Question', lecture before Brighton Liberal registration association reported in *Freeman's Journal*, 23 October 1869.

[5] R. D. Collison Black, *Economic Thought and the Irish Question, 1817–1870* (Cambridge: Cambridge University Press, 1960), p. 81; John Stuart Mill, 'Of the Laws of Interchange between Nations; And the Distribution of the Gains of Commerce Among the Countries of the Commercial World [1844]', in John Stuart Mill, *The Collected Works of John Stuart Mill* [hereafter *CW*], vol. IV, ed. John M. Robson, intro. V. W. Bladen, online edn (33 vols., Toronto: Toronto University Press, 1965), pp. 234–5; Dadabhai Naoroji, 'The Wants and Means of India', in Dadabhai Naoroji, *Essays, Speeches, Addresses and Writings of the Hon'ble Dadabhai Naoroji*, ed. C. L. Parekh (Bombay: Caxton Printing Works, 1887), p. 101.

[6] Eugenio F. Biagini, *Liberty, Retrenchment and Reform: Popular Liberalism in the Age of Gladstone, 1860–1880* (Cambridge: Cambridge University Press, 1992), pp. 167, 189–90.

[7] Henry Fawcett, *Pauperism: Its Causes and Remedies* (London: Macmillan & Co, 1871), pp. 111–12.

political economy. Failing this, the poor would continue to suffer from a lack of character since, like Naoroji's Indian helots, 'pauper labour had in fact many of the economic defects of slave labour'.[8] To this end, the organization of capital and labour into a unified system to the benefit of the 'whole community' was of paramount importance since the separation of the two classes into opposing blocs demoralized the latter because they had 'no direct interest in the success of their work'.[9] Another European, the freethinker Charles Bradlaugh, also expressed similar views on British poverty. Bradlaugh maintained that when people were living at a subsistence level one could hardly expect them to find the time and resources 'in which other emotions can be cultivated other than those of the mere desires for food and rest'.[10] Here, again, the absence of accumulated capital through the exercise of property in one's own person was a form of domination comparable to slavery – a sort of moral and political 'bondage' – the only cure for which was 'property' and a 'personal stake' in one's work.[11]

Fawcett and Bradlaugh's joint desire to remunerate labour more proportionately was always attenuated on account of their abiding belief in the wage fund doctrine.[12] This mainstay of early-nineteenth-century political economy considered the amount of labour any economic enterprise could employ as directly proportional to the capital fund set aside for that purpose before any business commenced. The productivity of labour, the value of commodities and the profit level had no bearing on labour demand. Labour's role in creating value was thus subordinated to the primacy of pre-existing capital or financial investment. Though Mill had publicly recanted the wage fund doctrine in 1868, it continued to be widely adhered to and curiously remained in his 1878 edition of *Principles of Political Economy*.[13] Naoroji endorsed and quoted Fawcett's analysis of Irish and Indian absenteeism, which claimed that 'the bane of our system was

[8] Ibid., pp. 6–7, 22, 118.

[9] Ibid., pp. 119–20.

[10] C. Bradlaugh, 'Poverty: The Effects on the Political Condition of the People' in John Saville, ed., *A Selection of the Political Pamphlets of Charles Bradlaugh* (New York, NY: Augustus M. Kelly Publishers, 1970), p. 4.

[11] Ibid., pp. 7–8; Zak Leonard has recently dubbed this the British rhetoric of 'virtual slavery'; see Zak Leonard, '"A Blot of English Justice": India Reformism and the Rhetoric of Virtual Slavery', *Modern Asian Studies* (FirstView, 20 March 2020).

[12] Bradlaugh, 'Poverty, p. 6; Henry Fawcett, *The Economic Position of the British Labourer* (London: Macmillan & Co, 1865), p. 120.

[13] J. S. Mill, 'Thornton on Labour and Its Claims', *Fortnightly Review* 5 (May 1869), pp. 505–18, and (June 1869), pp. 680–700; Eugenio F. Biagini, 'British Trade Unions and Popular Political Economy, 1860–1880', *Historical Journal* 30, no. 4 (1987), pp. 824–6; Biagini, *Liberty, Retrenchment and Reform*, p. 135.

that the advantages were reaped by one class and the work was done by another'.[14] Yet Fawcett could not envisage an India in which the agriculturalist was not dependent on a pre-existing stock of capital. In this crucial regard, he emphasized that India had to import European capital in order to augment its wage fund and employ labour.[15] In his estimation, the colonial state's land revenue was irrelevant in making this calculation.[16]

Unencumbered by a wage fund theory, Naoroji's Indian peasant was a generator of capital and therefore a potential engine of sociability under the correct conditions. This chapter of the book explains how Naoroji became an advocate of reforming the Indian revenue system and the colonial state with the goal of reining in a kleptocracy influencing Indian economic exchange through their status as hallowed civil servants. Not only were they enriching themselves, in Naoroji's view, but colonial officialdom was also distorting the natural terms of trade both domestically and internationally to the detriment of commercial society and the prospects of Indian civil peace.

## Commercial Society, Capital and the Colonial State

Having calculated individual subsistence and the potential for production in India through his labour theory of value, Naoroji turned his attention to international trade. Just as one could augment personal property through trade with other Indians, international trade was the most effective way in which Indians could collectively augment their stock of capital given the global division of labour and India's competitive advantage in particular labour-intensive sectors. The most well-known instance of popular protest against the terms of Anglo-Indian trade before the Gandhian era was Bengal's *swadeshi* movement (the promotion of indigenous manufacturing and the boycotting of British products), which had exploded in the wake of Viceroy Curzon's plan to partition the province along religious lines in 1905. Amid this furore, as president of the 1906 Indian National Congress meeting in Calcutta, Naoroji reminded delegates that the promotion of domestic manufacturing was 'not a thing of to-day' but that on the contrary it had 'existed in Bombay as far as I know for many years past'. Bombay had led the way, albeit tentatively, by promoting Indian industry through Indian capital investment, and it was only through Bombay's example of indigenous economic agency that the profits of trade would augment Indian production and consumption. Naoroji

[14] Naoroji to Lord Welby, quoting Henry Fawcett's speech to parliament of 5 May 1868, (undated) October 1895, DNP, N-1 (2599).

[15] Fawcett, *British Labourer*, p. 122.

[16] Ibid., pp. 136–8.

embraced the label of a 'freetrader', having been on the executive of the Cobden Club since 1886, but in the context of the Indian drain he insisted that the parameters of what Westminster, Whitehall and imperial mandarins in Calcutta called free trade had to be rethought.[17]

Naoroji had clarified in his maiden speech to the Cobden Club the conviction that he 'regarded free trade as one of the greatest discoveries of the present age' and that its practice 'was allied with every principle involved in the freedom of humanity'.[18] In line with his Macaulayite understanding of free trade among 'civilized men', Naoroji envisaged the 'conditions of a natural trade' to be reciprocal and mutually beneficial. In the case of Indian accumulation from a *fair* trade, if bullion was included in the official trade figures, for every 100 pounds exported the same amount should return with a margin of profit, resulting in a general 'excess of imports over exports'.[19] However, in the context of the drain, Naoroji noted that so-called free trade 'between England and India in a matter like this is something like a race between a starving, exhausted invalid and a strong man with a horse to ride on'.[20] Fixing this dilemma was paramount because, as Naoroji's critique of the expansion of the colonial rail network in India suggests, fair international trade was the only means of supplementing the value already created by labour.

Naoroji's drain theory had been challenged throughout the 1870s by the India Office statistician and former colleague of J. S. Mill during his East India Company days, Charles Danvers. Regarding railways, Danvers averred that they augmented the value of food grains and the wealth of the districts through which they ran.[21] It was naïve to suggest, Naoroji responded, that just because the wheat was priced at one level in Punjab and fetched a greater sum in Bombay that one had created value or wealth. Perhaps reflecting on the legal travails with banks and

---

[17] Naoroji, 'Presidential Address' at the twenty-second session of the Congress in Calcutta, 1906, in Dadabhai Naoroji, *The Grand Little Man of India: Dadabhai Naoroji, Speeches and Writings*, vol. I, ed. Moin Zaidi (2 vols., New Delhi: Indian Institute of Applied Political Research, 1985), p. 95; Richard Gowling, secretary of the Cobden Club, to Naoroji, 13 May 1886, DNP, C-203.

[18] 'Extract Report of the Annual Meeting of the Cobden Club', 17 July 1886, DNP, notes and jottings, group 5: extracts, serial number 12.

[19] Naoroji, 'East India Revenue Account, Amendment for a Full and Independent Parliamentary Enquiry, 14 Aug. 1894', in Dadabhai Naoroji, *Poverty and Un-British Rule in India* (London: Swann Sonnenschein & Co, 1901), p. 281.

[20] Dadabhai Naoroji, 'Poverty of India, Part I', in Naoroji, *Essays, Speeches, Addresses, and Writings*, p. 217.

[21] 'Memorandum on Mr. Danvers's Papers of 28th June 1880 and 4th January 1879', in Naoroji, *Poverty and Un-British Rule*, pp. 443–4; F.C. Danvers, 'Memorandum on a Letter from Mr. Dadabhai Naoroji, dated 24th May, 1880', *JEIA* 13 (1881), pp. 145–6.

moneylenders in the conduct of his own business in the 1860s, Naoroji insisted that the difference in price was merely that owed to unproductive middlemen and the wealth it was drawn from had already existed in Bombay before the wheat was moved an inch.

There was a faint echo of Mill's attention to the economic function of distributors and retailers who stole a proportion of wealth due to producers. Labour and capital could undertake this role themselves if they were better organized.[22] Naoroji's innovation was to subsume labour and capital into a single relation of production, exclaiming that '"railway wealth" does not exist', and adding that if 'the mere movement of produce can *add* wealth, India can become rich in no time.... But there is no Royal (even railway) road to material wealth. It must be produced from the materials of the Earth till the great discovery is made of converting motion into matter'. If India's railways were moving goods to ports for export under unjust terms of trade, in which Indian labour would not get a profitable return, then what were India's railways but a tax on producers who were already labouring for barely subsistence returns?[23] This was compounded by the colonial state's irregular practice of guaranteeing the profits of railway companies should their initial investments not yield a return. Comparing figures with the United States, where American citizens were on the hook for the original outlay and interest on the loans, Indian taxpayers were contributing an additional sum to mitigate the risk posed to European capital.[24]

Refusing to see state–market relations in terms of negative or positive liberty, Naoroji's observations showed that the colonial state facilitated more efficient exploitation of peasant-producers and diminished their productive capacities. Naoroji's European friends and interlocutors, like the former *Times of India* editor W. Martin Wood, were also critics of the official liberalism of laissez faire. Wood, though he regularly used Naoroji's writings to bolster his argument, disclaimed 'any wish to raise political questions'.[25] Wood's usefulness to Naoroji was his ability to 'formulate' their common ideas 'from the standpoint of the popular mind' and 'to make our politicians and conventional economists *believe*

---

[22] John Stuart Mill, 'Principles of Political Economy with Some of Their Applications to Social Philosophy, Books III–IV', in Mill, *CW*, vol. III, pp. 248–9.

[23] Naoroji, 'Condition of India: Correspondence with the Secretary of State for India, 1880', in Naoroji, *Essays, Speeches, Addresses, and Writings*, pp. 443–4 (emphasis in original).

[24] American and British trade and railway figures with notes, DNP, notes and jottings, group 1: accounts/economic/trade, serial number 21.

[25] W. Martin Wood, 'India's Un-adjusted Trade Balance: Its Effect on the Industrial and Commercial Condition of the People', *Political Science Quarterly* 2, no. 4 (1887), pp. 681–2.

that India does send out millions more than she receives'.[26] While Wood advocated government-funded public works to augment productivity and prosperity, Naoroji's ideal sphere of circulation was one in which sufficient surplus capital would return to its originator – labour. Absolved of their dependence on the mediating and exploitative logic of colonial capital, Indian 'helots' would become a propertied yeomanry raised to a new state of commercial non-domination. Naoroji used the colonial governor Richard Temple's analysis of the Punjab during the Indian 'Mutiny' of 1857 to illustrate his point. The province was endowed with natural fertility and a high level of investment in irrigation works and yet suffered because its land revenue paid for the salaries of Indian army regiments based at Oudh. However, upon returning to the Punjab, soldiers' salaries and additional plunder were remitted back to their villages, leading to an 'increase in agricultural capital, a freer circulation of money, and a fresh impetus to cultivation'.[27] Naoroji substituted plunder for the profits of international trade in Temple's example, claiming that the Raj would experience analogous benefits if there were a 'just adjustment of the financial relations between India and England'.[28]

The generation of surplus value by trade was tied directly to the process of creating civil subjects by augmenting their productive and consumptive capacity. Quantifying Indian production in terms of exports and imports per capita, Naoroji carried out a comparative political economy of development with other countries to show how Indian political actualization based upon free trade was a myth. Naoroji noted that Britain exported goods worth 6 pounds per capita and Australia 19 pounds, whereas India managed a paltry 4 shillings.[29] Likewise, India imported a mere 9 shillings per capita to Britain's 9 pounds.[30] It was only the semi-independent native states that exhibited a surplus of imports over exports; Indian economic activity in British territory saw its surpluses appropriated via the revenue and council bill system and the profits on European capital returned to the pockets of metropolitan investors.[31] A summary comparison with agriculture, trade and railway investment statistics of Britain and the settler colonies showed that they

[26] W. M. Wood to Naoroji, 31 October 1884, DNP, W-153 (20); W. M. Wood to Naoroji, 30 October 1887, DNP, W-153 (64) (emphasis in original).
[27] See Dadabhai Naoroji, 'Financial Administration of India', in Naoroji, *Essays, Speeches, Addresses, and Writings*, p. 138n.
[28] Ibid., p. 138.
[29] Naoroji, 'On the Commerce of India', in ibid., p. 116.
[30] Naoroji, 'The Wants and Means of India', in ibid., pp. 102–3.
[31] 'British India Import and Export Statistics', DNP, notes and jottings, group 1: accounts/economic/trade, serial number 19.

enjoyed significant import surpluses, whereas India did not.[32] Other Indians with a background in business, like the Bengali Bholanath Chandra, echoed Naoroji's concerns, commenting that 'nothing is more sensibly felt by them [peasants] now-a-days than that the so-called trade of their country, is properly speaking, no trade of India'.[33] Chandra also harboured similar views on labour, capital and circulation, suggesting that labour, the land and mineral resources were the only sources of value and that predatory rural moneylenders only existed because the British revenue settlement, British capitalists and European shippers appropriated the re-investable profits due to workers.[34]

Certain proactive measures could be undertaken to ensure that India traded on a more equal footing with Britain. When in the 1890s the colonial government faced considerable deficits due to the falling value of the rupee and rising military expenditure, Naoroji advocated raising revenue by placing a protective tariff on imports of cotton piece-goods from Britain. This was partly to encourage indigenous manufactures as well. Naoroji even quoted Mill on the need for protection in 'young colonies' irrespective of the short-term issue of falling state revenue.[35] To Mill's mind, this reform would leverage Indian exports into a more equitable position so that new industries could stand on their own two feet in time. However, Naoroji's use of protection was even more nuanced than this. In the light of his labour theory of value, he acknowledged that capitalists enjoyed an unjust share of profits in both Britain and India. After all, it was 'only some people of the United Kingdom of the higher classes' who drew 'all the benefit from the connection with India'. Both the British labourer and Indian *ryot* did 'not derive that benefit'.[36] Naoroji suggested that protection would not harm the Lancashire millworker and that if duties were imposed in India, then the additional cost of production and consumption would be thrown onto 'the better-able shoulders' of British capitalists and well-to-do Indian customers buying from abroad.[37] Protectionism served to balance the class interest on both sides of the trade as well

[32] American and British trade and railway figures with notes, DNP, notes and jottings, group 1: accounts/economic/trade, serial number 21.
[33] Bholanath Chandra, 'A Voice for the Commerce and Manufactures of India', *Mookherjee's Magazine* 2 (1873), p. 85.
[34] Ibid., pp. 85–6, 95; Naoroji made similar comments about British shipping and marine insurance; see Naoroji, 'Poverty of India, Part II', in Naoroji, *Essays, Speeches, Addresses, and Writings*, pp. 278–80; HC Deb 28 February 1893, vol. 9, cols. 653–8.
[35] Naoroji, 'Poverty of India, Part I', p. 217.
[36] Naoroji, 'Presidential Address', at the ninth session of the Congress in Lahore, 1893, in Naoroji, *The Grand Little Man of India*, vol. I, p. 42.
[37] Ibid, p. 56.

as to mitigate colonial state-backed capital's mediation in the natural productivity of the peasant-producer.

Alongside the concurrent and related debate on protectionism, Naoroji also waded into the controversy over the state manipulation of Indian currency in order to thwart what he regarded as the parasitic practice of the European financial classes to rig the natural sphere of circulation unduly in their favour. The abundance of American silver in the global market, of which the Government of India was the largest purchaser until the 1890s, brought major inflationary pressures. The 1893 Herschell Committee recommended the closure of the mints to free coinage in gold and silver in 1893 with the intention of transitioning to a gold exchange standard. The 1898 Indian Currency Committee, before which Naoroji gave evidence, eventually recommended pegging the silver rupee to the British gold standard at a fixed rate of 1 shilling 4 pence. The imperative behind this move was to reverse the declining value of the rupee against the pound, which was placing pressure on the servicing of gold-denominated Indian debt as well as disturbing the terms of colonial trade.[38] Naoroji demanded a return to the free coinage of silver on the grounds of upholding the honesty and transparency of commercial contracts given that existing economic agreements, including those pertaining to the state's revenue demand, had already been 'contracted on a silver basis'.

Naoroji opined that since the revenue demand was largely paid for in produce, a change in the value of gold or silver would not change the fact that an absolute quantity of produce would have to be exported to cover the debt on state securities held in London. Only if the price of actual commodities increased would the financial burden of the drain on the Indian taxpayer reduce. In fact, in increasing the value of the rupee through monetary stringency, the salaries of colonial officials and money owed to domestic creditors would be artificially inflated to the detriment of the 'poorer classes' and 'the rayats', with unilateral transfers of up to 138,000 pounds to European banks. The arbitrary fabrication of a 'false rupee' was thus an 'illegal, dishonourable and despotic act'.[39] Naoroji argued that this system of fiat money served the interests of 'the few wealthy men who hold permanent promissory notes of other bonds' because the fixed value of the 'false

[38] *Report of the Committee Appointed to Inquire into the Indian Currency* (London: Her Majesty's Stationary Office, 1899), pp. 3, 9–11; A. G. Chandavarkar, 'Money and Credit', in Dharma Kumar and Meghnad Desai, eds., *The Cambridge Economic History of India* (Cambridge: Cambridge University Press, 1983), p. 770.

[39] Naoroji, 'Statement Submitted to the Indian Currency Committee of 1898', in Naoroji, *The Grand Little Man of India*, pp. 54, 314–56.

rupee' now gave them 'more than they lent'. Inevitably, this policy pandered to 'British capitalists, bankers, merchants etc.'[40] The professional interest of a foreign administrative elite who superintended economic governance was thrown into stark relief during this episode. The civil service salaries, which catered to their sumptuous English lifestyles in India, and, more importantly, their pensions were also fixed under the freely coined rupee. Naoroji calculated that these would now be unnaturally inflated to the tune of 45 per cent. Collectively, these measures tore up the 'distinct contract between the Government and taxpayers based upon the fundamental principle of sound currency' simply to pander to the 'convenience of the foreign exploiter, official and non-official'.[41]

To Naoroji's mind, the logical consequence of enacting his recommendations was growth in the productive and consumptive capacity of the *ryot* and the completion of the Macaulyite circle of trade within India but also across the British Empire. It was necessary for him to exhort his British readers to the potential for trans-imperial prosperity for this reason. The market for British textiles in India would be so vast if British commercial governance was rectified that 'England would be able to eliminate altogether the word "unemployed" from her dictionary'.[42] In reality, Naoroji's global business pursuits and experience of colonial capital in India had taught him that the British imperial trade was characterized by the 'merchant or capitalist of every kind' who wanted 'to save himself in his trade-risks at the cost of the taxpayer, besides using to no small extent, or to the extent of the deposits of revenue in the banks, the revenues of the taxpayers, as his capital for trade'.[43]

Nevertheless, it is only by working with his trans-imperial ideal of sociality in the form of commercial society that we can make full sense of Naoroji's connecting of Indian peasant prosperity with that of the British working classes. In 1869, he pointed out that he regarded 'India as a firm managed by England'. As such, 'the firm had a right to expect that the manager should so manage the concern as to produce his own salary and something more [for his workers]'.[44] This was a universal principle. It is no surprise then that Naoroji reemployed the trope when electioneering in Holborn in 1886, insisting that the discrete parts of the empire could be socialized internally but also to each other through natural economic laws as trading partners in a larger 'Imperial Firm'.[45]

[40] Naoroji draft evidence to the currency committee, (undated) 1899, DNP, C-299.
[41] Naoroji, 'Statement Submitted to the Indian Currency Committee', pp. 315, 330.
[42] Naoroji, 'England and India', in Naoroji, *The Grand Little Man of India*, pp. 160–1.
[43] Naoroji, 'Statement Submitted to the Indian Currency Committee', p. 331.
[44] Naoroji's comments during a discussion following Hyde Clarke, 'Transport in India', *JEIA* 3 (1869), p. 163.
[45] Naoroji, 'At a Meeting of the Electors of the Holborn Division', 27 June 1886, in Naoroji *Essays, Speeches, Addresses, and Writings*, p. 307.

## Commercial Society, Capital and the Princely States

The so-called native states, the patchwork of approximately 600 princely sovereignties through which Britain ruled indirectly, were a regular case study in Naoroji's comparative political economy. Naoroji subdivided the exports of India into three categories. Those produced in British India, those produced in the native states and those from the European plantation economy. Naoroji only regarded the latter two as getting a full return on the cost of production of their commodities plus profit. That was not to say the returns in the native states and on the plantations necessarily returned to labourers but as economic units they functioned in a condition of relative freedom. It was only the Indian economic actors of British India who laboured in a state of domination and were forced by the revenue demand and home charges to export commodities on which they would never receive a fair return.[46] In this tripartite formulation, the native states offered an invaluable laboratory for how natural economic laws could work successfully in India as a whole. Naoroji's championing of native state independence from external economic domination and his short term as *dewan* (prime minister) of the princely state of Baroda illustrate his understanding of how an administration could be reformed and run by Indians in order to operate in accordance with natural law.

Naoroji's earliest efforts to protect the rights of princely states were with Major Thomas Evans Bell of the Madras Staff Corps.[47] Throughout the 1850s, Evans Bell was based at the court of the Rajah of Nagpur and became heavily involved in the succession crisis of that state when the king died without an heir in 1853. The Government of India pursued their policy of lapse, insisting that the succession to an heirless monarch was an issue of British policy and not of dynastic right and proceeded to annex the state. Bell became a liaison between the deceased king's family and adopted son and the colonial government, seeking to secure them their just rights of inheritance and title. Petitioning the government he proclaimed that the British 'had not either by ancient custom and precedent, or by the test of treaties, any right to interfere with the Hindoo law of inheritance and the family arrangements on the death of the late Rajah of Nagpore'.[48] Developing his views throughout this episode and the disastrous impact the doctrine of lapse had in sparking the 1857 Indian 'Mutiny', Evans Bell would become a confidant of

---

[46] 'British India Imports and Exports Statistics' DNP, notes and jottings, group 1: accounts/economic/trade, number 19.
[47] Masani, *Dadabhai Naoroji*, p. 251; Major Evans Bell to Naoroji, 1 Mar. 1869, DNP, B-81 (3).
[48] Memo 2, Thomas Evans Bell to G. F. Edmonstone, 14 September 1858, BLAPAC, IOR L/PS/6/477 Coll 36/2, f. 265.

Naoroji's on princely politics and a regular contributor at the latter's East India Association.

One such collaboration was Evans Bell's representation of Chamarajendra Wadiyar X of Mysore. Mysore was ruled directly by the British from 1831, and the Wadiyars successfully campaigned through Bell and others to have their sovereignty restored. In the 'rendition of 1881' Chamarajendra took over the reins of the principality's internal government, and Mysore became an instructive example of how British interference could detach the sovereign from governance but also how sovereignty could successfully be restored via agitation.[49] Bell's pronouncements on the native states influenced Naoroji's thinking about the necessity for Indianization in the civil service and princely sovereignty. Bell believed that the native states offered the best opportunity for the regeneration of India because it was a field in which indigenous agency could be most freely implemented.[50]

Indian agency in government was essential because the problem of bureaucratic rule in British India was that an 'administration' managed the territory but did not behave like a 'government'. If a state were an individual, its 'government' would be like a person's 'constitution', defined as 'that more or less perfect co-ordination of all the animal, moral and intellectual energies, under the guidance of a central organ, upon which, in a community as in a person, depends healthy and harmonious life'. Administration might supply the basic necessities of the body, like nutrition and daily ablutions, but it could not improve its constitution.[51] On the other hand, princes empowered with full executive authority, influenced by liberal education, could become reformers of their respective states' constitutions.[52] Indianizing native administration and the civil service, Bell claimed, would reverse the moral degradation inflicted on depoliticized Indian elites.[53] Bell hinted, in a diluted form of Naoroji's moral drain, that inducting the native elites into the covenanted civil service (the largely European and well-paid upper echelons of the bureaucracy) would cultivate higher material wants, augment consumption and encourage industrialization in order to pay for them.[54] Naoroji and Bell disseminated their views on princely states in the East India Association, imploring

[49] Aya Ikegame, *Princely India Re-imagined: A Historical Anthropology of Mysore from 1799 to the Present* (London: Routledge, 2013), pp. 16–30.
[50] Evans Bell, *The Rajah and the Principality of Mysore* (London: T. Richards, 1865), pp. 46–7.
[51] Evans Bell, *Our Great Vassal Empire* (London: Trübner & Co, 1870), p. 6.
[52] Evans Bell, *Remarks on the Mysore Blue Book* (London: Trübner & Co, 1866), p. 53.
[53] Evans Bell, *The English in India: Letters from Nagpore, Written in 1857–58* (London: John Chapman, 1859), pp. 53, 124.
[54] Ibid., pp. 66, 97.

Britain to abide by non-interference in its treaties with native states, and suggesting neutral tribunals to arbitrate between the British government and the native states when conflicts arose.[55]

Naoroji also undertook agency work on behalf of Indian princes independently of Evans Bell, aiding the Gujarati and Kathiawadi states with which he was familiar and earning 100,000 rupees from 1871 to 1872 to fund his East India Association.[56] Between 1868 and 1869, Naoroji also represented the Rao of Cutch's interests to the British government. The Rao objected to the British contravening their pledges of non-interference in the criminal and civil jurisdiction of the state laid down by the treaty of December 1819.[57] The Government of Bombay accused the Rao of misgovernment of his *bhayads*, the kinsmen of the top chiefs of the state who shared the Rao's ancestry (the word literally means 'brothers'). The Rao insisted that customarily the *bhayads* were 'zamindar vassals' and that the British attempt to secure to them 'all but sovereign positions' over their lands was 'to introduce innovations directly opposed to the usages of the country'.[58] Naoroji corroborated the Rao's objections, claiming that elevation of the *zamindars* entrenched a decentred feudal hierarchy and was inimical to the growth of a spontaneous and contractual 'constitutionalism' between the people and the Cutch state.[59] Naoroji viewed a rational and integrative Indian executive as an indispensable tool for defining the parameters of the Indian social. He pointed out that the first rule of the Government's draft agreement would disintegrate the social fabric of the state. It proposed to apportion civil jurisdiction to the *bhayads* in accordance with the amount of property they owned while fixing the royal council's powers to

---

[55] Evans Bell, 'Claims of the Natives of India to a Share in the Executive Government of Their Country', *JEIA* 2 (1868), pp. 182–300; 'On Trust as the Basis for Imperial Policy', *JEIA* 6 (1872), pp. 145–74; 'A Privy Council for India', *JEIA* 9 (1876), pp. 289–325.

[56] Naoroji to Dewan of Cutch, 5 September 1871, New Delhi, Nehru Memorial Museum and Library [NMML], Dadabhai Naoroji Collection, vol. I, p. 493; Masani, *Dadabhai Naoroji*, p. 137; Col. Robert Phayre to the governor of Bombay, 29 April 1873, BLAPAC, *Baroda Administration Report, 1872–73* and *1873–74*, IOR/R/2/481/55, pp. 74–5; Phayre to the secretary of the government political department, Poona, 15 August 1874, Mumbai, Maharashtra State Archive [MSA], political department: Baroda, 1874/11, ff. 99–103.

[57] C. Gonne, secretary to the Government of Bombay, to the secretary to the Government of India, 7 September 1868, BLAPAC, IOR/L/PS/6/560, coll. 12, f. 3; John Clunes, *An Historical Sketch of the Princes of India: Stipendiary, Subsidiary, Protected, Tributary, and Feudatory* (London: A. Shortrede, 1833), p. 110.

[58] Clunes, *An Historical Sketch of the Princes of India*, pp. 111–12; Khureeta from H. H. Rao Shree Pragmuljee of Kutch to the governor of Bombay, 13 August 1868, BLAPAC, IOR/L/PS/6/560, Coll. 12, f. 4.

[59] Dadabhai Naoroji memorandum, 3 November 1868, Dadabhai Naoroji memorandum, 3 November 1868, BLAPAC, IOR/L/PS/6/560, Coll. 12, f. 11.

intercede in *bhayad* affairs according to the 'different classes' of these notables. However, Rule 7 of the agreement undermined this principle because it allowed the British to arbitrarily elevate a *bhayad* controlling, for instance, only five villages to the jurisdictional authority of one governing twelve.[60] Naoroji worried that 'if some bhayads are sufficiently ambitious and clever', they might 'manage under Rule 7 to convert the whole territory into a few first class jurisdictions and leave to the Council to look after and control murder, homicides and sentence to death only'.[61]

It was certainly true that the royal executive needed modernizing into 'new administrative departments', but to disperse sovereign authority to local feudal hierarchies was 'a retrograde movement' because it was only an 'efficient administration' and 'strong central power' that was capable of 'developing the resources of the territory to the best advantage'. It is important to note that Naoroji was opposed to not the status of the *bhayad*s as local notables, or their wealth, but simply the location of sovereign power, its managing of economic affairs and the consequences for civil society. Quite the opposite, Naoroji was attentive to the fact that the *bhayad*s were the largest single contributors (40 per cent of total income) to Cutch's treasury. That they were indigenous elites contributing to a pot of capital that returned to a central treasury which might be used to further augment the productive capacities of the people was not lost on Naoroji. He had no qualms about *bhayad*s properly educated in the science of government and political economy employed on the royal council or in the ranks of modern administrative departments. The net result of that would be the socially productive distribution of *bhayad* resources throughout the territory as an investment multiplier. For Naoroji, this was the foundation of an elite, public-spirited and socially reproductive administration.[62]

As the *dewan* of Baroda between 1873 and 1875, Naoroji had an opportunity to put his theory, that a rational and public-spirited bureaucracy run by Indians would be more socially productive than the European colonial state, into practice. So important was the task of turning Baroda into an exemplar of Indian self-government that Naoroji referred to it as 'the cause'.[63] Naoroji was offered the *dewan*'s role in Malharrao IX's Baroda as the maharajah's administration came under intense scrutiny for profligate spending, excessive taxation and arbitrary corporal punishment of political enemies. In the winter of 1873, the Government

[60] Ibid., ff. 11–12.
[61] Ibid., f. 13.
[62] Ibid., ff. 13–17; Clunes, *Princes of India*, p. 111.
[63] Masani, *Dadabhai Naoroji*, p. 148.

of India appointed a commission to investigate.[64] The 'Baroda crisis' from 1873 to 1877 ultimately ended in the attempted poisoning of the British Resident, Colonel Robert Phayre, and the deposition of the maharajah in 1875. As this court intrigue came to a head, Sir Lewis Pelly was appointed to replace the incompetent Colonel Phayre in late 1874. The details of the whole crisis are too lengthy to enter into here; what is germane is that Naoroji was asked to act as *dewan* by Malharrao in 1873 alongside the former prime minister who was given the honorary title of 'Pritinidhe'. As the British government rightly guessed, this was an attempt by the corrupt Baroda court to hide behind Naoroji's reputation while continuing their former practices and obstructing and obfuscating the commission's task.[65] Nonetheless, the government was keen to give Naoroji an opportunity to reform the state despite vociferous objections to Naoroji's appointment by Phayre.[66]

In late 1873, Naoroji accepted the maharajah's offer after much consideration. He was concerned that he could 'do no good unless' he had 'the moral and official support of the Bombay Government'. Encouragement from Erskine Perry and Bartle Frere allayed these fears.[67] Naoroji arrived in Baroda a fortnight before the commission completed its review.[68] His first executive decision was an act upholding princely sovereignty by interrogating the viceroy on the right of the British to appoint a commission into the domestic affairs of a 'sovereign' state.[69] The commission's recommendations, particularly of reducing taxes on Brahmin notables, were a foregone conclusion by this stage, so Naoroji set about appointing

[64] Report by the viceroy, Lord Northbrook, giving his view on the conduct of affairs in Baroda, 9 April 1875, BLAPAC, Lewis Pelly Papers, MSS Eur F126/93, ff. 1–2; Philip Wodehouse, governor of Bombay to Phayre, 22 April 1873, MSA, political department: Baroda, 1873/11, ff. 33–8.

[65] The secretary to the government of Bombay to the secretary of the government of India, 5 March 1874, BLAPAC, *Bluebook Containing Report of Commissioner Appointed to Enquire into the Administration of Baroda with Connected Correspondence*, IOR/R/2/536/312A 1873–5, p. 64.

[66] Wodehouse to Phayre, 14 August 1874, MSA, political department: Baroda, 1874/11, ff. 42–3; for a general survey of events and varying interpretations of the Baroda crisis, see E. C. Moulton, 'British India and the Baroda Crisis 1874–5: A Problem in Princely State relations', *Canadian Journal of History* 3, no. 1 (1968), pp. 68–94; Ian Copland, 'The Baroda Crisis of 1873–7: A Study in Governmental Rivalry', *Modern Asian Studies* 11, no. 2 (1968), pp. 97–123; Judith Rowbotham, 'Miscarriage of Justice? Postcolonial Reflections on the "Trial" of the Maharajah of Baroda, 1875', *Liverpool Law Review* 28, no. 3 (2007), pp. 377–403.

[67] Naoroji to Erskine Perry, DNP, 6 December 1873, N-1 (28).

[68] Phayre to the secretary of the government political department, 16 June 1874, *Baroda Administration Reports, 1872–3* and *1873–4*, pp. 268–9.

[69] Quoting Naoroji's letter to the viceroy on 31 December 1873 in Phayre to governor general of Bombay, 2 November 1874, ibid., p. 431.

a competent team of bourgeois professionals to assist him in reforming the state.[70] He asked Shahabuddin, the former *dewan* of Cutch, and the barristers B. M. Wagle and H. A. Wadia to take up the offices of revenue commissioner, joint supreme court judge and joint chief of police respectively.[71] The three of them had also been members of Naoroji's association and were dubbed the 'East India Association School' of administration by Phayre.[72] Far from being an empty epithet, as soon as Shahabuddin arrived in Baroda he was met with a copy of Naoroji's drain theory, which he subsequently published in the local newspaper, *Gaekwari Dawn*.[73]

In Baroda, as in Cutch, Naoroji was confronted with local notables who were securing as much freedom from state control and taxation as possible. The Bijapur *thakurs* objected to the state taxing their villagers directly in place of the system of revenue farming that allowed the *thakurs* to act as collectors, leading to considerable abuses of power, blackmail and disproportionate exaction from the labourers.[74] However, one of the reasons the *thakurs* exploited the *ryots* was because of the 'accession nazarana', a state tax on hereditary titles at the point of their inheritance, which was in essence a form of secular simony levied on the landholding class by the state and which the commission had wanted to abolish.[75] Naoroji and his colleagues were circumspect about relinquishing this important source of state revenue, not least because it was a way of reclaiming the unearned exactions upon labour and returning it to them via productive investment. By the late 1870s, 10 per cent of all Baroda's land had been alienated under this system, and Naoroji's desire to institute central control over the territory's economic surplus brought him into conflict with Phayre.[76] Naoroji told Phayre that immediate cessation of collecting the *nazarana* would have 'a very bad political effect' and that for the time being he would enter it into the official accounts as *baki* (outstanding balance). As Phayre reported, Naoroji deemed this measure expedient in order to 'maintain His Highness' sovereignty' in matters of domestic economy. Thus, at Naoroji's behest,

[70] *Report of the Commission Appointed to Inquire into the Administration of the Baroda State* (London: Her Majesty's Stationary Office, 1875), BLAPAC, IOR/L/PARL/2/215, p. 72.

[71] Phayre to the secretary of the government political department, 16 June 1874, *Baroda Administration Reports* for *1872–3* and *1873–4*, p. 289.

[72] Ibid., pp. 269–70.

[73] K. Shahabuddin to Naoroji, DNP, 24 June 1874, S-97.

[74] *Report of the Baroda Enquiry Commission on the Administration of the Government of Malhar Rao, Gaekwar of Baroda*, February 1874, BLAPAC, Lewis Pelly Papers, MSS Eur F126/78, p. 7; H. Fukazawa, 'Agrarian Relations. Western India', in Kumar and Desai, eds., *The Cambridge Economic History of India*, p. 189.

[75] Phayre to the secretary of the government of Bombay, 27 May 1874, *Bluebook Containing Report of Commissioner*, p. 351.

[76] Fukazawa, 'Agrarian Relations: Western India', p. 190.

Shahabuddin demanded that the tax be paid but that the state allow ample time for existing arrears to be cleared.[77]

In 1874, the land revenue settlement for Baroda was also due for review. The level had been set in 1864 when the price of agricultural products, especially cotton, was significantly higher because of the American Civil War and hence the prevailing revenue demand was regarded as too exacting.[78] As a result of the inability of landowners to pay over the past decade, the treasury had arrears of 8 million rupees. Naoroji's initial attempts at retrenchment in what he considered to be unproductive expenditure were met with opposition from British officials. The *sirdar*s (nobles with military functions) had their *nemnook*s (allowances paid to office holders) reduced by a quarter on Naoroji's order. However, there was significant opposition from the nobles who made representations to the British agent. Additionally, the *sirdar*s were less creditworthy in the eyes of the *sowcar*s (moneylenders), thus affecting their economic prosperity and, in the eyes of the British, their loyalty and military usefulness. Consequently, Naoroji was forced to rescind the order.[79]

There were also allegations that Phayre had been accepting bribes from the *sirdar* class to increase their allowances. Even before Naoroji's administration it seems Phayre had been actively usurping the sovereign power of the maharajah, even using the power of the residency office to remove a village in Koellee without consulting the royal court.[80] Pelly admitted that Phayre was using the residency as a 'sort of Court of Appeal' against Naoroji's reforms.[81] Naoroji's efforts were thus blocked and sabotaged from the outset since Phayre feared a rival to his proxy government, dubbing Naoroji a 'political adventurer'.[82] Phayre preferred Naoroji's predecessor, the pliable and deferential Nanasahib Khanvilkar, because he was 'an easy going, quiet man', 'gentlemanly in his manners' and a 'good medium of

[77] Phayre to the secretary of the government political department, Poona, 7 October 1874, MSA, political department: Baroda, 1874/11, ff. 20–38.

[78] *Report of the Baroda Enquiry Commission*, p. 41; Minute by the viceroy, 29 April 1875, BLAPAC, Lewis Pelly Papers, MSS Eur F126/88, ff. 22–6.

[79] Lewis Pelly to Lord Northbrook, 13 December 1874, BLAPAC, Lewis Pelly Papers, MSS Eur F126/83, ff. 2–3; Memorandum, 2 December 1874, BLAPAC, Lewis Pelly Papers, F126/81, f. 120.

[80] Representation from Atmaram Jugannath Burway against the arbitrary proceedings of Colonel Phayre, the Resident, addressed to the governor of Bombay, 20 October 1873, MSA, political department: Baroda, 1870/13, ff. 89–110.

[81] Lewis Pelly to the secretary of the Government of India, 7 January 1875, ibid., f. 83.

[82] Phayre to the governor of Bombay, 29 April 1873, *Baroda Administration Reports, 1872–3* and *1873–4*, p. 73.

communication with the Resident and English officers'.[83] Naoroji, on the other hand, tersely dubbed Nanasahib and his colleagues 'informers'.[84]

Naoroji did succeed in instituting some reforms. Shahabuddin's initial plans for rationalizing the revenue system were to extend it across the entire state and to take half of the revenue demand in kind rather than in coin. Malharrao rejected this scheme on the advice of his former courtiers.[85] However, the agreed revenue code did reduce the overall demands on the *ryot* and removed the opportunities for oppression through tax farming by introducing harsh penalties for abuse.[86] Before Naoroji resigned in December 1874 due to endless obstructions, the state had been divided into four administrative districts, each with a district commissioner reporting to a central executive headed by the *dewan* and the monarch. Given Naoroji's antipathy to unproductive financial institutions and their practices, the outlying city and state banks were abolished and amalgamated into a central state treasury.[87] The judicial system was modernized by founding a high court, a small cause court and a police court, all of which employed new head officers in each department.[88] Judicial reforms were generally intended to rationalize the administration of justice after Malharrao's arbitrary imprisonments and floggings had caused indignation. However, it is likely that Naoroji also hoped that the reforms would ensure the credibility and therefore continued independence of Baroda's justice system. In recent years Baroda's sovereignty had been eroded by the practice of neighbouring British village police pursuing criminals who robbed British subjects into Malharrao's territory because the king's justice could not be relied upon.[89] Given Naoroji's criticisms of the British civil service as a major channel of the drain, it is telling that ascertaining the competence and salaries of

---

[83] Phayre to the governor of Bombay, 25 March 1873, 'Correspondence on Deaths of Bhow Scindia and Govind Naik', *Report of the Commission Appointed to Inquire into the Administration of the Baroda State*, p. 7.

[84] Dadabhai Naoroji, 'The Baroda Administration in 1874', in Dadabhai Naoroji, *Essays, Speeches, Addresses and Writings*, p. 394.

[85] Phayre to the secretary of the government political department, 16 June 1874, *Baroda Administration Reports, 1872–3* and *1873–4*, pp. 292–3.

[86] Translation of durbar yad 1458, 17 August 1874, MSA, political department: Baroda, 1874/11, ff. 150–3.

[87] Lewis Pelly to Lord Northbrook, 28 December 1874, BLAPAC, Lewis Pelly Papers, MSS Eur F126/83, f. 6; To the secretary of the foreign department, Government of India, (undated) 1875, BLAPAC, *Baroda Administration Report, 1875*, IOR/R/2/488/73, p. 4.

[88] *The Pioneer*, 3 February 1874.

[89] The political secretary of the government of Bombay to the Baroda residency, 28 September 1874, MSA, political department: Baroda, 1874/15, f. 168; for Baroda's 'quasi-sovereignty', see Lauren Benton, *A Search for Sovereignty: Law and Geography in European Empires, 1400–1900* (Cambridge: Cambridge University Press, 2010), chs. 5–6.

Baroda's administrative officials was one of Naoroji's first acts as *dewan*.[90] From Naoroji's perspective his most successful and significant reform was the creation of a meritocratic and generously salaried indigenous administrative service purged of simony and nepotism.[91]

After his resignation, Naoroji wanted his highly publicized episode as *dewan* to be an example to other native states, and as such he continuously, though unsuccessfully, pushed for his version of events (as opposed to Phayre's) to be officially accepted as a parliamentary blue book.[92] Naoroji's experience and reforms in Baroda convinced him that a just legal system and a centralized administration could augment the state income for productive investment while also reducing the disproportionate extraction of surplus from the poorest *ryots*.[93] The key to successful government in the princely states was having 'well paid, competent and honest officials' because '[n]o matter how good laws may be they are non-effective without proper men to give effect to them'. Naoroji would advise the future monarch Sayajirao III that educated officials were essential to a government that wished to promote constitutionalism in the face of British strategies, entrenched feudal hierarchy and social disintegration. The creation of a professional, public-spirited and propertied indigenous bureaucracy from the revenues generated by labour and fair trade was of paramount importance. Naoroji surmised that an indigenous middle-class technocracy would not abuse their status for private gain nor would there be an exodus of salaried wealth from the territory upon retirement. Public-spiritedness and rational administration brought unfair exactions on labour under control, allowing peasants to accumulate while also securing a sufficient re-investable surplus for the state to invest in socially generative institutions. Leaving princely administration behind, Naoroji would continue to exhort Baroda's rulers from afar that it was 'an absolute economic, or material, industrial and moral necessity' that Baroda's bureaucracy originated in the 'territory itself'.[94]

## Indianization of the Civil Service and 'Self-Government'

Dadabhai Naoroji had campaigned on behalf of Indian candidates to have the same access to the Indian civil service as their European counterparts throughout the 1850s. He argued in general terms that the setting of the maximum age of

---

90 *The Pioneer*, 20 January 1874.

91 Translation of durbar yad 1460, 17 August 1874, MSA, political department: Baroda, 1874/11, ff. 154–6.

92 George Hamilton, undersecretary of state for India to Naoroji, 18 April 1877, DNP, H-11; Naoroji to W. Taylor, 15 March 1879, NAI, Dadabhai Naoroji Papers, N-1 (56).

93 Naoroji, 'The Baroda Administration in 1874', pp. 395–6.

94 Naoroji to M. M. Mehta, secretary to the Gaikwad, 20 November 1900, DNP, N-1 (2676).

applicants to twenty-one debarred Indians 'who have to struggle under the peculiar disadvantages' of having, first, to educate themselves to the standard of their British counterparts and, second, of securing the necessary funding and community sanction to travel abroad.[95] Naoroji regarded Indian access to the civil service as the silver bullet for alleviating the drain and making India safe for commercial society. The anglicized colonial state suffered from the same defects as the corruptly managed princely state under British domination that Naoroji had direct experience of. Highly remunerated British bureaucrats were the pernicious unnatural mechanism by which the bulk of Indian-generated value was coercively exported abroad through the council bill system. To add insult to injury, this political elite was also a rentier class that consumed a part of that wealth abroad in the form of inflated salaries and pensions.

Although they were entitled to compete in England on a par with Europeans, religious and financial obstacles prevented Indians from travelling abroad to sit the civil service exams.[96] At any rate, only subordinate and modestly paid junior positions were available to Indians in the uncovenanted service. Though a statutory service was established in 1870 for Indians, it was only via official nomination, the majority of Indians remaining uncovenanted. This subordinate service, British officials argued, gave greater scope for Indian professionals because there were 352 positions available in Bombay compared to only 84 appointments in the senior covenanted service.[97] Privately, British officials considered the racial and cultural unity of the covenanted servants as indispensable to the 'common feeling and common interest' that underpinned the 'esprit de corps of the service'.[98] Simultaneous exams held in Britain and India, Naoroji thought, enabled Indians to compete on an equal footing with Britons for access to the covenanted section. This was paramount even if in gaining access on equal terms meant the abolition of statutory appointments for Indians in the lower echelons of the service and potentially reducing the total number of Indians employed.[99]

---

[95] Naoroji to Lord Stanley, secretary of state for India, 18 March 1859, DNP, N-1 (12); John Melvill, India Office to Naoroji, 26 March 1859, DNP, I-13 (2).

[96] Naoroji to Kharshedji Cama, 4 June 1856, DNP, N-1 (1).

[97] Notes from Crawley Boevey's 'Natives of India and the Civil Service, 1884', BLAPAC, Arthur Godley Papers, MSS Eur F102/45B, ff. 172–4.

[98] Lee Warner, Bombay civil service, to secretary of the government general department, 28 June 1875, BLAPAC, Lee Warner Papers, F92/2.

[99] Naoroji, 'The Indian Civil Service', in Naoroji *Essays, Speeches, Addresses, and Writings*, p. 352; Naoroji's evidence, section II, witness XXVL, 28 January 1887, in *Proceedings of the Public Service Commission: Bombay Presidency (including Sind)*, vol. IV, sections I–III (Calcutta: Superintendent of Government Publishing, 1887), BLAPAC, IOR/L/PARL/2/239/1, pp. 126–9.

Critiquing a proposed reform to the uncovenanted service by the Secretary of State for India in 1870, Naoroji noted how the plan transferred 221 better-remunerated uncovenanted offices held by Indians into the covenanted service. The effect was that fewer Indians would be employed because of the European advantage in competing for that service. More importantly, the highest salary attainable in the uncovenanted section would be reduced to 500 rupees per month compared to the 4,000 rupees per month currently attainable for the most senior officer.[100] British rationalization of the scheme insisted that because there were more Indians employed, they took home a larger share of the overall wage bill. Naoroji retorted that this was still 'unfair' and one should compare 'the higher posts only' in which the annual salary was 1,000 pounds or more.[101]

What Naoroji hoped for was the accumulation of Indian-produced agrarian capital in the hands of a counter-class of indigenous bureaucrats which could be deployed to undo the rusticating logic of colonial capital under the superintendence of a largely anglicized colonial state. Even at the scanty 'rate of production' achieved under British rule, some of the 'yearly abstraction' by the state would be saved and used as an 'addition to capital'.[102] Naoroji thus proclaimed that it was an issue of 'life and death' for 'the whole of British India' and that the Indianization of the services represented a '*complete gain* to the whole extent of salary'.[103] It was the freedom to use agricultural revenue in Indian industry or state-led agricultural improvement that made 'all the difference' by returning surplus value to the labourers themselves. Expressing this in distinctly neo-Roman terms, Naoroji wrote that this was the key distinction that set 'bleeding poverty' and 'British slavery' apart from 'citizenship'.[104]

In pushing this agenda, Naoroji and some of his colleagues saw themselves as guardians of the British Whig tradition. However, they also realized that the restitution of English liberty in their age was to occur first in India, not Europe. It is for this reason that they framed the policies of the colonial bureaucracy as

[100] Dadabhai Naoroji, 'Another Rendering of the Patronage Despatch: To the Editor of the Times', *Times of India*, 4 June 1872.
[101] 'Evidence of Mr. S. Jacob, C.S.I.', *Royal Commission on the Administration of the Expenditure of India* (Calcutta: Superintendent of Government Publishing, 1895), BLAPAC, IOR L/AG/49/5 part I, p. 325.
[102] Naoroji, 'Poverty of India, Part I', p. 212.
[103] Discussion at a meeting of the East India Association at which M. A. K. Connell read a paper on the 'Indian Civil Service', July 1887, in Naoroji, *Essays, Speeches, Addresses, and Writings*, p. 378; Naoroji, 'Third Day's Proceedings at the First Indian National Congress', 30 December 1885, in ibid., p. 330 (emphasis in original).
[104] Naoroji to the undersecretary of state for India, 26 May 1900 and 4 September 1900, BLAPAC, IOR/L/PJ/6/555, f. 2168.

'inveterate' and 'obdurate Conservatism' to be challenged by Indian liberalism.[105] What is more, Bombay had an especially important role to play since it was the 'centre of the best political thought in India'. Unlike that other locus of colonial criticism, Bengal, the 'Deccan Sirdars' co-operated with Bombay traders, native princes and middle-class advocates of the rural labourer in organizations like the Poona Sarvajanik Sabha. Western India had less of the 'factionalism' of landlord versus peasant that led to a 'self-destructive' politics. Bombay's 'broad political views' were defined by a merchant-led united front against a species of Indian Tory Party that was epitomized by a colonial state that seemed to characterize all of the classic Whig bugbears of coercive government, a corrupt landed gentry and an irrational 'un-British' attitude associated with Catholic clericalism.[106]

In this regard, Naoroji's critique of the colonial state had considerable moral overtones that went beyond straightforward allegations of economic mismanagement. In European thought, the socially disintegrating effects of modern commerce and international trade were countered by the nineteenth-century rise of economic nationalism. In Germany, Friedrich List's 'economic science of states' institutionally and geographically inscribed a national political economy through doctrines of industrial nationalization, national customs unions and preferential tariffs. However, sociality depended upon accepting the ethno-cultural nation as a counteracting force to the cosmopolitics of the international free market.[107] For Naoroji, it was ethnicity and religion that were antagonistic and, when coupled with economic slavery, prevented a commercial civility from emerging. Oriented differently to the German Historical School of economics then, Naoroji thought that membership of a largely Indianized civil service – that is to say, the executive power of the colonial state – had its own socially transformative power to re-organize the antagonistic divisions of religion, caste and community into a pluralist commercial society. This is where Naoroji's concept of the economic drain dovetailed with that of the moral drain.[108]

Naoroji identified the moral drain as the flight of 'all experience of knowledge and statesmanship' and 'of high scientific or learned professions' as Europeans

---

[105] 'The Inarticulate Stage of Native Politics and the Next Reform', *Indian Spectator*, 10 February 1884.

[106] 'Bombay as "the Centre of the Best Political Thought in India"', *Indian Spectator*, 9 September 1883.

[107] Istvan Hont, *The Jealousy of Trade: International Competition and the Nation-State in Historical Perspective* (Cambridge, MA: Cambridge University Press, 2005), pp. 141–2, 150.

[108] Moral drain described as colonial officials returning to Britain; see Bayly, *Recovering Liberties*, p. 197.

retired.[109] However, far from being just a brain drain, what Naoroji lamented was that every country except India possessed a bureaucratic clerisy of middle-class professionals who made natural governors. European monopoly of the colonial state precluded Indian middle classes from receiving the instruction and example of 'nobility of intellect and soul' that Indian state officials might otherwise acquire and which Naoroji had tried to assemble in Baroda.[110] Dinshaw Wacha strongly supported Naoroji's identification of the moral drain from India and pressed for simultaneous examinations instead of official appointments on the grounds that this elevated whole 'classes' by example rather than a few select 'individuals'. Meritocracy was a collective affair that forced the various communities 'to improve themselves' and 'put their shoulders to the wheel' with the most 'advanced' vanguard classes leading the way.[111] Even as the Muslim gentry voiced their concern that simultaneous exams would lead to the Hinduization of the bureaucracy, Naoroji insisted that the duty of all professional classes was to represent the social development of their respective communities. As such, the Indian intelligentsia regarded themselves as a vanguard class engaging in meaningful liberal acts in order to encourage the masses and even disgruntled elites in other communities 'to be true to themselves'.[112] There were after all, as Malabari observed, Muslims from 'the old literary classes and nobility' who could successfully compete for the civil service and be exemplars for their own community.[113]

## Indian Political Economy

By the late nineteenth century, a number of Hindu interlocutors had also joined in Naoroji's investigations into Indian political economy.[114] Mahadev Govind Ranade had acknowledged Naoroji's drain in 1892 but, unlike Naoroji, launched a much broader attack on the fundamental principles of classical political economy,

[109] Naoroji, 'Poverty of India, Part I', p. 212.
[110] Ibid., p. 213.
[111] Wacha to Naoroji, 11 October 1896, in Patwardan, ed., *Dadabhai Naoroji Correspondence*, vol. II, part II, pp. 514–5; Wacha's evidence, section II, witness LXXVI, 29 January 1887, *Proceedings of the Public Service Commission*, pp. 363–4; Naoroji made the same argument in 'Replies to Questions Put by The Public Service Commission', 4 January 1887, DNP, N-1 (679).
[112] Malabari to Naoroji, 31 August 1893, DNP, M-32 (354).
[113] Malabari's evidence, section III, witness XXI, replies received by persons not examined by the commission in *Proceedings of the Public Service Commission*, p. 121.
[114] For a more detailed overview of these individuals, see Vikram Visana, 'Decolonising Capital: Indian Political Economy in the Shadow of Empire', in Maureen E. Ruprecht Fadem and Michael O'Sullivan, eds., *The Economics of Empire: Genealogies of Capital and the Colonial Encounter* (London: Routledge, 2020), ch. 2.

especially the fictitious notion of individual contract.[115] As we saw in Chapter 3, Ranade's overweening desire to renovate Hindu religion meant that he never countenanced a wholesale critique of its social relations. As such, he subordinated his economics to the ethical world of Hindu life in which status and the Hindu undivided family not only did, but ought to triumph over contract.[116] Indeed, this was also true of the Bengali Hindu Romesh Chunder Dutt to whom Naoroji's drain is often erroneously compared. Unlike Naoroji, Dutt's drain focused exclusively on the revenue burden of Indian agriculturalists and did not imagine a disordered uncivil liberal capitalism restored to an equitable logic through simultaneous examinations or Indianization of the bureaucracy – a fact Naoroji demanded he consider before he falsely equated their respective economic histories of India under the British.[117] Moreover, the life of the 'Indian village weaver' and his family was regarded as fundamentally more 'responsible and dignified' than his proletarian counterpart.[118] In this echo of Henry Maine's sociology, Indian co-operation and social harmony were existing faculties of the wider population.

What Ranade wanted was a means to coax capital inefficiently hoarded in urban banks to the countryside through initiatives like rural credit cooperatives and the elevation of the concentrated resources of the colonial state to the 'sole customer' of the land. In this latter instance, Ranade had something like the Dutch Java culture system in mind, whereby European private enterprise made cash payments for crops with money loaned by the government but also with the state as the guaranteed buyer. This had the double advantage of using government loans as a way of paying the farmer a minimum from which he might pay the revenue demand. Moreover, the fixing of prices would ensure long-term stability and that the labourer would get more than if he was at the mercy of the market.[119] In this regard, Ranade thought Naoroji's drain was overblown since India was not suffering from an absolute dearth of resources but merely their imbalanced allocation.[120] However, as Anirban Karak has recently observed, this left Ranade's

[115] M. G. Ranade, 'Indian Political Economy', in Mahadev Govind Ranade, *Essays on Indian Economics* (Madras: G. A. Natesan & Co, 1906), pp. 8–9, 25.

[116] M. G. Ranade, 'The Re-organisation of Rural Credit in India', in Ranade, *Essays on Indian Economics*, p. 45.

[117] R. C. Dutt to Naoroji, (undated) July 1903, DNP, D-161 (24); R. C. Dutt, *India in the Victorian Age: An Economic History of the People* (London: Kegan Paul, Trench, Trübner & Co, 1904), pp. 343–4.

[118] Romesh C. Dutt, 'Industrial India: A Review', *Indian Review* 5, no. 7 (1904), p. 440.

[119] M. G. Ranade, 'Netherlands India and the Culture System', in Ranade, *Essays on Indian Economics*, pp. 70–104.

[120] M. G. Ranade, 'Industrial Conference, 1890', in Ranade, *Essays on Indian Economics*, p. 200.

modernizing project largely unfinished since he was unable to resolve his status-based Indian political economy – and its caste and gender discrimination – with the modern ideals of freedom and equality that his wider liberalism demanded.[121]

If Ranade believed that capital was languishing in urban banks, then Kashinath Trimbak Telang thought the customary commerce of the Indian countryside was preventing investment from feeding the modern industry that would accelerate India's journey from status to contract. Since the countryside was 'stereotyped by custom', there was 'so little knowledge both of the real resources of the country, and of the proper mode of developing those resources', Telang thought a regime of industrial protectionism and subsidy would not only insulate nascent Indian industries from British competition but also redirect cautious capital from traditional channels to 'modernising' ones in the cities.[122] In this regard, Telang's views differed starkly from Ranade. While the latter dabbled in social reform and economic reform in his ambiguous project to both liberalize India and retain some of the character of Indian custom, Telang had a much more Naorojian attitude towards the transformative power of capital. If rural wealth reinforced customary relationships, as Telang thought, this was 'not in fact capital strictly speaking' until it was employed in the urban industry.[123] Telang called upon the state to nurture Indian modernity by using protectionism to redirect rural capital but, unlike Ranade, not through state ownership or state trading. Like Naoroji, Telang did not regard the state as separate from society and in fact thought its predominant role was to usher illegitimate capital into legitimate avenues that encouraged sociality.[124]

## Conclusion

It was not until 1903, in a message to the Madras Congress, that Naoroji shifted the discussion from partial Indianization of the civil service to Indian 'self-government under British paramountcy' or 'swaraj'.[125] Naoroji officially announced this as the goal of the Indian National Congress at its 1906 meeting in Calcutta. He seems

[121] Anirban Karak, 'What Was "Indian" Political Economy? On the Separation of the "Social", the "Economic" and the "Ethical" in Indian Nationalist Thought, 1892–1948', *Modern Asian Studies* 55, no. 1 (2021), pp. 75–115.

[122] K. T. Telang, 'Free Trade and Protection from an Indian Point of View', in K. T. Telang, *Selected Writings and Speeches* (Bombay: Manoranjan Press, 1916), pp. 116–18.

[123] Ibid., p. 117.

[124] For an opposing view on the primacy of the political as a separate domain, see Niraja Gopal Jayal, *Citizenship and Its Discontents: An Indian History* (New Delhi: Permanent Black, 2013), pp. 121–2.

[125] 'A Call to Arms', II, *Hindustan Review and Kayastha Samachar*, December 1903, p. 474.

to have been encouraged to speak publicly about this following the Bishop of Bombay's sermon in 1901 in which he used the same phrase to define the end goal of India's 'resuscitated national existence'.[126] To ensure the British public was aware that other Britons were advocating home rule for India, Naoroji insisted the sermon be circulated in *India*, the British Committee of the Indian National Congress' journal.[127]

It is important to note that what Naoroji termed 'responsible self-government for India' did not imply self-determination, much less universal suffrage. Nor can it really be regarded as the first step in a nationalist genealogy that culminates in the Indian National Congress' 1928 demand for *purna swaraj* (or complete independence – politically, economically and culturally from Britain). In fact, Naoroji compared Indian 'self-government' to the status that Indian native states like Baroda and Mysore enjoyed. They were self-governing because the use of indigenous officials put an end to the British capacity to dominate their economic affairs, but in all other respects this system of indirect rule entailed a subordination to British political sovereignty.[128] Thus, Indian self-government was intended as a developmentalist project in which Naoroji was quite happ. to accept that India would have a very narrow franchise for the foreseeable future until an Indian bureaucracy had sufficiently mitigated the effects of the drain and elevated the country to a proper commercial society. In calculating the rate of this change, Naoroji noted that in Britain the 10-pound householder franchise had only been enacted in 1884 giving 60 per cent of the male population the vote in a country where the annual per capita income averaged 40 pounds. Indian income was still 20–25 times smaller than this.

Indian society required a lengthy period of elite stewardship before the indigenized state might undo the disintegrating effects of British economic monopoly, and only then might Indians be moulded into a unitary people with a 'truly national character' that could authorize its own sovereignty.[129] Naoroji drew these conclusions from a congeries of individual and community experiences over the preceding decades but also from the careful deconstruction of colonial political economy. The philosophical discovery of the colonial state as a political and economic monopoly was, however, a seminal moment in the history of Indian

[126] *India*, 17 May 1901.
[127] Gordon Hewart to Naoroji, 14 May 1901, DNP, H-97 (4).
[128] 'Responsible Self-government for India', DNP, notes and jottings, group 7: political, serial number 1.
[129] 'Self-government for India like Other Colonies', DNP, notes and jottings, group 7: political, serial number 2.

political thought. In Bombay, it allowed for the growth of a capitalist critique (as opposed to a critique of capitalism) of the colonial project that simultaneously presented an integrative political programme of generating sociality without resorting to the ethno-cultural or religious pigeonholing of particular communities. Moreover, with this discovery, the numerous native states of India hooved into view as an alternative model for upholding natural economic laws and fostering commercial society.

In the end, Naoroji's settled policy for India was that the educated elements of the country's many communities, in competing for the civil service and directing the ship of state, would put an end to European economic domination and form a new class of mercantile public servant 'working together for the common good' and labouring to 'improve good feeling' between India's communities.[130] However, these Indian perspectives on the relationship between labour, capital and the state under colonial monopoly also influenced Naoroji's attitudes towards the situation in the British Isles. How Naoroji transposed his theory of Indian sociality onto British politics and used it to intervene in several significant debates of the day is the subject of the next chapter.

[130] 'Irish Self-government and Related Questions', DNP, notes and jottings, group 7: political, serial number 9.

# 6 Making Commercial Society in Britain

On 3 December 1893, Dadabhai Naoroji returned to Bombay with great fanfare as an elected member of the House of Commons. Up to half a million Indians had gathered to congratulate India's Grand Old Man for his successful election to London's Central Finsbury constituency the previous year.[1] Naoroji's successful contesting of a parliamentary seat was undoubtedly a milestone in British and Indian history; nevertheless, this chapter avoids a detailed retelling of Naoroji's wrangles with the British press, the party system and the issue of cultural 'performance' within colonialism's representational order. This has been covered extensively by other scholars, focuses overmuch on identity and leaves the agency of Indian ideas underdetermined.[2] This chapter traces the reception and use of Naoroji's political thought within the relevant British social debates of the day. It was in the discrete context of British political argument that Naoroji was appreciated as a political thinker rather than simply a cultural curiosity. Naoroji used his prominence as the first Indian MP to intervene in the British liberal and radical canon, arguably leaving a subtler and longer lasting legacy than the symbolism of his short three-year term as an MP.

Naoroji entered British electoral politics immediately after the 1884 Reform Act which had prompted liberals and conservatives to compete for the working-class vote in London. Troubled by this democratic shift, middle-class anxieties around poverty, character and the partial enfranchisement of the 'residuum' were

[1] *India and Mr. Dadabhai Naoroji: An Account of the Demonstrations Held in His Honour as M.P. for Central Finsbury, During His Visit to India* (Bombay: Commercial Press, 1898), p. 425.

[2] For a further interpretation of the extensively covered themes of race, culture and representation in Naoroji's electioneering in Britain, see Antoinette Burton, 'Making a Spectacle of Empire: Indian Travelers in Fin-de-Siècle London', *History Workshop Journal* 42 (Autumn, 1996), pp. 126–46; Antoinette Burton, 'Tongues Untied: Lord Salisbury's "Black Man" and the Boundaries of Imperial Democracy', *Comparative Studies in Society and History* 42, no. 3 (2000), pp. 632–61; Matthew Stubbings, 'The Partisan Nature of Race and Imperialism: Dadabhai Naoroji, M. M. Bhownaggree and the Late Nineteenth-Century Politics of Indian Nationalism', *Journal of Imperial and Commonwealth History* 44, no. 1 (2016), pp. 48–69.

catapulted to the heart of British political debate.[3] The last quarter of the nineteenth century also saw the burgeoning of the labour movement and new unionism as rising prices and wage cuts culminated in the Cotton Lockout of 1887 and the Great London Dock Strike of 1889.[4] Much of the working-class politics expressed in major newspapers like *Reynolds* continued to articulate radical concerns in the language of 'Old Corruption' and a critique of the state rather than through the language of class war.[5] While London's new radical and labour associations advocated an attack on privilege and monopoly, they also persisted with the nonconformist and 'puritanical' tradition of radical reformism. The latter strain was frequently characterized by the sort of public moralism exemplified by the Temperance Movement.[6] At any rate, London's industrial geography of small-scale production and manufacturing differentiated it from the large, concentrated industrial landscapes of the North. In 1887, 'the manufacturing parts of London' were said to 'lie between the city and suburbs', constituting 'a sort of debatable land that is neither city nor suburb'.[7] The relative quantity of skilled artisanal labour was higher in London compared to the mechanized factory floors of Cottonopolis. Concerns about the imperial capital's poverty from both the middle and working artisanal classes tended to reflect a preoccupation with bourgeois respectability, social mobility and character. *The Times* succinctly linked these themes when it observed that East London constituencies were 'among the poorest in England', not necessarily in absolute terms, but because of the 'absence of any middle class'.[8]

Naoroji's ideas would enter the British public arena at a time when such questions of the rights and social function of labour were increasingly on the lips of intellectuals, activists and electors. This chapter traces the insertion and impact

---

[3] Gareth Steadman Jones, *Outcast London: A Study in the Relationship Between Classes in Victorian Society*, new edn (New York, NY: Oxford University Press, 1984), p. 290; James Thompson, *British Political Culture and the Idea of 'Public Opinion', 1867–1914* (Cambridge: Cambridge University Press, 2013), p. 77.

[4] Jose Harris, *Private Lives, Public Spirit: Britain 1870–1914* (London: Penguin Books, 1994), pp. 142–3.

[5] Eugenio F. Biagini, *Liberty, Retrenchment and Reform: Popular Liberalism in the Age of Gladstone, 1860–1880* (Cambridge: Cambridge University Press, 1992), p. 54; Marc Brodie, *The Politics of the Poor: The East End of London, 1885–1914* (Oxford: Oxford University Press, 2004), p. 150.

[6] John Davis, *Reforming London: The London Government Problem, 1855–1900* (Oxford: Oxford University Press, 1988), p. 119.

[7] *Routledge's Diamond Jubilee Guide to London and Its Suburbs* (London: George Routledge & Sons, 1887), p. 23.

[8] *The Times*, 6 July 1886, cited in Alex Windscheffel, *Popular Conservatism in Imperial London, 1868–1906* (Woodbridge: Boydell and Brewer, 2007), p. 51.

of the drain theory's anti-monopolistic analysis of land, labour and capital into a plethora of British conversations on land nationalization, land taxes, workers' rights, municipal reform and anti-imperialism. In concluding with a section on the appeal of Naoroji's ideas to his would-be constituents in Central Finsbury, this chapter also emphasizes the appeal of Naorojian grassroots politics beyond the subcontinent.

## Landed Capital in Britain and Ireland

From the 1880s, the British land question piqued Naoroji's interest. The debates of the Irish Land War were an international affair, attracting attention from both the United States and Britain. In radical circles like the Irish National Land Leagues, on both sides of the Atlantic, questions of the right to property in land took on a republican flavour. This ideology invoked the language of the anti-slavery crusade in order to claim that just as natural rights precluded the ownership of other human beings, so too did it prohibit the ownership of land since the monopolization of this natural factor of production led to the enslavement of the labourer.[9]

The American political economist Henry George did much to popularize this republican sentiment in Britain through the publication of his *Progress and Poverty* in 1879.[10] The work appeared in England in 1880 and began to fly off the shelves after George's lecture trips to Britain between 1881 and 1883.[11] George echoed many of the claims Naoroji had made in the 1860s and 1870s. Indeed, it is not implausible that through their common interests and critiques, the two men may have had occasion to meet during George's British lecture tours. It was the British Marxist Henry Mayers Hyndman – Naoroji's close confidant and collaborator – who organized George's first transatlantic trips. Moreover, the land nationalizer and naturalist Alfred Russel Wallace was acquainted with both men and was instrumental in endorsing and promoting their work on 'social economy' in Britain. Naoroji was even dubbed an influential member of the so-called New Party of radical political economists who sought to recalibrate British economics

---

[9] *Irish World*, 16 November 1878; Andrew Phemister, '"Our American Aristotle": Henry George and the Republican Tradition during the Transatlantic Irish Land War, 1877–1887' (unpublished PhD thesis, University of Edinburgh, 2016).

[10] Henry George, *Progress and Poverty: An Inquiry into the Cause of Industrial Depressions and of Increase of Want with the Increase of Wealth, the Remedy* (London: William Reeves, 1884 [1879]).

[11] Elwood P. Lawrence, 'Henry George's British Mission', *American Quarterly* 3, no. 3 (1952), p. 232.

in the interests of social harmony.[12] George offered a republican critique of land ownership, considering the private ownership of this resource as a 'monopoly', labour as the sole generator of value and production as the 'mother of wages'.[13] Like Naoroji's analogy of the coerced and asocial Indian 'helot' who merely extracted natural resources for British appropriation, George claimed that the man who sacrifices self-directed productivism 'becomes a slave' and added that 'the veriest savage could not afford to exchange' with such degraded producers.[14] George and Naoroji's popularity is hardly surprising given the ongoing Irish Land War and the fact that the value of land in Britain had increased from 1.8 billion pounds in the late 1860s to 2 billion pounds by the late 1870s, accounting for 25 per cent of the national wealth by 1878.[15] The tenor of the radical movement in the 1880s and 1890s was, therefore, in favour of greater remuneration of naturally productive labour and against the unearned proceeds of unnatural economic monopoly.

Departing from many sympathetic Irish Land Leaguers, Naoroji's identification of the colonial state's interest in acting as India's landlord made him suspicious of land nationalization in Britain. He noted that because in India the 'National land lord as Government' was 'all powerful and virtually despotic – the tenant is squeezed mercilessly by laws made at the Rulers' will!'[16] In Britain, this was also a possibility where parliament did not effectively represent labour as the true producer of wealth.[17] Instead, the legislative power was in the hands of the self-interested 'classes' of the middle and upper classes in the House of Commons, with the House of Lords presenting a 'total barrier' to changing the economic landscape from one of 'compulsion' to one of free 'competition'.[18] This species of labour republicanism was a major point of radical liberal electioneering in Central Finsbury and the foundation of Naoroji's desire to enter parliament besides his Indian lobbying.[19] As Naoroji clarified to Herbert Gladstone in 1903, he had represented a labour constituency and had always regarded himself as a

---

12 Phemister, *Henry George and the Republican Tradition*, p. 103; Andrew Reid, ed., *The New Party* (London: Hodder Brothers, 1894), pp. 179, 429.

13 George, *Progress and Poverty*, pp. 6–8, 26, 32–3, 43, 409–11.

14 Ibid, pp. 220–1.

15 Harris, *Private Lives*, p. 97.

16 'Relations Between Landlords and Tenants. Notes', (undated), National Archives of India [NAI], Dadabhai Naoroji Papers [DNP], notes and jottings, group 1: Accounts/Economic/Trade, serial number 64.

17 *Birmingham Daily Post*, 19 February 1894; *Daily News*, 19 February 1894 and 2 March 1894; 'Labour Questions', DNP, group 9: social, serial number 20.

18 Ibid.

19 'Central Finsbury Radical Club: Two Labour Questions', *Holborn and Finsbury Guardian*, 9 January 1892.

spokesperson for general labour issues even when the press had lazily dubbed him 'the Member for India'.[20]

Naoroji's solution to the labour question reflected his experience as *dewan* of Baroda, when taxation upon the local landowners was rationalized, institutionalized and contributed to a central treasury intended to subsidize peasant production through state investment. Though Naoroji was making these arguments in the midst of the Georgeist *Zeitgeist* of the 1880s and 1890s, they were ideas and policies he had personally pioneered in India five years before the American's publication of *Progress and Poverty*. His notes reveal that India was repeatedly used as the comparison through which he considered British issues of land and labour. The episodes and enquiries of Naoroji's Indian career, discussed in previous chapters of this book – the *zamindari* system, the colonial state and Baroda reform – were all used to identify counter-productive mediation in natural law and the general policies that would restore natural justice and reinstate an equitable contract between landlord and tenant.[21] The principles to be observed were those that stemmed from the labour theory of value he developed in India, which regarded land as a 'gift of nature' belonging to and worked by the 'whole human race' and the 'universal people' and consequently that 'the whole rent accruing from it ought to go for the benefit of the whole of the people'.[22]

As a member of the Land Restoration League and the United Committee of the Taxation of Ground Rents and Values, both supported by Henry George, Naoroji was associated with organizations whose aim was 'the abolition of landlordism' via 'the abolition of all taxes upon labour and the products of labour; and the increase of taxation upon land values until the whole annual value of land is taken in taxation'.[23] However, it is not clear whether Naoroji was for the total confiscation of the profit accruing from landlordism or simply redistributing it as he had in Baroda in order to make the contract with the tenant more equitable. In his pronouncements to the British public, he seemed to favour the latter:

> Unfortunately in India the same vicious principle is maintained; there [colonial officials] take not from the great land lords but from the poor cultivators, who have,

[20] Naoroji to Herbert Gladstone, 4 May 1903, DNP, N-1 (2768); Pall Mall Gazette, 30 April 1889.

[21] 'Relations Between Landlords and Tenants. Notes'.

[22] 'Land and Capital', DNP, Notes and Jottings. Group 1: Accounts/Economic/Trade, serial number 52.

[23] Fred Verinder to Naoroji, 18 May 1889, DNP, E-54 (1); 31 January 1890, NAI, Dadabhai Naoroji Papers, E-54 (2); R. P. Cottam and Fred Verinder to Naoroji, 3 March 1891, DNP, U-12 (1).

> perhaps, a field or maybe three fields and have to pay their rent, whilst, however, the land lord in India pays his quota into the gross revenue of the Country, here in England the ground land lord deserving and enjoying the abnormally augmented increment in the worth and value of his property pays only two or three per cent of the national burden. And it should be remembered that the mere rental of the land in England is equal to the production of the whole of the land in India. You will now see that whilst your laws relating to the land enforce certain principles it adopts different principles in other parts of the empire.

Naoroji calculated that if the English landlord (8 per cent tax burden) paid the same as the Indian peasant-cultivator (16 per cent tax burden excluding the baneful impact of the drain), the British treasury could raise an additional 40 million pounds.[24] The revenue earned could then be productively redistributed to employ more British labour significant above subsistence levels 'for the benefit of the whole of the people'.[25] For instance, by 1905 some advanced liberals were suggesting that revenues from the taxation of land values could be used for building affordable housing and reducing unemployment all at once.[26] Naoroji was especially keen on revenues funding public goods that might promote civil society like secular education.[27] The question of taxation was really about the free contract between landlord, the state and the autonomous tenant-producer. This was a more natural market condition under which the productive capacity of the producer was maximized by securing his right to labour-property and the socializing interdependency that followed from this. Naoroji's policy of differential property rates depending on the aggregate demand for tenancies in the British economy also reflected this thinking. Only if national tenancy demand was high could landlords justify including a portion of the rates in their rental charge. If tenant demand was low and real estate oversupplied, then landlords across the country ought to be compelled to pay the entire rate themselves, thereby penalizing the passive capital that contributed nothing to social economy.[28]

---

[24] 'Extract from Speech', among US, Ireland, UK Trade Figures and Ground Values (undated), DNP, notes and jottings, group 1: accounts/economic/trade, serial number 22.

[25] 'Land and Capital'.

[26] *The Unemployed* (London: n.p., 1905), Bristol, University of Bristol Library (UBL), National Liberal Federation Collection, JN1129.

[27] 'Extract from a Speech', DNP, notes and jottings, group 1: accounts/economic/trade, serial number 22.

[28] 'Proceedings of Land and Capital Discussion at Central Finsbury Radical Club', 5 April 1891, ibid., serial number 66.

## The Irish Connection

The land issue also brought Naoroji together with Fabians like Sidney Webb as well as Irish nationalists like Michael Davitt and John Dillon. In 1888, Naoroji wrote to Webb because he took 'an interest in the question of ground rents' and wanted to be supplied 'with all the literature upon it'.[29] It was at this time that Webb was articulating views close to Naoroji's own, such as the idea of interest and rent as resulting from 'opportunity and chance' rather than production.[30] Though Webb later described himself as a socialist, it was his positivist leanings that shaped his attitude towards encouraging the 'social good' over 'individual happiness' and the promotion of a moralized capitalism.[31] Some positivists like Alfred Russell Wallace accepted land nationalization, whereas Frederic Harrison and Webb had rejected it in favour of the confiscation of land values, suggesting that the 'unearned increment' be taxed at 20 per cent.[32] Equally, they promoted leaseholder enfranchisement and the abolition of short-term leases in London in order to punish idle rentiers and the sapping of the productive energies of the working classes.

Naoroji exclaimed that for 'the tenant to do his work with all his might and heart, which will be to the benefit of the whole community in the larger production of wealth ... [he] must not be allowed to be exploited by the landlord whoever he may be'.[33] Positivists thus had a much closer ideological affinity with Naoroji when it came to what they regarded as Britain-only questions even as the Member for Central Finsbury regarded land monopolization and the 'unearned increment' as comparable to the arbitrary control the state exercised over the land revenue in India. Naoroji was the Strand Liberal Association's delegate to the Liberals' radical Newcastle programme of 1891 which committed the party to the taxation of land values.[34] The government never brought any legislation forward when in power, so

[29] Naoroji to Sidney Webb, 18 October 1888, DNP, N-1 (1234).

[30] Sidney Webb, 'Rate of Interest and Laws of Distribution', *Quarterly Journal of Economics* 2, no. 2 (1888), 203.

[31] Sidney Webb, 'The Ethics of Existence', 1880–1, London, British Library of Political and Economic Science (BLPES), Passfield Papers, VI/3; Gregory Claeys, *Imperial Sceptics: British Critics of Empire, 1850–1920* (Cambridge University Press: 2010), p. 197.

[32] Sidney Webb, *A Plea for the Taxation of Ground Rents* (London: United Committee for the Taxation of Ground Rents, 1887), p. 12; Sidney Webb, *Socialism in England* (London: Swann Sonnenschein, 1890), pp. 87–8; Frederic Harrison to Alfred Russell Wallace, 11 June 1885, London, British Library, Alfred Russell Wallace Papers, Add MS 46440, ff. 94–5.

[33] Naoroji to Unknown, 6 Mar. 1891, DNP, N-1 (1760).

[34] Naoroji to A. O. Hume, 8 September 1891, DNP, N-1 (1985); Malabari to Naoroji, 30 September 1891, DNP, M-32 (263).

it was left to Naoroji to unsuccessfully table two private members' bills giving local authorities the power to tax landed capital.[35]

Naoroji's friendship with Irish nationalists facilitated 'strategic interventions' by both parties in British politics but was also defined by ideological convergence.[36] Jennifer Regan-Lefebvre refers to Naoroji, Webb, Davitt and F. H. O'Donnell's friendship as an example of 'cosmopolitan nationalism' in which social and political capital was built through 'multicultural interaction' and networking.[37] It is certainly true that all these men were united by a certain professional liberal sensibility.[38] This middle-class civility notwithstanding, there is a need to explain why Naoroji kept up a much more consistent relationship with some of these figures over others. The answer lies in the fact that the political thought of individuals like Davitt resonated more with Naoroji's understanding of the importance of a sound political economy to social regeneration. Davitt's connection of land, labour and social economy identified the coercion of the Anglo-Irish state's 'official mercenaries' as monopolistic and so made common cause with the labour republicanism of Naoroji's drain theory.[39] This differed markedly from F. H. O'Donnell and his brother Charles's distinction between land reform and civic nationalism as separate issues. This is all the more surprising because the O'Donnells' internationalism and championing of Irish Home Rule and greater Indian representation in parliament intended to use Irish nationalism to push for a freer association of nations under British paramountcy – a goal similar to Naoroji's ideal of *swaraj*.[40] O'Donnell even educated himself on Indian famines and raised the issue in parliament, as the MP. for Dungarvin, pestering his brother in the Bengal civil service, C. J. O'Donnell, for information. The latter, dubbed the 'l'enfant terrible of the I.C.S.', had accused the Bengal government of incompetence and tardiness in its famine policy.[41]

---

[35] 'Central Finsbury Parliamentary Election 1895, D. Naoroji Addresses to his Fellow Electors in Central Finsbury', 5 July 1895, DNP, F-34 (37); *The Standard*, 17 March 1894.

[36] Michael Silvestri, *Ireland and India: Nationalism, Empire, Memory* (Basingstoke: Palgrave, 2009), pp. 17–18.

[37] Jennifer Regan-Lefebvre, *Cosmopolitan Nationalism: Ireland, India and the Politics of Alfred Webb* (Basingstoke: Palgrave, 2009), pp. 3–4.

[38] Carla King, 'Michael Davitt, Irish Nationalism and the British Empire in the Late Nineteenth Century', in Peter Gray, ed., *Victoria's Ireland? Irishness and Britishness, 1837–1901* (Dublin: Four Courts P., 2004), pp. 116–30.

[39] *Freeman's Journal*, 25 May 1888.

[40] *Freeman's Journal*, 13 August 1878; Brasted, 'Irish Home Rule Politics and India', pp. 25–6, 58–60.

[41] F. H. O'Donnell, *A History of the Irish Parliamentary Party*, vol. I (2 vols., London: Longman, Green & Company 1910), p. 105; *The Pioneer*, 1 March 1882; C. J. O'Donnell, *The Black Pamphlet of Calcutta: The Famine of 1874* (London: William Ridgway, 1876).

Yet the two brothers' calls for Naoroji's attention fell on deaf ears. F. H. O'Donnell had a 'fortuitous meeting' with Naoroji in Paris, where the latter put him in touch with other 'Parsis and Mahrattas' (presumably other Indians from the Bombay Presidency).[42] No correspondence between the two took place after this event, nor does Naoroji mention him to others. C. J. O'Donnell only wrote to Naoroji in 1902 wanting to 'make Naoroji's acquaintance' since they both worked 'for the same excellent end'.[43] These attempts bore little fruit in terms of fostering a long-term working relationship, with C. J. O'Donnell complaining that Naoroji failed to recognize him at a political gathering.[44] Naoroji's antipathy to the O'Donnells was likely because they had delinked land reform from the question of bureaucratic or customary domination through the colonial state. At the same time C. J. O'Donnell was trying to get Naoroji's attention, he was advocating a council of conservative notables to balance the opinions of the Indian middle class as well as downplaying the necessity of legislative council reforms. Land reform, he claimed, would be enough to placate Indians without having to grant them any significant political concessions.[45] For many nationalists in Ireland, Land League-ism from 1879 represented a compromise between social reform and political devolution. Parnell was forced to promise that none of the funds of the Irish Land League would be used for parliamentary purposes.[46] F. H. O'Donnell never reconciled himself to the promotion of land reform over Home Rule and from 1885 drifted further and further away from the Parnellite mainstream. Though he remained a tenant-righter, his attacks on absentee landlordism were diluted compared to those of Parnell, Davitt and Naoroji.[47]

In Michael Davitt, Naoroji found a like-minded intellectual collaborator on the question of labour republicanism. This relationship was all the more striking given the antipathy of many Indian critics of empire to Davitt's radicalism, believing the association would make Naoroji's name synonymous with 'rebellion'.[48] Naoroji's enthusiasm for Davitt should not be simplified to the fact that the Irishman was energetic in trying to find Naoroji a potential Irish constituency in 1886 and 1892 – especially when it seemed that the Liberal Party machine in Britain

[42] O'Donnell, *A History of the Irish Parliamentary Party*, vol. II, p. 423.
[43] C. J. O'Donnell to Naoroji, 3 March 1902, DNP, O-10.
[44] C. J. O'Donnell to Naoroji, 11 November 1903, DNP, O-10 (2)a.
[45] *India*, 30 March 1906, p. 150.
[46] Brasted, 'Irish Home Rule', p. 288.
[47] *The Times*, 10 August 1880.
[48] Dinshaw Wacha to Naoroji, 26 June 1888, quoted in Anil Seal, *The Emergence of Indian Nationalism: Competition and Collaboration in the Later Nineteenth Century* (Cambridge: Cambridge University Press, 1968), p. 284.

was pulling strings behind the scenes against Naoroji's campaigns.[49] Davitt was also a 'close and intimate friend' of Hyndman and both developed their political and economic views in collaboration with Naoroji.[50] Davitt and Naoroji had advocated an imperial critique that prefigured John A. Hobson's attack on the political and economic monopoly of the military-aristocracy. More than this, Davitt agreed wholeheartedly with Naoroji's natural rights basis of free labour. While in prison in 1881, Davitt opined that if man 'revels not in the possession of all that Nature has so beauteously placed within reach of his industry, he has but to blame modern society for having placed a law between him and the enjoyment of his natural rights'.[51] If natural justice prevailed, Davitt believed that a better state of socialization would ensue as 'a condition of social peace and harmony' proliferated by rewarding 'the industry of the people' and expunging unproductive 'privileged idleness'.[52]

Both Naoroji and Davitt believed that establishing the political sovereignty of labour in parliament was the long-term solution to monopoly by electing labour MPs who would 'make a holocaust of privilege'.[53] Both men admitted that an Indian representing a constituency from Connaught would 'intensify largely the present general sympathy' between India and Ireland.[54] That Naoroji believed economics was the factor around which mutual sympathies would arise is evident from the annotated extracts he kept of Davitt's speeches. These spoke of landlordism, the monopoly of capital and the degradation of the Irish labourer. If in India the colonial bureaucracy and extractive mechanism was subsidized by wealth generated exclusively by the *ryot*, Davitt spoke of landlords in Ireland who 'have to pay for agents, solicitors etc and the labourer is forced to make up the cost from his rent'.[55] He heaped praise on Naoroji's drain theory but also his general idea of commercial society which linked the plight of the European working class with the Indian peasant:

[49] R. P. Masani, *Dadabhai Naoroji: The Grand Old Man of India* (London: George Allen & Unwin, 1939), p. 139; Naoroji to Davitt, 16 February 1892, DNP, N-1 (2218).

[50] H. M. Hyndman, *Record of an Adventurous Life* (London: Macmillan, 1911), pp. 2, 225.

[51] Michael Davitt, 'Random Thoughts on the Irish Land War', in Carla King, ed., *Jottings in Solitary* (Dublin: University College Dublin Press, 2003), p. 187.

[52] Michael Davitt, 'English Civilisation', in ibid, p. 24.

[53] Michael Davitt, *Leaves from a Prison Diary or Lectures to a 'Solitary' Audience*, vol. II (2 vols., London: Chapman and Hall, 1885), pp. 160–1.

[54] Notes by Dadabhai Naoroji on the back of a letter from Franz Baum, 8 July 1886, DNP, B-65 (1).

[55] 'Extracts from Mr. Davitt's Speech at St. James' Hall, (undated), DNP, notes and jottings, group 1: accounts/economic/trade, serial number 23.

> [T]he struggle of the working population for material and social betterment ... will give to the economic and popular aspect of the Indian question a relationship in similarity of motive and purpose, which will ensure a hearing and a sympathy from the industrial democracy.[56]

Davitt's support for Naoroji's co-founding of the London Reform Union in 1892, an organization working for municipal socialism, stemmed from both men's desire to combat the 'demoralized' character of London labour as a major step towards 'good citizenship'.[57] It was perhaps Davitt's greater sympathy for Naoroji's linking of national politics with the rights of producers that prompted Naoroji to offer him the presidency of the Indian National Congress ahead of Alfred Webb (who eventually presided anyway) in 1894. Davitt replied that he was not the 'wisest selection' since his Fenian 'delinquencies' would damage the Indian cause.[58] None of this is to say that alliances based on political pragmatism were insignificant. The Irish National League, for example, worked with Naoroji's 1895 election campaign in order to help him register more working-class voters in Finsbury, and Naoroji contributed funds towards the effort.[59] As Davitt wrote to Francis Schnadhorst, the secretary of the National Liberal Federation and the party's grassroots organizer, registering the poorer industrial classes and Irish migrants was essential since the labour and Home Rule causes were sympathetic to one another. Campaigning on both of these causes would yield more liberal parliamentarians and further the Irish cause.[60]

After having been ousted from parliament in 1895, it was land-reforming associations like the United Irish League that occupied most of Naoroji's attention.[61] For other Indians too, like Gopal Krishna Gokhale, who had been weaned on the economic arguments of Naoroji and Ranade, the Irish nationalists were most interesting when they critiqued British political economy and shared potential reforms. For instance, the Irish nationalist MP John Swift MacNeill and Gokhale discussed the Irish Agricultural Organisation Society and its promotion

---

56 *India*, 1 December 1893, pp. 369–70.

57 'Proceedings of the London Reform Union', 1 November 1892, NAI, DNP, L-109; F. W. Galton, secretary of the London reform union to Naoroji, 14 April. 1904, DNP, L-109 (11).

58 Davitt to Naoroji, 5 November 1894, DNP, D-59 (4).

59 Clerkenwell branch of the Irish national league to Naoroji, 20 June 1895, DNP, I-42 (7).

60 Davitt to Francis Schnadhorst, 7 October 1890, Birmingham, Cadbury Research Library, Francis Schnadhorst Papers, MS170, box 3.

61 John Keating and J. J. Bunting, secretaries of the United Irish League to Naoroji, 7 February 1906, DNP, U-20 (1).

of agricultural co-operatives at length.[62] The organization had set up 'hundreds of village societies' in Ireland, and MacNeill was advising Gokhale on the practicality of opening a small number of rural banking co-operatives around Pune.[63] The co-operative model also appealed to Naoroji's ideal of commercial society as a way of realigning British producers and consumers on more natural economic lines. This and other types of economic arbitration became necessary in the short term since unnatural capital could not be dislodged from its influence over the state.

## Securing the Rights of Labour in the British World

Naoroji was vexed at the inability of British working-class voters to unify behind a pro-labour agenda. Even though 60 per cent of male labourers had been enfranchised in the 1867 and 1884 Reform Acts, they had failed to enact a raft of anti-monopoly and anti-class legislation. At a meeting of the National Municipal Vestry Employees Labour Union in 1892, Naoroji claimed that labour was reduced to slavery in years past because the upper classes had rigged the economy through parliament. However, 'now the sovereign power was in the hands of the working men, it would be their own fault if that state of things continued to exist'.[64] The House of Lords was still a bastion of inherited privilege, urging Naoroji to demand its abolition; ultimately, however, he believed that 'labour organisation' was at fault and that if 'the whole labour party put their shoulders to the wheel – they can send a body as large as the Irish' to parliament.[65] The liberal split over Home Rule did not help the situation, even during Naoroji's successful 1892 campaign, and it was supposed that radicals and liberals had missed out on as many as twelve seats in the capital on account of the Irish controversy.[66]

However, as with his experience of the Indian native states, it was really sovereign command of labour-synthesized value and the limiting of parasitical monopoly and mediation that Naoroji was concerned with. Far from being a principled democrat, parliamentary representation and the ability to legislate in the interests of labour was a means to an end in a country where representative government was already established but whose institutions were dominated by

---

[62] J. Swift MacNeill to Gokhale, 30 September 1901, British Library, Asia, Pacific and Africa Collection, London [BLAPAC], Gokhale Papers, IOR Neg 11704.

[63] J. Swift MacNeill to Gokhale, 26 November 1901, BLAPAC, Gokhale Papers, IOR Neg 11704.

[64] *Reynolds Newspaper*, 23 October 1892.

[65] *Birmingham Daily Post*, 19 February 1894; *Daily News*, 19 February 1894 and 2 March 1894; 'Labour questions', DNP, notes and jottings, group 9: social, serial number 20.

[66] *Daily Chronicle*, 9 July 1892.

monopolistic capital. In British and princely India, the state was not representative but had institutionalized bureaucratic parasitism in the ways discussed in the previous chapter. For this reason, promoting labour democracy in India was out of the question given the absence of a unitary Indian 'people' defined by class rather than cultural interest. Naoroji's career as a social reformer, in which he delicately avoided moralizing on social matters beyond his own community, had made this eminently clear. But reforming the bureaucratic institutions which prevented a commercial society – the prerequisite for a people defined by individual economic interest – from emerging was the order of the day. The subordination of political representation and state sovereignty to the problem of arrested social development is explored in greater detail next in the context of Naoroji's municipal politics in London and Bombay.

Since British labourers were not making the most of their democratic weight to 'work out their own redemption', Naoroji proposed a number of industrial interventions into the existing process of accumulation.[67] Rearticulating his labour theory of value in Britain, he claimed that the workers 'had as much claim to a proper share in everything as capital, for after all capital was merely crystalized labour, stored up and preserved'. Returning to his suspicion of banking, Naoroji insisted that if manufacturers claimed a right to surplus value because it was their capital that was invested, they ought to remember that credit was merely the lending of pre-existing wealth created by the act of labour upon the natural bounty of the land. Britain's institutional arrangements ought to be reformed 'so that the national life blood might be distributed in such a way as to supply nourishment to all classes as nature intended it for them'.[68]

In order to encourage this 'natural' ordering of economic society in the absence of a political system which represented labour's sovereignty, Naoroji mooted the idea of industrial courts to adjudicate for a fair wage bargain, claiming that it was necessary to find alternative ways to institutionalize the rights of labour.[69] Not only was the existing wage bargain a 'forced contract' preying on workers' indigence but labour would also never see the wealth it created return to the community of producers. Naoroji observed how copyright and patent law protected mental labour by creating a monopoly on intellectual innovation for a limited time only before making it available for the benefit of the whole community, whereas in the case of wage labour the capitalist absconded with the wealth indefinitely.

[67] Dadabhai Naoroji, *The Rights of Labour*, 2nd edn (London: Fred W. Evans, [undated]), p. 11.
[68] 'Finsbury Politics', *Holborn and Finsbury Guardian*, 18 June 1892.
[69] N, 'The Rights of Labour', *Westminster Review* 134, no. 1 (1890), pp. 95–103; Naoroji revealed as the author in *Manchester Guardian*, 30 September 1890, p. 9.

Once again conceptualizing the state as the midwife of society, Naoroji asked whether it was not the duty of the state to protect 'sacred labour-property' not by nationalization but by adjudicating the relationship between labour and capital. Industrial courts might level the playing field by electing an equal number of court assessors from capital and labour who would go into the costs of production and calculate fair remuneration based on labour-hours, rather than a spurious market wage based on compulsion. Such innovations would safeguard labour-property through a balanced and uncoerced calculation in order to create an economic contract that was 'an unalloyed benefit to the whole nation'.[70]

Colonial critics also used Naoroji's model of commercial society in Africa. Naoroji was an ally and correspondent of the radical Scottish Baptist Joseph Booth, who had worked to encourage African commercial self-sufficiency in British Central Africa. Booth began with the establishment of the Zambesi Industrial Mission in 1892 and the African Cooperative Society in 1900.[71] His 1897 work *Africa for the African* criticized the habit of the Europeans to 'seize upon property and permanently drain the wealth of Africa and the African's labor into European channels'.[72] While it is not clear whether Booth borrowed these ideas from Naoroji's 1860s drain formulations, he did recognize the common thrust of their respective works. He informed Naoroji that he and an African colleague were distributing Naoroji's *Poverty and Un-British Rule* in Edinburgh and Glasgow.[73] Booth's slogan of 'Africa for the African' would outlive his personal activism and pass to militant indigenous movements like the Zulu Rebellion of 1906.[74]

Naoroji was particularly interested in Booth's arguments which highlighted the increased prosperity of indigenously administered African provinces. Booth reported that in 'Bechenanaland, the country is practically ruled by the African Chief Kahma' where 'a greatly improved state of things exist ... the land has been preserved for the people who cultivate it ... in a sort of commonweal principle under the direction of their chiefs'. Booth believed, like Naoroji, that the principal resources were 'both people and land', and if control of these factors of production remained under indigenous guardianship, the European could get no more than

[70] N, 'The Rights of Labour', pp. 96–9, 103.

[71] Harry W. Langworthy, 'Joseph Booth: Prophet of Radical Change in Central and South Africa, 1891–1915', *Journal of Religion in Africa* 16, no. 1 (1986), pp. 25–6, 32.

[72] Joseph Booth, *Africa for the African*, ed. Laura Perry (Blantyre: Christian Literature Association in Malawai, 1996 [1897]), p. 12; 'Africa for the African by Joseph Booth 1897', DNP, extracts, E-72.

[73] Joseph Booth to Naoroji, 20 August 1906, DNP, B-181 (9).

[74] J. Stuart, *A History of the Zulu Rebellion, 1906* (London: Macmillan, 1913), p. 521.

'the reimbursement for the necessary and economical outlay incurred'.[75] Where the Europeans had drained Africa, Booth promoted industrial missions funded by American and British donations (as reparation for the drain) at a rate of 2 cents per capita per day for a decade. This would yield 75 million dollars for industrial missions on a co-operative basis so that Africans could cultivate their own enterprises and provide for their own wants, like education, which the colonial state denied them.[76]

As with Naoroji's ideal of an Indianized bureaucracy, Booth also identified African-Americans as an intellectual and commercial clerisy that ought to be encouraged to relocate to Africa for the running of industrial missions.[77] Both men's mutual correspondence reveals Booth's support for the Indianization of the Raj's civil service as well as Naoroji's encouragement for industrial missions in Africa as means of promoting African gentrification.[78] The only criticism Naoroji had was that Africa's condition would ameliorate faster if Booth advocated Africanization of the bureaucracy as an immediate solution to the drain rather than as a gradual outgrowth of his mission system under European expertise.[79]

Naoroji also latched on to the economic reciprocity inherent in the co-operative model in Britain as another means of institutionally overcoming the dependent relationship between labour and capital. The appeal of the co-operative movement to ethical positivists, radicals and socialists was its moralizing of economic relations into a system of equitable mutual dependence.[80] One of the leading lights of this movement was the freethinker George Holyoake with whom Naoroji was well acquainted.[81] For Holyoake, the cultivation of individual 'morality' had both educational and 'material conditions'.[82] Co-operation entailed self-supporting and self-sufficient economic activity in which profits were divided among the shareholders in which 1 pound would buy you a share, but a one-man-one-vote system operated regardless of how many shares you owned. Stores were run democratically and the trading surplus was reinvested into community services

[75] 'Africa for the African by Joseph Booth 1897', DNP, extracts, E-72.
[76] Booth, *Africa for the African*, pp. 28–9, 68.
[77] Ibid., pp. 14–15.
[78] Joseph Booth to Naoroji, 18 June 1906, DNP, B-181 (1); 15 August 1906, DNP, B-181 (iv); 29 August 1906, B-181 (10); C. R. D. Halisi, *Black Political Thought in the Making of South African Democracy* (Bloomington, IN: Indiana University Press, 1999), p. 51.
[79] Naoroji to Joseph Booth, 5 July 1905, in Masani, *Dadabhai Naoroji*, p. 443.
[80] Peter Gurney, *Co-operative Culture and the Politics of Consumption in England, 1870–1930* (Manchester: Manchester University Press, 1996), p. 22.
[81] Naoroji to G. J. Holyoake, 8 November 1888, DNP, N-1 (1305).
[82] G. J. Holyoake, *The Co-operative Movement Today*, 4th edn (London: Methuen & Co, 1905 [1891]), p. 74.

like education.[83] It was the processes of exchange, rather than the core relations of production, that were to be reformed. Monetized commodities and private ownership persisted but with the absence of middlemen, speculation and rent extraction.[84] It was assumed that being rewarded proportionately for one's work would transform the unskilled labourer into a virtuous yeomanry or artisanal class in which it was recognized that

> worker has skill and good will latent in him, but, as a rule, they are not evoked, as no one offers a price for these qualities. As human nature is constructed, participation in profits is the talisman which awakens interest and calls out efficiency which would otherwise sleep.

Added to this factor was the sharing of social burdens and labouring for the good of the whole community. If the 'rapid workman' increased productivity, earned a higher wage and, consequently, a 'higher dividend' accrued, then the less skilled labourers would 'have the advantage of that'.[85] One such advantage, education, was intended to be explicitly socially oriented, as a 'school of social citizenship' that the simple 'erudition' of state education did not supply.[86] Both Naoroji and Holyoake were also frequent platform speakers and discussants on political, economic, social and religious issues at that well-known nursery of Victorian positivism and radical liberalism, the South Place Ethical Society.[87]

Co-operation also seemed to solve a fundamental defect of existing capitalism that Naoroji's labour theory of value had revealed. Genius and innovation were rightly remunerated through patents and intellectual property rights; yet, when innovators died, their inventions and machines were monopolized by capitalists and manufacturers who used them as an excuse to extract surplus value from labour. Naoroji claimed that upon the death of the patent holder, this 'knowledge' actually became 'public property', and it was no exaggeration to say that every

---

[83] Gurney, *Co-operative Culture*, p. 19.

[84] Ibid., p. 172.

[85] G. J. Holyoake, 'Co-operation as an Industrial Policy', 11 June 1902, in *National Liberal Club, Political and Economic Circle: Transactions*, vol. IV (London: n.p., [1904?]), pp. 39–42, UBL, Papers of the National Liberal Club, DM668.

[86] G. J. Holyoake, *Essentials of Co-operative Education* (London: Labour Association for Promoting Cooperative Production, 1898), p. 7.

[87] Matikkala, *Empire and Imperial Ambition: Liberty, Englishness and Anti-Imperialism in Late Victorian Britain* (London: Bloomsbury, 2010), p. 136; Lawrence H. Mills to Naoroji, 28 September 1888, DNP, M-127 (2); Naoroji to Malabari, 12 October 1888, DNP, N-1 (1225); Arthur Bonner to Naoroji, 22 September 1892, DNP, B-175 (a); see ethical society documents, London, Bishopsgate Institute, George Jacob Holyoake Papers, HOLYOAKE/9.

'machine therefore owes a certain "rent" to the Community'. Labour also used its own genius to create wealth, but because it used 'land and matter', some of the profits had to be 'in the possession of the community'. Co-operatives, Naoroji claimed, thus brought capital 'down from its unjust high position' and responsibly allocated a proportion of the dividend from labour to the social economy.[88] In this regard, Naoroji led by example by joining the Labour Association for Promoting Co-operative Production alongside Holyoake (its president) and the economist Alfred Marshall.[89] Naoroji also owned shares in numerous co-operatives and made a concerted effort to place various 'orders' with co-operative enterprises.[90] He purchased shoes, boots, hats, suits and rugs from co-operatives across London and was keen for an appreciation of co-operative methods to proliferate among Indians as well.[91] After the turn of the century, Naoroji was encouraging fellow co-operator Henry Vivian to write articles for the *India* journal and for various co-operative societies to host Indian lecturers.[92]

## Municipal Politics in London via Bombay

Municipal government was another tool that Naoroji used to promote natural justice and social economy. While the bulk of Naoroji's endeavours in this sphere took place in London, his short stints on the Bombay town council in 1875 to 1876 and 1883 to 1886 were formative. Commercial crisis and the fiscal profligacy of Bombay's municipal commissioner, Arthur Crawford, between 1865 and 1871 ignited a period of intense debate on representative local government by the city's ratepayers and their representatives.[93] Opinion was divided as to whether the executive powers of the commissioner should be collectivized in the council

---

[88] 'Proceedings of [the] Land and Capital Discussion at Central Finsbury Radical Club', 5 April 1891, DNP, notes and jottings, group 1: accounts/economic/trade, serial number 66.

[89] 'Co-operative Labour', *Leicestershire Chronicle and the Leicestershire Mercury*, 17 August 1895.

[90] Edmund W. Greening, London productive society to Naoroji, 5 October 1889, DNP, L-107d (1); C. Cooper, secretary to the guild of co-operators to Naoroji, 15 January 1891, DNP, G-127 (3).

[91] Henry Vivian, 'The Objects and Methods of the Co-operative Movement', 28 September 1895, BLPES, Political Pamphlets Collection; Henry Vivian, manager of the London Co-operative Institute Society, to Naoroji, 18 November 1893, DNP, C-252; Vivian to Naoroji, 19 March 1894, DNP, C-252 (2); Vivian to Naoroji, 31 December 1895, DNP, C-252 (11).

[92] Henry Vivian to the British Committee of the Indian National Congress, 17 August 1904, in *Minutes of Meetings of the British Committee of the Indian National Congress*, vol. VI, NAI, Private Archives Section, New Delhi, accession number 1943, microfilm reel 3, pp. 63–5.

[93] Christine Dobbin, *Urban Leadership in Western India: Politics and Communities in Bombay City* (Oxford: Oxford University Press, 1972), p. 138.

(argued by Furdoonji) or whether the commissioner could continue to exercise executive functions but with the power for financial audit and control in the hands of council members.[94] Pherozeshah Mehta came to dominate the debate from 1871 by invoking Mill's *Considerations on Representative Government* and suggesting that it was only when a corporation elected by the ratepayers, rather than appointed by the government, was instituted that real responsibility was exercised over spending.[95] He wanted to maintain the executive power of the commissioner because, despite Crawford's poor financial management, he had used his office to bring about 'the wonderful transformation of Bombay' through municipal works.[96]

By 1872, the new Local Government Act created a half-elected corporation of sixty-fourmembers which was free to vote on the rates and appoint all officers except the commissioner. Importantly, the council had been invested with powers of audit, with Naoroji's friend and colleague Ardeshir Framji Moos appointed as the first auditor.[97] By 1883, the debate renewed over the extension of the franchise.[98] Naoroji was sufficiently satisfied with the existing arrangement to allow the government to bring forward its proposals for reform and then pass judgement on them rather than setting out a demand for a newly constituted corporation. While Telang and others insisted on sketching a plan for increased powers and representation, Naoroji sided with Dosabhai Framji and V. N. Mandlik, who were of the opinion that as long as the corporation had sufficient control of municipal finances, it already had self-government.[99]

Naoroji argued, as he did for Indianization of the civil service, that while municipal finances were in the hands of public representatives, they could exercise sufficient financial sovereignty to counter the monopolism of unproductive capitalists. Even from Britain, he made sure his followers were following the school of municipal politics. Wacha wrote in 1891 that at 'corporation meetings I have always fought for the principles you suggest. I am fully with you that the days of the monopolist are past. That the City itself should monopolise for the sake of

[94] *Native Opinion*, 9 July 1871; D. E. Wacha, *Rise and Growth of Bombay Municipal Government* (Madras: G. A. Natesan & Co, 1913), pp. 129–30.
[95] Dobbin, *Urban Leadership*, p. 139; P. M. Mehta, 'Bombay Municipal Reform Question of 1871', in P. M. Mehta, *Speeches and Writings of the Honourable Sir Pherozeshah M. Mehta*, ed. Dinshaw Edulji Wacha (Allahabad: The Indian Press, 1905), p. 117.
[96] P. M. Mehta quoted in Wacha, *Rise and Growth*, p. 214.
[97] Ibid., p. 58; Prashant Kidambi, *The Making of an Indian Metropolis: Colonial Governance and Public Culture in Bombay* (Aldershot: Routledge, 2007), p. 46.
[98] Kidambi, *The Making of an Indian Metropolis*, p. 47.
[99] *Times of India*, 18 June 1883 and 17 September 1883.

the City'.[100] In the spirit of civic solidarity, Naoroji suggested that the corporation set up its own pawn bank to lend on a favourable rate to Bombay's citizens and use the interest to reinvest in the community. Naoroji, Furdoonji and Telang believed this would introduce competition against the domination of Marwari bankers and their 'exorbitant' rates of interest.[101]

While it is true that the colonial state and municipality comprised the dominant class functions of Bombay's wealthy ratepayers, after 1871 the council members from the professional classes did criticize the monopoly that manifested in the racial and class divisions of the city.[102] Many municipal functions were provided by private contractors paid by council funds raised through the rates or a separate cess for the specific service. For instance, the *halalkhor* caste of scavengers and sweepers were employed to empty latrines but they often demanded an additional bribe for their services, knowing full well that higher castes would not perform the task. By default, only the moneyed areas of the city were serviced, meaning that the municipal cess was not a charge for a universal service but actually a 'tax' on the urban citizenry that subsidized the rich.[103] Similar arguments were emerging in Britain in the 1870s, legitimated by Mill's postulation that natural monopolies were more efficient under public control and by Joseph Chamberlain's municipal socialism in Birmingham.[104]

The water supply was the most monopolized of Bombay's utilities. The rapid growth of the urban population and industry rapidly outstripped supply. In the 1850s the Vehar waterworks were undertaken to create an artificial lake north of the city and provide a daily supply of 9.5 million gallons.[105] The construction of the lake and pipes were contracted out to a private company, but the infrastructure

---

[100] Wacha to Naoroji, 19 December 1891, in R. P. Patwardan, ed., *Dadabhai Naoroji Correspondence: Correspondence with Dinshaw Wacha,* vol. II, part I (2 vols., Bombay: Allied Publishers Private Limited, 1977), pp. 271–2.

[101] *Times of India*, 9 July 1883.

[102] Sandip Hazareesingh, *The Colonial City and the Challenge of Modernity: Urban Hegemonies and Civic Contestations in Bombay, 1900–1925* (Himayatnagar: Orient Longman, 2007), p. 216; Kidambi, *Making of an Imperial Metropolis*, p. 41.

[103] Wacha, *Rise and Growth*, pp. 193–4; Mehta, 'Bombay Municipal Reform Question of 1871', p. 84.

[104] Martin Daunton, *Wealth and Welfare: An Economic and Social History of Britain, 1851–1951* (Oxford: Oxford University Press, 2007), pp. 107–110; Mill, 'Principles of Political Economy, Book IV', in John Stuart Mill, *The Collected Works of John Stuart Mill*, vol. II, ed. John M. Robson, intro. V. W. Bladen, online edn (33 vols., Toronto: University of Toronto Press, 1965), ch. 11.

[105] S. M. Edwardes, *The Gazetteer of Bombay City and Island*, vol. III (Bombay: The Times Press, 1909), p. 34; 'Report of the Health Officer', in *Annual Report of the Municipal Commissioner of Bombay, 1876* (Bombay, 1877), p. 61; 'Bombay Water Supply', DNP, B-173.

costs and the subsequent charge to pay for the water and cover the repayment of the loan were meticulously worked out by the government beforehand at 9 annas per person per annum.[106] However, as costs mounted and the water rate increased by the 1860s, claims of corruption on the part of the government contractors proliferated, all the while the municipality was burdened with the additional expenses of mending the defective dam.[107]

Naoroji took a keen interest in the issue from the beginning, since it was generally considered to be the 'first municipal project in India'.[108] The renewed cry of the ratepayers was that their streets showed a conspicuous lack of Vehar water even though they paid for the service.[109] Naoroji resorted to his statistical liberalism once more to show that the contract between the British government and the municipality had been distorted by accounting errors, thus the cost of water per capita was artificially high and universal provision artificially depressed. Submitting a long minute to the town council in 1876 and 1884, Naoroji showed that the original contract between the government and the municipality agreed to charge 4.50 per cent simple interest on the loan. However, the government's accountant-general had calculated compound interest which placed an additional burden of 6.9 million rupees on the ratepayer.[110] After having been repeatedly pressured, the government agreed that the municipality should form a committee to investigate the matter. Naoroji recommended Furdoonji to ensure a sympathetic voice since colleagues like Telang insisted that the accountant-general's calculations were correct.[111] For Naoroji, this question was intimately connected with the economic welfare of the community. Alongside his own calculations of interest, Naoroji wished to know exactly how the government arrived at its calculation of 1,840 gallons per head per day, commenting, 'I doubt we have such supply and

[106] *Selections from the Records of the Bombay Government on the Supply of Water to Bombay* (Bombay: Bombay Education Society's Press, 1854), pp. 138–48.

[107] Wacha, *Rise and Growth*, p. 70; 'Nowrozji Furdoonjji Examined', 25 June 1873, *Third Report from the Select Committee on East India Finance; Together with the Proceedings of the Committee, Minutes of Evidence and Appendix*, BLAPAC, IOR/L/PARL/2/210, p. 402.

[108] Mariam Dossal, *Imperial Designs and Imperial Realities: The Planning of Bombay City, 1845–1875* (Oxford: Oxford University Press, 1991), pp. 95–8.

[109] *Jam-e-Jamsed*, 21 May 1868, week ending 23 May 1868; *Bombay Chabuk*, 31 March 1869, week ending 31 April 1869, Report on the Native Papers, Bombay.

[110] Masani, *Dadabhai Naoroji*, p. 181; Wacha to Naoroji, 18 November 1884, in Patwardan, ed., *Dadabhai Naoroji Correspondence*, vol. II, part I, pp. 3–4.

[111] E. C. K. Ollivant to Naoroji, 4 December 1883, DNP, O-22 (1); Naoroji to E. C. K. Ollivant, 5 December 1883, DNP, N-1 (130); Nowrosji Furdoonji to Naoroji, 2 November 1883, DNP, F-96.

I want to be sure of this.'[112] Direct comparisons were drawn by Naoroji with the domestic and industrial water provision for London in order to show that despite the municipality's financial independence, reliance on state credit was distorting economic development in India.[113]

In Britain, a municipal revolution was underway when Naoroji entered London politics. Elected school boards were established in 1870 (for which women were enfranchised), country and borough councils were introduced in 1888, and by 1894 parish and district councils replaced the vestries, widening the sphere of popular democracy. Local authorities were empowered to raise public loans and build local and civic amenities.[114] The creation of the London County Council in 1889 politicized local government and gave expression to the issues of Georgeism, unionism, unemployment and sweated labour.[115]

Naoroji's notes reveal that he welcomed these reforms as a way of achieving the '[f]ull development of man and woman's gifts of nature'.[116] When Naoroji critiqued the municipal franchise, it was on the grounds of institutionalizing economic monopoly. The vestry elections attracted little over 3 per cent of the existing franchise. Since it was the vestries that elected the municipal board of works, the city's local government was gifted to men of property in a manner not dissimilar to parliament.[117] It was not until the Local Government Act in 1894 that the prohibitive qualification for vestry membership was removed and women were admitted.[118] It seems that Naoroji's concern around popular control of municipal institutions in London mirrored his view of the House of Commons. Working-class representatives were essential because the United Kingdom had already institutionalized a form of representative government through which local economy was managed. By contrast, the stronger executive powers for the commissioner in Bombay meant that only that office and its financial probity were the objects of Naoroji's Indian reform.

To this end, Naoroji was intimately involved in the affairs of the vestry in Clerkenwell after his successful election in 1892, insisting upon attending the

[112] Naoroji to E. C. K. Ollivant, 20 October 1885, DNP, N-1 (437).
[113] Naoroji to E. C. K. Ollivant, 30 October 1889, DNP, N-1 (1525).
[114] Harris, *Private Lives*, pp. 18–19.
[115] Davis, *Reforming London*, pp. 115, 120.
[116] Quoting Lord Rosebery in 'Various Points', 31 May 1894, DNP, notes and jottings, group 3: miscellaneous, serial number 66; William Phillips, *"'Home Rule" for London: An Appeal and a Warning* (London, n.p., 1888), p. 1.
[117] 'Local Government Notes', DNP, notes and jottings, group 7: political serial number 8; Davis, *Reforming London*, p. 87.
[118] Ibid., p. 197.

committees and demanding that all 'minutes, agenda notices, and other papers' be sent to him.[119] Naoroji also consistently gave his backing to the progressive candidates for the London county council in his ward: Ashley Ponsonby and William Farewell Blake.[120] He was also a member of the London municipal reform league and a founding member of the London reform union with Sidney Webb.[121] Webb would champion the progressive 'London Programme' via the county council in an effort to secure labour's sovereignty within the 'social machinery', buttress their 'corporate existence' in the face of the monopolists and 'develop their character as citizens'.[122]

A residual bourgeois elitism permeated Webb's thought as it did Naoroji's. Just as Naoroji believed his class could best represent the public interests of Indian labour in the Indian civil service, so too did Webb support a new class of professional representatives in local and central government administrations as well as in the unions and co-operatives. These professionals would maintain an 'intimate and reciprocal' relationship with the working-class electorate in order to raise 'the ordinary man into active political citizenship'.[123] Webb desired the promotion of sociality and the 'lofty ideal of civil life'.[124] The elective principle in the London Council was designed to promote an equitable contract between capital and labour to just such an effect by re-claiming control of institutions which directed the capital investment, such as the Board of Works and water and gas companies, so that a 'natural evolution' followed which developed labour's sovereign command of its surplus and capacity for contract.[125]

Naoroji dissected the reports of the municipality as soon as the London County Council was created in an effort to promote the above aims, noting the regressive nature of local taxation before 1888. He observed that the rate levied across London parishes varied from 3 shillings to 3 shillings and 6 pence in the

---

[119] Vestry meeting, 7 July 1892, *Minutes and Proceedings of the Board and Committees from May 1892 to May 1893*, London, Islington Local History Centre (ILHC), Clerkenwell Vestry Minutes.

[120] London county council voting instructions for ward 4, Central Finsbury, DNP, L-95 (3); A. Ponsonby to Naoroji, 12 March 1892, DNP, F-34 (3); Naoroji to A. Ponsonby, (undated), DNP, N-1 (3196).

[121] J. F. Torr, secretary to the London municipal reform league, to Naoroji, 23 March 1889, DNP, L-106 (1); 'Proceedings of the London Reform Union', 1 (November 1892), DNP, L-109.

[122] Sidney Webb, *The London Programme* (London Swan Sonnenschein & Co, 1891), pp. 6–8.

[123] Sidney Webb and Beatrice Webb, *Industrial Democracy* (London: Longman, Green & Co, 1920 [1897]), pp. 70–1.

[124] *Glasgow Herald*, 28 February 1894.

[125] 'Municipalities Elected by the People', DNP, notes and jottings, group 7: political, serial number 56.

pound 'irrespective of the poor rate' in each parish and concluded that 'the poorer parishes have the heaviest burden'. He also proposed that the council build a 'competing supply' of water reservoirs, gas works and workmen's housing since the municipality could borrow money with a rate of interest 33 per cent lower than that of joint stock companies. With a critique unmistakably like his attack on the Indian colonial state, Naoroji noted that since the county council was not obliged to pay huge dividends to shareholders, or 'large salaries and pensions' to its contractors, economies could be passed onto the urban citizen to aid their social development.[126] Naoroji also wanted to legally obligate the county council to force capitalists to invest in civic amenities in the name of a better working environment and labour productivity.[127] He unsuccessfully tabled an amendment to the County Council Bill of 1894, obligating all 'owners of houses' to light every 'stairwell and passage ... from sunset to sunrise' thus absolving lower income ratepayers of any undue burden. Naoroji even suggested that failure to comply should result in the property owner paying the punitive fine of 5 pounds per night.[128]

Alongside utility companies, one of the more dubious examples of monopolistic rent extraction in London was the city's ancient guilds and liveries. A royal commission on London's livery companies instituted in 1880 reported four years later that these institutions ought to use some of their funds for 'public purposes'. The minority report claimed that state had a right to dis-endow the various worshipful companies but recommended that members be compensated first.[129] Naoroji was baffled as to why this ought to be the case, scribbling: 'To what benefit!?' He observed that there were seventy-four livery companies in London, administering 15 million pound worth of property, with an income of 750,000 pounds per annum. While 25 per cent of this income went to charitable trusts, 600,000 pounds was solely for the disposal of its members with 60,000 pounds paid in salaries. Naoroji thought that the organizations should simply be abolished, all funds used for public purposes like education and the rights of the companies transferred to the county council.[130] Recourse to representative institutions to combat monopoly followed the same logic as promoting workers' co-operatives and industrial courts. Naoroji invoked all these tools to foster a commercial society

---

[126] 'London Financial Matters', DNP, notes and jottings, group 1: accounts/economic/trade, serial number 25.

[127] Adjourned vestry meeting, 7 June 1894, ILHC, *Minutes and Proceedings of the Board and Committees from May 1894 to May 1895*, Clerkenwell Vestry Minutes.

[128] HC Deb 29 May 1894 vol. 24, cc. 1509–1510.

[129] *Royal Commission Appointed to Inquire into the Livery Companies of the City of London, 1880*, vol. I (5 vols, London: n.p., 1884), c. 4073.

[130] 'London Financial Matters'; 'Local Government Notes'.

through the subordination of monopolistic capital to worker oversight that brought a fairer contractual bargain and a more natural basis for market exchange.

## The Rights of Labour and Naoroji's Finsbury Campaign

The language of the Indian drain and labour rights was instrumental in Naoroji's successful election to Central Finsbury in 1892. The constituency was overwhelmingly working class, with the middle classes constituting less than 10 per cent of the electorate. This was a marked difference from Naoroji's failed 1886 campaign in Holborn in which the middle class constituted 33–40 per cent of the electorate and where Naoroji lost by about 30 per cent of the total votes cast.[131] Naoroji's loud proclamations in favour of Irish Home Rule in 1886 did not win him much support among a predominantly conservative electorate, one that exclusively returned Tory or Unionist members from 1885 until the seat's abolition in 1950.[132] The 1881 and 1891 Finsbury censuses show that the constituency was working class but that it was characterized mostly by artisanal labour. Skilled and semi-skilled bricklayers, wicker workers, watchmakers, glass blowers, cabinetmakers and jewellers fill the census pages with sons apprenticed to their father's trade or in similar trades elsewhere in the borough. Localized artisanal workshops were interspersed with housing.[133] The tens of thousands of cabmen, dockworkers and chimney sweeps that constituted the bulk of the labouring poor of the East End were few and far between in Finsbury.[134] By 1891, electrical engineers, surgical instrument makers and machinists began to make an appearance, suggesting an increase in skilled labour on the eve of Naoroji's election.[135]

Naoroji's strict adherence to the Newcastle Programme, with its focus on housing legislation and the taxation of land values, attracted working-class voters during the upswing in unemployment after 1891.[136] However, Naoroji continued to advocate the type of labour reform that the Gladstonians had rejected, like the Fabian proposal for the eight-hour working day and demands for municipal

---

[131] Paul Thompson, 'Liberals, Radicals and Labour in London 1880–1900', *Past and Present* 27 (April 1964), pp. 96–7.

[132] Masani, *Dadabhai Naoroji*, p. 240.

[133] 1881 Census Report, London, Islington Local History Centre (ILHC), RG11 345–49; Charles Booth, *Life and Labour of the People of London, Second Series: Industry* (London: Macmillan, 1903), pp. 114–15.

[134] Based on 1891 census data for the East End in Marc Brodie, *The Politics of the Poor: The East End of London, 1885–1914* (Oxford: Oxford University Press, 2004), p. 25.

[135] 1891 Census Report, ILHC, RG12 221–223.

[136] Thompson, 'Liberals, Radicals and Labour', pp. 91–2.

control of London's gas and water markets.[137] He thus capitalized on the new unionism of this period, which was to decline after 1892, obtaining the support of union leaders like A. P. Borgia, the chairman of the North-side District Council Federation of Trades and Labour Unions. Naoroji agitated for key planks in their platform like the Employers' Liability Bill of 1886 that was ultimately defeated in the House of Lords. The language from Naoroji's drain theory was used to suggest neat solutions to Finsbury's labour problem. Naoroji exclaimed that since Finsbury's family-owned workshops were wealth creators, the landlord or factory owner should be prohibited from denying workers the fruits of their labour and a comfortable working environment. This also applied to the problem of 'aliens' ostensibly undercutting English labour. Naoroji suggested that if Irish Home Rule were granted and the Irish worker could enjoy the fruits of international trade would he not return to Ireland and enjoy the prosperity of his homeland?[138] India was also included in this logic, with Naoroji giving talks at the Finsbury Liberal and Radical Club entitled the 'British Masses and India'. In this lecture, Naoroji implored the British worker to take an interest in Indian affairs in the name of free trade. If the drain were stopped, the increased consumptive powers of the subcontinent would mean a precipitate increase in the British worker's market for exports, thereby putting an end to unemployment and low pay in London.[139] A pro-Naoroji campaigner in Finsbury, Oscar Eisengarten even offered to translate Naoroji's 'poverty of India' into German. Such enthusiasm for Indian issues was, Naoroji wrote, 'a good sign from a member of our club'.[140]

Asking British producers to act in their own self-interest by agitating on behalf of Indian interests was a persistent theme that Naoroji would use throughout the 1890s.[141] With a focus on both general labour issues and those specific to the artisanal classes, Naoroji bridged the radicalism of the 1880s and the labourism of the 1890s. As John Davis notes, the politics of the radical club in the 1890s brought different branches of the labour movement into single social centres in which a language of shared experience created deeper sense of solidarity compared to the artisanal proselytizing of the 1880s.[142]

---

[137] Ibid., p. 84.

[138] 'Finsbury Politics', *Finsbury and Holborn Guardian*, 18 June 1892.

[139] Naoroji to Griffith, 10 July 1891, DNP, N-1 (1902); Talk given on the 25 August 1891, DNP, F-34.

[140] Naoroji to Griffith, 29 January 1891, DNP, N-1 (1718).

[141] 'Mr. Naoroji on the Needs of India, East Manchester Liberal Association', *Manchester Guardian*, 15 November 1898.

[142] John Davis, 'Radical Clubs and London Politics, 1870–1900', in David Feldman and Gareth Steadman Jones, eds., *Metropolis London: Histories and Representations since 1800* (London: Routledge, 1989), p. 115.

The labour vote in 1892, mobilized through workers unions and clubs, was crucial in getting Naoroji's message heard. Naoroji had taken on board the advice imparted to him after the Holborn election that a significant proportion of the constituency had not turned out to vote and that these were more than likely apathetic radicals who suffered from a 'want of organization'.[143] Mustering support via key conduits in the labour movement in London became of paramount importance. The enthusiasm of figures like the East Finsbury MP James Rowlands was called upon to get organizations like the Metropolitan Radical Association to throw their weight behind Naoroji.[144] The impact of Naoroji's grassroots organization and propaganda should not be underestimated. Some of the most popular radical newspapers in London like *The Star* had intervened against Naoroji's candidature from the beginning, viewing Indian candidates as gifting the seat to the Tories.[145] On the ground, however, Naoroji's message struck a chord. A 'working man', writing to the *Weekly News and Chronicle*, declared that he was 'ready and willing to give up a considerable portion' of his time to 'promote the interests' of Naoroji.[146] By 1892, Naoroji was confident that labour organizations in Finsbury now firmly considered him 'their candidate'.[147] Under Naoroji's leadership, the Central Finsbury United Liberal and Radical Association was, for a brief period between 1893 and 1895, able to combine progressive British politics with vociferous support for Indian reform when it supported Naoroji's presidency of the Lahore Congress in 1893 and demanded simultaneous examinations for the Indian Civil Service.[148]

## The Drain Theory and Global Critics of Empire

The neo-Roman liberty implicit in Naoroji's drain theory also appealed to a number of imperial critics who regarded colonialism as a negative externality of a malfunctioning capitalism. In this intellectual genealogy, Naoroji's theory was not only an antecedent to John A. Hobson's 1902 work *Imperialism: A Study* but his labour theory of value also placed the dominated British labourer in a unified framework with their Indian counterpart. Hobson's theory did not countenance this. Drawing on the positivist tradition, Hobson tended to rail

---

[143] Naoroji underlining these points in R. A. Taylor Loban to Naoroji, 31 August 1887, NAI, DNP, L-80 (2).
[144] *Pall Mall Gazette*, 5 June 1891.
[145] *The Star*, 17 August 1888 and 18 August 1888.
[146] *Weekly News and Chronicle*, 15 September 1888.
[147] Naoroji to Griffith, 18 August 1892, NAI, Dadabhai Naoroji Papers, N-1 (2331).
[148] Central Finsbury United Liberal and Radical Association, rules, (undated), DNP, C-84 (4); *India* 4, no. 9 (1893), p. 271.

'more against jingoism at home than imperialism in Africa'.[149] Other Positivists within the ranks of the British Committee of the Indian National Congress, like Henry Cotton, were also circumspect about the possibility of a self-regulating Indian civil or commercial society. Cotton believed that the best the peasant could hope for was to be led by a 'patrician aristocracy' of the higher castes.[150] Economic monopolists, aristocrats and militarists in Britain were the targets of their radical broadsides; hence, Hobsoniant anti-imperialism and its allies promoted a historical conception of 'Englishness' and English liberty that stood in opposition to overseas imperium but also ignored the rights of indigenous peoples.[151] Naoroji was even acquainted with members of the 'Rainbow Circle', the coterie of New Liberal thinkers, towards the end of the nineteenth century, so it is not improbable that Hobson drew on Naoroji's earlier theories.[152] Naorojian ideas may also have been disseminated through several prominent associations of liberal economic debate of which he was also a member. In addition to the Cobden Club, he frequented Alfred Marshall's British Economic Association, and the political and economic circle of the National Liberal Club.[153]

William Digby, the critic of the economics of empire, had honed his version of India's economic predicament through Naoroji and by 1902 was describing himself as Naoroji's 'disciple'.[154] In a letter to the National Liberal Federation in 1881, before he had met Naoroji, Digby mentioned the Indian drain when asking the federation's council to take greater account of the subcontinent's grievances.[155] However, by the late 1880s after he had been Naoroji's election agent for Holborn in 1886, Digby was citing Naoroji's articles from the *Contemporary Review* and his 'Poverty of India'.[156] By the time Digby published *Prosperous British India* in

---

[149] Bernhard Porter, *Critics of Empire: British Radicals and the Imperial Challenge* (London: I. B. Tauris, 2008), p. 91.

[150] Sir Henry John Steadman Cotton, *New India or India in Transition*, new edn (London: Kegan, Paul, Trench, Trübner & Co, 1904), p. 12.

[151] Matikkala, *Empire and Imperial Ambition*.

[152] William Clarke, J. A. Hobson, and G. H. Perris to Naoroji, 3 February 1899, DNP, C-172.

[153] British Economic Association to Naoroji, 20 December 1890, DNP, B-217 (ii); *National Liberal Club, Political and Economic Circle: Transactions*, vol. I (London: n.p., 1891), UBL, Papers of the National Liberal Club, DM668; *The Times*, 30 October 1890.

[154] William Digby to Naoroji, 5 October 1902, DNP, D-118 (219).

[155] William Digby, *Indian Problems for English Consideration: A Letter to the Council of the National Liberal Federation* (Plymouth: Latimer & Son, 1881), p. 46.

[156] William Digby, 'The Condition of India', *Manchester Guardian*, 24 January 1891; Dadabhai Naoroji, 'Sir M. E. Grant Duff's Views About India. – I', *Contemporary Review* 52 (August 1887), pp. 221–35 and 'Sir M. E. Grant Duff's Views About India. – II', *Contemporary Review* 52 (November 1887), pp. 694–711.

1901, he had adopted a much more sophisticated drain paradigm for colonial rule, acknowledging its debt to Naoroji.[157] It even abstracted India's position at the periphery of global capitalism as the 'labourer' in hock to Britain's global capitalist and pointed to the English banking and council bill systems as mechanisms of subordination.[158]

Likewise, W. Martin Wood's interest in the inaccuracy of official opinion and statistics on Indian political economy stemmed from his time as a journalist in India. Wood asked Naoroji to browse his 1887 article on Britain and India's skewed 'trade balance' and offer suggestions.[159] Wood admitted that his initial work 'may seem very incomplete' to Naoroji and requested further direction based on Naoroji's 'elaborate and emphatic exposition'.[160] To the dismay of some English positivists, of all the Europeans on the British Committee, Wood remained the most committed to Naoroji's thesis because 'the smell of the "drain"' was 'ever in his nostrils'.[161] English followers of Comte, like Henry Cotton, believed that poverty was an accepted fact in India but the state had no role in it. India's transformation was to be entirely organic and spontaneous, the role of the state relegated to a Mainite 'conservancy' of custom in order to prevent the disintegration of traditional communities.[162]

Naoroji also influenced the leading British socialist of the day, Henry Mayers Hyndman, the founder of the Social Democratic Federation. Hyndman reminisced that he began his long study of India after having met James Geddes, after which he fortuitously discovered Naoroji's work in 1878.[163] At this time, Hyndman had already begun to analyse the economic side of colonial exploitation and was penning an article for the journal *Nineteenth Century*. Stumbling upon a copy of Naoroji's 'Poverty of India' at the parliamentary booksellers 'completed [Hyndman's] own work'.[164] It is unsurprising that Naoroji's theory ought to appeal to Hyndman's Marxist understanding of colonialism. The latter subscribed to Marx's labour theory of value as evidenced by his critique of Jevons's equivalent

[157] William Digby, *Prosperous British India: A Revelation from Official Records* (London: Fisher Unwin, 1901), p. xxiv.
[158] Ibid., pp. 105–6, 142, 201–2.
[159] W. Martin Wood, 'India's Un-adjusted Trade Balance: Its Effect on the Industrial and Commercial Condition of the People', *Political Science Quarterly* 2, no. 4 (1887), pp. 666–83.
[160] W. M. Wood to Naoroji, 30 October 1887, DNP, W-153 (64); Wood to Naoroji, 20 Dec. 1887, DNP, W-153 (65).
[161] Albert Louis Cotton to Harry Evan Auguste Cotton, 28 January 1904, BLAPAC, Sir Henry John Steadman Cotton Papers, IOR Neg 12038.
[162] Cotton, *New India*, pp. vi–vii; *India*, 7 November 1902, p. 224.
[163] H. M. Hyndman to Naoroji, 12 September 1901, DNP, H-221 (98).
[164] H. M. Hyndman, *Record of an Adventurous Life*, p. 175.

which Hyndman read to mean that labour had no intrinsic value save the final price of the commodity. Thus, Jevons's price was determined more by utility and quantity of supply than embodied labour hours.[165] Hyndman attempted to popularize the Marxist theory of value and surplus value for a British audience in his *England for All*, an analysis of land, labour and capital in Britain and the colonies. It also embraced Naorojian and Georgeist republican principles of land ownership and securing to the labourer the fruits of his transformation of natural resources.[166]

Hyndman's work was likely a meditation on Naoroji's thesis, and Hyndman's correspondence with Karl Marx from February 1881 shows that the manuscript was prepared in dialogue with Naoroji, whom he wanted Marx 'very much to meet'.[167] There is even evidence to suggest that Marx's own views were shaped either directly by Naoroji or through Hyndman's popularizing of his ideas in socialist circles. Later that February, Marx emphasized the institutional subordination of India under British capitalism wherein Indians lived under the arbitrary will of metropolitan interests. He wrote to *Narodnik*'s Nicolai Danielson:

> In *India* serious complications, if not a general outbreak, is in store for the British government. What the English take from them annually in the form of rent, dividends for railways useless to the Hindus; pensions for military and civil service men, for Afghanistan and other wars, etc., etc. – what they take from them *without any equivalent* and quite apart from what they appropriate to themselves annually *within* India, speaking only of the *value of the commodities* the Indians have gratuitously and annually to *send over* to England – it amounts to *more than the total sum of income of the sixty millions of agricultural and industrial labourers of India!* This is a bleeding process, with a vengeance![168]

By 1885, Naoroji's ideas were reproduced even more explicitly as Hyndman drew attention to the non-remunerative 'home charges', the excess of exports over imports and the class dominance of an increasingly anglicized Indian civil

[165] H. M. Hyndman, 'The Final Futility of Final Utility', 28 February 1894, in *National Liberal Club, Political and Economic Circle: Transactions*, vol. 2 (London: n.p., 1895), UBL, Papers of the National Liberal Club, DM668, pp. 126–9.

[166] H. M. Hyndman, *England for All* (London: E. W. Allen, 1881).

[167] Hyndman to Naoroji, 9 December 1881, DNP, H-221 (5); Marcus Morris, 'From Anti-Colonialism to Anti-Imperialism: The Evolution of H.M. Hyndman's Critique of Empire, c.1875–1905', *Historical Research* 87, no. 236 (2014), pp. 293–314.

[168] Karl Marx to Nicolai Danielson, 19 February 1881, in *K. Marx and F. Engles on Colonialism* (Moscow: Foreign Languages Publishing House, n.d.), p. 337 (emphasis in original).

service.[169] Emphasizing the unified global framework of Naoroji's paradigm, Hyndman claimed that both Indian peasants and British workers suffered as a result of 'middle class economics'.[170] Hyndman continued to promote this model after Marx's death, forwarding *Poverty and un-British Rule* to Karl Kautsky in 1902.[171]

Naoroji's theories also crossed the Atlantic Ocean. In the 1890s, Naoroji carried on an extensive correspondence with the American-Irish journalist and socialist George Freeman. Failing to get re-elected in 1895, and frustrated by his inability to secure simultaneous civil service examinations for Indians, Naoroji looked to international collaborators to feed him information about retaliation against un-British and uncivil liberalism beyond Britain and India.[172] Freeman's analysis of global events was encouraging to Naoroji since it seemed to show a demand for reform proliferating in every corner of the globe. Unfortunately, Freeman used the drain theory's account of financial domination to buttress his anti-Semitism, confiding in Naoroji that in Canada Joseph Chamberlain's aggressive stewardship of the Colonial Office was creating a movement for independence where 'the Canadian sheep [was] turning at last'.[173] Whatever pro-British and pro-imperialist sentiment existed, Freeman blamed on 'Jewish papers', which he curiously claimed were all the more conciliatory to Britain because Lord Curzon's wife was the 'daughter of that old Chicago Jew speculator, Levi Lecter'.[174] Naoroji never expressed any interest in Freeman's anti-Semitic rants but continued to enquire after growing anti-British sentiment around the world and the prospect of imminent reform, such as the efforts of the Canadian Independence Club.[175]

Freeman was more useful in getting Naoroji's views a hearing by the Democratic Party's populist presidential candidate for the 1896, 1900 and 1908 elections, William Jennings Bryan. Freeman had sent Bryan both Naoroji and Hyndman's works on imperialism in India as well as Naoroji's statements before the Indian Currency Committee of 1898.[176] Bryan's 'Cross of Gold' speech at the 1896 Democratic convention had famously pulled the rug out from under the

169 H. M. Hyndman, *The Bankruptcy of India: An Enquiry into the Administration of India under the Crown* (London: Swan Sonnenschein & Co, 1886), pp. 25–9, 53–7, 87.
170 Ibid., pp. 154–5, 181–2, 211.
171 Hyndman to Naoroji, 30 January 1902, DNP, H-221 (105).
172 G. Freeman to Naoroji, 3 December 1900, DNP, F-87 (64).
173 Freeman to Naoroji, 26 May 1899, DNP, F-87 (34).
174 Freeman to Naoroji, 1 January 1901, DNP, F-87 (65).
175 Freeman to Naoroji, 23 October 1900, DNP, F-87 (62).
176 Freeman to Naoroji, 2 December 1898, DNP, F-87 (14); Freeman to Naoroji, 12 December 1898, DNP, F-87 (15).

Populist Party by advocating the abandonment of the gold standard and a return to the free coinage of silver. This was a welcome measure with American farmers since it proposed to re-inflate agricultural prices after their continuous fall from the end of the Civil War. Bryan's moral economy was consciously future-orientated, proposing a harmonized industrial capitalism in which agriculturalists and workers could be re-socialized and reclaim their autonomy in a neo-Jeffersonian republic.[177] This dovetailed with Naoroji's own views on financial domination, with Jennings Bryan claiming that the struggle was between the 'idle holders of capital and the struggling masses who produce the wealth and pay the taxes of the country'. Like Naoroji, the Jennings Bryan Democrats would not abandon the 'producing masses of the nation and the world' and refused to 'crucify mankind upon a cross of gold'.[178]

In the case of India, the British decided to close the mints in 1893 to free coinage in gold and silver because the declining value of the rupee against sterling was placing pressure on servicing Indian debt and was a disturbance to international trade.[179] Like Jennings Bryan, Naoroji demanded a return to the free coinage of silver because all existing economic contracts, including those pertaining to the state's revenue demand, had been 'contracted on a silver basis'. Naoroji opined that since the economic monopoly of India was largely paid for in produce, a change in the value of gold or silver would not change the fact that an absolute quantity of produce would have to be exported to cover, for instance, a 20 million pound debt in Britain. Only if the price of the commodity itself increased would the level of drain on the Indian taxpayer reduce. In fact, in increasing the value of the rupee through monetary stringency, the salaries of colonial officials and money owed to domestic creditors would be artificially inflated to the detriment of the 'poorer classes'. The fabrication of a 'false rupee' was thus an 'illegal, dishonourable and despotic act'.[180] Like the American populists, Naoroji argued that fiat money served the interests of 'the few wealthy men who hold permanent promissory notes

[177] Charles Postel, *The Populist Vision* (Oxford: Oxford University Press, 2007), p. 4.
[178] *Official Proceedings of the Democratic National Convention Held in Chicago, Illinois, 7, 8, 9, 10 and 11 July 1896* (Logansport, IN: Wilson, Humphreys & Co, 1896), pp. 226–34.
[179] *Report of the Committee Appointed to Inquire into the Indian Currency* (London Her Majesty's Stationary Office, 1899), pp. 3, 9–11; A. G. Chandavarkar, 'Money and Credit', in Dharma Kumar and Meghnad Desai, eds., *The Cambridge Economic History of India* (Cambridge: Cambridge University Press, 1983), p. 770.
[180] Naoroji, 'Statement Submitted to the Indian Currency Committee of 1898', in Dadabhai Naoroji, *The Grand Little Man of India: Dadabhai Naoroji, Speeches and Writings*, vol. I, ed. Moin Zaidi (2 vols., New Delhi Indian Institute of Applied Political Research, 1985), pp. 314–56.

of other bonds' because the fixed value of the 'false rupee' now gave them 'more than they lent'. Inevitably, this policy pandered to 'British capitalists, bankers, merchants etc'.[181] Since they reinforced his own views about American labour, Jennings Bryan asked Freeman if he could use Naoroji's pamphlets on the Indian drain publicly in his own speeches.[182]

Naoroji's drain theory also helped Jennings Bryan to combine his anti-imperialist position against the American annexation of the Philippines with his pro-producer and anti-trust positions at home. In his 'Imperialism' speech at the 1900 Democratic national convention, Jennings Bryan had vowed to end the policy of annexation and plunder so reminiscent of the European empires and institute a truly 'American' policy in the Philippines that granted self-government and security.[183] A year before, he had quoted Naoroji's comments from a talk at the London Indian Society stating that the current American policy in the Philippines would lead to a system of colonial labour in which the Filipinos, like the Indians, would be compelled 'to make brick, not only without straw, but even without clay'. The American added that, according to Naoroji, Indians were there 'to pay taxes and to slave' and it was 'the business of the government to spend those taxes to their own benefit'. Jennings Bryan thought it inconceivable that the 'principles of politics, of commerce, of equality which are applied to Great Britain are not applied to India. As if India were not inhabited by human beings!'[184] It is evident that Naoroji's theory of uncivil liberalism, with its focus on monopoly capitalism, had a distinct impact on fellow critics of empire. With Naoroji's labour theory of value, it seemed obvious to Jennings Bryan that Indians and Filipinos were entitled to the same autonomy that he wanted restored to American labour in the name of a modern social economy. Had Jennings Bryan taken his cue from J. A. Hobson's imperial criticism, it is unlikely that he would have arrived at the same determination.

## Conclusion

Hobson understood imperialism as symptomatic of an impoverished, under-consuming proletariat; in turn, this inexorably led to the extension of state power abroad to satiate an over-producing capitalist class in their search for new markets

[181] Naoroji draft evidence to the currency committee, (undated) 1899, DNP, C-299.
[182] Freeman to Naoroji, 1 January 1899, DNP, F-87 (17).
[183] William Jennings Bryan, 'Imperialism', in William Jennings Bryan, ed. *Under Other Flags: Travels, Lectures, Speeches* (Lincoln, NE: Woodruff-Collins Printing Co, 1904), pp. 305–39.
[184] William Jennings Bryan, *Republic or Empire? The Philippine Question* (Chicago, IL: The Independence Company, 1899), p. 76.

and a greater rate of return.[185] He prescribed state intervention in the economy in order to alleviate poverty and stimulate demand, thereby undercutting the need for military-aristocratic adventures abroad in the search for new markets. Much like English positivism's imperial critique, the normative thrust of this critique was focused on the social and political future of the British Isles, not of India. Hobson's focus on the distributive imbalance between producers and consumers seemed to echo Naoroji's own, pointing out that if miners in successful businesses get remunerated on the same level as those in failing ones, then the capitalist appropriated surplus value. Equally, Hobson's rationale for social reform was akin to Naoroji's post-1860s claims in India, 'to raise the wholesome standard for private and public consumption for a nation, so as to enable the nation to live up to its highest standard of production'.[186] Nevertheless, Hobson could not go so far as to apply the same language to India and, like the positivists, he concluded that the abstractions of classical political economy could not be applied to 'low-typed unprogressive races'. Whether independent or supported by European guidance, Hobson believed that India ought to be encouraged to supply raw materials for the socially reproductive processes of European industry because, left to their own devices, indigenous peoples did not possess the 'ordinary economic motives and methods of free exchange to supply the growing demand for tropical goods'.[187]

This chapter has shown how Naoroji's drain theory had intellectual and political significance in Britain. His labour theory of value allowed Naoroji to generate intellectual capital across a range of contemporary debates from Irish Home Rule and American populism to working-class politics and municipal radicalism. Though Naoroji relied on networks of collaborators to facilitate these interactions, the purchase of his ideas was not reducible to these connections; indeed, it facilitated and sustained some personal relationships, while those without intellectual synergies with Naoroji's thought withered and died. This radical universalism was simply absent from Hobson's imperial critique in which capital still retained its right to a higher rate of return on account of its ability to organize production. The state was to intervene in the market to augment working-class consumption where it was deficient, which would reinvigorate the domestic profitability of capital.[188] In Hobson's view, the capitalist producers and the consuming public were conceptualized as potentially antagonistic groups who, nonetheless, needed one another. Thus, Hobson supported workers' co-operatives

[185] J. A. Hobson, *Imperialism: A Study* (London: James Nisbet & Co, 1902).
[186] Ibid., pp. 89, 93–4.
[187] Ibid., pp. 237–8.
[188] Hobson, *Imperialism*, pp. 88, 95.

only insofar as they generated an investible surplus for consumption by eliminating waste and allowing capitalists to raise their rate of return at home.[189]

Naoroji's Indian experience was coloured by the state-reinforced domination of capital and the economic enslavement of Indians. His development of a labour theory of value, therefore, placed producers and consumers on an equal footing with one another and sought to relegate capital to an ancillary rather than formative factor of production. The result was to decentre the industrial capital of the 'West' as the driver of global economic and social development and also to subordinate state autonomy to the task of social development. The producer of re-investible value and property in Naoroji's imagination was the humblest peasant or worker. It was only when both were remunerated according to natural law that they had the consumptive power to reproduce labour and generate property or capital which might then support industry. This process was to remain subject to the systematic arbitration of economic legislation or institutions like industrial courts. Hobson, however, never assented to the displacement or management of capital, casually dismissing republican arguments about co-operation and land taxes as an 'interesting testimony to the naiveté of the British mind'.[190]

If Naoroji's drain theory and liberalism received a sympathetic hearing among radical circles in Britain and beyond, then it was also taken up in his homeland but by a more motley collection of thinkers. The final chapter of the book examines some of these curious ideological legacies in India.

---

[189] J. A. Hobson, *Confessions of an Economic Heretic: The Autobiography of John A. Hobson*, ed. Michael Freeden (Hassocks: Harvester Press, 1976 [1938]), p. 27.
[190] Ibid., p. 27.

# 7 The Afterlives of Naoroji's Political Thought

In 1917, at the venerable age of ninety-one and only four months before his death, Naoroji reassured the Indian Legislative Council that the new problem of terrorist 'anarchism in India' resulted from 'propaganda' and 'dangerous conspirators' rather than the innate Indian propensity for political violence.[1] The Grand Old Man's reassurances allayed British fears about anti-colonial revolution but also reflected the creeping worry among Indian 'moderates' that a harmonious society predicated on a liberal model of civil peace was moving further out of view.

The rise of an antagonistic politics buttressed by British strategies of divide and rule threatened to undermine any long-term dreams of multicultural sociality. The founding of the Muslim League in 1906, and its lobbying for minority representation for Muslims, culminated in the separate electorates of the 1909 Morley–Minto Reforms. It is telling that Naoroji welcomed such reforms that increased Indian political representation in order to train a larger Indian clerisy of reformers. This was a means to an end, that of plugging the drain rather than a plebiscitary upscaling of Indian popular sovereignty and the establishing of a constituent power. Instead, Naoroji focused on a rules-based 'constitutionalism' to govern social issues and replacing the arbitrary will of British officials. He continued to believe that Indian peoplehood depended on a commercial sociality and implored the British that the scrapping of all despotic economic monopolies was the only way to reach that goal. It is hardly surprising, then, that all of Naoroji's letters on the topic of constitutional reform were qualified with the primary demand for simultaneous civil service examinations.[2]

The new question of political representation did dilute the relevance of Naoroji's drain theory for card-carrying Indian liberals for whom political economy was, by this stage, an epiphenomenal but not a fundamental factor in imagining Indian liberal subjectivity. Surendranath Banerjea, V. S. Srinivasa Sastri

[1] Dadabhai Naoroji's speech in the Indian Legislative Council, 8 February 1917, National Archives of India, New Delhi [NAI], Home Political, 1917, August, proceedings 225–32.

[2] Dadabhai Naoroji to Lord Morley and Lord Minto, 26 January 1909, NAI, Dadabhai Naoroji Papers [DNP]; Naoroji to Morley and Minto, 3 April 1909, DNP, N-1 (2856).

and Tej Bahadur Sapru founded the Indian National Liberal Federation in 1910 as the Indian National Congress became more radical in its aims and tactics. Pushing for greater political representation, they promoted federalism and decentralization as a gradualist solution to Indian responsible government, which increasingly obscured Naoroji's ideal of commercial society and elided the question of social interdependence. For communitarian liberals like M. M. Malaviya and Lala Lajpat Rai, the new democratic rubric also shifted the question from one of creating a multicultural but unitary society which could claim sovereignty to that of engineering a democratic majority in whom sovereignty could be invested.[3] In this understanding, Malaviya and Lajpat Rai subordinated the drain and questions of Indian labour to anxieties about the forces that allegedly undermined Hindu self-confidence.[4] Malaviya was especially concerned with how coerced labour interfered with the caste system's occupational structure.[5] He supported simultaneous examinations but only so that Hindu males could take cultural pride in being on an equal footing with Europeans.[6] If overcoming economic subordination had an overarching agenda in these communitarian accounts, it was to maximize the efficiency of the Hindu social organism in the shadow of domestic and international competition rather than a programme for creating an interdependent civil society.[7]

But Naoroji's interventions were kept alive in other political spheres which did not shy away from the conceptual conundrum of Indian sociality after his death. The economist and vice-chairman of postcolonial India's planning commission, D. R. Gadgil, would comment in 1958 that India had no concept of a cohesive 'cultural society' but merely a 'territorial' unity overlaid with new political institutions.[8] Similarly, the country's first Indian-born governor-general and founder of the conservative Swatantra (Freedom) Party in 1959, Chakravarti Rajagopalachari (affectionately known as Rajaji), lamented that the technocrats of the newly independent union were so preoccupied with the

[3] C. A. Bayly, *Recovering Liberties: Indian Thought in the Age of Liberalism and Empire* (Cambridge: Cambridge: University Press, 2011), pp. 219–22.
[4] Ibid., pp. 225–30.
[5] M. M. Malaviya, 'The Abolition of Indentured Labour', in M. M. Malaviya, *Speeches and Writings of Pandit Madan Mohan Malaviya* (Madras G. A. Natesan & Co, 1919), pp. 331–2, 380–1.
[6] Ibid., pp. 357–8.
[7] Lala Lajpat Rai, *Lala Lajpat Rai: The Man in His World* (Madras: G. A. Natesan & Co, 1907), pp. 70–3, 158.
[8] D. R. Gadgil, 'Social Change and Liberal Democracy in New States', in Sulabha Brahme, ed., *Selected Writings of D. R. Gadgil: The Indian Economy Problems and Prospects* (Oxford: Oxford University Press, 2011), pp. 356.

atomizing impulses of the ship of state that they paid no attention to 'the ship of society', which was the ultimate guarantor against fragmentation.[9] This chapter is not an exhaustive account of the drain theory's intellectual legacy, nor does it seek to draw a straight line from Naoroji to later thinkers; instead, it focuses on the abiding anxieties about the politically constitutive power of social relations and how Naoroji's ideas – among others – remained useful for addressing this question.

## The Drain and Village Traditionalism: G. Birdwood, M. K. Gandhi and D. R. Gadgil

During Naoroji's lifetime, the drain theory attracted interest from unexpected quarters. Even as Dadabhai's liberalism sought to differentiate Indian individuals from a colonial representational order based on custom, others interpreted the drain theory in a way that sought to reinforce this conservative Maineite interpretation. One such interlocutor was the British expert on Indian arts and manufactures, George Birdwood, who was a retired Indian administrator and naturalist based at the Grant Medical College and University in Bombay, where he was also curator of the government museum, and after which he returned to Britain, where he indulged his interest in Indian arts and crafts from 1868.[10] Birdwood was among Naoroji's oldest European friends, the two having been acquainted since the 1850s, with the Englishman saying that there was not a single one of his 'friends dead or alive' of whose character or 'moral ideals' he could use the words 'loyal and true' to the extent that he could of Naoroji.[11] Yet in politics, Birdwood always displayed disappointment at Naoroji's affiliation with the Liberal Party. In 1886, he offered to help Naoroji in his Holborn candidacy but admitted that he 'would not like to do anything that would augment the Gladstonian camp'.[12] Birdwood made no bones about his intellectual position, informing Naoroji that 'it is emphatically as a Tory' that he wanted 'to serve the Congress party' while

[9] C. Rajagopalachari, 'Peasant Ownership', undated, Nehru Memorial Museum and Library [NMML], New Delhi, C. Rajagopalachari Papers [CRP] (Instalment VI to XII), Speeches/Writings/Articles, serial number 87.

[10] Valentine Chirol, 'Birdwood, Sir George Christopher Molesworth (1832–1917)', rev. Katherine Prior, *Oxford Dictionary of National Biography*, Oxford University Press, 2004 (http://www.oxforddnb.com/view/article/31896, accessed 21 June 2015).

[11] Birdwood remarked that they had been friends for over thirty years in George Birdwood to Naoroji, 4 June 1886, DNP, B-140 (2).

[12] Birdwood to Naoroji, 11 June 1886, NMML, Dadabhai Naoroji Collection, vol. I, pp. 69–76.

simultaneously subscribing to the drain theory even if he 'never agreed with all the aims of [Naoroji's] Political Faith'.[13]

Birdwood's love of traditional Indian art motivated his active intellectual engagement with the Royal Society of Arts and the Imperial Institute.[14] In 1878, he published his *Industrial Arts of India*, a handbook of Indian crafts for the Paris Exhibition.[15] As Birdwood saw it, the pre-industrial social relations and techniques that produced Indian architecture and arts were being destroyed by the incursion of capitalism and Western commodities.[16] Echoing Maine, Birdwood saw authentic art as 'indissolubly bound up with the popular institutions of the country' and whatever the aims of reformers may be in advocating modern political institutions, for Birdwood the 'spiritual consciousness' of the Hindu could only find 'natural and coordinated unity' in 'cooperative village communities'.[17] So keen was Birdwood on the self-directed evolution of Hindu society that he opined that allowing Indian widows to remarry was one of the primary causes of the 1857 rebellion. Defending his ideal of Indian tradition, he believed that 'the laws of Hindoos have created the highest type of family life known' to the world.[18]

British administration, according to Birdwood, militated against realizing the 'natural' order of Hindu civilization. Britain's 'will in India [was] all too political'; it ignored the region's 'literature, art, philosophy' and 'religion' and as a direct consequence the educated classes of India were 'too political in their expectations and aims'. It was economic reform that India required to create a commerce 'based on its own interests, not those of Manchester'.[19] From the perspective of his life-world, therefore, Birdwood bifurcated the political and economic aspects of Dadabhai's drain theory, but it was still to Naoroji he turned when he wanted

---

[13] Birdwood to Naoroji and Wedderburn, (undated) 1898, DNP, B-140 (36); Birdwood to Naoroji, 26 May 1907, DNP, B-140 (66); For Birdwood's close relationship and common interests with fellow Tory Muncherjee Bhownaggree, see John McLeod, 'Mourning, Philanthropy, and M. M. Bhownaggree's Road to Parliament', in John R. Hinnells and Alan Williams, eds., *Parsis in India and the Diaspora* (London: Routledge, 2008), pp. 136–55.

[14] Minutes of the Committee on India, 10 May 1871, Royal Society of Arts, minutes of the various committees, 1871–3, PR/GE/112/12/101; Special committee for Indian collections in *Imperial Institute Annual Report for 1893* (London: n.p., 1893), p. 10.

[15] Abigail McGowan, *Crafting the Nation in Colonial India* (Basingstoke: Palgrave MacMillan, 2009), p. 46.

[16] Partha Mitter, *Much Maligned Monsters: A History of European Reactions to Indian Art* (Chicago, IL: University of Chicago Press, 1992), p. 236.

[17] George Birdwood, *Two Letters on the Industrial Arts of India* (London: W. B. Whittingham & Co, 1879), pp. 8–9.

[18] *India* 2, no. 21 (1891), p. 167.

[19] Birdwood to G. K. Gokhale, 2 December 1908, British Library Asia, Africa and Pacific Collections [BLAPAC], London, Gokhale Papers, IOR Neg 11697.

to calculate how much village-disintegrating English capital there was in India.[20] He sympathized with Naoroji's talk of land reform and co-operative agricultural banking, and tried to generate support for it among Britons and Indians alike, seeing it as addressing the 'supreme question' for India by bolstering 'the integrity of the social' and returning Indians to pre-industrial hierarchies.[21]

That Birdwood was using the drain theory as an orientalist critique of European industrialism was epitomized by his article on the 'Mahratta Plough'. In the simple plough, built by the village farmer and blacksmith, Birdwood saw not only a tool but also a work of art perfectly in harmony with the 'social organization' of the Indian village. Considering the plough, he stated that 'there could not be a stronger proof than this of the thoroughly practical and scientific character of Indian agriculture'.[22] The drain theory in Birdwood's hands took on a different moral dimension to Naoroji's intention, in which British economic monopoly did not prevent socialization in the face of customary separation but actually engaged in active dismantling of what Birdwood regarded as the organic political economy and social order of the Indian village. It was very much in this conservative vein that Mohandas K. Gandhi also deployed Naoroji's drain theory in his own political thought.

Laying out the fundamentals of his political thought in *Hind Swaraj*, Gandhi insisted that Indians 'must admit' that Dadabhai Naoroji was 'the author of nationalism' and that authorship began with the Grand Old Man's seminal observation that 'the English had sucked' India's 'life-blood'.[23] He would later attest in a 1925 speech that accused Britain of conquering India's labour, that he was a 'disciple' of Naoroji's and worked 'along his lines', repeating in 1928 that Naoroji's 'terrible drain' was still the correct heuristic for comprehending Indian poverty.[24] During his South African activism, Gandhi had co-operated with Naoroji in order to secure the rights of Indians in the Transvaal and the South African Union. From a trading caste background himself, it is notable that Gandhi's critique focused on the rights and social contributions of productive Indian merchant classes which were contrasted with the desire of Europeans in South Africa to promote

[20] Birdwood to Naoroji, 3 December 1888, DNP, B-140 (11).
[21] Appendix: extracts from a lecture given by Dr Birdwood before the Society of Arts, 26 February 1879, on 'Indian Pottery at the Paris Exhibition', in Birdwood, *Two Letters on the Industrial Arts*, pp. 17, 21; Samuel Digby to Birdwood, 8 September 1891, BLAPAC, George Birdwood Papers, MSS Eur F216/23; Birdwood to Naoroji, 2 October 1906, DNP, B-140 (84).
[22] 'Sir George Birdwood on the Mahratta Plough', *Indian Spectator*, 28 October 1888.
[23] M. K. Gandhi, *Hind Swaraj or Indian Home Rule* (Ahmedabad: Navajivan Publishing House, 1938 [1909]), pp. 14–15.
[24] M. K. Gandhi, 'Talk to Students at Dacca', *Young India*, 28 May 1925, in *The Collected Works of Mahatma Gandhi* [hereafter *CWMG*], vol. XXVII, pp. 122–3; M. K. Gandhi, 'Our Poverty', *Young India*, 6 September 1923, in *CWMG*, vol. XXXVII, p. 236.

only *coolie* manual labour and so represent all Indians as 'slaves'.[25] Transmitting the complaints of his associates in South Africa via Naoroji to London, Gandhi complained that the system of relocating Indian businesses away from white areas to 'Locations' on account of poor hygiene was not about 'the right of residence' as many Asians stated but concerned, in Naorojian terms, 'the right of trade' and of 'bread and butter'.[26]

After penning *Hind Swaraj* in 1909 and returning to India in 1915, Gandhi's rejection of European capitalism and liberalism would lead him to invert the orientalism of British observers like Birdwood in order to reaffirm their belief that the village was the foundation of Indian cultural life. But Gandhi also flipped the civilizational polarity of colonialism in order to claim that the traditional village generated a morally superior non-desiring subjectivity that promoted reciprocal self-sacrifice instead of individual or group interest. The result was a diverse society based on cultural difference that retained a model for living together without violence.[27] Sympathy and ethical conduct based on sacrifice and death trumped the inauthenticity of utilitarian self-interest and the 'will to life'.[28] Despite this pivot to radical conservatism, Gandhi retained the vestiges of the Naorojian critique of British poverty through the language of natural law. If British and Indian industrialists produced the ever-increasing material desires that undermined the Mahatma's new moral order, it was because they kept more than they required for their own subsistence. Invoking Naoroji directly, Gandhi insisted that the village thrived because there it was accepted that 'the farmer is the father of the world' and it was his economic freedom under conditions of non-domination from the colonial state and foreign capital that sustained village autarky.[29] Gandhi also re-oriented the language of the drain theory to apply it to indigenous as well as foreign distortions of the Indian economy, with modern capitalists portrayed as 'thieves in a way' since 'Nature' produced enough for day-to-day wants and 'pauperism' could be eradicated through self-denial.[30]

---

[25] M. K. Gandhi to Naoroji, 5 July 1894, in *CWMG*, vol. I (100 vols., Ahmedabad: Navajivan Press, 1960–94), pp. 139–40.

[26] Statement from Gandhi forwarded to India Office via Naoroji, 16 November 1903, BLAPAC, IOR/L/PJ/6/628, file 402.

[27] Faisal Devji, *The Impossible Indian: Gandhi and the Temptation of Violence* (Cambridge, MA: Harvard University Press, 2012).

[28] Shruti Kapila, 'Self, Spencer and Swaraj: Nationalist Thought and Critiques of Liberalism, 1890–1920', *Modern Intellectual History* 4, no. 1 (2007), pp. 112–19.

[29] 'Speech at the Gujarati Bandhu Sabha', *Indian Opinion*, 10 October 1919, in *CWMG*, vol. XVI, pp. 18–22.

[30] M. K. Gandhi, *The Speeches and Writings of Mahatma Gandhi*, 4th edn (Madras: G. A. Natesan, 1933), pp. 384–5; *Harijan*, 4 February 1942.

Britain's industrial dominance manifested as a monopoly over Indian rural labour, by deindustrializing the countryside and creating a 'nation of idlers'. The system enforced servility since villagers were not free to exercise their will to both self-sufficiency and ascetism, which inspired the duty of reciprocal self-sacrifice that maintained Indian social relations.[31] Additionally, it was only if Indian capitalists could morally transform themselves and embrace the doctrine of 'trusteeship' on behalf of rural labour that the latter's 'enslavement' would come to an end.[32] Thus, Gandhi expanded on Naoroji's litany of mediating institutions that arbitrarily absconded with Indian capital, the goal of which was to firmly buttress the village as the only site generative of legitimate social relations and marginalize modern urban life. To this extent, Gandhi claimed that the only 'function of cities' was to 'serve as clearing houses for village products', not to exercise an economic influence over the countryside.[33] He even wrote in 1927 to the Indian Communist Member of the House of Commons, Shapurji Saklatvala, that one had to consider Indian cities as complicit in the drain and oppression of the Indian villager.[34] Unlike Naoroji, the Mahatma said he could not 'prove this with statistics' but doubled-down in 1940 exhorting Indians to make a choice between the 'India of the cities', created by the foreign monopoly exercised over labour, and the 'India of the villages', which currently suffered under this 'organised violence'.[35] All manifestations of modern urban life that facilitated this state of affairs would have to be abolished, including the legal profession which defended the industrial and urban interest by feeding off the value generated by rural labour to the detriment of village autonomy.[36]

Gandhi's neo-orientalist conviction that the Indian village contained the seed-corn from which an authentically Indian society might grow under the correct circumstances was also reflected in the economic theory of D. R. Gadgil. He had taken a keen interest in the roots of Indian economic inequality through the works of Naoroji and economic historians like R. C. Dutt, founding the Gokhale

[31] Gandhi, 'Talk to Students at Dacca', p. 123; M. K. Gandhi, 'A Great Disease', *Navajivan*, 30 August 1925, in *CWMG*, vol. XXVIII, pp. 135–6.
[32] M. K. Gandhi, 'The Secret of Swaraj', *Young India*, 19 January 1921, in *CWMG*, vol. XIX, pp. 239–42.
[33] M. K. Gandhi, 'Discussion with Economists', *Harijan*, 28 January 1939, in *CWMG*, vol. LXVIII, pp. 258–9.
[34] M. K. Gandhi, 'No and Yes', *Young India*, 17 March 1927, in *CWMG*, vol. XXXIII, p. 163.
[35] M. K. Gandhi, 'Why Only Khadi?', *Harijan* 20 January 1940, in *CWMG*, vol. LXXI, pp. 102–3.
[36] Gandhi, 'Speech at the Gujarati Bandhu Sabha', *Indian Opinion*, 10 October 1919, in *CWMG*, vol. XVI, pp. 18–22; M. K. Gandhi, 'The Hallucination of Law Courts', *Young India* 6 October 1920, in *CWMG*, vol. XVIII, pp. 321–3.

Institute for Politics and Economics in 1930.[37] Gadgil was not quite so scathing in his attack on Indian cities as the Mahatma, but he did acknowledge the need to place the social interdependence of the village at the centre of any economic plan which sought to engender a modern Indian society through industrialization. Unlike Europe's civil society, which had ostensibly inherited civic virtue from the Greek *polis*, India could claim no such urban solidarity.[38] The growth of Indian towns was the result of a drain of financial and human capital through the displacement of famine and the rent extraction of a wealthy class or urban landlords. With the exception of the powerhouses of indigenous manufacturing in Ahmedabad and Bombay, Gadgil believed there was no industrial basis for Indian social interdependence.[39] Historically, it was only in the self-contained economies of individual villages that one could speak of interdependence, with the only external trade being in salt.[40] British railways had hastened the disintegration of the rural economy by linking its surplus with the cities and the ports and also by introducing a market mechanism but without the industrialization that would give the countryside the bargaining power to trade on fairer terms.[41] Without an Indian analogue of civic virtue, Gadgil seemed to riff on Naoroji's commercial society by envisioning reciprocal trade between equals in a 'co-operative commonwealth' as the only solution to India's social disintegration.[42]

Co-operation inveighed against state ownership of the means of production, and it was for this reason that Gadgil proposed it as an alternative to the so-called Mahalanobis model of Indian planning which focused developmental energies on state-owned heavy industry and urban institutions like tertiary education. For Gadgil, this attitude to planning amounted to little more than an exacerbation of the already concentrated capital in the hands of urban interests and 'unsocial' forces that were sapping the productive capacities of individuals in the countryside.[43] Government intervention was called for to break up this monopolistic concentration of capital through cooperative rural banking,

---

[37] C. A. Bayly, 'The Ends of Liberalism and the Political Thought of Nehru's India', *Modern Intellectual History*, 12, no. 3 (2015), p. 620.

[38] Gadgil, 'Social Change and Liberal Democracy in New States', pp. 356–7.

[39] D. R. Gadgil, *The Industrial Evolution of India*, 4th edn (Oxford: Oxford University Press, 1944), p. 148.

[40] Ibid., pp. 9–12.

[41] Ibid., p. 137, 199.

[42] D. R. Gadgil, 'Co-operation and the Transformation of Economic Society', in Brahme, ed., *Selected Writings of D. R. Gadgil*, p. 302.

[43] D. R. Gadgil, 'Towards Self-Reliance', in ibid., pp. 102–3; D. R. Gadgil, 'A Note on Co-operative Farming', in ibid., pp. 293–4.

restrictions on speculation, and the promotion of rural industrialization. The resulting small-scale industrial production would imply a return to a modicum of rural autarky, limiting the drain of capital to the cities and into the pockets of the technocrats, who through arbitrary decision-making and corruption perpetuated an urban bias.[44] To ensure the that co-operative enterprises operated strictly on non-monopolistic terms, Gadgil suggested that they should be overseen by the local *panch* (village council) which, in an ideal world, could be constituted to represent all regional stakeholders and come to a deliberative consensus about the fair allocation of local resources.[45]

Sunil Khilnani has observed that Gadgil sought to reinvigorate 'village habits and psychology' through an 'industrial outlook' and 'new innovations' in technology, occupying a middle ground between Gandhian libertarianism and Nehruvian planning.[46] One cannot escape the conclusion that, like Gandhi, Gadgil's preoccupation with the organic unity of village political economy owed something to a conservative reading of Naoroji's drain theory, which viewed modern India's urban sphere as a by-product of both external and internal monopoly capital. Unlike Gandhi, Gadgil recognized the role industrialism had to play in reforging some semblance of economic interdependence but was convinced that this could only occur under conditions in which the terms of trade between the countryside and the city had been equalized through rural investment and systems of non-arbitrary deliberation. In the context of communal tensions and Partition at the moment of independence, Gadgil was as convinced as Naoroji that non-monopolistic economic relations would inculcate a plural commercial society that was India's and the world's best hope for civil peace.[47]

## The Drain and Urban Modernity: J. Nehru, K. T. Shah and C. N. Vakil

Jawaharlal Nehru had read Naoroji's works on Indian economic history and adapted these accounts to his own Fabian and scientific views.[48] The Nehrus were also intimately acquainted with the Naoroji family, remaining lifelong friends

---

[44] D. R. Gadgil, 'Notes on Rural Industrialisation', in ibid., pp. 207–9.

[45] D. R. Gadgil, 'A Note on Co-operative Farming', in ibid., p. 296.

[46] Sunil Khilnani, *The Idea of India* (London: Penguin, 2003), p. 87; Bayly, 'Ends of Liberalism', pp. 621–2.

[47] D. R. Gadgil, 'An Approach to Indian Planning' and 'Economic Challenges on World Scale', in Brahme, ed., *Selected Writings of D. R. Gadgil*, pp. 54, 371–2.

[48] Bayly, 'The Ends of Liberalism', p. 623; Benjamin Zachariah, *Developing India: An Intellectual and Social History* (Oxford: Oxford University Press, 2005), p. 234.

with Naoroji's daughter and grandson.[49] Perhaps more than any other post-independence thinker, Nehru repeated, in a repackaged form, the fundamental insight of Naoroji's political thought that sustainable civil relationships required economic non-domination. In this respect before the late 1960s, the republican votaries of the Nehruvian economic consensus included both state planners and indigenous capitalists. As Benjamin Zachariah notes, although Nehru was not himself a signatory of the 1944 Bombay Plan proposed by key Indian industrialists, its agreement on state intervention to alleviate the dependence of the post-colonial economy on European capital marched in lockstep with the prime minister's aims.[50] A. D. Shroff, whose ideas are parsed later, was one signatory of the plan who did come to critique the monopolistic tendencies of Nehruvian state ownership; nevertheless, both he and the prime minister believed they were working towards a broadly Naorojian social economy of free and interdependent commercial agents.

On the eve of India's independence in December 1946, Jawaharlal Nehru's speech on the objects and aims of the Constituent Assembly, charged with framing India's post-colonial constitution, argued for committing his colleagues to founding a 'sovereign Indian republic'. In the absence of any all-India dynasty, Nehru was adamant that the new union could be 'nothing but a republic'. Nevertheless, on the question of political democracy, Nehru remained non-committal, believing it was for the assembly to ultimately decide what form popular representation must take. Nehru resiled from burdening the resolution with excess verbiage, given the fact that the word 'republic' implied, for him, popular authorization. He qualified this to add that not only did 'republic' imply 'democracy' but, more specifically, it implied 'economic democracy'.[51]

Nehru would later reflect that the goal of the constitution was to secure a republic through political liberty and equality but also through the socio-economic justice and the 'equality of status' through which one could ensure civil concord, which he termed 'fraternity'.[52] This vision was based on a core assumption about legitimate politics that mirrored Naoroji's understanding of communal violence as a problem unique to dominated rustics rather than an autonomous *homo economicus*. Nehru also believed that in matters of political interest people ought not 'to function as religious groups' and that parties should

---

[49] J. Nehru to J. A. D. Naoroji, in S. Gopal, ed., *Selected Works of Jawaharlal Nehru*, vol. 8 (New Delhi: Orient Longman, 1973), p 853.

[50] Zachariah, *Developing India*, p. 220.

[51] *Constituent Assembly Debates*, vol I, 13 December 1946, 1.5.5 to 1.5.17, https://www.constitutionofindia.net/constitution_assembly_debates/volume/1/1946-12-13 (accessed 17 December 2020).

[52] J. Nehru, 'Changing India', *Foreign Affairs* 41, no. 3 (1963), pp. 453–65.

'be formed with economic ideals' alone.[53] The demand for 'separate electorates' among India's minority communities was little more than a vestigial medievalism weaponized by religious leaders. A concession to this form of narrowly defined 'political democracy' would be ruinous if, as with Naoroji's drain theory, the country's arrested development rendered it incapable of forming a cohesive society. Economic democracy was for Nehru the 'something more' India required to make political democracy a sustainable reality.[54]

In strikingly Naorojian terms, Nehru also insisted that the masses were not chiefly moved by religious considerations but were naturally driven by material subsistence. Unlike political mischief-makers, they understood all too well that poverty would never be expunged if 'economic life' was 'to be led in isolation'. To any economic agent free to act according to their needs, it was plainly obvious that commerce demanded that they were 'interdependent in daily life'.[55] Nehru thus implored employees to unionize so that they would not be 'denied the fruits' of their work while attaching to this the warning that any 'swaraj' without free labour was a 'mockery'.[56] This could never be realized under 'monopoly conditions' in which the 'concentration of economic power' was in the hands of a 'few vast organisations in India', many of whom were in hock to the arbitrary financial will of foreign capital.[57] Nehru's commercial society also demanded the equalization of bargaining power in international trade, with the hope that a rational system of global planning would prevent an arbitrary global economic development in which the growth of the powerful came at 'the expense of foreign markets'. This shrinking of the world was a strictly economic and institutional enterprise, with India and other countries free to develop their cultures according to their respective 'natural genius'.[58]

The economist and founder of the Bombay School of Indian Economics, C. N. Vakil, made his name chiding P. C. Mahalanobis's model of state

[53] J. Nehru, 'The Parting of the Ways', in *The Unity of India: Collected Writings, 1937–40* (New York, NY: The John Day Company, 1942), p. 386.

[54] J. Nehru, 'On Minorities and Nationalism', in S. Gopal, ed., *Selected Works of Jawaharlal Nehru*, vol. 5 (New Delhi: Orient Longman, 1973), pp. 283–5; J. Nehru, 'Freedom and Equality', in S. Gopal, ed., *Selected Works of Jawaharlal Nehru*, vol. 14 (New Delhi: Orient Longman, 1973), pp. 40–1.

[55] Nehru, 'On the Riots in Kanpur', in Gopal, *Selected Works of Jawaharlal Nehru*, vol. 5, pp. 281–2.

[56] Nehru, 'The Congress and Mill Workers', in Gopal, *Selected Works of Jawaharlal Nehru*, vol. 5, p. 287.

[57] J. Nehru to Lal Bahadur Shastri, 'Self Sufficiency', 20 May 1959, in S. Gopal, ed., *Selected Works of Jawaharlal Nehru*, vol. 49 (New Delhi: Orient Longman, 1973), pp. 464–5.

[58] Nehru, 'Freedom and Equality', in Gopal, *Selected Works of Jawaharlal Nehru*, vol. 14, pp. 551–2.

planning for failing to focus on worker consumption and wage goods. As with A. D. Shroff, these criticisms still functioned within a wider agreement about the need to nurture an Indian commercial society, but they differed on the best way to alleviate economic monopoly. Nehru had leaned on nationalization, industrialization and the production of heavy capital goods to spur a demand for employment so that villages could be 'urbanised in a small way'.[59] Vakil was in agreement about renovating Indian society through village urbanization and industrialization but pointed to Naoroji's economic theory as demonstrating that the dearth of basic consumables meant that the Indian worker was never going to be fit for production unless the availability of subsistence wage-goods was drastically increased.[60]

The first two five-year plans' preoccupation with heavy industry was a distraction. Contrary to the view that one needs a fixed sum of capital to coax traditional agricultural labour into modern wage-labour, Vakil adapted Naoroji's labour theory of value. Villages could produce small-scale capital unaided though agricultural accumulation and cottage industry if they were liberated from the 'English charges', and their post-colonial equivalent, the 'forced saving' imposed by Nehruvian economic planning for future investment in nationalized heavy industries.[61] Left to their own devices, full employment would produce increases in household productivity and a concomitant increase in worker consumption. The manifold rise in the taxable capacity of individual labourers in the countryside would allow the state to then invest and pursue capital-intensive growth without a period of protracted rural austerity.[62] In the same way Naoroji had abstracted *homo economicus* from British discourses on the moral and material progress of ethnographic groups by calculating gross domestic product per capita, Vakil accused the planning commission of working far too much in the aggregate and obsessing about fixed capital when it should be concerned with how individual income was the taproot of national wealth.[63]

The emergence of the debate around Indian taxable capacity occurred in the context of inter-war imperial criticism and became a major pillar of what Eleanor

---

[59] Nehru, 'Public Meeting Cooperative Farming, Rajaji's New Party', 1 June 1959, in Gopal, *Selected Works of Jawaharlal Nehru*, vol. 49, pp. 40–3.

[60] C. N. Vakil, *Financial Developments in Modern India, 1860–1924* (Bombay D. B. Taraporevala Sons & Co, 1924), pp. 308–10, 516–21.

[61] Ibid., pp. 541–2.

[62] C. N. Vakil and Brahmanand, *Planning for an Expanding Economy* (Bombay: Vora & Co Publishers, 1956), pp. xvi–xviii.

[63] Ibid., p. xv.

Newbigin has called 'national accounting' in India.[64] Like Naoroji, scholars like Vakil and K. T. Shah regarded the worker's right to the property constituted by surplus production over consumption as sacrosanct and promoted 'social institutions' that countered the 'degraded and dehumanised nation' enslaved to the economic monopolists who 'own this human property'.[65] Shah based his insights on Naoroji's 'field investigations' even deriving his own figures on taxable capacity by interrogating jail and famine statistics.[66] Like his forerunner, Shah was cognizant of the importance of family and caste in daily life but also proclaimed that the individual had to be the 'basic unit' for 'work, consumption, or taxation'. In these realms the family had to 'yield place' if a society of 'free associations and combinations' was to arise in India.[67]

Naoroji's strict theory of value, positing that the human fabrication of new commodities was the only means by which wealth was created, was also the basis of Shah's social economy.[68] Existing capital was merely the 'crystalised surplus of past labour' and large land owners and capitalists were but 'passive factors of production'.[69] Regarding the service and financial sectors as unproductive parasites, Shah demanded that the interdependence of the commercial contract was to be based solely on those who could productively sustain it.[70] Shah was decidedly less squeamish than Naoroji on the issue of state ownership; a product of his age, he had a Nehruvian faith in the scientific neutrality of the state and the ability of experts to rise above arbitrary acts of self-interest. In this regard Shah was a radical Naorojian, moving beyond Dadabhai's progressive equalizing of gendered inheritance to abolishing inheritance entirely. For Shah, marriage, like the economy, was to be a perfectly balanced 'civil contract', anything outside of which – including the sacred – was to 'not be recognised by the State'.[71]

---

[64] Eleanor Newbigin, 'Accounting for the Nation, Marginalizing the Empire: Taxable Capacity and Colonial Rule in the Early Twentieth Century', *History of Political Economy* 52, no. 3 (2020), pp. 455–72.

[65] K. T. Shah and K. J. Khambata, *Wealth and Taxable Capacity of India* (Bombay: D. B. Tarapolevara Sons & Co, 1924), p. 254.

[66] Ibid., pp. 253–60.

[67] K. T. Shah, *National Planning, Principles and Administration* (Bombay: Vora & Co, 1948), pp. 70–1.

[68] K. T. Shah, *Ancient Foundations of Economics in India* (Bombay Vora & Co, 1954), p. 37.

[69] Shah, *National Planning*, p. 75.

[70] Ibid., vii; Shah, *National Planning*, p. 21.

[71] Shah, *National Planning*, p. 72.

## The Drain and the Swatantra Party

India's Swatantra Party was a short-lived experiment in indigenous free-market conservatism from 1959 to 1974. Swatantra stood apart from other groups typically associated with the Indian right-wing which, far from being conservative, promoted a radical reconstitution of India along the lines of the European nation-state through the ideology of Hindu nationalism. The party emerged in protest at the ruling Congress Party's 1959 Nagpur Resolution that committed the country to a policy of collectivized farming. The intellectual genealogy of this right-wing opposition has been eruditely linked by Aditya Balasubramanian to a pursuit of negative liberty, 'free economy' and American modernization theory during the Cold War.[72] This section complicates such accounts to show how some pushers of the 'free economy' articulated a neo-Roman account of commercial liberty appropriated from Naoroji's drain theory. In doing so, they cast the Nehruvian state as a monopolistic neo-colonial actor seeking to return Indians to a state of dependence.

The Parsi economist and co-founder of the Forum of Free Enterprise and Swatantra, Ardeshir Darabshaw Shroff, maintained in 1964 that the 'basic economic problem before our country' was 'the same one as pointed out by ... Dr Dadabhai Naoroji'.[73] In the manifesto of the Forum, Shroff also displayed a capacious definition of entrepreneurship as a natural human faculty – from the first man to discover fire to the farmer and the manufacturer – and as such the ideal of 'free enterprise' was not necessarily state non-intervention in the economy but a distinction between legitimate profit and anti-social profiteering.[74] Indeed, the figurehead of Swatantra, Rajaji, identified social democratic Sweden as the model of good free enterprise.[75] With this in mind, the following discussion evaluates the ideas of high-profile leaders of the party like Rajaji, Minoo Masani and A. D. Shroff.

Rajaji was a part of the Gandhian old-guard, a Congress conservative who left the party because the post-independence Nehruvian consensus was, in his view, lurching too far to the left. In claiming that his whole outlook on political-economy was synonymous with the Gandhian doctrine of 'trusteeship', Rajaji had to be conversant with Gandhi's re-interpretation of Naoroji's drain theory, which, as we saw earlier, was repeatedly invoked by the Mahatma as the correct

[72] Aditya Balasubramanian, 'Contesting Permit-and-License *Raj*: Economic Conservatism and the Idea of Democracy in 1950s India', *Past and Present* 251, no. 1 (2021), pp. 189–227.

[73] A. D. Shroff, *Will Democratic Socialism Help India?* (Bombay: Forum for Free Enterprise, 1964).

[74] Forum of Free Enterprise, *Manifesto* (Bombay: Forum for Free Enterprise, 1956); A. D. Shroff, *Our Economic Future* (Bombay: Forum for Free Enterprise, 1958), p. 17.

[75] C. Rajagopalachari, 'Drastic Surgery', draft article, undated, pp. 2–3, CRP (Instalment V), Speeches/Writings/Articles, serial number 59.

heuristic for understanding Indian economic problems.[76] That Rajaji conceived of trusteeship in neo-Roman terms was clear from the fact that he contrasted 'swatantra' – or freedom from the 'soulless leviathan' – not with state interference but with 'paratantra' – or dependence – on the bureaucratic class which wiped out individual will 'through a scheme of compulsion'.[77] The technocrats of the planned state were described in recognizably Naorojian terms as a 'hereditary' or 'congenital middle class' that dominated and distorted individual labour through the compulsion of status rather than any identifiable acts of interference (although Rajaji could also point to instances of this).[78] The result was a universal 'serfdom' not because of daily obstacles to liberty but due to the inequality of status under which all Indian citizens had to 'work in dread of and as inferiors to that class'.[79] Others recognized the republican thrust of Rajaji's critique, with one supporter writing approvingly that he had learned that the virtues of the Roman republic were corrupted by state trading in food grains.[80]

Real individualism for Rajaji consisted in a gentrified patchwork of rural and urban middle classes whose security of property guaranteed the emergence of an honest commercial society that could displace 'the new class of exploiters' who through their direction of political economy constituted a type of social artifice.[81] In such a system, where civil liberty and society were not based on natural law but were beholden to the arbitrary will of the socialist state, the political liberties enshrined in a democratic constitution were a nonsense. As Rajaji declared in 1964, the 'Constitution' was 'itself the indenture' since under a planned state 'the only choice left is as to who shall be your masters'.[82] Rajaji's spiritualism meant that his faith in the community's capacity to impose moral order on anarchic individualism made him more of a communitarian liberal idealist than Naoroji. Nevertheless, he was not a Hindu majoritarian like Malaviya or Lajpat Rai, but as with Naoroji his ideas prioritized the labourer's and consumer's total independence in order to knit together an Indian society, with this process prefiguring any naïve attachment

[76] C. Rajagopalachari, 'The Quest for an -Ism', 28 October 1938, CRP, Speeches/Writings/Articles, serial number 48.

[77] Rajagopalachari, 'Peasant Ownership'; C. Rajagopalachari, 'What Is Wanted', *Broadway Times*, 11 May 1959, in ibid., serial number 51.

[78] C. Rajagopalachari, 'To the Middle Classes', undated draft of an article, p. 1, in ibid., serial number 54.

[79] Rajagopalachari, 'What Is Wanted'.

[80] M. R. Pai to Rajagopalachari, 31 July undated, NMML, Swatantra Party Papers, serial number 41, part II, item 741.

[81] C. Rajagopalachari, 'Swatantra Party to Be People's Group', *Free Press Journal*, 18 June 1959, in NMML. C. Rajagopalachari Papers (Instalment VI to XIII), Subject Files, serial number 41, item 238.

[82] C. Rajagopalachari, 'Inaugural Address', in *The Swatantra Party Third National Convention: A Report* (Bombay: Inland Printers, 1964), pp. 13–15, in ibid., item 129.

to the universal franchise as an expression of freedom. There was 'no power in votes', Rajaji exclaimed, so long as 'there are numerous classes that depend on the labour of other classes and such physical dependence is essential for existence'. The 'power' was 'in work' and 'not in the votes'; thus, like the assumptions underlying Naoroji's developmentalism, Rajaji believed that 'the writ of democracy does not run by divine right but by force of social and economic organization'.[83]

Minoo Masani, the son of Naoroji's biographer R. P. Masani and onetime employee of the Tata Corporation, was also a founding member of Swatantra. He too leaned on the free-trade arguments of American modernization theorists who sought to export light consumer goods from India while augmenting the country's capacity to import American commodities. Masani traced his intellectual genealogy to nineteenth-century liberals like Naoroji – around whose feet Masani played as a boy – and the doctrine of trusteeship inherited from Gandhi. This liberalism with a social conscience, Masani insisted, constituted the 'new liberalism' of Swatantra.[84]

Masani regarded the interdependence of international trade governed by an ethical outlook as the surest foundation for a world federation of independent nation-states.[85] Yet, in comparing his party with the anti-communist Hungarian Independent Smallholders, Agrarian Workers and Civic Party rather than the American Republican Party, Masani insisted that Swatantra was not ideologically laissez-faire in the conventional sense. Shroff also insisted that those who accused Swatantra of a classical liberal recidivism were 'tilting at imaginary windmills'.[86] It was an independent yeomanry of wealthier peasant owner-occupiers that Masani was protecting from monopoly and was even willing to tolerate state ownership of heavy industry so long as the bureaucracy was barred from 'entering the field of trade' or agricultural 'management'.[87] The consequences of this were aligned with Rajaji's criticism that the state would drain the profits of common labour, thereby rendering all 'individuals' as 'employees of one kind or another of the state'.[88] It was hardly surprising, then, that in his conviction that the future of a cohesive society lay with Swatantra, Masani complained that pundits dubbed them liberals or conservatives when they were really a 'people's party'.[89]

---

[83] Rajagopalachari, 'To the Middle Classes', pp. 4–5.

[84] M. R. Masani, 'Liberalism', in *Freedom First*, April 1985.

[85] Balasubramanian, 'Contesting "Permit-and-License *Raj*"', pp. 204, 214.

[86] A. D. Shroff, *The Future Is with Free Enterprise* (Bombay: Forum of Free Enterprise, 1959), p. 12.

[87] M. R. Masani, 'The Swatantra Party', in *Minoo Masani 90* (Bombay: Freedom First, 1995), pp. 40–1.

[88] M. R. Masani, 'Planning', in ibid., pp. 15–16.

[89] Masani in 'Minutes of the Madras Meeting of the Swatantra Party', 4 June 1959, in C. Rajagopalachari, *Protect Farm and Family Birth of the Swatantra Party* (Bangalore: undated), in NMML, Swatantra Party Papers, serial number 41, part I.

This individual freedom in matters of political economy was couched in the same terms of basic Indian subsistence that Naoroji had founded his drain theory upon. In any 'free economy', Masani railed, 'the consumer is king' because the basic function of political economy is to provide 'his wants'. If tied to a state trading monopoly, 'he must purchase or perish' and in turn is unable to influence production through consumer demand.[90] To compound the issue, Shroff observed how the state's licencing system for new enterprises was riddled with corruption as industrialism established through monopoly had already drained the common man through the state's revenue demand and was using the same wealth as graft for future concessions from the bureaucracy.[91] These were the same enterprises that benefited from the state's import controls in order to engage in 'profiteering' when prices rose for the extraction of further value from subordinated citizens – an activity Shroff deemed 'anti-social'.[92] This amounted to little more than the council bill system criticized by Naoroji, wherein bills of exchange were bought in London by traders to finance exports and who then exchanged these bills for rupees extracted from Indian labourers through the land revenue.

Masani accused Indian planning of reproducing the 'ruler–ruled' complex in which the 'managerial state' was in fact run arbitrarily by a 'small clique'. The country could overcome this situation if there was more scope for 'free co-operation' in 'smaller decentralised industrial units'. This was an ideal that would become reality, Masani believed, when the disastrous impact of urban industrial bombing during the Second World War was fully appreciated.[93] Even in matters of currency and finance, the Nehruvian state resembled its colonial predecessor. Its gold bonds scheme was an amnesty that allowed hoarders who had violated the Gold Control Act to invest the metal in government bonds. Masani regarded gold control as penalizing socially productive artisans like goldsmiths and the amnesty as rewarding a single class of people who could help the state in its foreign exchange crisis but whose day-to-day practices contributed nothing to the 'social economy'.[94] In 1966, Masani re-stated the necessity of Swatantra as a party committed to actualizing Indian social economy and society by emancipating individuals from

---

[90] M. R. Masani, *Economics of Freedom* (Bombay: Forum of Free Enterprise, 1965), p. 5.

[91] A. D. Shroff, 'Nehru Government Flayed – Analysis of Financial Chaos', *Indian Libertarian* 5, no. 20 (1958), pp. 21–2.

[92] Shroff, *Our Economic Future*, p. 13.

[93] M. R. Masani, *Socialism Reconsidered* (Bombay: Padma Publications, 1944), pp. 28–9, 50–1.

[94] M. R. Masani on Gold Bonds, speech delivered to the Lok Sabha on 12 November 1965, pp. 14–15, NMML, Swatantra Party Papers, Subject File, serial number 44, 1962, 1965–6, 1969–70. Issues of 'Swatantra Newsletter' and 'Swatantra in Parliament' containing Swatantra Party's participation in the proceedings of Lok Sabha and Rajya Sabha.

alleged neo-colonial monopoly. It was in this spirit that Masani quoted Leonard T. Hobhouse on the 'self-directing power' of individuals as the only foundation upon which modern 'society' and 'true community' could be built. Liberty was an individual right but found its true meaning 'as a necessity of society'.[95]

## Conclusion

This book began with an anecdote about a communal riot and Dadabhai Naoroji's analysis that civil peace depended upon the gentrification of the benighted 'lower orders'. From the middle of the nineteenth century, the Grand Old Man had pursued sociality through a programme of liberal social reform until events prompted a reconsideration of the origins of civil society. His new drain theory took stock of Britain's uncivil liberalism in order to promote a new model for commercial society founded upon labour republicanism. This drain theory was liberal in its origins but was detached from an exclusively liberal repertoire because of its ability to speak to a concern that persisted after independence. This concern was the absence of a unitary Indian society and the need for a culturally neutral language – political economy – with which to diagnose and resolve this problem.

This book ends with a summary of Naoroji's intellectual legacy by tracing the varied uses of his thought by a new generation of Indian thinkers. These new articulations were undoubtedly palimpsests over-laying the drain theory with new economic doctrines from Fabianism and Laskian guild socialism to Hayekian free market economics. Nevertheless, what emerges is a ubiquitous language of labour republicanism and social economy which was deployed to legitimize the village, the planned economy and the free market in the name of anti-monopolism and anti-dependence. The drain theory's legacy entailed that 'development' became the common vocabulary of India's moral economy, allowing for a variety of political interpretations on how to secure commercial society through free labour. More than just identifying the impoverishing mechanism of colonialism, the lasting impact of the drain theory was to establish common developmentalist parameters that were also open to ideological contestation about how to promote free labour and commercial society. In other words, the drain theory provided a shared but competitive language for modern Indian politics.

95 M. R. Masani, *Congress Misrule and the Swatantra Alternative* (Bombay: Manaktalas, 1966), p. 23.

# Conclusion

Naoroji travelled to Amsterdam and Stuttgart in 1904 and 1907 to participate in the two Congresses of the Socialist International. Invited by the organizers to represent the 'East', Naoroji was keen to promulgate his analysis of uncivil liberalism far and wide but demanded that Hyndman make it clear to his leftist colleagues that this was a 'direct personal invitation independent of Socialism as Socialism'.[1] With this qualification established, Naoroji and Hyndman co-authored a resolution for the 1904 gathering that carefully steered the former's politics away from any association with revolutionary action, calling instead for the 'abandonment' of the 'nefarious system' of exploitation. Naoroji even edited the initial draft Hyndman sent to him by adding the gradualist qualification of 'present nefarious system', signalling his continued faith in a reformed British Empire.[2] To his last, Dadabhai remained a reformer holding out hope for a redeemed liberal order in which labour – and its powers of social reproduction – were restored to their natural condition.

This book began by summarizing exclusionary 'official liberalism' as well as the wider British post-Enlightenment debates about the civil and commercial registers of modern sociality. The first chapter also considered the romanticist critics of these registers before considering how far these ideas were convincing beyond Europe. The following chapter explored the nineteenth-century Parsi life-world with a focus on faith, commerce and philanthropy as engines of civil interdependence in the context of brewing social and communal tensions. We saw how Naoroji matured into a community that was in a state of political and social flux. We then examined the fragility of this world as the eyes of young Parsi professionals like Naoroji turned to debates on community governance and social reform in an effort to define their minority's boundaries and internally stabilize its social norms. This was achieved by challenging the domination of the Parsi *panchayat* with a self-regulating civil society based on liberal self-fashioning and

[1] H. M. Hyndman to Dadabhai Naoroji, 29 June 1904, New Delhi, National Archives of India, Dadabhai Naoroji Papers [DNP], H-221 (110).

[2] Hyndman to Naoroji, 24 June 1904, DNP, H-221 (108).

individual autonomy guaranteed by property ownership. Chapter 4 recounted the financial collapse, personal bankruptcy and famine that prompted Naoroji to formulate his iconic drain theory as a model of commercial society through statistical liberalism. This pivot to political economy allowed him to conceptualize what individual labour and contract in India might look like when abstracted from the ethnographic groupings and customary categories of colonial liberalism.

The second half of the book commenced with the application of Naoroji's drain theory to British and princely India and his programme to reform state and financial monopolies to the benefit of free labour. We then considered Naoroji's application of his drain theory's labour republicanism to the working classes of the United Kingdom, which led to the winning of a working-class constituency in 1892. Naoroji's solutions aligned with those he proposed for the Raj, that of enacting a programme of anti-trust legislation buttressed by industrial courts to arbitrate the relationship between monopoly capital and labour. The final chapter offered an indicative look at the ideological twists and turns the drain theory made as it was appropriated by a new generation of Indian thinkers. From Gandhian village economics to state planning, Naoroji's liberalism was cannibalized and hybridized with political and economic theories of the day for a panoply of divergent ideological goals. Yet the thread uniting these new articulations of the drain was the normative political language of Naoroji's labour republicanism.

## Implications for Liberalism and Empire

If the reality of colonial liberalism was that it bifurcated those it governed into 'modern' and 'traditional' subjects, it also presented indigenous thinkers with a foil against which new local alternatives were pioneered. Naoroji's liberal political economy was one such example that incorporated the colonized peasant and the downtrodden British proletarian into a renewed narrative of civil progress. By arguing for the labourers' right to retain a higher proportion of the property they created, but without advocating the collective ownership of the means of production, Naoroji's ideal of commercial society was a capitalist critique of both colonial and metropolitan inequality. What was striking about this global analysis was that it had been incubated within the life-world of India's smallest religious community. In excavating this genealogy of Parsi liberalism, this book has emphasized the way in which this modern political language could achieve 'Western' currency even though it was initially innovated within a social and intellectual ecology of the Global South. Moreover, an attentiveness to the liberal debates within these locales shows how ideas which achieved future legitimacy under the rubric of 'anti-colonialism' or 'nationalism' were, in their day, indicative of a much more capacious Indian imagination. Naoroji's project wanted to realize free association in the domestic context of Indian cultural difference but also the international area of civilizational difference. As a result, Naoroji's thought was not 'nationalist' in the conventional sense of that term.

Dadabhai Naoroji's drain theory was also a way of rendering the tumult of nineteenth-century Parsi social travails both intelligible and controllable with an eye to the restitution of internal community stability and external civil peace. In tracing the link between political economy and social theory in Parsi liberalism, this study has refocused attention on the materialist dimensions of liberalism in the colonial setting. Far from an intuitive desire to abolish poverty as a moral evil, we reinterpreted Naoroji's thought in order to clarify his liberal reform as a programme for establishing civil peace through the interdependence of property-constituting labour in a commercial society. Scholars like Onur Ulas Ince have written convincingly on the need to parse the abstract universalism and representational order of imperial liberalism through a closer analysis of the specific social and capitalist histories in which these ideologies were 'differentially evaluated' and their component parts 'conscripted into imperial ideologies of rule, dispossession, and domination'.[3] In the same vein, this book has shown how Parsi liberalism – deeply indebted to the sphere of circulation for its conceptual repertoire – also sought to address in new ways the incongruous relationship between liberty and capitalism. This uniquely Parsi liberalism addressed 'Western' liberalism's tendency to overlook structural inequality and domination by seeding it with a powerful labour republicanism. This liberalism from the Global South implores us to attend to the critical possibilities of this ideology in the hands of indigenous thinkers.[4]

In common with other liberalisms, Naoroji's theory sought to put an end to theo-political conflict. New global analogues of this liberal practice, like the United States, offered an ascriptive civic identity that was predicated on both Christian morality and a secular bifurcation of religious and political commitments. However, the Parsi minority, desperate to protect its cultural distinctiveness, could not countenance a majoritarian process of socialization. From this dilemma came Naoroji's rigid attitude towards the relationship between the material register of liberal capitalism and social theory under the aegis of British trade. In an effort to realize a commercial society founded upon individual abstract labour and

[3] Onur Ulas Ince, *Colonial Capitalism and the Dilemmas of Liberalism* (Oxford: Oxford University Press, 2018), pp. 16–17.

[4] I. M. Young, *Global Challenges: War, Self-Determination and Responsibility for Justice* (Cambridge: Polity Press, 2007), p. 177.

property-ownership, Parsi liberalism was preoccupied with India's social realm – or more accurately, its underdeveloped civil relationships – as the essence of its arrested modernization. Naoroji's materialist drain theory aspired to undo this arrested social development by realizing the Enlightenment and Macaulayite ideal of commercial society and subordinated the role of the state to this programme. Establishing this fact makes it much easier to see why the drain theory's socially subordinated politics were amenable, in the hands of certain Indians, to a conservative re-inscription that buttressed the social theory of Henry Maine.

## Implications for Indian Political Thought

The drain theory's openness to interpretation is key to understanding why Naoroji's ideas retained their currency in India after decolonization. Even as the nascent republic witnessed sometimes rancorous debates around constitutionalism and liberal rights, key planks of Naoroji's liberal political economy were near universally accepted. In the twilight of empire and in the immediate decades after independence, his ideas were mostly kept alive by socialists, conservatives and Gandhians. For these three political groups, a particular alignment of social relations prefigured legitimate agency in the political domain. Whether society had to be engineered out of the fragmentation of caste and custom by the state or whether it was a pre-political domain that had an organic and ethical durability, Naoroji's labour republicanism was regarded as a necessary step in the search for legitimate civil relations between different categories of Indian. Gandhi's village republic, Nehru's social democracy and a host of conservative visions of Indian peoplehood all owed something to Naoroji's concept of worker autonomy.

Naoroji's liberalism has been at the heart of Indian political modernity in one way or another. As Shruti Kapila notes, modern political languages were remade in India by reconceptualizing what it meant to live together under conditions of cultural difference. The quest for Indian sovereignty was inextricably linked with the question of Indian unity – variously conceptualized – in such a way as to throw the question of politics back onto the social.[5] The architects of Indian republicanism worked in the shadow of a liberal imperialism in which the question of property and the interests it generated were ever present. While religious figures like Gandhi and Muhammad Iqbal sought to efface the communal tensions created by the state and its politics of propertied interest, Muhammed Ali Jinnah and Bhimrao Ambedkar regarded the colonial institution of property as truncated

[5] Shruti Kapila, *Violent Fraternity in the Indian Age* (Princeton, NJ: Princeton University Press, 2021).

and sought to fulfil it politically through republican constitutionalism.[6] The contention of this book has been that Naoroji's was another contribution to this debate which firmly foregrounded the social as the realm in which propertied interests could be managed and rationalized. Unlike Jinnah and Ambedkar, Naoroji's ambition was to resolve theo-political conflict completely, rather than to render it non-violent by institutionalizing it through political competition. Competitive politics was a secondary concern given that Naoroji had diluted the state of the European imagination – insofar as it was autonomous of society – with the categorical imperatives of the Indian social realm. As far as Naoroji was concerned, the priority was a sort of functional interdependence defined by political economy, which I have called 'sociality', while for others it would be a more consciously held sense of social unity defined by cultural considerations.

In restricting his politics to the language of basic life processes, property and sociality, Naoroji's commercial society epitomized what Hannah Arendt would have regarded as the apolitical world of the *animal laborans*. Naoroji's politics were constituted exclusively through concerns about subsistence and social conditions without the absolute political freedom to imagine alternative futures that characterized the Greek *polis*, where labour was scrupulously confined to the private sphere.[7] And yet, as we saw in both India and Britain, Naoroji's career was built around the Parsi condemnation of excluding labour from the gentrified society that its work had created. So long as this constitutive lack, in which labour could create commercial society – but not partake of it – persisted, Naorojism urged a radical collective politics of producers against monopoly capital in all its forms.[8] What Naoroji believed would come after the final political victory of restored workers' rights across the empire is not clear. It is apparent, however, that he did not regard national self-determination as the sine qua non of achieving these ends.

It was only by linking the social and economic experiences of the Parsi community with the seemingly uniform liberal lexicon which Naoroji engaged with that we have arrived at a far better understanding of the numerous and contested meanings of this ideology in its Indian, imperial and global contexts. Appreciating

[6] Faisal Devji, *The Impossible Indian: Gandhi and the Temptation of Violence* (Cambridge, MA: Harvard University Press, 2012); Faisal Devji, *Muslim Zion: Pakistan as a Political Idea* (Cambridge, MA: Harvard University Press, 2013); Shruti Kapila, 'Ambedkar's Agonism: Sovereign Violence and Pakistan as Peace', *Comparative Studies of South Asia, Africa and the Middle East* 39, no. 1 (2019), pp. 184–95.

[7] Hannah Arendt, *The Human Condition*, new edn (Chicago, IL: Chicago University Press, 1998), p. 214.

[8] Ibid., pp. 218–19.

these meanings has allowed us to overcome the simplistic imperialism–nationalism dyad and successfully recover Naoroji's liberalism as an ideology that moulded critiques of economic monopoly around the world and which continues to shape India's political modernity. The sophistication and international reach of the Grand Old Man's ideas force us to recognize that his status as an intellectual should not be qualified with the parochial epithets of 'nationalist' or 'Indian'. On the contrary, like some of his white contemporaries, we ought to think of Dadabhai Naoroji as simply a liberal political thinker of global significance.

# References


## Primary Sources

### *Archival Collections*

#### *New Delhi, National Archives of India*

Dadabhai Naoroji Papers.
Minutes of the British Committee of the Indian National Congress, microfilm reels 1940–3.

#### *New Delhi, Nehru Memorial Museum and Library*

B. G. Tilak Papers.
C. Rajagopalachari Papers.
Dadabhai Naoroji Collection, vols. I–II.
Reports of the Indian Social Conference, 1895–9.
Servants of India Society Collection.
Swatantra Party Papers

#### *Mumbai, Maharashtra State Archives*

Commercial Department: 1830.
General Department: 1824; 1890.
Judicial Department: 1863; 1874.
Political Department: Baroda, 1873; 1874.
Public Department: 1792.
Revenue Department: 1875; 1887.

#### *Mumbai, Bombay (Mumbai) University Library*

Jamsetji Jeejeebhoy Letterbooks.

#### *Pune, Tata Central Archives*

J. N. Tata Papers.

### *London, British Library*

#### Personal Papers

Alfred Russell Wallace Papers, Add MS 46440.
Florence Nightingale Papers, Add. MS 45800.
George Birdwood Papers, MSS Eur F216.
G. K. Gokhale Papers, IOR Neg 11697-11698, 11701–11705.
Lee Warner Papers, MSS Eur F92.
Lewis Pelly Papers, MSS Eur F126.
National Indian Association Minute Books, MSS Eur F147.
Sir Henry John Steadman Cotton Papers, IOR Neg 12038.
William Digby Papers, MSS Eur D767.

#### India Office Records

Bombay Proceedings, IOR/L/P/350.
Compilations and Miscellaneous Records 1860–1948, IOR/L/PJ/5.
Committee and Commission Reports, IOR/V/26/860.
India Acts 1831–40, IOR/V/8/31.
Indian State Residencies, IOR/R/2.
Political Correspondence with India, IOR/L/PS/6.
Public and Judicial Departmental Papers, IOR/L/PJ/6.

### *London, The Women's Library, London School of Economics*

British Committee of the Continental & General Federation for Abolition of Government Regulation of Prostitution, 3BGF.

### *London, Royal Society of Arts Library*

Minutes of the Society, RSA/AD/MA/100/12/1.
Minutes of the Various Committees, 1871–3, PR/GE/112/12/101.

### *London, Bishopsgate Institute*

George Holyoake Papers, HOLYOAKE/9.

### *London, Islington Local History Centre*

Minutes and proceedings of the board and committees, 1892 to 1895.
Census Reports, 1881 and 1891.

### *London, National Liberal Club Archives*

Rules, regulations, bye-laws and list of members, 1886.
Elections sub-committee minutes, 1889–98.

### *Birmingham, Cadbury Research Library, University of Birmingham*

Francis Schnadhorst Papers, MS170.

### *Bristol, University of Bristol Library*

National Liberal Federation Collection, JN1129.
Papers of the National Liberal Club, DM668.
Schnadhorst Papers, DM668, box 1.

### *Cambridge, Cambridge University Library*

Elizabeth Adelaide Manning Correspondence and Papers, MS Add. 6379/30.

## Printed Primary Sources

### *Dadabhai Naoroji Essays and Collections*

Anon. *The First Indian Member of The Imperial Parliament, Being A Collection of The Main Incidents Relating to The Election of Mr Dadabhai Naoroji to Parliament.* Madras, 1892.

———. *India and Mr. Dadabhai Naoroji: An Account of the Demonstrations Held in His Honour as M.P. for Central Finsbury, During His Visit to India*. Bombay: Commercial Press, 1898.

N. 'The Rights of Labour'. *Westminster Review* 134, no. 1 (1890), pp. 95–103.

Naoroji, Dadabhai. 'Sir M. E. Grant Duff's Views about India. – I'. *Contemporary Review* 52 (August 1887), pp. 221–35

———. 'Sir M. E. Grant Duff's Views about India. – II'. *Contemporary Review* 52 (November 1887), pp. 694–711.

———. *Essays, Speeches, Addresses and Writings of The Hon'ble Dadabhai Naoroji.* Edited by C. L. Parekh. Bombay, 1887.

———. *On the Duties of Local Indian Associations in Connection with the London Association*. London, 1868.

———. *Poverty and Un-British Rule in India*. London, 1901.

———. *The Grand Little Man of India: Dadabhai Naoroji, Speeches and Writings*, 2 vols. Edited by Moin Zaidi. New Delhi, 1985.

Patwardan, R. P. (ed.). *Dadabhai Naoroji Correspondence: Correspondence with Dinshaw Wacha*, 2 vols. Bombay, 1977.

### *Official and Institutional Publications*

'Dadabhai Naoroji and Another *v.* the Chartered Bank of India, Australia and China, 4 May 1868'. In *The Law Journal Reports for the Year 1868,* vol. 37. London, 1868), pp. 221–5.

*Annual Report of The Bombay Presidency*. 1864–5.

*Annual Report of The Council of the National Sunday League*. London, 1886.
*Annual Report of the Municipal Commissioner of Bombay, 1876*. Bombay, 1877.
*Baroda Administration Report, 1872–73* and *1873–74*.
*First Report of The Royal Commission on The Administration of The Expenditure of India; With Minutes of Evidence*. London, 1896.
*Gazetteer of the Bombay Presidency, Ahmedabad*, vol. 4. Bombay, 1879.
HC Deb. 14 August 1894, vol. 28.
HC Deb. 29 May 1894, vol. 24.
Howell, A. P. *Notes on Jails and Jail Discipline in India, 1867–8*. Calcutta, 1869.
*Imperial Institute Annual Report for 1893*. London, 1893.
*Measures Taken to Give Effect to The Recommendations of a Committee Appointed to Report on the State of Jail Discipline and to Suggest Improvements*. Calcutta, 1867.
Mouat, F. J. *Report on the Statistics of the Prisons of the Lower Provinces of the Bengal Presidency for 1861, 1862, 1863, 1864 and 1865*. Calcutta, 1868.
*Official Proceedings of the Democratic National Convention Held in Chicago, Illinois, 7, 8, 9, 10 and 11 July 1896*. Logansport, IN, 1896.
*Proceedings of the Public Service Commission: Bombay Presidency (including Sind)*, vol. IV, sections I–III. Calcutta, 1887.
*Proceedings of the Students' Literary and Scientific Society, 1854–5 and 1855–6*. Bombay, 1857.
*Proceedings of the Students' Literary and Scientific Society, 1856–7, 1857–8 and 1858–9*. Bombay, 1860.
*Public Department Diary of the Bombay Government*. 1792, vol. 100.
*Rahnuma-e-Majdisna Sabha* [Gujarati]. Bombay, 1861.
*Report of the Board of Education, Bombay*. Bombay, 1845.
*Report of the British Branch of the British, Continental, & General Federation for the Abolition of the State Regulation of Vice*. London, 1887.
*Report of the Commission Appointed to Enquire into the Working of the Cotton Frauds Act (1863); With Minutes of Evidence and Other Appendices*. Bombay, 1875.
*Report of the Commission Appointed to Inquire into the Administration of the Baroda State*. London, 1875.
*Report of the Committee Appointed to Inquire into the Indian Currency*. London, 1899.
*Report of the Political Administration of the Rajpootana States, 1868–9*. Calcutta, 1869.
*Royal Commission Appointed to Inquire into the Livery Companies of the City of London, 1880*, vol. I. London, 1884.
*Royal Commission on the Administration of the Expenditure of India*. Calcutta, 1895.
*Selections from the Records of the Bombay Government on the Supply of Water to Bombay*. Bombay, 1854.
*Servants of India Society Report*, vol. I. Poona, 1918.

*Statement of the Moral and Material Progress of India, 1864–5/1866–7/1868–9.*

*The Seventh Report of the Proceedings of the Bombay Native Education Society*. Bombay, 1833.

*The Sixth Annual Report of the Society for Promoting the Education of the Poor within the Government of Bombay*. Bombay, 1821.

*The Third Report of the Proceedings of the Bombay Native School-Book and School Society*. Bombay, 1827.

*Third Report from the Select Committee on East India Finance; Together with the Proceedings of the Committee, Minutes of Evidence and Appendix*. London, 1873.

*Third Report of the Students' Literary and Scientific Society and Its Vernacular Branch Societies*. Bombay, 1852.

Wacha, Dinshaw (ed.). *Indian Abkari Administration, Being Notes on the Despatch of the Government of India, Relating to the System of Licenses for the Distillation and Sale of Spiritous Liquors in Force in the Various Provinces of India, Presented to the House of Commons*. Bombay, 1888.

### Newspapers and Journals

*Abkari: The Quarterly Organ of the Anglo-Indian Temperance Association*

*Amrita Bazaar Patrika*

*Asiatic Journal and Monthly Register*

*Biographical Magazine*

*Birmingham Daily Post*

*Blackburn Standard and Weekly Express*

*Bombay Gazette*

*Bombay Times and Journal of Commerce*

*Daily Chronicle*

*Daily News*

*Eastern Post*

*Englishwoman's Review*

*Freeman's Journal*

*Hindustan Review and Kayastha Samachar*

*Holborn and Finsbury Guardian*

*India: A Journal for the Discussion of Indian Affairs*

*Indian Libertarian*

*Indian Opinion*

*Indian Review*

*Indian Spectator* (Bombay, 1880–1913)

*Journal of the East India Association*

*Journal of the National Indian Association*

*Journal of the Society for Arts*

*Leicestershire Chronicle and the Leicestershire Mercury*
*Manchester Guardian*
*Manchester Times*
*Native Opinion*
*Pall Mall Gazette*
*Parsiana*
*Quarterly Journal of the Poona Sarvajanik Sabha*
*Report on Native Papers, Bombay*
*Reynolds Newspaper*
*Sunday Times*
*The Economist*
*The Pioneer*
*The Standard*
*The Star*
*The Times*
*Times of India*
*Weekly News and Chronicle*
*Western Daily Mercury*
*Young India*

## Books, Pamphlets and Collections

Anon. 'Political and Economical Heterodoxy: Cliffe Leslie'. *Westminster Review* 64 (October 1883), pp. 221–33.

———. *K. Marx and F. Engles on Colonialism*. Moscow: Foreign Languages Publishing House, n.d.

———. *The Unemployed*. London: n.p., 1905.

Banaji, Koshru Navrosji. *Memoirs of the Late Framji Cowasji Banaji*. Bombay, 1892.

Banerjea, Surendranath. *A Nation in The Making: Being Reminiscences of Fifty Years of Public Life*. Bombay: Oxford University Press, 1963 [1925]).

Bengalee, Sorabjee Shapoorjee (ed.). *The Parsee Marriage and Divorce Act 1865* (Act no. XV of 1865), *the Parsee Chattels Real Act* (Act no. IX of 1837), *the Parsee Succession Act* (Act no. XXI of 1865), with an appendix and Guzerattee translation. Bombay: Parsee Law Association, 1868.

Bentham, Jeremy. 'A Fragment on Government' [1776]. In Ross Harrison (ed.), *Cambridge Texts in the History of Political Thought* (Cambridge: Cambridge University Press, 1988), pp. 36–114.

———. *The Theory of Legislation* (ed.), C. K. Ogden (London: Paul, Trench, Tübner & Co, 1931[1840]).

Birdwood, George. *Two Letters on the Industrial Arts of India*. London: W. B. Whittingham & Co, 1879.

Booth, Charles. *Life and Labour of the People of London, Second Series: Industry*. London: Macmillan, 1903.

Booth, Joseph. *Africa for the African*. Edited by Laura Perry. Blantyre: Christian Literature Association in Malawi, 1996 [1897].

Bradlaugh, C. *A Selection of the Political Pamphlets of Charles Bradlaugh*. Edited by John Saville. New York, NY: Augustus M. Kelly Publishers, 1970.

Bright, John. *Speeches on Questions of Public Policy*, vol. I. Edited by James E. Thorold Rogers, 2 vols. London: Macmillan & Co, 1868.

———. *Speeches on Questions of Public Policy by the Right Honourable John Bright MP*. Edited by James E. Thorold Rogers. London: T. Fisher Unwin, 1898.

Bryan, William Jennings. *Republic or Empire? The Philippine Question*. Chicago, IL: The Independence Company, 1899.

———. 'Imperialism'. In William Jennings Bryan (ed.), *Under Other Flags: Travels, Lectures, Speeches*. Lincoln, NE: Woodruff-Collins Printing Co, 1904, pp. 305–39.

Callcott, Maria Dundas Graham. *Journal of a Residence in India*. Cambridge: Cambridge University Press, 2012 [1813].

Cama, K. R. *The Collected Works of K. R. Cama*, 2 vols. Bombay: K. R. Cama Oriental Institute, 1968.

Carlyle, Thomas. *On Heroes, Hero-Worship, and the Heroic in History*. London: James Frasier, 1841.

———. *Past and Present*. Boston, MA: Charles C. Little & James Brown, 1843.

———. *Critical and Miscellaneous Essays*, vol. I. 4 vols. London: Chapman & Hall, 1887 [1838–57].

———. *The Last Words of Thomas Carlyle: On Trade-Unions, Promoterism and the Signs of the Times*. Boston, MA: Dana Estates & Company, 1892.

———. *Latter Day Pamphlets*. London: Chapman & Hall, 1897.

———. *The Collected Letters of Thomas and Jane Welsh Carlyle*, vol. 20. Durham, NC, Duke University Press, 1970–.

———. *Sartor Resartus*. Oxford: Oxford University Press, 1987.

Chandra, Bholanath. 'A Voice for the Commerce and Manufactures of India'. *Mookherjee's Magazine* 2 (1873), pp. 77–121.

Chirol, Valentine. *Indian Unrest*. London: Macmillan, 1910.

Cliffe Leslie, T. E. 'On the Philosophical Methods of Political Economy' [1876]. In T. E. Cliffe Leslie, *Essays in Political Economy*, new edn. London: Longman, Green & Co, 1888, pp. 171–80.

Clunes, John. *An Historical Sketch of the Princes of India: Stipendiary, Subsidiary, Protected, Tributary, and Feudatory*. London: A. Shortrede, 1833.

Cotton, Sir Henry John Steadman. *New India or India in Transition*, new edn. London: Kegan, Paul, Trench, Trübner & Co, 1904.

Cursetjee, Manockjee, *The Parsee Panchayet, Its Rise, Its Fall and the Causes That Led to the Same: Being a Series of Letters in the Bombay Times of 1844–5, Under the Signature of Q in the Corner, Published at the Request of Some Gentlemen of the Parsee Community and with the Permission of the Author*. Bombay: L. M. De Souza, 1860.

Davitt, Michael. *Leaves from A Prison Diary or Lectures to a 'Solitary' Audience*, 2 vols. London: Chapman and Hall, 1885.

———. 'Random Thoughts on the Irish Land War'. In Carla King (ed.), *Jottings in Solitary*. Dublin: University College Dublin Press, 2003, pp. 170–93.

De Tocqueville, Alexis. *The Old Regime and the French Revolution*. Translated by S. Gilbert. New York, NY: Doubleday, 1955.

———. *Democracy in America*. Translated by G. Lawrence. New York, NY: Harper and Row, 1966.

Dickinson, John. *India: Its Government under a Bureaucracy*. London: Saunders and Stanford, 1853.

Digby, William. *Indian Problems for English Consideration: A Letter to the Council of the National Liberal Federation*. Plymouth: Latimer & Son, 1881.

———. *Prosperous British India: A Revelation from the Official Records*. London: Fisher Unwin, 1901.

Dobson Collet, Sophia (ed.). *Keshub Chunder Sen's English Visit*. London: Strahan, 1871.

Edwardes, S. M. *The Gazetteer of Bombay City and Island*, 3 vols. Bombay: The Times Press, 1909.

Evans Bell. *The English in India: Letters from Nagpore, Written In 1857–58*. London: John Chapman, 1859.

———. *The Rajah and the Principality of Mysore*. London: T. Richards, 1865.

———. *Remarks on the Mysore Blue Book*. London: Trübner & Co, 1866.

———. *Our Great Vassal Empire*. London: Trübner & Co, 1870.

Evans, E. P. *Evolutional Ethics and Animal Psychology*. London, 1898.

Fawcett, Henry. *The Economic Position of the British Labourer*. London: Macmillan & Co, 1865.

———. *Pauperism: Its Causes and Remedies*. London: Macmillan & Co, 1871.

Gadgil, D. R. *The Industrial Evolution of India*, 4th edn. Oxford: Oxford University Press, 2004.

———. *Selected Writings of D. R. Gadgil: The Indian Economy Problems and Prospects*. Edited by Sulabha Brahme. Oxford: Oxford University Press, 2011.

Gandhi, M. K. *The Speeches and Writings of Mahatma Gandhi*, 4th edn. Madras: G. A. Natesan & Co, 1933.

———. *Hind Swaraj or Indian Home Rule*. Ahmedabad: Navajivan Publishing House, 1938.

———. *The Collected Works of Mahatma Gandhi*, 100 vols. Ahmedabad: Navajivan Press, 1960–94.

George, Henry. *Progress and Poverty: An Inquiry into the Cause of Industrial Depressions and of Increase of Want with the Increase of Wealth, the Remedy*. London: William Reeves, 1884 [1879].

Gidumal, Dayaram (ed.). *The Life and Life-Work of Behramji M. Malabari*. Bombay: Education Society Press, 1888.

Gokhale, G. K. *Speeches of the Honourable Mr. G. K. Gokhale*. Madras: G. A. Natesan & Co, 1908.

———. *Speeches of Gopal Krishna Gokhale*. Madras: G. A. Natesan & Co, 1916.

Hobson, J. A. *Confessions of an Economic Heretic: The Autobiography of John A. Hobson*. Edited by Michael Freeden. Hassocks: Harvester Press, 1976 [1938].

———. *Imperialism: A Study*. London: James Nisbet & Co, 1902.

Holyoake, G. J. *Essentials of Co-Operative Education*. London: Labour Association for Promoting Cooperative Production, 1898.

Hyndman, H. M. *England for All*. London: E. W. Allen, 1881.

———. *The Bankruptcy of India: An Enquiry into the Administration of India under the Crown*. London: Swan Sonnenschein & Co, 1885.

———. *Record of An Adventurous Life*. London: Macmillan, 1911.

Judius. 'Poetry, Poets, and Poetical Powers'. *Westminster Review* 149, no. 6 (1898), pp. 667–79.

Karaka, Dosabhai Framji. *History of the Parsis*, 2 vols. London: Macmillan & Co, 1884.

Lajpat Rai, Lala. *Lala Lajpat Rai: The Man in His World*. Madras: G. A. Natesan & Co, 1907.

*Lloyd's Register of British and Foreign Shipping, 1862/3*. London: Wyman & Sons, 1862.

Locke, John. *An Essay Concerning the True Original and Extent of Civil Government*. Dublin: George Bonham, 1798.

———. 'Second Treatise on Government'. In John Locke, *Two Treatises on Government*, edited by Peter Laslett, 3rd edn. Cambridge: Cambridge University Press, 1988.

———. *An Essay Concerning the True Original and Extent of Civil Government*. Dublin: George Bonham, 1798.

Macaulay, Thomas Babington. *The History of England from the Accession of James the Second*, 5 vols. London: Longman, Green, Reader & Dyer, 1877 [1848–59].

———. *The Miscellaneous Writings and Speeches of Lord Macaulay*, vol. 4. London: Longmans, Green & Co, 1880.

———. *The Works of Lord Macaulay*, 12 vols. London: Longman & Co, 1898.

Maine, Henry. *Ancient Law: Its Connections with the Early History of Society and Its Relation to Modern Ideas* (London: John Murray, 1861).

———. *Village Communities in the East and West, With Other Lectures, Addresses and Essays*, 3rd edn. London: John Murray, 1890 [1871].

Malabari, Behramji M. *Gujarat and the Gujaratis: Pictures of Asian Men and Manners Taken from Life*, 3rd edn. Bombay: W. H. Allen & Co, 1889 [1882].

Malaviya, M. M. *Speeches and Writings of Pandit Madan Mohan Malaviya*. Madras: G. A. Natesan & Co, 1919.

Marx, Karl. *A Contribution to the Critique of Political Economy*. Moscow: Progress Publishers, 1977 [1859].

Masani, R. P. *Dadabhai Naoroji: The Grand Old Man of India*. London: George Allen & Unwin, 1939.

Masani, Rustom. *The Religion of the Good Life: Zoroastrianism*. London: George Allen, 1954 [1938].

Masani, Minoo. *Socialism Reconsidered*. Bombay: Padma Publications, 1944.

———. *Economics of Freedom*. Bombay: Forum for Free Enterprise, 1955.

———. *Congress Misrule and the Swatantra Alternative*. Bombay: Manaktalas, 1966.

———. *Why Swatantra? On the Programme and Policy of the Swatantra Party*. Bombay, 1966.

———. *Minoo Masani 90*. Bombay: Freedom First, 1990.

Mehta, P. M. *Speeches and Writings of the Honourable Sir Pherozeshah M. Mehta*. Edited by C. Y. Chintamani. Allahabad: The Indian Press, 1905.

Mill, John Stuart. *The Collected Works of John Stuart Mill*. Edited by John M. Robson, introduced by V. W. Bladen. 33 vols., online edn. Toronto: University of Toronto Press, 1965.

———. 'Thornton on Labour and Its Claims'. *Fortnightly Review* 5 (May 1869), pp. 505–18, and (June 1869), pp. 680–700.

*Minute of Proceedings of the Bombay Association*. Bombay: Bombay Association, 1852.

Narayan, Govind. *Mumbai: An Urban Biography from 1863*. Translated by Murali Ranganathan. London: Anthem Press, 2008 [1863].

Nehru, Jawaharlal. *The Unity of India: Collected Writings 1937–40*. New York, NY: John Day Company, 1942.

———. *Selected Works of Jawaharlal Nehru*, 85 vols. New Delhi: Orient Longman, 1973.

O'Donnell, C. J. *The Black Pamphlet of Calcutta: The Famine of 1874*. London: William Ridgway, 1876.

O'Donnell, F. H. *A History of the Irish Parliamentary Party*, 2 vols. London: Longman, Green & Co, 1910.

Patell, B. B. *Parsee Prakash: Being a Record of Important Events in the Growth of the Parsee Community in Western India, Chronologically Arranged*, vol. I [Gujarati]. 3 vols. Bombay: Duftur Ashkara Press, 1888.

Phillips, William. *"Home Rule" or London: An Appeal and a Warning*. London: n.p., 1888.

Potter, George (ed.). *The Monthly Record of Eminent Men*. London: George Potter, 1891.

Ranade, Mahedeva Govind. *Religious and Social Reform: A Collection of Essays and Speeches*. Edited by M. B. Kolasker. Bombay: Gopal Narayan & Co, 1902.

———. *Essays on Indian Economics: A Collection of Essays and Speeches*. Madras: G. A. Natesan & Co, 1906.

Ricardo, David. 'On the Principles of Political Economy and Taxation' [1817]. In David Ricardo, *The Works and Correspondence of David Ricardo,* vol. I, edited by Pierro Sraffa. 11 vols. Cambridge: Cambridge University Press, 1951, pp. 24–258.

*Routledge's Diamond Jubilee Guide to London and Its Suburbs*. London: George Routledge & Sons, 1887.

Ruskin, J. *Unto his Last and Other Writings*. Edited by Clive Wilmer. London: Penguin, 1997 [1862].

Shah, K. T. *National Planning, Principles and Administration*. Bombay: Vora & Co, 1948.

———. *Ancient Foundations of Economics in India*. Bombay: Vora & Co, 1954.

Shah, K. T. and K. J. Khambata. *Wealth and Taxable Capacity of India*. Bombay: D. B. Tarapolevara Sons & Co, 1924.

Shapurji, Sorabji. *The Evil Social Customs at Present Prevalent among the Parsees and the Best Means of Eradicating Them*. Bombay: Ripon Printing Press, undated.

Shroff, A. D. *Forum for Free Enterprise Manifesto*. Bombay: Forum for Free Enterprise, 1956.

———. *Our Economic Future*. Bombay: Forum for Free Enterprise, 1958.

———. *The Future Is with Free Enterprise*. Bombay: Forum for Free Enterprise, 1959.

———. *Will Democratic Socialism Help India?* Bombay: Forum for Free Enterprise, 1964.

Siraj-al-Dīn Muḥammad ibn Muḥammad al-Sajāwandī. *Al Sirajiyyah; or, the Mahommedan law of Inheritance*. Translated by Sir William Jones with notes and appendix by Almaric Rumsey. London: Thacker, Spinck & Co 1869 [1792].

Smith, Adam. *The Glasgow Edition of the Works and Correspondence of Adam Smith: The Theory of Moral Sentiments*. Edited by D. D. Rapheael and A. L. Macfie. Oxford: Oxford University Press, 1976.

———. *The Wealth of Nations*, books I–III. London: Penguin, 1982.

Smith, Samuel. 'The Nationalization of the Land'. *Contemporary Review* 44 (December 1883), pp. 850–71.

———. 'India Revisited'. *Contemporary Review* 49 (June 1886), pp. 794–819.

Stuart, J. *A History of the Zulu Rebellion, 1906*. London: Macmillan, 1913.

Taleyarkhan, Dinshah Ardeshir. *The Riots of 1874: Their True History and Philosophy*. Bombay: Vining & Co, 1874.

Telang, K. T. *Selected Writings and Speeches of K. T. Telang*. Bombay: Manoranjan Press, 1916.

Temple, Richard. *India in 1880*. London: John Murray, 1880.

Thorold Rogers, J. E. *A History of Agriculture and Prices in England from 1259 To 1793*, 7 vols. Oxford: Clarendon Press, 1866–1902.

Tilak, B. G. *Bal Gangadhar Tilak: His Writings and Speeches*. Madras: G. A. Natesan & Co, 1919.

Vakil, C. N. *Financial Developments in Modern India, 1860–1924*. Bombay: D. B. Taraporevala Sons & Co, 1924.

Vakil, C. N. and Brahmanand. *Planning for an Expanding Economy*. Bombay: Vora & Co Publishers, 1956.

Vicaji, Veerbaiji F. *Home: Its Duties and Comforts*. Bombay: Parsee Girls' School Association, 1888.

Wacha, Dinshaw. *A Financial Chapter in the History of Bombay City*, new edn. Bombay: A. J. Combridge & Co, 1910.

———. *Rise and Growth of Bombay Municipal Government*. Madras: G. A. Natesan & Co, 1913.

———. *The Life and Work of J. N. Tata*, new edn. Madras: Ganesh & Co, 1915 [1914].

———. *Shells from the Sands of Bombay: Being My Recollections and Reminiscences, 1860–1875*. Bombay: Bombay Chronicle Press, 1920.

Watcha, P. B. *Firdousi and the Parsis: What We Owe to Him*. Bombay: n. p., 1911.

Watts, Isaac. *The Improvement of the Mind: Or a Supplement to the Art of Logick*. Edinbugh: D. Shaw, 1801 [1727].

Webb, Sidney. 'Rate of Interest and Laws of Distribution'. *Quarterly Journal of Economics* 2, no. 2 (1888), pp. 188–208.

———. *The London Programme*. London: Swan Sonnenschein & Co, 1891.

Webb, Sidney and Beatrice Webb. *Industrial Democracy*. London: Longman, Green & Co, 1920 [1897].

Wood, W. Martin. 'India's Un-adjusted Trade Balance: Its Effect on the Industrial and Commercial Condition of the People'. *Political Science Quarterly* 2, no. 4 (1887), pp. 666–82.


## Secondary Literature

### *Books, Articles and Chapters*


Ambirajan, S. 'Economic Thinking of Dadabhai Naoroji'. In P. D. Hajela (ed.), *Economic Thoughts of Dadabhai Naoroji*. New Delhi: Deep and Deep Publications, 2001, pp. 1–36.

Anon. *The Parsee Voice* 1, no. 19 (2004), pp. 1–4.

Arendt, Hannah. *The Human Condition*, new edn. Chicago, IL: Chicago University Press, 1998.

Arnold, David. 'The Colonial Prison: Power, Knowledge and Penology in Nineteenth Century India'. In *Subaltern Studies 8: Essays in Honour of Ranajit Guha*, edited by David Arnold and David Hardiman. New Delhi: Oxford University Press, 1994, pp. 148–84.

———. *Science, Technology and Medicine in Colonial India*. Cambridge: Cambridge University Press, 2000.

———. 'Agriculture and "Improvement" in Early Colonial India: A Pre-history of Development'. *Journal of Agrarian Change* 5, no. 4 (2005), pp. 505–25.

———. 'Labouring for the Raj: Convict Work Regimes in Colonial India, 1836–1939'. In Christian Giuseppe de Vito and Alex Lichtenstein (eds.), *Global Convict Labour* (Leiden: Brill, 2015), pp. 199–221.

Asad, Talal. *Formations of the Secular: Christianity, Islam, Modernity*. Stanford, CA: Stanford University Press, 2003.

Balasubramanian, Aditya. 'Contesting Permit-and-License *Raj*: Economic Conservatism and the Idea of Democracy in 1950s India'. *Past and Present* 251, no. 1 (2021), pp. 189–227.

Banerjee, Prathama. 'The Abiding Binary: The Social and the Political in India'. In Stephen Legg and Deana Heath (eds.), *Michael Foucault and the Question of Postcolonial Orderings* (Cambridge: Cambridge University Press, 2018), pp. 81–105.

Banerjee, Milinda. '"All This Is Indeed Brahman" Rammohun Roy and a "Global" History of the Rights-Bearing Self'. *Asian Review of World Histories* 3, no. 1 (2015), pp. 81–112

———. *The Mortal God: Imagining the Sovereign in Colonial India*. Cambridge: Cambridge University Press, 2018.

———. 'Sovereignty as a Motor of Global Conceptual Travel: Sanskritic Equivalents of "Law" in Bengali Discursive Production'. *Modern Intellectual History* 17, no. 2 (2020), pp. 487–506.

———. 'How "Dynasty" Became a Modern Global Concept: Intellectual Histories of Sovereignty and Property'. *Global Intellectual History*. Advanced online publication, 2020, pp. 1–32.

Banerjee, Sukanya. *Becoming Imperial Citizens: Indians in the Late Victorian Empire*. Durham, NC: Duke University Press, 2010.

Bayly, C. A. 'Patrons and Politics in Northern India'. *Modern Asian Studies* 7, no. 3 (1973), pp. 349–88.

———. *Rulers, Townsmen and Bazaars: North Indian Society in The Age of British Expansion, 1770–1870*. Cambridge: Cambridge University Press, 1983.

———. *Empire and Information: Intelligence Gathering and Social Communication in India*. Cambridge: Cambridge University Press, 1996.

———. *Origins of Nationality in South Asia: Patriotism and Ethical Government in the Making of Modern India*. Oxford: Oxford University Press, 1998.

———. 'Rallying around the Subaltern'. In Vinayak Chaturvedi (ed.), *Mapping Subaltern Studies and the Postcolonial*. London: Verso, 2000, pp. 116–26.

———. 'Ireland, India and the Empire: 1780–1914'. *Transactions of the Royal Historical Society* 6, 10 (2000), pp. 377–97.

———. 'Liberalism at Large: Mazzini and Nineteenth Century Indian Thought'. In C. A. Bayly and Eugenio F. Biagini (eds.), *Giussepe Mazzini and the Globalisation of Democratic Nationalism, 1830–1920*. Oxford: Oxford University Press, 2008.

———. *Recovering Liberties: Indian Thought in the Age of Liberalism and Empire*. Cambridge: Cambridge University Press, 2011.

———. 'Empires and Indian Liberals'. In Catherine Hall and Keith McClelland (eds.), *Race, Nation and Empire: Making Histories, 1750 To the Present*. Manchester: Manchester University Press, 2011, pp. 74–93.

———. 'The Ends of Liberalism and the Political Thought of Nehru's India'. *Modern Intellectual History* 12, no. 3 (2015), pp. 605–26.

Bell, Duncan. 'What Is Liberalism?' *Political Theory* 42, no. 6 (2014), pp. 682–715.

———. *Reordering the World: Essays on Liberalism and Empire* (Princeton, NJ: Princeton University Press, 2016).

Benton, Lauren, *Law and Colonial Cultures: Legal Regimes in World History*. Cambridge: Cambridge University Press, 2002.

Biagini, Eugenio F. 'British Trade Unions and Popular Political Economy, 1860–1880'. *Historical Journal* 30, no. 4 (1987), pp. 811–40.

———. *Liberty, Retrenchment and Reform: Popular Liberalism in the Age of Gladstone, 1860–1880*. Cambridge Cambridge University Press, 1992.

———. 'Liberalism and Direct Democracy: John Stuart Mill and the Model of Ancient Athens'. In Eugenio Biagini (ed.), *Citizenship and Community: Liberals, Radicals and Collective Identities in the British Isles, 1865–1931*. Cambridge: Cambridge University Press, 1996, pp. 21–44.

———. 'Neo-roman Liberalism: "Republican" Values and British Liberalism, ca. 1860–75'. *History of European Ideas* 29, no. 1 (2003), pp. 55–72.

Birla, Ritu. *Stages of Capital: Law, Culture, and Market Governance in Late Colonial India*. Durham, NC: Duke University Press, 2009.

Boehmer, Elleke. *Empire, the National, and the Postcolonial, 1890–1920: Resistance in Interaction*. Oxford: Oxford University Press, 2002.

Bose, Sugata and Ayesha Jalal. *Modern South Asia: History, Culture and Political Economy*. London: Routledge, 1998.

Bose, Sugata and Kris Manjapra (eds.). *Cosmopolitan Thought Zones: South Asia and the Global Circulation of Ideas*. Basingstoke: Palgrave Macmillan, 2010.

Brodie, Marc. *The Politics of the Poor: The East End of London, 1885–1914*. Oxford: Oxford University Press, 2004.

Broomfield, J. H. *Elite Conflict in a Plural Society: Twentieth-Century Bengal*. Cambridge: Cambridge University Press, 1968.

Brown, Judith. *Gandhi's Rise to Power: Indian Politics 1915–1922*. Cambridge: Cambridge University Press, 1972.

Burrow, John. *A Liberal Descent: Victorian Historians and the English Past*. Cambridge: Cambridge University Press, 1985.

Burton, Antoinette. 'Fearful Bodies into Disciplined Subjects: Pleasure, Romance and the Family Drama of Colonial Reform in Mary Carpenter's "Six months in India"'. *Signs* 20, no. 3 (1995), pp. 545–74.

———. 'Making a Spectacle of Empire: Indian Travelers in Fin-de-Siècle London'. *History Workshop Journal* 42 (Autumn, 1996), pp. 126–46.

———. 'The White Woman's Burden: British Feminists and the Indian Woman, 1865–1915'. *Women's Studies International Forum* 13, no. 4 (1990), pp. 295–308.

———. 'Tongues Untied: Lord Salisbury's "Black Man" and the Boundaries of Imperial Democracy'. *Comparative Studies in Society and History* 42, no. 3 (2000), pp. 632–61.

Chakrabarty, Dipesh. *Re-Thinking Working Class History: Bengal 1890–1940*. Princeton, NJ: Princeton University Press, 1989.

———. *Provincializing Europe: Postcolonial Thought and Historical Difference*. Princeton, NJ: Princeton University Press, 2000.

Chandavarkar, A. G. 'Money and Credit'. In Dharma Kumar and Meghnad Desai (eds.), *The Cambridge Economic History of India*. Cambridge: Cambridge University Press, 1983, pp. 762–803.

Chandavarkar, Rajnarayan. *The Origins of Industrial Capitalism in India: Business Strategies and the Working Classes in Bombay*, 2nd edn. Cambridge: Cambridge University Press, 2002.

———. 'Bombay's Perennial Modernities'. In Jennifer Davis, Gordon Johnson and David Washbrook (eds.), *History, Culture and The Indian City: Essays by Rajnarayan Chandavarkar*. Cambridge: Cambridge University Press, 2009, pp. 12–30.

Chandra, Bipan. *The Rise and Growth of Economic Nationalism in India: Economic Policies of Indian National Leadership*. New Delhi: People's Publishing House, 1966.

Chandra, Sudhur. 'The Cultural Component of Economic Nationalism: R. C. Dutt's "The Lake of Palms"'. *Indian Historical Review* 12, nos. 1–2 (1985–6), pp. 106–20.

Chatterjee, Partha. 'Whose Imagined Community?' In Gopal Balakrishnan (ed.), *Mapping the Nation* (London: Verso, 1996), pp. 214–25.

———. 'On Civil and Political Society in Postcolonial Democracies'. In Sudipta Kaviraj and Sunil Khilnani (eds.), *Civil Societies: History and Possibilities*. Cambridge: Cambridge University Press, 2001, pp. 165–78.

Chatterji, Joya. 'Nationalisms in India, 1857–1947'. In John Breuilly (ed.), *The Oxford Handbook of The History of Nationalism*. Oxford: Oxford University Press, 2013, pp. 242–62.

Chirol, Valentine. 'Birdwood, Sir George Christopher Molesworth (1832–1917)'. Revised by Katherine Prior. In *Oxford Dictionary of National Biography*. Oxford: Oxford University Press, 2004.

Claeys, Gregory. *Imperial Sceptics: British Critics of Empire 1850–1920*, new edn. Cambridge: Cambridge University Press, 2012.

Clarkson, Chris. *Domestic Reforms: Political Visions and Family Regulation in British Columbia, 1862–1940*. Vancouver: University of British Columbia Press, 2007.

Cockram, Gill. *Ruskin and Social Reform: Ethics and Economics in the Victorian Age*. London: Bloomsbury, 2007.

Cocks, R. C. J. *Sir Henry Maine: A Study in Victorian Jurisprudence*, new edn. Cambridge: Cambridge University Press, 2004.

Codell, Julie F. 'Reversing the Grand Tour: Guest Discourse in Indian Travel Narratives'. *Huntingdon Library Quarterly* 70, no. 1 (2007), pp. 173–89.

Cohn, Bernard S. *Colonialism and Its Forms of Knowledge: The British in India*. Princeton, NJ: Princeton University Press, 1996.

Collini, Stefan. 'The Idea of "Character" in Victorian Political Thought'. *Transactions of the Royal Historical Society* 35, no. 1 (1985), pp. 29–50.

Collison Black, R. D. *Economic Thought and the Irish Question, 1817–1870*. Cambridge: Cambridge University press, 1960.

Ian Copland. 'The Baroda Crisis of 1873–7: A Study in Governmental Rivalry'. *Modern Asian Studies* 11, no. 2 (1968), pp. 97–123.

Cumpston, Mary. 'Some Early Indian Nationalists and Their Allies in the British Parliament, 1851–1906'. *English Historical Review* 76 (April 1961), pp. 279–97.

Das Gupta, Uma. 'The Indian Press 1870–1880: A Small World of Journalism'. *Modern Asian Studies* 11, no. 2 (1977), pp. 213–35.

Davis, John *Reforming London: The London Government Problem, 1855–1900*. Oxford; Oxford University Press, 1988.

———. 'Radical Clubs and London Politics, 1870–1900'. In David Feldman and Gareth Steadman Jones (eds.), *Metropolis London: Histories and Representations Since 1800*. London: Routledge, 1989, pp. 103–28.

Deshpande, Prachi. *Creative Pasts: Historical Memory and Identity in Western India, 1700–1960*. New York, NY: Columbia University Press, 2007.

Devji, Faisal. 'Apologetic Modernity'. *Modern Intellectual History* 4, no. 1 (2007), pp. 61–76.

———. *The Impossible Indian: Gandhi and the Temptation of Violence*. Cambridge, MA: Harvard University Press, 2012.

———. *Muslim Zion: Pakistan as a Political Idea*. Cambridge, MA: Harvard University Press, 2013.

Dirks, Nicholas B. *Castes of Mind: Colonialism and the Making of Modern India*. Princeton: NJ: Princeton University Press, 2001.

Dobbin, Christine. *Urban Leadership in Western India: Politics and Communities in Bombay City*. Oxford: Oxford University Press, 1972.

Dossal, Mariam. *Imperial Designs and Imperial Realities: The Planning of Bombay City, 1845–1875*. New Delhi: Oxford University Press, 1991.

Downing, Arthur. 'The Friendly Planet: "Oddfellows", Networks, and the "British World" c. 1840–1940'. *Journal of Global History* 7, no. 3 (2012), pp. 389–414.

Finestein, Israel. 'A Modern Examination of Macaulay's Case for the Civil Emancipation of the Jews'. *Transactions and Miscellanies (Jewish Historical Society of England)* 28 (1981–1982), pp. 39–59.

Freeden, Michael. *Liberal Languages: Ideological Imaginations and Twentieth-Century Progressive Thought*. Princeton, NJ: Princeton University Press, 2005.

Fukazawa, H. 'Agrarian Relations: Western India'. In Dharma Kumar and Meghnad Desai (eds.), *The Cambridge Economic History of India*. Cambridge: Cambridge University Press, 1983, pp. 177–206.

Gadamer, Hans-Georg. *Truth and Method*. Translated by Joel Weinscheimer and Donald G. Marshall. London: Bloomsbury, 2013.

Gallagher, John and Ronald Robinson. 'The Imperialism of Free Trade'. *The Economic History Review* 6, no. 1 (1953), pp. 1–15.

Gallagher, John, Gordon Johnson and Anil Seal (eds.). *Locality, Province and Nation: Essays on Indian Politics 1870–1940*. Cambridge: Cambridge University Press, 1973.

Geuss, Raymond. *Philosophy and Real Politics*. Princeton, NJ: Princeton University Press, 2008.

———. *Politics and The Imagination*. Princeton, NJ: Princeton University Press, 2010.

Green, Nile. 'Waves of Heterotopia: Toward a Vernacular Intellectual History of the Indian Ocean'. *American Historical Review* 123, no. 3 (2018), pp. 846–74.

Gopal Jayal, Niraja. *Citizenship and Its Discontents: An Indian History*. New Delhi: Permanent Black, 2013.

Goswami, Manu. *Producing India: From Colonial Economy to National Space*. Chicago, IL: Chicago University Press, 2004.

Guha, Ranajit. *Elementary Aspects of Peasant Insurgency in Colonial India*. Durham, NC: Duke University Press, 1999.

———. 'On Some Aspects of the Historiography of Colonial India'. In Vinayak Chaturvedi (ed.), *Mapping Subaltern Studies and The Postcolonial*. London: Verso, 2000, pp. 1–7.

Gupta, Narayani. *Delhi Between Two Empires, 1803–1901*. New Delhi: Oxford University Press, 1981.

Gurney, Peter. *Co-Operative Culture and the Politics of Consumption in England, 1870–1930*. Manchester: Manchester University Press, 1996.

Habermas, Jürgen. *The Theory of Communicative Action*, vol. I. 2 vols. Boston, MA: Beacon Press, 1984.

———. *The Structural Transformation of the Public Sphere: An Inquiry into the Category of Bourgeois Society*. London: Polity Press, 1989.

Halisi, C. R. D. *Black Political Thought in the Making of South African Democracy*. Bloomington, IN: Indiana University Press, 1999.

Hall, Catherine and L. Davidoff. *Family Fortunes: Men and Women of the English Middle Class 1780–1850*. London: Routledge, 2002.

Hall-Matthews, David. *Peasants, Famine and the State in Colonial Western India*. Basingstoke: Palgrave Macmillan, 2005.

Hansen, Kathryn. 'Languages on Stage: Linguistic Pluralism and Community Formation in Nineteenth-century Parsi Theatre'. *Modern Asian Studies* 37, no. 2 (2003), pp. 381–405.

———. 'Making Women Visible: Gender and Race Cross-dressing in the Parsi Theatre'. *Theatre Journal* 51, no. 2 (1999), pp. 127–47.

Harnetty, Peter. *Imperialism and Free Trade: Lancashire and India in the Mid-Nineteenth Century*. Vancouver: University of British Columbia Press, 1972.

Harris, Jose. *Private Lives, Public Spirit: Britain 1870–1914*. London: Penguin Books, 1994.

Harrison, Robert. 'Dickinson, John (1815–1876)'. Revised by Peter Harnetty. In *Oxford Dictionary of National Biography*. Oxford: Oxford University Press, 2004; online edn, October 2007.

Hasan, Mushirul. 'The Myth of Unity: Colonial and National Narratives'. In David Ludden (ed.), *Contesting the Nation: Religion, Community and the Politics of Democracy in India*. Philadelphia, PA: University of Pennsylvania Press, 1996, pp. 185–210.

Hatcher, Brian. 'Remembering Rammohan: An Essay on the (Re-)Emergence of Modern Hinduism'. *History of Religions* 46, no. 1 (2006), pp. 50–80.

Haynes, Douglas. *Rhetoric and Ritual in Colonial India: The Shaping of a Public Culture in Surat City, 1852–1928*. Oakland, CA: University of California Press, 1992.

Hazareesingh, Sandip. 'The Quest for Urban Citizenship: Civic Rights, Public Opinion, and Colonial Resistance in Early Twentieth-Century Bombay'. *Modern Asian Studies* 34, no. 4 (2000), pp. 797–829.

———. *The Colonial City and the Challenge of Modernity: Urban Hegemonies and Civic Contestations in Bombay, 1900–1925*. Himayatnagar: Orient Longman, 2007.

Hilton, Boyd. *The Age of Atonement: The Influence of Evangelicalism on Social and Economic Thought, 1785–1865*, new edn. Oxford: Oxford University Press, 2001.

Hinnells, John R. *Zoroastrianism and the Parsis*. London: Wardlock Educational Co, 1981.

———. *Zoroastrians in Britain: The Ratanbai Katrak Lectures, University of Oxford 1985*. Oxford: Oxford University Press, 1996.

Hinnells, J. R. 'The Flowering of Zoroastrian Benevolence'. In H. Bailey (eds.), *Papers in Honour of Professor Mary Boyce, Homages Et Opera Minora*, vol. 10. 11 vols.. Leiden: Brill, 1985, pp. 261–326.

Hinnells, John R. and Alan Williams (eds.). *Parsis in India and the Diaspora*. London: Routledge, 2008.

Hont, Istvan. *Jealousy of Trade: International Competition and the Nation-State in Historical Perspective*. Cambridge, MA: Harvard University press, 2005.

———. *Politics in a Commercial Society: Jean-Jacques Rousseau and Adam Smith*. Edited by Béla Kapossy and Michael Sonnenscher. Cambridge, MA: Harvard University Press, 2015.

Hunter, Emma. *Political Thought and the Public Sphere in Tanzania: Freedom, Democracy and Citizenship in the Era of Decolonization*. Cambridge: Cambridge University Press, 2015.

Ikegame, Aya. *Princely India Re-Imagined: A Historical Anthropology of Mysore from 1799 to the Present*. London: Routledge, 2013.

Ince, Onur Ulas. *Colonial Capitalism and the Dilemmas of Liberalism*. Oxford: Oxford University Press, 2018.

Irshick, Eugene. *Politics and Social Conflict in South Asia: The Non-Brahman Movement and Tamil Separatism, 1916–1929*. Berkley, CA: University of California Press, 1969.

Jacobs, Harland J. *Builders of Empire: Freemasons and British Imperialism, 1717–1927*. Chapel Hill, NC: University of North Carolina Press, 2007.

Jaffe, James. *Ironies of Colonial Governance: Law, Custom and Justice in Colonial India*. Cambridge: Cambridge University Press, 2015.

Kapila, Shruti. 'Self, Spencer and Swaraj: Nationalist Thought and Critiques of Liberalism, 1890–1920'. *Modern Intellectual History* 4, no. 1 (2007), pp. 109–27.

———. 'Global Intellectual History and the Indian political'. In Darrin M. McMahon and Samuel Moyn (eds.), *Rethinking Modern European Intellectual History*. Oxford: Oxford University Press, 2014, pp. 253–74.

———. 'Ambedkar's Agonism: Sovereign Violence and Pakistan as Peace'. *Comparative Studies of South Asia, Africa and the Middle East* 39, no. 1 (2019), pp. 185–95.

———. *Violent Fraternity in the Indian Age*. Princeton, NJ: Princeton University Press, 2021.

Karak, Anirban. 'What Was "Indian" Political Economy? On the Separation of the "Social", the "Economic" and the "Ethical" in Indian Nationalist Thought'. *Modern Asian Studies* 55, no. 1 (2021), pp. 75–115.

Kaviraj, Sudipta. 'The Imaginary Institution of India'. In Partha Chatterjee and Gyanendra Pandey (eds.), *Subaltern Studies 7*, new edn. Delhi: Oxford University Press, 1994.

Khilnani, Sunil. *The Idea of India*. London: Penguin, 2003.

Kidambi, Prashant. *The Making of an Indian Metropolis: Colonial Governance and Public Culture in Bombay, 1890–1920*. Aldershot: Ashgate, 2007.

King, Carka. 'Michael Davitt, Irish Nationalism and the British Empire in the Late Nineteenth Century'. In Peter Gray (ed.), *Victoria's Ireland? Irishness and Britishness, 1837–1901*. Dublin: Four Courts P., 2004, pp. 116–30.

Koditschek, Theodore. *Liberalism, Imperialism and the Historical Imagination: Nineteenth-Century Visions of Greater Britain*. Cambridge: Cambridge University Press, 2011.

Koot, Gerard M. *English Historical Economics, 1870–1926: The Rise of Economics History and Neomercantilism*. Cambridge: Cambridge University Press, 1987.

Kopf, David. *The Brahmo Samaj and the Shaping of the Modern Indian Mind*. Princeton, NJ: Princeton University Press, 1979.

Kulke, Eckehard. *The Parsees in India: A Minority as Agent of Social Change*. Munich: Weltforum Verlag, 1974.

Lally, Jagjeet. 'Trial, Error and Economic Development in Colonial Punjab: The Agri-Horticultural Society, the State and Sericulture Experiments, c. 1840–70'. *Indian Economic and Social History Review* 52, no. 1 (2015), pp. 1–27.

Langworthy, Harry W. 'Joseph Booth: Prophet of Radical Change in Central and South Africa, 1891–1915'. *Journal of Religion in Africa* 16, no. 1 (1986), pp. 22–43.

Lawrence, Elwood P. 'Henry George's British Mission', *American Quarterly* 3, no. 3 (1952), pp. 232–43.

Lloyd Kelly, Robert, *The Transatlantic Persuasion: The Liberal-Democratic Mind in the Age of Gladstone*, new edn. London: Routledge, 1990.

Lokhandwalla, S. T. 'Islamic Law and Ismaili Communities'. *Indian Economic and Social History Review* 4, no. 2 (1967), pp. 155–76.

Lubenow, William C. *Liberals and Public Culture in Modern Britain, 1815–1914*. Woodbridge: Boydell and Brewer, 2010.

Lyndon Shanely, Mary. *Feminism, Marriage and the Law in Victorian England, 1850–1895*. Princeton, NJ: Princeton University Press, 1989.

Mander, W. J. *British Idealism: A History*. Oxford: Oxford University Press, 2011.

Marashi, Ahshin. *Exile and the Nation: The Parsi Community of India and the Making of Modern Iran*. Austin, TX: University of Texas Press, 2020.

Mason, Michael. *The Making of Victorian Sexuality*. Oxford: Oxford University Press, 1994.

Masselos, J. *Towards Nationalism: Group Affiliations and the Politics of Public Associations in Nineteenth Century Western India*. Bombay: Popular Prakashan, 1974.

Matikkala, Mira. *Empire and Imperial Ambition: Liberty, Englishness and Anti-Imperialism in Late Victorian Britain*. London: Bloomsbury, 2010.

McCully, Bruce Tiebout. *English Education and the Origins of Indian Nationalism*. New York, NY: Columbia University Press, 1940.

McGowan, Abigail. *Crafting the Nation in Colonial India*. Basingstoke: Palgrave MacMillan, 2009.

Mehrota, S. R. 'The British India Society and Its Bengal Branch, 1839–46'. *Indian Economic and Social History Review* 4 (June 1967), pp. 131–54.

Mehta, Uday S. *Liberalism and Empire*. Chicago, IL Chicago University Press, 1999.

Mehta, Uday S. 'Liberal Strategies of Exclusion'. In Ann Laura Stoler and Frederick Cooper (eds.), *Tensions of Empire: Colonial Cultures in a Bourgeois World*. Berkley, CA: University of California Press, 1997, pp. 59–86.

Mitter, Partha. *Much Maligned Monsters: A History of European Reactions to Indian Art*. Chicago, IL: Chicago University Press, 1992.

Morris, Marcus. 'From Anti-Colonialism to Anti-Imperialism: The Evolution of H.M. Hyndman's Critique of Empire, c.1875–1905'. *Historical Research* 87, no. 236 (2014), pp. 293–314.

Moulton, E. C. 'British India and the Baroda Crisis 1874–5: A Problem in Princely State Relations'. *Canadian Journal of History* 3, no. 1 (1968), pp. 68–94.

Moyn, Samuel and Andrew Sartori. *Global Intellectual History*. New York, NY: Columbia University Press, 2013.

Muthu, Sankar (ed.). *Empire and Modern Political Thought*. Cambridge: Cambridge University Press, 2012.

Naik, J. V. 'Forerunners of Dadabhai's Naoroji's Drain Theory'. *Economic and Political Weekly* 36, nos. 46/47 (2001), pp. 4428–32.

Nair, Janaki. 'Beyond Nationalism: Modernity, Governance and a New Urban History for India'. *Urban History* 36, no. 2 (2009), pp. 327–41.

Naregal, Veena. *Language Politics, Elites, and the Public Sphere: Western India under Colonialism*. London: Permanent Black, 2002.

Newbigin, Eleanor. 'Accounting for the Nation, Marginalizing the Empire: Taxable Capacity and Colonial Rule in the Early Twentieth Century'. *History of Political Economy* 52, no. 3 (2020), pp. 455–72.

Norgate, G. Le G. 'Smith, Samuel (1836–1906)'. Revised by H. C. G. Matthew. In *Oxford Dictionary of National Biography*. Oxford: Oxford University Press, 2004.

O'Hanlon, Rosalind. *Caste, Conflict and Ideology: Mahatma Jotirao Phule and Low-Caste Protest in Nineteenth-Century Western India*. Cambridge: Cambridge University Press, 1985.

Oldenberg, Veena Talwa. *The Making of Colonial Lucknow, 1856–77*. Princeton, NJ: Princeton University Press, 1984.

Omidsalar, Mahmoud. *Poetics and Politics of Iran's National Epic, the Shahnameh*. New York, NY: Palgrave, 2011.

O'Sullivan, Michael. 'Vernacular Capitalism and Intellectual History in a Gujarati Account of China, 1860–68'. *Journal of Asian Studies* 80, no. 2 (2021), pp. 267–92.

Owen, Nicholas. *The British Left and India: Metropolitan Anti-Imperialism 1885–1947*. Oxford: Oxford University Press, 2010.

———. 'British Progressives and Civil Society in India 1905–1914'. In Jose Harris (ed.), *Civil Society in British History: Ideas, Identities, Institutions*, new edn. Oxford: Oxford University Press, 2005, pp. 149–76.

Palsetia, Jesse S. *The Parsis of India: Preservation of Identity in Bombay City*. Leiden: Brill, 2001.

———. 'The Parsis of India and the Opium Trade in China'. *Contemporary Drug Problems* 35 (Winter, 2008), pp. 647–78.

Parekh, Bikhu. 'The Cultural Particularity of Liberal Democracy'. *Political Studies* 40 (August 1992), pp. 160–5.

Patel, Dinyar. *Naoroji: Pioneer of Indian Nationalism*. Cambridge, MA: Harvard University Press, 2020.

Pettit, Philip. *Republicanism: A Theory of Freedom and Government*. Oxford: Oxford University Press, 2007.

Pitts, Jennifer. *A Turn to Empire: The Rise of Imperial Liberalism in Britain and France*. Princeton, NJ: Princeton University Press, 2005.

Pocock, J. G. A. *The Machiavellian Moment: Florentine Thought and the Republican Tradition*. Princeton, NJ: Princeton University Press, 2016.

Porter, Bernhard. *Critics of Empire: British Radicals and the Imperial Challenge*, new edn. London: I. B. Tauris, 2008.

Postel, Charles. *The Populist Vision*. Oxford: Oxford University Press, 2007.
Ranade, Rekha. *Sir Bartle Frere and His Times: A Study of His Bombay Years, 1862–1867*. New Delhi: Mittal Publications, 1990.
Rawal, Munni. *Dadabhai Naoroji: A Prophet of Indian Nationalism, 1855–1900*. New Delhi: Amol Publications, 1989.
Regan-Lefebvre, Jennifer. *Cosmopolitan Nationalism: Ireland, India and the Politics of Alfred Webb*. Basingstoke: Palgrave Macmillan, 2009.
Rowbotham, Judith. 'Miscarriage of Justice? Postcolonial Reflections on the "Trial" of the Maharajah of Baroda, 1875'. *Liverpool Law Review* 28, no. 3 (2007), pp. 377–403.
Sagar, Paul. *The Opinion of Mankind: Sociability and the Theory of the State from Hobbes to Smith*. Princeton, NJ: Princeton University Press, 2018.
Sartori, Andrew. *Bengal in Global Concept History: Culturalism in the Age of Capital*. Chicago, IL: Chicago University Press, 2008.
———. *Liberalism in Empire: An Alternative History*. Berkley, CA: University of California Press, 2014.
Schneer, Jonathan. *London: The Imperial Metropolis*. New Haven, CT: Yale University Press, 1999.
Schwan, Ann. '"Dreadful Beyond Description": Mary Carpenter's Prison Reform Writings and Female Convicts in Britain and India'. *European Journal of English Studies* 14, no. 2 (2010), pp. 107–20.
Schabas, Margaret. *The Natural Origins of Economics*. Chicago, IL: Chicago University Press, 2005.
Seal, Anil. *The Emergence of Indian Nationalism: Competition and Collaboration in the Later Nineteenth Century* (Cambridge: Cambridge University Press, 1966).
———. 'Imperialism and Nationalism in India'. In John Gallagher, Gordon Johnson and Anil Seal (eds.), *Locality, Province and Nation: Essays on Indian Politics 1870–1940*. Cambridge: Cambridge University Press, 1973, pp. 19–25.
Sharafi, Mitra. *Law and Identity in Colonial South Asia: Parsi Legal Culture, 1772–1947*. Cambridge: Cambridge University Press, 2014.
Silvestri, Michael. *India and Ireland: Nationalism, Empire and Memory*. Basingstoke: Palgrave Macmillan, 2009.
Skinner, Quentin. 'The Limits of Historical Explanations'. *Philosophy* 41, no. 157 (1966), pp. 199–215.
———. 'Meaning and Understanding in the History of Ideas'. *History and Theory* 8, no. 1 (1969), pp. 3–53.
———. *Liberty before Liberalism*. Cambridge: Cambridge University Press, 1997.
———. 'Freedom as the Absence of Arbitrary Power'. In Cecile Laborde and John Maynor (eds.), *Republicanism and Political Theory*. Oxford: Oxford University Press, 2008, pp. 83–101.

Stedman Jones, Gareth. *Outcast London: A Study in the Relationship between Classes in Victorian Society*, new edn. New York, NY: Oxford University Press, 1984.

Sultan, Nazmul. 'Self-Rule and the Problem of Peoplehood in Colonial India'. *American Political Science Review* 114, no. 1 (2020), pp. 81–94.

Sunstein, Cas. 'Beyond the Republican Revival'. *Yale Law Journal* 97 (1988), pp. 1539–90.

Thompson, Andrew. 'The Power and Privilege of Association: Co-Ethnic Networks and the Economic Life of the British Economic World'. *South African Historical Journal* 56, no. 1 (2006), pp. 43–59.

Thompson, James. *British Political Culture and the Idea Of 'Public Opinion', 1867–1914*. Cambridge: Cambridge University Press, 2013.

Thompson, Paul. 'Liberals, Radicals and Labour in London 1880–1900'. *Past and Present* 27 (April, 1964), pp. 73–101.

Tomlinson, B. R. *The Economy of Modern India: From 1860 to the Twenty-First Century*. Cambridge: Cambridge University Press, 2013.

Tosh, John. *A Man's Place: Masculinity and the Middle-Class Home in Victorian England*. New Haven, CT: Yale University Press, 1999.

Tripathi, Dwijendra. *The Oxford History of Indian Business*. Oxford: Oxford University Press, 2003.

Tully, James. *Public Philosophy in A New Key*, vol. II: *Imperialism and Civic Freedom*. 2 vols. Cambridge: Cambridge University Press, 2008.

Udin, Layly. '"Enemy Agents at Work": A Microhistory of the 1954 Adamjee and Karnaphuli Riots in East Pakistan'. *Modern Asian Studies* 55, no. 2 (2021), pp. 629–64.

Varouxakis, Georgios. *Mill on Nationality*. London: Routledge, 2002.

Vaughn, I. Karen. 'John Locke and the Labour Theory of Value'. *Journal of Libertarian Studies* 2, no. 4 (1978), pp. 311–26.

Veevers, David. *The Origins of the British Empire in Asia, 1600–1750*. Cambridge: Cambridge University Press, 2020.

Vernon, James. *Distant Strangers: How Britain Became Modern*. Berkley, CA: University of California Press, 2014.

Visram, Rosina. *Asians in Britain: 400 Years of History*. London: Pluto Press, 2002.

Visana, Vikram. 'Savarkar before Hindutva: Sovereignty, Republicanism, and Populism in India c. 1900–1920'. *Modern Intellectual History* (FirstView, 2020), pp. 1–24.

———. 'Decolonizing Capital: Indian Political Economy in the Shadow of Empire'. In Maureen Ruprecht E. Fadem and Michael O'Sullivan (eds.), *The Economics of Empire: Genealogies of Capital and the Colonial Encounter*. London: Routledge, 2020, ch. 2.

Wahrman, Dror. *The Making of the Modern Self: Identity and Culture in Eighteenth-Century England*. New Haven, CT: Yale University Press, 2004.

Waldron, Jeremy. 'Theoretical Foundations of Liberalism'. *Philosophical Quarterly* 37, no. 147 (1987), pp. 127–50.

Walhof, Darren R. 'Friendship, Otherness, and Gadamer's Politics of Solidarity'. *Political Theory* 34, no. 5 (2006), pp. 569–93.

Washbrook, David. 'Progress and Problems: South Asian Economic and Social History, c. 1720–1860'. *Modern Asian Studies* 22, no. 1 (1988), pp. 57–96.

Watt, Anthony Carey. *Serving the Nation: Cultures of Service, Association, and Citizenship in Colonial India*. Oxford: Oxford University Press, 2005.

———. *Serving the Nation: Cultures of Service, Association, and Citizenship in Colonial India*. Oxford: Oxford University Press, 2005.

Watts, Ruth. 'Mary Carpenter and India: Enlightened Liberalism or Condescending Imperialism?' *Paedagogica Historica: International Journal of History and Education* 37, no. 1 (2001), pp. 193–210.

Welch, Cheryl B. 'Social Science from the French Revolution to Positivism'. In Gareth Steadman Jones and Gregory Claeys (eds.), *The Cambridge History of Nineteenth Century Political Thought*. Cambridge: Cambridge University Press, 2011, pp. 171–99.

White, David L. 'From Crisis to Community Definition: The Dynamics of Eighteenth-Century Parsi Philanthropy'. *Modern South Asia* 25, no. 2 (1991), pp. 303–20.

White, Stuart. *The Civic Minimum: On the Rights and Obligations of Economic Citizenship*. Oxford: Oxford University Press, 2003.

Windscheffel, Alex. *Popular Conservatism in Imperial London, 1868–1906*. Woodbridge: Boydell & Brewer, 2007.

Wood, Neal. *John Locke and Agrarian Capitalism*. Berkley, CA: University of California Press, 1984.

Young, I. M. *Global Challenges: War, Self-Determination and Responsibility for Justice*. Cambridge: Polity, 2007.

Zachariah, Benjamin. *Developing India: An Intellectual and Social History c. 1930–1950*. Oxford: Oxford University Press, 2005.

Zastoupil, Lynn. *Rammohun Roy and the Making of Victorian Britain*. Basingstoke: Palgrave Macmillan, 2010.

## *Talks and Lectures*

Bayly, C. A. 'Indian Thought in the Shadow of Macaulay'. Macaulay Lecture, Rothley Court, Leicester, 13 October 2014.

Devji, Faisal. 'Ambedkar and the Politics of Interest'. Tata Institute of Social Sciences, 8 August 2014.

### *Unpublished Dissertations*


Brasted, Howard V. 'Irish Home Rule Politics and India, 1873–1886: Frank Hugh O'Donnell and Other Irish "Friends of India"'. Unpublished Ph.D. thesis, Edinburgh University, 1974.

Jordan, Alexander. '"Noble Just Industrialism": Saint Simonism in the Political Thought of Thomas Carlyle'. Unpublished Ph.D. thesis, European University Institute, Florence, 2015.

Morrow, Margot D. 'The Origins and Early Years of the British Committee of the Indian National Congress, 1887–1907'. Unpublished Ph.D. thesis, University of London, 1977.

Marwah, Inder Singh. 'A Matter of Character: Moral Psychology and Political Exclusion in Kant and Mill'. Unpublished Ph.D. thesis, University of Toronto, 2002.

Patel, Simin. 'Cultural Intermediaries in a Colonial City: The Parsis of Bombay, c. 1860–1921'. Unpublished Ph.D., thesis, University of Oxford, 2015.

Phemister, Andrew. '"Our American Aristotle": Henry George and the Republican Tradition during the Transatlantic Irish Land War, 1877–1887'. Unpublished Ph.D. thesis, University of Edinburgh, 2016.

Stevens, John A. 'Colonial Subjectivity: Keshub Chandra Sen in London and Calcutta, 1870–1884'. Unpublished Ph.D. thesis, University College London, 2011.

# Index


accumulation process, 18
administration and civil service, 134
Africa, 25–6, 51, 59, 163, 164, 175–6
Agri-horticultural Society, 112
Ambedkar, Bhimrao, 205–6
America, 35
American Civil War, 99
Anglophile Parsi community, 20
*anjuman* (assembly/association), 62–3
anti-imperialism, 152
Asad, Talal, 7
Asiatic Banking Corporation, 107, 108–9
Auguste Comte's positivism, 31

Back Bay scheme, 99
Banerjea, Surendranath, 44, 113, 184–5
banking, 75, 100, 107–9, 119, 161, 177, 188
Baroda, 20–1, 23, 25, 133, 136–41
the 'Baroda crisis', 137
Baroda's justice system, 140
Bartle Frere, Henry, 51, 137
Bayly, C. A., 6, 14, 19
Bell, Duncan, 7
Bell, Thomas Evans, 133
Bengal, 33, 38, 44, 56, 67, 74, 90, 112, 121, 126, 130
The Bengal Renaissance, 56
Bengal's *swadeshi* movement, 126
Bentham, Jeremy, 32, 87
*bhayads*, 135–6
Bhownaggree, Mancherjee, 82–3
Birdwood, G., 22, 186–9
Bombay, 5–6, 15, 24, 35, 52, 56, 73–5, 101–2
  Cotton Act of 1869, 105
  Education Society, 20
  Legislative Council, 21
  Municipal Corporation, 21
  mercantile communities, 99
  'modernization', 52
Bonnerjee, Womesh Chunder, 66–67
Booth, Joseph, 163–4
Bradlaugh, Charles, 125
Bright, John, 36, 37, 65–7
Britain, 152–5
British Committee of the Indian National Congress, 22
British firms, 98
British strategies, 141
British working-class voters, 161–6
Bryan, William Jennings, 179–81
bureaucracy, 25, 134, 136, 141, 143–6, 148, 159, 164, 199–200
business, 15, 16, 20, 24, 30, 37, 48, 61, 64, 72, 100, 103–7

Cairnes, J. E., 124
Calcutta, 16, 21, 66, 113, 114, 126–7, 147
Cama, Kharshedji Nasarvanji, 72

Cama, Kharshedji Rustomji, 24, 56–7
Cambridge School, 3
Cambridge school of Indian history, 52
capitalism, capital, capitalists, 2, 3, 14–16, 47, 100–2, 107, 115
Carlyle, Thomas, 23, 46–7, 49
Carpenter, Mary, 67–8, 82, 111, 113
Carpenter's National Indian Association, 68
*Cato's Letters*, 17
Central Bank of Western India, 107, 108–9
Central Finsbury, 1, 21, 25, 150, 152–3, 156, 173, 175
Chakrabarty, Dipesh, 8
Chandra, Bipan, 2
Chandra Sen, Keshub, 49, 67–8
character, 28, 31, 34–8, 44, 47, 50–1, 54–5, 58, 64, 69, 71–2, 74, 77–8, 89, 96, 101, 124
character and civil society, 34–8
charity. *See* philanthropy
China, 58–60, 75, 109
Christianity, 28, 54, 73, 86
civility, civil peace, 24, 37, 40–2, 44–5, 48, 63, 66, 73, 77, 126, 144, 157, 184, 192, 201, 204
civil service, 25, 67, 132, 134, 140–5, 157, 164, 171, 178–9, 184
civil service examinations, 184
civil society, 2, 7, 14–15, 23–4, 28, 34–6, 38, 50, 61, 70–3, 75, 77–9, 95–96, 98–9, 106, 136, 155, 185, 191, 201–2. *See also* civility
client firm, 104
Cliffe Leslie, Thomas Edward, 33, 38
Cobden, Richard, 86, 126–7, 176
colonial age, 1
colonialism, 3, 5, 9, 16, 93, 150, 175, 177, 189, 201
colonialism's representational order, 150
'colonialist and neo-colonialist', 4
colonial lawmakers, 30
colonial officials, 115
commentators, 102
commerce reports, 105
commercial crises, 107
commercial pragmatism, 100
commercial society, 15, 25, 27–8, 38–48, 98, 106, 115–16, 123, 133–4
  natural born Englishmen, 42–5
  natural law, 38–41
  romanticism's critique, 46–8
communal, 1, 23–4, 38, 63, 72–8, 91, 192, 193
  rioting, 72
  tensions, 73–8
Comte, Auguste, 31, 177
concept of *asha*, 53
conservatism, 4, 143–4, 189, 197
consumption, 38, 45, 104, 114–16, 119–20, 122, 126, 130, 134, 182–3, 194–6
contract, 16, 29–30, 34, 38, 40, 109, 120, 132, 145–6, 154–5, 162, 169, 171, 196, 203
cooperatives, 146, 161, 163, 187, 191–2
'cosmopolitan nationalism', 157
'cosmopolitan thought zones', 6
cotton, 20, 27, 59–60, 100, 105–6, 139, 151, 176
Cotton Lockout (1887), 151
cotton supply association, 105
Cowasji, Framji, 74
Crawfurd, John, 27, 32
cultural education, 87–92
cultural inheritance, 33
currency, 8, 103, 131–2, 179, 200, 203, 205

Dadabhai Naoroji & Co, 20, 104, 106, 108–9
Davitt, Michael, 123, 156 158–60
Devji, Faisal xiii
*dewan*'s role, 136–7
Dickinson, John, 65–6
Digby, William, 22, 176–7
Dillon, John, 156
divorce and inheritance, 62
drain theory, 1–2, 6–7, 18–19, 21, 25–6, 97–115, 175–80
drama, 88–90
*Duties of Zoroastrians, The*, 55
Dutt, Romesh Chunder, 90–1, 146

East India Association, 20, 22, 66, 83, 113–14, 133–5, 138
East India Finance Committee (1871–3), 114
economic crisis, 38, 97–104, 106
'the edifice of industrialism', 101
education, 24, 28, 31–2, 52, 54–5, 61, 67–8, 72–4, 78–84
educational and healthcare schemes, 100
election, 21, 36, 123, 150, 160, 170–1, 173, 175–6, 179
Elphinstone College, 20, 33, 54–5, 79, 92, 106, 121
'England's Duties to India', 114
enlightenment empiricism, 111
entrenched feudal hierarchy, 141
European banks, 131
Evans Bell, Thomas, 133–5
'exclusionary thrust', British liberalism, 7

Fabian, 156, 173–4, 192
Fawcett, Henry, 114, 123–6
female education, 78–84
Ferdowsi, 55–6
finance, 60, 67–8, 101, 103–10, 114, 118–20, 167, 200
Finance Committee, 114
Fort area of Bombay, 77
free economy and property ownership, 98
*Freeman's Journal*, 23
freemasonry, 63–4
free trade, 127
Frere, Henry Bartle, 51
Furdoonji, Naoroji, 20, 24, 63, 84, 86, 92–3, 117–18, 168–9

Gadamer, Hans-Georg, 10–11
Gadgil, Dhananjay Ramchandra, 185–92
Gadgil, D. R., 185, 186–9
*Gaekwari Dawn* (newspaper), 138
Gandhi, Mohandas Karamchand, 186–92, 197–9, 205
generosity and benevolence, 101
George, Henry, 152, 154
Geuss, Raymond, 10–11
Gladstone, Herbert, 153–4
Gladstone, William Ewart, 123, 153–4
Gladstonian, 37, 173–4, 186
Gokhale, Gopal Krishna, 22, 58, 160–1
Gold Control Act, 200
Goswami, Manu, 3
government intervention, 191
government mismanagement, 124
Great London Dock Strike (1889), 151
Gujarat, 19, 20, 24, 53, 55, 58, 60–1, 81, 117

Harrison, Frederic, 156
Heidegger, Martin, 10, 12
Herschell Committee (1893), 131
'heterotopia' arrangements, 6
*Hind Swaraj* (1909), 189

Hindu, 1, 30, 33, 44, 56, 58, 60–1, 70, 73, 75, 77, 81, 85–90
*History of Agriculture and Prices in England*, 34
Hobson, John A. 159, 175–6, 181–3
Holborn, 132, 173, 176, 186
home charges, 98, 133, 178–9
House of Commons, 21, 150, 153, 170, 190
House of Lords, 153, 161, 174
Hume, David, 23, 39
Hyndman, Henry Mayers, 152, 159, 177–9, 202

*Illustrated Mirror of Knowledge, The* (1851), 75
imperialism, 2, 8, 175–6, 179, 181, 205
*Improvement of the Mind, The*, 55
Indian capital investment, 126
Indian Communist Member of the House of Commons, 190
Indian Companies Act (1882), 30
Indian Currency Committee (1898), 131
Indian Education Commission, 80
Indian 'falsehoods', 32
Indian 'Mutiny' 129, 133–4
Indian National Association, 113
Indian National Congress, 21–2, 66, 92, 126, 147–8, 160, 176, 185
Indian nationalism, 3
Indian National Liberal Federation, 184–5
Indian political economy, 145–7
Indian politics
  local and global, 5–9
  state and capital, 2–5
Indian social interdependence, 191
Indian social relations, 190
Industrial Revolution, 28
infrastructure projects, 100
inheritance, 92–5
interstitial financial institutions, 108
Iqbal, Muhammad, 205
Iran, 53, 55–7
Iranian Zoroastrians, 57
Ireland, 23, 25–6, 33, 37, 44, 83, 114, 123–4, 152–5, 162–5
Irish, 25, 33, 43–4, 70, 81, 123–4, 156–60
Irish Agricultural Organisation Society, 160–1
The Irish Connection, 156–61
Irish Home Rule, 25, 70, 123, 157, 173–4, 182
Irish Land League, 25, 123, 153, 158
Islam, 53, 55–8, 85, 87, 90–1, 94

jails, 111–14
Jeejeebhoy, Jamsetjee, 60–1, 78–9, 100
Jews, 54, 60–1
Jinnah, Muhammed Ali, 205–6
judicial reforms, 140

Kapila, Shruti xiii, 8, 205
Kautsky, Karl, 179
Kaviraj, Sudipta, 5
Khan, Sayyid Ahmed, 91–2
Knight, Robert, 108
Koditschek, Theodore, 19

labour-intensive sectors, 126
labour republicanism, 158
labour theory of value, 116–20
landed capital, 152–5
Land, Landlord, 116–20
land nationalization, 152
Land Restoration League, 154
*Land Systems and Industrial Economy of Ireland, England the Continental Countries*, 33
land taxes, 152

Lawrence, John, 111–12
Leslie, T. E. Cliffe, 33
liberal education, 72
liberalism, 13–17
Liberal Party, 21, 25, 158–9, 186
liberty, 14–15, 17, 35, 39–40, 42–45, 72–3, 98, 128, 143, 175
List, Friedrich, 32, 144
literature, 5, 79–80, 83, 86, 88–9, 91, 159, 187
Liverpool, 20, 27, 64, 103, 105–6
local government, 58, 166–7, 170
Locke, John, 13–14, 37, 41, 108, 120–2
London, 1, 18, 20–4, 27, 151, 166–73
London County Council. *See* local government
London Ethnological Society, 27
'the lower orders', 1

Macaulay, Thomas Babington, 42–5
Madras Staff Corps, 133
Magna Carta, 42, 44
Mahalanobis, Prasanta Chandra, 91, 194–5
Maine, Henry Sumner, 23, 28–9
Malabari, Behramji, 24, 43, 68, 81–3, 88, 145
Malaviya, Madan Mohan, 185, 198–9
Manning, Elizabeth, 68–9
Marx, Karl. *See* Marxism
Masani, Minoo, 197–9
Masani, Rustom Pestonji, 18, 46
Masselos, Jim, 5–6
Mehta, Pherozeshah, 167
Mehta, Uday Singh, 7
member of parliament (MP), 1
metropolitan investors, 129
Mill, James, 27
Mill, John Stuart, 23, 30–5, 123, 127
'the modalities of spatialization', 3
modern liberalism, 29
monopoly, 2, 18, 25, 38, 41, 45–6, 48–9, 72, 77, 88–9, 97–8, 110, 115–16, 123, 145, 148–9, 151, 153, 156–7, 159
Montesquieu, 41
Moos, Ardeshir Framji, 80, 109, 167
Morley–Minto Reforms, 184
multicultural sociability, 54
municipal. *See* local government
municipal politics, 166–73
municipal reform, 152
Muslim, 1, 44, 57, 60, 63, 75–7, 85, 87, 90–2, 94–5, 145, 184

Namierite politics, 3
Naoroji, Dadabhai, 18–21, 53–7
National Archives of India, 97
National Indian Association, 67–9
*National System of Political Economy* (German), 33
nationalism, 1–4, 19, 144, 157, 188, 197, 203–4, 206–7
'nationalist and neo-nationalist', 4
National Liberal Club, 69–70, 176
National Liberal Federation, 160, 176, 184–5
Native Literary Society, 79
native merchants, 101
natural born Englishmen, 42–5
natural law, 18, 28, 30–1, 37–42, 45, 98, 118, 122, 154, 183, 189, 198
Negotiable Instruments Act (1881), 30
Nehru, Jawaharlal, 26, 192–6
Nehru Memorial Museum, 22
Newcastle programme, 156
New Party of radical political economists, 152–3
Nightingale, Florence, 68, 111
'Notes and Jottings' files, 21

'object orientation' concept, 8
O'Donnell, Frank Hugh, 157–8
'official' liberalism, colonial rule, 28–34
'official mercenaries', 157
opium, 58, 60, 75, 104
'oriental peasant mentality', 4

*Pall Mall Gazette,* 1, 23
*panchayat*, 24, 58, 62–3, 70–9, 93–5, 202–3
Parnell, Charles Stewart, 158
Parsee Marriage and Divorce Act, 74
Parsee Succession Act of 1865, 74
Parsi landholders, 101
Parsi Law Association, 63, 74
*Parsi Mission to Iran, A*, 57
Parsi sociality and commerce, 58–62
Parsis of western India
  city planning and economic interests, 52
  community's historical role, 51
peasant-producers, 128
Perry, Erskine, 54, 78, 137
Persia. *See* Iran
personal profit maximization, 103
Pettit, Philip, 17–18
Phayre, Robert, 137–9, 141
philanthropy, 15, 20, 24, 34, 37, 53, 61–2, 70–1, 73
Pitts, Jennifer, 7
poetry, 88–9
Poona Sarvajanik Sabha, 22, 144
populism, 182
positivism, 31, 165, 182
poverty, 20, 34, 36, 38, 57, 97–8
*Poverty and Un-British Rule* (1901), 21
prejudices, 11–13
princely states, 65–6, 132–5, 141
*Principles of Political Economy*, 30, 125–6
Prisons. *See* jails
production, 2, 8, 33, 38, 45, 48, 65, 97–8, 102, 111, 115–16, 118–22, 126, 128–30, 133, 143
productive and consumptive capacity, 129
*Progress and Poverty*, 152, 154
proletarian wage-earners, 102
property, 2, 5, 14, 17–18, 24–5, 33, 37–9, 41–2, 45, 47–8, 57, 62, 73, 76, 92–5
protectionism, 130–1, 147
public-spiritedness, 141
Punjab Agri-horticultural Society in 1851, 111

radical reformism, 151
Rai, Lala Lajpat, 185, 198–9
railways, 46, 127–30, 178, 191
Rajagopalachari, Chakravarty, 185–6
Ranade, Mahadev Govind, 49, 58, 82, 88, 91, 115, 145–7, 160
rational administration, 141
regional Indian patriotisms and liberalism, 6
religion, 7, 14, 22, 29–30, 43, 51, 56, 64, 78, 82, 85–9, 95, 144
*Religion of the Good Life, The*, 54
religious reform, 84–7
*Renowned Prophets and Nations, The* (1873), 75
rent, 115–16, 118–19, 121, 154–6
Report of the Board of Education, 54
representation, 14, 25, 43, 105–6, 134, 139, 150, 157, 161–2, 184–5
republicanism, 13, 17–19, 26, 37, 41, 157
revenue settlement, 115
Ricardo, David, 30–1, 116, 121
Richard Temple, 111, 129

The Rights of Labour, 173–5
right to property, 92–5
riot, 1, 24, 38, 63, 72, 75, 77, 84, 88, 201
*Rise and Growth of Economic Nationalism*, 2
Rogers, James Edwin Thorold, 34
Rogers, Thorold, 34
Ruskin, John, 23, 46–8

Saklatvala, Shapurji, 190
Sarkar, Benoy Kumar, 33
Sartori, Andrew, 8–9, 121
Savarkar, Vinayak Damodar, 91
Schabas, Margaret, 30
Schnadhorst, Francis, 160
Schroff, H. R., 108
Scottish Enlightenment, 34, 39, 42, 110–11
self-directed productivism, 153
self-government, 25, 136, 141–5, 147–8, 167, 181
'self-improvement' process, 54
'self-sacrifice' process, 54
Shahabuddin, Kazi, 114, 138–40
Shah, Kushal Talaksi, 192–6
*Shahnameh* (the *Book of Kings*), 55–6
Shia Muharram festival, 75
Shroff, Ardeshir Darabshaw, 193, 195, 197, 200
Skinner, Quentin, 9–10, 17
slavery, 17, 37, 65, 125, 143–4, 152, 161
Smith, Adam, 23, 34, 39–42, 44, 49, 64, 188
sociability, 14–15, 34, 39, 41–2, 54, 64, 67, 69, 73, 75, 94, 126
social disintegration, 141
socialism, 160–8, 201–2
social reform, 12, 20, 22, 24, 30, 49, 67, 72
Society for the Encouragement of Arts, Manufactures and Commerce, 112
South–South intellectual connections, 57
sovereignty, 5, 26, 39, 43, 91, 120, 133, 134, 137–40, 148, 159, 162, 167, 171
'state of civilization', 31
'state of society', 31–2
statistical liberalism, 110–16
'Status to Contract', 29
Stead, W. T., 23
Strand Liberal Association, 156
'strategic interventions', 157
Students' Literary and Scientific Society (SLSS), 79
'sturdy independence', 37
subaltern, 4–5
*swaraj*. *See* self-government
Swatantra party, 197–201
sympathy and ethical conduct, 189

Taleyarkhan, Dinshah, 76
Tata Corporation, 199
taxation, taxes, taxpayers, 25, 65, 98, 111, 115, 119, 128, 131–2, 137, 152, 154–5, 180–1, 183
Telang, Kashinath Trimbak, 33, 85, 109, 147, 167
Temperance Movement, 151
Thompson, James, 36
Tocqueville, Alexis de, 35
trade, international trade, 45, 98, 110, 114, 119, 126–7, 129, 144, 174, 180, 194, 199
Tyabji, Badruddin, 66

United Committee of the Taxation of Ground Rents and Values, 154
utilitarian, 27–9, 189

Vakil, C. N., 192–7
value, theory of, 18, 116–21, 123, 126, 130, 154, 162, 165, 175, 177–8, 181–3, 195–6
vendor firm, 104
vernacular journals and newspapers, 99
*Village-Communities in the East and West* (1871), 29

Wacha, Dinshaw, 24, 77, 99–101, 145, 167
Wadia, H. A., 138
Wagle, B. M., 138
Webb, Sidney, 156, 171
'Westernized middle class', 3
Whig, Whiggism, 42, 122, 143–4
Wodehouse, Philip, 76
women, 22, 63, 67–8, 71, 73, 78–82, 89, 93, 112–13
Wood, W. Martin, 128
workers' rights, 152

'young colonies', 130

the *zamindari* system, 154
*Zend Avesta* (Zoroastrian scripture), 56
Zoroastrian heritage, 55
zoroastrianism, 53–7, 84–6